Psychoeducational Approaches to Family Therapy and Counseling

Ronald F. Levant, Ed.D. (Editor) is Associate Clinical Professor of Counseling Psychology at Boston University, and Director of the Fatherhood Project, a service for men and their families offered by the Boston University School of Education. He earned his doctorate from Harvard in 1973 and joined the faculty at Boston University in 1975. His interests lie in family therapy, men's family roles, and the development of psychoeducational programs for families. He has published over 40 articles and chapters, nine monographs and curriculum packages, and two books: *Family Therapy: A Comprehensive Overview* and *Client-Centered Therapy and the Person-Centered Approach,* co-edited with John Shlien. He was recognized for his contributions to the field of psychotherapy by being named the 1984 recipient of the Jack Krasner Memorial Award from the Division of Psychotherapy of the American Psychological Association.

Psychoeducational Approaches to Family Therapy and Counseling

Ronald F. Levant, Ed.D.

Editor

Springer Publishing Company / New York

Copyright © 1986 by Springer Publishing Company, Inc.

Springer Publishing Company, Inc.
536 Broadway
New York, New York 10012

86 87 88 89 90 / 5 4 3 2 1

Library of Congress Cataloging-in-Publication Data

Main entry under title:

Psychoeducational approaches to family therapy and counseling.

   Includes bibliographies and index.
   1. Family psychotherapy.   2. Family life education.
I. Levant, Ronald F.   [DNLM: 1. Family Therapy—methods.
WM 430.5.F2 P9736]
RC488.5.P785   1986   362.8′286   85-26236
ISBN 0-8261-4850-6

Printed in the United States of America

Contents

106044

Contributors

Sylvia J. Bruce, Ed.D., is Professor and Chair, Department of Advanced Studies (Programs in Parent-Child, Primary Care, Community Health, and Psychiatric Nursing) at the Boston University School of Nursing. She earned her doctorate from Boston University in 1970, and has published numerous articles, chapters, and reviews in the fields of nursing and childbirth education.

Nicole Bussod, M.A., received her M.A. from UCLA, where she is a doctoral candidate in clinical psychology. Her publications lie in the area of marital and family therapy, with a particular focus on cognitive behavioral approaches.

Myron R. Chartier, Ph.D., is Professor of Ministry and Director of Doctoral Programs at The Eastern Baptist Theological Seminary in Philadelphia, where he has taught since 1974. He earned his doctorate from the University of Denver and is the author of numerous articles and three books, including *Preaching as Communication: An Interpersonal Perspective* for which he received the 1981 Religious Speech Communication Book Award. Together with his wife Jan (Professor of Christian Education at EBTS), he leads Marriage Enrichment groups and other seminars and workshops. They are editors of the 11-volume Judson Family Life Series (1984–1986).

David G. Fournier, Ph.D., is Associate Professor of Family Relations and Child Development at Oklahoma State University. He is author or co-author of six diagnostic instruments and numerous articles and scholarly papers on marriage preparation, early marital adjustment, diagnosing family relationships, and conflicts between family life and employment. Dr. Fournier received his doctorate from the University of Minnesota in Family Social Science.

Anthony M. Graziano, Ph.D., is Professor of Clinical-Community Psychology at the State University of New York at Buffalo, where he has taught since 1969. He earned his doctorate from Purdue in 1960. He is the author of numerous journal articles and chapters and six books, with a focus on behavior modification of child and family systems. His most recent book, co-authored with K.C. Mooney, is *Children and Behavior Therapy*.

Neil S. Jacobson, Ph.D., is Associate Professor of Psychology at the University of Washington, where he has taught since 1979. He earned his doctorate from the University of North Carolina in 1977. He has published over 65 articles and chapters and four books on topics such as behavioral marital therapy, depression, cognitive and behavioral therapies, research design and clinical psychology, and clinical/political issues. He served as the Associate Editor of the *American Journal of Family Therapy* and received an award from the American Family Therapy Association in 1983 for Innovative Contributions to Family Therapy Research.

Patricia A. Kiladis, M.S., received her B.S. degree from Worcester State College (Summa Cum Laude) and her M.S. degree in Parent-Child Nursing from Boston University.

Wesley A. Lamb, Ph.D., is a clinical psychologist at Permanente Medical Group in Hayward, California, and was formerly associated with the Institute for Juvenile Research in Chicago from 1974 to 1982. He earned his doctorate from the University of Arizona in Tucson. His publications are in the areas of child clinical psychology and parent education. With his wife Jackie he co-authored *Parent Education and Elementary Counseling*.

David H. Olson, Ph.D., is Professor and Director of Graduate Studies, Department of Family Social Science, University of Minnesota, where he has been a member of the faculty since 1973. He earned his doctorate from Pennsylvania State University in 1967. He has published over 50 articles and chapters, numerous instruments, and 12 books in the area of family studies. He is the developer of the "Circumplex Model of Marital and Family Systems," which serves as the theoretical foundation for extensive research on marriage and family systems and therapy, as well as preventive programs for couples and families. Dr. Olson received the 1983 award for "Distinguished Contribution to Family Therapy Research" from the American Family Therapy Association.

Douglas Sprenkle, Ph.D., is an Associate Professor and Director of the Marriage and Family Therapy Program, Purdue University, West Lafayette, Indiana. He earned his doctorate from the University of Minnesota in 1975. He has published over 40 articles and one book (*Divorce Therapy*) in the area of family therapy and family studies. He is a Fellow and Approved Supervisor in the American Association of Marriage and Family Therapy Education.

Cheryl L. Storm, Ph.D., is an Assistant Professor in the Department of Social Work and Marriage and Family Therapy, Pacific Lutheran University, Tacoma, Washington. She earned her doctorate from Purdue University in 1982. Her publications are in the areas of divorce, strategic family therapy, and supervision. She is a Clinical Member and Approved Supervisor in the American Association of Marriage and Family Therapy. Dr. Storm was previously the director of a conciliation courts program in Anoka, Minnesota, and on the faculty at Auburn University.

Windell Williamson, M.Ed., is a doctoral student specializing in community counseling, Counselor Education, Auburn University, Auburn, Alabama. He is a Licensed Professional Counselor in the State of Alabama and was formerly a counselor at a rehabilitation center in Opelika, Alabama.

Preface

The purpose of this book is to spotlight a new professional field which is now emerging, a field which applies the concepts and techniques of the psychoeducator to help families solve problems or prevent their occurrence.

Families today are in great need of attention. During the past 25 years tremendous changes have taken place in the social landscape. The traditional pattern of breadwinner-father and housewife-mother has been all but replaced by a plethora of new family forms: single parents, stepfamilies, dual-earner/co-parents, househusbands, joint custody, and childless couples. Fathers as sole breadwinners are now outnumbered two-to-one in the work place by dual earners and single parents.

It is not easy to see all of these changes in perspective and a number of related social trends are involved. Separating out their interacting effects is difficult, but it is possible to point out a few important features. First of all, there was the development of effective methods of birth control in the late 1950s and early 1960s, which liberated sexuality and served to separate the pursuit of intimacy from the responsibility of parenting. This was followed by an explosion in the divorce rate, which more than doubled from 1965 to 1980. Currently there are over two million marriages each year and over one million divorces. Families undergoing divorce have, on the average, slightly more than one child per family, so that each year there are over one million children affected by divorce. These figures mount up over time; there are now more than 12 million children under the age of 18 whose parents have divorced. The major stresses on these children stem from two primary sources: continuing conflict between their parents and the disruption of their relationships with their fathers. There are presently over eight million father-excluded families.

Many children thus live at least part of their lives in a single-parent family and until recently, that meant for the majority a female-headed household. However, awards for father-custody and joint custody have increased significantly in recent years, and in many states joint custody has become the norm. On the other hand, the difficulties of joint custody are now beginning to surface: split weeks; every other week; Tuesday and Thursday evenings and every other weekend—these patterns represent difficult feats of juggling and much added stress for all concerned. The problems increase geometrically when divorcing parents do not live in the same community, because then there are different school systems, disruptions of children's friendships, and the like.

This, then, is the situation after divorce in single-parent families. But many divorced parents do not stay single, and most eventually remarry, forming "reconstituted" families. Such blended families may include children from prior marriages of one or both spouses (increasingly with joint custody) and possibly children from the current marriage. The stresses on such families often stem from there being too many adults for the two parental roles. These stresses usually involve complex issues of loyalty and inclusion.

Another major trend that has contributed to the changes is the sharp increase in the employment of women. This is a result of many factors, including the women's movement as well as the divorce rates. This trend is expected to continue, so that by 1990 over half of the work force will be female. The results are seen in the delaying of marriage, the postponement of parenthood, and smaller family size. Another facet is the increase in the dual-earner or two-paycheck family, which often creates role-overload for both spouses. In the late sixties and early seventies, time-use studies indicated that husbands spent little time in child care and increased their involvement only slightly, if at all, in response to their wives' employment. However, more recent studies indicate that husbands' and wives' levels of time expenditure in family work are converging: wives are spending less time, and husbands are spending more. This trend is projected to continue, and by 1990 sixty percent of employed fathers will have wives in the labor force and will be sharing more direct family responsibilities.

The common themes that run through these new family variations are balancing, adjustment, learning new roles, role overload, and stress. The need for short-term problem-focused and coping-oriented family counseling programs has never been greater. At the same time we now have available an expanding array of programs, based on the psychoeducator model, designed specifically for families.

The psychoeducator model draws inspiration from such diverse sources as the American philosopher John Dewey and the Chilean biologist Humberto Maturana. It is based on the constructivist principles that people are self-creating, self-evolving entities, that dysfunction and psychopathology represent not "illness" but rather problems in living, that people can solve such problems if they have sufficient skills, and that psychological skills (such as communication, problem solving, conflict resolution) can be taught.

Applications of the psychoeducator model to families have arisen from diverse fields. Within the field of professional psychology, two traditions have contributed heavily to these developments: client-centered therapy and behavior modification. These are certainly unlikely bedfellows, if one recalls the debates of Carl Rogers and B.F. Skinner in the sixties. And there indeed are major differences in perspective. Both traditions, however, share certain optimistic assumptions about human nature, and both subscribe to an educational/growth versus a medical model. Although their respective family psychoeducational programs evolved for different reasons, reasons intrinsic to each tradition, both developments were strongly influenced by trends within psychology as a whole. These include George Miller's widely appealing plea to "give psychology away;" the community mental health movement, with its emphasis on the use of nonprofessionals and on primary prevention; and the growing interest in families and family therapy.

Outside of the field of psychology, several kindred disciplines have made major contributions to this new field. *Parent education* is probably the oldest of these, dating back to 1815 in this country. Growing out of the humanist wave of the late 1960s, *marriage enrichment* originated within the ministry, but later expanded to include secular bases. Somewhat less recently, the field of *family life education* developed within the home economics profession, and has formulated course offerings on the secondary school and college level designed to prepare young adults for the life transitions involved in marriage and parenthood. *Childbirth education* developed within the nursing profession in the early 1900s, and for many years offered programs which focused on the health care needs of mothers during pregnancy and on preparing them for childbirth and the care of the newborn infant. Recently the outlook within this field has broadened to include fathers in childbirth preparation classes and to incorporate the topic of transition to parenthood in its curriculum. As such it serves as an extremely well-positioned prevention program and deserves increased attention from professionals in related fields. *Premarital counseling* dates back to 1932 as a recognized profession in the United States. For many years it was the province of ministers and physicians, who were most directly in contact with prenuptial couples. Programs were often unsystematic and haphazard until the late 1960s, when family social scientists began formulating and researching programs aimed at both pre- and neo-marital stages. Finally, there is *divorce counseling*, an emerging field which arose in response to the escalating needs of divorcing couples in the seventies and eighties, and has involved a range of professions including law, education, and social work, as well as psychology.

As a whole, these fields have contributed a growing number of programs of increasing sophistication. The programs focus on either marriage or parenting at various stages of the life cycle. They are in general short-term skills-training psychoeducational programs designed to prevent or resolve problems and/or to facilitate life transitions. As a group, they have increasingly been subjected to empirical scrutiny, and a good deal is known about their effects and efficacy. In short, there is much to recommend them.

This book is organized to provide readers with a conceptual overview of the range of programs available, and with detailed discussions of each major field or set of programs. The discussions include attention to the historical development of each field, the types of programs that are available, the issues of concern within the field, a review of the evaluative research, and practical implications.

Chapter 1, by Ronald F. Levant, sets out the conceptual orientation to the field as a whole and provides a classification system for the various programs according to four dimensions: (1) the educational objective of the program; (2) the particular problem, relationship, role, or developmental transition to which it is applied; (3) the professional field within which the program originated; and (4) the theoretical orientation which has influenced its development. The subsequent chapters take up in turn the major sets of programs.

The programs that have originated within the field of professional psychology are treated in Chapters 2, 3, and 4. The client-centered programs are discussed by Ronald F. Levant in Chapter 2. The programs considered include Relationship Enhancement, Human Resource Development, Microcounseling, Parent Effectiveness Training, and Levant's own Personal Development Program. The behavioral approaches have seen so much development that their treatment requires two chapters. The field of Behavioral Parent Training will be covered in Chapter 3 by Anthony Graziano, who brings a child and family systems perspective to the discussion. And the field of Behavioral Marital Therapy will be discussed by Nicole Bussod and Neil Jacobson in Chapter 4, with an accent on the newer cognitive and self-control approaches.

The approaches that have arisen in kindred fields are treated in Chapters 5 through 9. The first two of these chapters deal with parenting, at the beginning and middle stages. Childbirth education is the topic of Chapter 5, written by Sylvia Bruce and Patricia Kiladis. Wesley Lamb writes on parent education in Chapter 6. The final three chapters deal with marriage, at the pre/neo, middle, and post stages. David Fournier and David Olson are the authors of Chapter 7, devoted to pre- and neomarital counseling. Marriage enrichment is the topic of Chapter 8, written by Myron Chartier. And, finally, the field of divorce counseling is addressed in Chapter 9 by Cheryl Storm, Douglas Sprenkle, and Windell Williamson.

R.F.L.

1

An Overview of Psychoeducational Family Programs*

Ronald F. Levant

Introduction

This book is addressed to the task of taking stock of an expanding array of programs designed for families which use psychoeducational and skills-training approaches. These are generally brief or time-limited, systematic or structured, experiential and didactic training programs designed to remediate individual and family problems and/or enhance aspects of family life. These programs have arisen in the last 15 years from several sources and amount to what some are calling a "new professional field" (L'Abate, 1981; Smith, Shoffner & Schott, 1979). They form the basis for an approach to family therapy in which the promotion of well-being is given status at least equal to that of the remediation of dysfunction, and educational approaches are seen as serious alternatives to approaches based on the medical model.

Classification of Skills-training Programs

The skills-training programs can be classified in a nested schema with four dimensions. The first dimension concerns the *objective* of the program, along a continuum from the remediation of dysfunction to the enhancement

*This is a revised version of an earlier article: R. F. Levant (1983), "Toward a Counseling Psychology of the Family: Psychological-educational and Skills-training Programs for Treatment, Prevention, and Development." *The Counseling Psychologist, 11*(3), 5–28. Reprinted by permission of *The Counseling Psychologist*.

of functioning. Nested within the first dimension of program objective is the second dimension, which concerns the *focus* of the intervention, or the particular problem, relationship, role, or developmental transition to which it is applied. The third dimension concerns the *field* within which the program originated, whether therapy and family therapy, parent education, marriage enrichment, or whatever. Nested within the third dimension of field of origin is the fourth dimension, which concerns the theoretical *orientation* which has informed the development of the skills-training program.

Objective and focus of the program.   Within the broad framework of the shift from the medical to the educational model discussed above, there are three distinct approaches, varying according to their emphasis on remediation or prevention and development. The first and historically earliest position involves the training of family members as therapeutic helpers, who then treat another family member. This approach could be termed *training for treatment.* It has evolved from a larger class of programs concerned with the training of "significant others" or "symbionts" (Guerney, 1969). The training of symbionts is itself a component of the broader field of paraprofessional training. The rationale for the training of symbionts is that, by virtue of their close ties with clients, symbionts are in a good position to affect clients' functioning or development in positive and significant ways, if provided with the necessary training. The training of symbionts dates back to the early 1900s, when Freud (1959) trained the father to carry out the treatment of Little Hans. The current programs have retained this focus on training a parent to help a disturbed child.

The second approach focuses on training family members in certain skills (e.g., communication, problem solving, conflict negotiation) where deficiencies are thought to exist, as a means of helping the family resolve its problems. This approach, termed *training as treatment* by Carkhuff (1971a), takes an additional step in the shift toward the educational model: Human problems are conceptualized as deficits in psychological or interpersonal skills which can be learned, rather than as impairments which require a corrective experience administered by a helper. The training as treatment concept originated with the training of psychiatric inpatients in communicational and social skills (Pierce & Drasgow, 1969; Vitalo, 1971). The application of this approach to the family has usually focused on a dyadic relationship—either the marital partners or a parent–adolescent dyad––and has involved conjoint skills-training for both members of the pair. Recently, this approach has been applied to the family as a whole.

The third approach uses psychoeducational methods to enhance the quality of family life as a means of either preventing the emergence of problems or of stimulating the development of family members. When thought of as a preventive measure, the aim is primary prevention— reduction of the incidence of mental health problems by strengthening the coping capacity of individuals who do not yet have but are at risk for the development of clinical problems (Caplan & Grunebaum, 1967). When viewed as a developmental intervention, it reflects John Dewey's position that "true education *is* development." This approach will be termed *training for enhancement*. It has been applied to marriage, parenthood, and the family as a whole, at various stages of the life cycle. For marriage, there are programs designed for premarital (pre), newlywed (neo), married (mid or meso), and divorcing couples (post). For parenthood, there are programs designed to prepare adolescents and young adults for parenthood (pre), to support young marrieds through pregnancy and childbirth (neo), and to help parents improve their parenting functions (meso). For the family as a whole, programs have tended to concentrate on the stage when children have reached adolescence, although one program has modules for all stages of the family life cycle.

Field of origin and theoretical orientation. The psychoeducational, skills-training approaches can also be grouped according to the field of origin and theoretical framework from which they have been developed. The two groups of approaches which originated in the therapy field—client-centered and behavioral skills-training programs—are the broadest and most comprehensive. They include programs developed for all three objectives and most of the foci described above. The parent education and marriage enrichment fields have each produced a number of single-objective, single-focus programs from several theoretical orientations, as well as eclectic and atheoretical programs. Psychodynamic, Adlerian, Kohlbergian, systemic, transactional-analytic, rational-emotive, reality-therapeutic, eclectic, and atheoretical programs have been developed for parent education. Communication systems, Gestalt, transactional-analytic, Rankian, eclectic, and atheoretical programs have been developed for marriage enrichment.

Family life education, a separate field which developed within the home economics profession, has been concerned with the offering of courses on a college level (and more recently in secondary schools) designed to have a more personal impact on students' lives than the traditional fare of "cooking, sewing, and money management." These courses were intended to "improve the courtship and marriage of the students" (Broderick & Schrader, 1980, pp. 10–11) and prepare them for parenthood (Kerckhoff, Ulmschneider, & Adams, 1976). As such, this field shares the vision of the originators of "deliberate psychological education," whose work springs from a belief that education currently offers little help to adolescents or young adults *as people* who are trying to mature against unusual vicissitudes. Our objective is to make personal development a central focus of education. (Mosher & Sprinthall, 1971, p. 3)

The field of family life education will not be covered separately because of space limitations, but some of the preparenthood and premarital programs will be discussed in this chapter, grouped with the parent education and marriage enrichment programs, respectively.

Several smaller fields will also be brought into this discussion. These are childbirth education and divorce counseling, which in this chapter will be grouped with the parent education and marriage enrichment programs, respectively. It should also be mentioned that, due to space limitations, two related fields will not be treated in this volume: sex education (Scales, 1981) and sex therapy (Heiman, LoPiccolo, & LoPiccolo, 1981). Although obviously an important part of family life, these fields have mushroomed in the last 10 to 15 years and are large enough to deserve a book in their own right.

It should be pointed out that this nested classification of theories within fields does not yield mutually exclusive categories. The client-centered and behavioral approaches have produced several programs commonly grouped under the rubrics of parent education or marriage enrichment. However, it seems more parsimonious to include these particular programs under the umbrella of their theoretical orientation; it is also truer to their conceptual lineage.

The skills-training programs classified according to their objectives, foci, fields of origin, and theoretical orientation are displayed in Table 1-1. The next four sections of this chapter will provide overviews of the various programs, grouped according to the columns on Table 1-1: client-centered, behavioral, parenting, and marriage programs. The last section of the chapter will review comparative evaluation studies and suggest directions for the future.

Client-centered Programs

The client-centered skills training programs for families began in the early 1960s. These programs are based on the concepts that the client-centered facilitative conditions of empathy, genuineness, and regard (Rogers, 1957) are at the core of good interpersonal relationships in general (Rogers, 1961) and that people can be trained to improve their interpersonal functioning (Carkhuff, 1971b). During the 1960s, encouraged by the emerging psychotherapy research findings indicating the importance of the facilitative conditions for psychotherapy outcome (Bergin, 1967), and mobilized by an acute awareness of the shortages of mental health personnel (Albee, 1967), a growing number of client-centered therapists began to train professional and lay helpers to enhance their interpersonal functioning in terms of the facilitative conditions (Guerney, 1969; Truax & Carkhuff, 1967). The facilitative conditions became known as skills, and systematic skills-training programs emerged (Carkhuff, 1969a, 1969b). A concern with having an impact beyond the individual and on the smaller and larger social systems led to their application to the family.

Several groups have developed family skills-training programs from, or influenced by, the client-centered orientation. These include (1) the Relationship Enhancement (RE) programs based at Pennsylvania State University, under the leadership of Bernard Guerney, Jr. (1977); (2) two efforts related to RE—Dialoguing (van der Veen, 1977) and the Communication and Parenting Skills (CAPS) Program (D'Augelli & Weener, 1978); (3) Robert Carkhuff's (1971b) Human Resource Development (HRD) programs; (4) Ivey's (1971) related Microcounseling; (5) the Personal Development Program (PDP) of Levant and associates (1981); and (6) Thomas Gordon's (1970) Parent Effectiveness Training (PET).

Relationship Enhancement and Related Programs

Relationship Enhancement (RE) constitutes the best developed and evaluated set of family skills-training programs informed or influenced by the client-centered perspective. Although aspects of social learning theory and other theoretical perspectives have shaped the development of the RE programs (B. Guerney, 1984; Guerney & Vogelsong, 1980), I regard the influence of client-centered therapy to be of central importance. I take this position not only because of the content of training program closely parallels the facilitative conditions of empathy, genuineness, and regard, but also because the RE method of training is explicitly trainee centered (van der Veen, 1977). In addition, the RE approach originated as a self-avowed part of the Rogerian tradition (B. Guerney, 1964). The RE programs provide training in four sets of skills or behavioral modes: (1) *the expressor mode,* wherein the individual learns skills of self-awareness and genuine self-expression; (2) *the empathic responder mode,* which includes listening and reflective responding skills; (3) *mode switching,* which involves learning how to change modes in order to facilitate communication; (4) *the facilitator mode,* in which participants learn to help others develop the first three sets of skills. Recently two new sets of skills have been developed: (5) *problem-solving and conflict-resolution skills,* which are based on the use of the first three skills in a six-step

Table 1-1 Skill Training Programs for Families Classified According to Their Objectives, Foci, Fields of Origin, and Theoretical Orientation

Objective and Focus		Field of Origin and Theoretical Orientation			
		Family Therapy		Parent Education, Family Life Education, Childbirth Education	Marriage Enrichment, Premarital Counseling, Divorce Counseling
		Client-centered	Behavioral	Psychodynamic, Adlerian, Kohlbergian, Systemic, T.A., R.E.T., Reality Therapy, eclectic, a-theoretical	Communication Systems, Gestalt, T.A.. Rankian eclectic, a-theoretical
Training for Treatment		Filial Therapy & Extensions, Human Resource Development, Micro-counseling	Behavioral Parent Training		
Training as Treatment	Marital	Conjugal Relationship Therapy, Human Resource Development	Behavioral Marital Therapy		
	Parent-Adolescent	Parent Adolescent Relationship Therapy			
	Family	Relationship Enhancement, Dialoguing			

Training for Enhancement				
Marital (pre, neo, meso, post)	PRIMES, Conjugal Relationship Enhancement, Children of Divorce, Communication Skills for Divorcees	PREP, Mutual Problem Solving Program, Group Behavioral Marital Training		Pre-marital Programs (Various), Religious Programs (Marriage Encounter, Quaker, Methodist), ACME, Theoretical Programs (Gestalt, T.A., Marital Rebirth), Skills Training Programs (CCP, and others), Children of Divorce Programs, Family Mediation, Divorce Adjustment Groups
Parental (pre, neo, meso)	Filial Education, Parent Adolescent Relationship Dev., Commun. Parenting Skills, Human Resource Dev., Personal Dev. Program, Parent Effectiveness Training	Group Behavioral Parent Training		Exploring Childhood & other pre-parental programs, Childbirth educ. classes (various), Parent disc. groups (Psychodynamic), Didactic/disc. groups (Adlerian, Humanistic, Systemic, T.A., Rational Emotive, Reality Guidance, and eclectic), Skills Training Pro. (STEP & others).
Family				Moral Dev. Pro., Struc. Fam. Enrichment, Understanding US

method; and (6) *maintenance and generalization* skills, which involve the use of home practice, relying on the use of the facilitator mode (Vogelsong, Guerney, & Guerney, 1983). The programs are didactic and experiential and include homework.

RE programs have been developed for all three objectives and most of the foci described in the previous section (see Table 1-1). The first development was in the training for treatment area, with the Filial Therapy program which began in 1962 (L. Guerney, 1976). Filial Therapy involves training the parent (most often the mother) in the application of client-centered therapy as a method of treating mild to severe emotional disturbance in preadolescent children. In Filial Therapy, parents are trained in groups of six to eight parents which meet weekly for two hours for 12 to 18 months.

In the training as treatment area, there are marital and parent–adolescent programs, and whole family programs are being developed. The marital [Conjugal Relationship Enhancement (CRE), Rappaport, 1976] and parent–adolescent [Parent Adolescent Relationship Development (PARD), Grando & Ginsberg, 1976] programs involve training both members of the dyadic relationship, usually in a brief group program of 10 to 15 weeks (20 to 30 hours), although longer programs with varying formats have been tried. Family relationship programs are being developed for psychiatric inpatients and their families (Vogelsong et al., 1983), and for clinical families in general (Dialoguing, van der Veen, 1977).

In the training for enhancement area, both the CRE and the PARD programs, originally intended as therapeutic programs, are also used as preventive programs. In addition, there are five other programs: (1) a version of CRE has been developed for premarital couples [The Program for Relationship Improvement by Maximizing Empathy and Self-Disclosure (PRIMES), Ginsberg & Vogelsong, 1977]. (2) A didactic version of Filial Therapy has been developed as a parent education course (L. Guerney, 1976). (3) An RE-related program [Communication and Parenting Skills (CAPS), D'Augelli & Weener, 1978] has been developed for parents. (4) A divorce program for children [Children of Divorce (COD), L. Guerney & Jordan, 1979] is in the process of development. Finally, (5) a communication skills training program for divorcees has also been recently developed (Avery & Thiessen, 1982).

The evaluative research literature has been reviewed by Levant (1978, 1983) and B. Guerney (1984). The RE programs have demonstrated their efficacy in teaching the communication skills (assessed by independent judges), improving parental attitudes and the functioning of disturbed children (Filial Therapy), improving relationships (CRE, PRIMES, PARD), and facilitating the adjustment of stressed individuals (communication skills for divorcees); the latter four areas have been assessed by self-report or participant ratings. The communication skills have been shown to be maintained at three-month (CRE) and six-month (PARD, PRIMES) follow-up, parental attitudes and child adjustment at three-year follow-up (Filial Therapy), and relationship changes at three-month (CRE) and six-month (PARD) follow-up intervals. Compared to other treatments, RE has been found to be superior to the Couples Communication Program (CRE), Gestalt Relationship Awareness Facilitation (CRE), traditional couples therapy (CRE), lecture/discussion (PRIMES), and discussion group (PARD) approaches, and equivalent to a behavioral approach (CRE, PRIMES). Only the Filial Parent Education Program has received no empirical support; and the COD, Family RE, and Dialoguing programs have yet to be systematically evaluated. Future research should include more objective assessments of individual and relationship changes; testing with clinical populations (particularly for PARD) and with a broader socio-economic spectrum; and additional follow-ups and comparisons with alternative treatments to fill in various gaps in the empirical literature. Two such comparisons that would be particularly rigorous tests of RE would be Filial Therapy versus behavioral parent training and CRE versus behavioral marital therapy.

Human Resource Development Program and Microcounseling

Robert Carkhuff is one of the pioneers of the skills-training psychoeducational approaches and has been seen as the original prime mover in this area (Kagan, 1972). His Human Resource Development (HRD) program involves training in the "responsive" dimensions of empathy, respect, and genuineness, the "initiative" dimensions of self-disclosure, confrontation, and immediacy, and the general dimension of concreteness. Training occurs in a two-stage process of discrimination training followed by communication training. The trainers must be functioning at high levels on the facilitative conditions and provide a student-centered climate for the trainees (Carkhuff, 1969a). Microcounseling (Ivey, 1971) is conceptually related to, and a refinement of, Carkhuff's approach, focusing on more specific skills and using videotaped feedback. Both programs are didactic and experiential and include homework exercises.

The HRD program has been applied to all three objectives, but with limited foci. In the training for treatment area, it has been applied to training parents in interpersonal skills, in a brief group program, in order to help disturbed children (Carkhuff & Bierman, 1970). A version of Microcounseling has been similarly applied (Durrett & Kelley, 1974). In the training as treatment area, it has been applied to the marital relationship (Pierce, 1973) in a brief group training program. Finally, in the training for enhancement area, it has been applied to training parents as trainers of their children (Bendix, 1977).

Unfortunately, there is not much empirical support for the efficacy of the HRD and Microcounseling family programs. Only a few studies have been done, and these are limited in scope and complicated by methodological problems. The literature in this area is consistent with the larger HRD literature, which has been criticized on methodological grounds (Gormally & Hill, 1974; Lambert & De Julio, 1977; Resnikoff, 1972).

Personal Developmental Program

The Personal Developmental Program (PDP), developed by Levant and associates, is a client-centered skills-training program. It includes a set of modules focusing on specific skills, which can be used in varying combinations: attending, listening and responding to content; listening and responding to feelings; speaking for oneself—self-awareness; speaking for oneself—genuineness; acceptance; structuring; rules, limits, and consequences; conflict resolution; and skill integration. The program is a brief didactic and experiential group training program which includes homework exercises. It has been applied as a training for treatment program with lower socioeconomic minority foster mothers (Levant, Slattery, & Slobodian, 1981), as training for enhancement programs with working-class parents (Haffey & Levant, 1984; Kanigsberg & Levant, 1982) and with fathers of school-aged children who wanted to increase their parental role (Levant & Doyle, 1983). New training for enhancement programs has been developed for single parents, step-parents and their spouses, and dual-earner/co-parents. The evaluative research has provided modest support for this program, which is still in the early stages of development.

Parent Effectiveness Training

Parent Effectiveness Training (PET, Gordon, 1970, 1976) is used widely throughout the country. A training for enhancement program, it consists of eight three-hour group sessions, which are didactic and experiential and include homework. PET emphasizes "active listening," which involves acceptance and empathy; owning or "I-messages," in which the parent communicates feelings genuinely and directly, without blaming the child; and a specific program of conflict resolution called the "no-lose method," which involves a search for mutually acceptable solutions to problems.

The evaluative research literature has been reviewed twice in recent years. Rinn and Markle (1977) reviewed 14 studies dating up to 1975, which included five single-group outcome studies (all unpublished papers or masters' theses) and nine comparative-group studies (one unpublished study, seven doctoral dissertations, and one published study). They found these studies to be plagued with methodological flaws and concluded that "the effectiveness of PET as a prevention or intervention strategy was not supported." More recently, Levant (1983) reviewed the studies available through 1981, focusing only on doctoral dissertations (17) or published studies (6). After reviewing the methodological features of the group of studies, he categorized them according to their adequacy. Examining the findings of the adequate group of studies, he concluded that there is some support for the efficacy of PET. PET appears to result in positive changes in parent attitudes (self-report) and behavior (child-rated) and improvement in children's self-concept (self-report) and behavior (teacher-rated).

Clearly, many questions remain regarding the efficacy of PET. To help address these, the author and associates are undertaking a meta-analysis of the PET literature.

Behavioral Programs

Behavioral training programs for families began in the mid-1960s. Like the client-centered training programs, the initial focus was on training a parent to participate in the treatment of a child. The impetus for this development came from a combination of sources: dissatisfaction with the results of traditional child therapy; the growth in the application of the principles of the experimental analysis of behavior; the shortages of mental health manpower; and the potential expansion of the manpower pool through the use of paraprofessionals, particularly symbionts (Cone & Sloop, 1974). The major reasons for training parents in behavioral (particularly operant) techniques, however, was that the principles of behavior therapy logically required it: Although certain child behaviors may be brought under control in the treatment session, there is little reason to expect that they will *generalize* to the home, if the contingencies of reinforcement in the home remain unchanged (O'Dell, 1974).

Behavioral skill training programs for families cluster into two general categories: behavioral parent training (BPT) and behavioral marital therapy (BMT). Although all three behavioral theories—classical or respondent, operant and social learning, and self-control or cognitive—have been used, the major approach is operant-social learning theory. Operant-social learning theory is a loosely systematized collection of ideas which includes the principles of operant learning (reinforcement, extinction, etc.) and social psychological influencing processes such as modeling. Classical conditioning procedures have been used in BPT to treat enuretic children (Berkowitz & Graziano, 1972); in BMT classical conditioning procedures include systematic desensitization to reduce one spouse's dysfunctional emotional responses to the other's behavior (Epstein & Williams, 1981) and assertiveness training (Alberti & Emmons, 1974). Self-control strategies have started to emerge in BPT (Brown, Gamboa, Birkimer, & Brown, 1976) and BMT (Jacobson, 1980; O'Leary & Turkewitz, 1978), but have not yet been applied widely.

Another general characteristic of the behavioral training programs is their preponderant use in an individual family format. BPT does utilize some group training procedures, but in the more sophisticated studies the group approach is integrated with individual consultations (Johnson & Katz, 1973; O'Dell, 1974). When used alone, the group training format is most often used for preventive goals (Cone & Sloop, 1974). In BMT, group training procedures have been developed for teaching communication skills to couples in a preventive program (Witkin & Rose, 1978). Jacobson & Margolin (1979) have suggested group training in problem-solving skills for treatment programs, but caution that this approach is "still very much in the experimental stage."

The focus on individual families is based on the principle of specificity. Simply teaching family members the general principles of behavior therapy is not considered sufficient to enable them to alter dysfunctional patterns. What is required is a very specific application of these principles, based on a detailed idiographic analysis of the contingencies of reinforcement operative in the family and resulting in the construction of a carefully designed treatment plan. These are tasks which are not easily accomplished in a group training format.

Related to this is the preponderant emphasis on treatment rather than enhancement. Behavioral parent training fits the training for the treatment paradigm, and behavioral marital therapy fits the training as treatment model. Training for enhancement is not nearly as well developed as are the treatment-oriented programs and is represented by some of the group training programs in BPT (e.g., Brockway & Williams, 1976; Dubanoski & Tanabe, 1980; Hall, 1976) and BMT. For the latter, marital (Harrell & Guerney, 1976; Witkin & Rose, 1978), premarital (Markman & Floyd, 1980; Markman, Floyd, Stephen, & Stanley, 1981; Ridley, Avery, Harrell, Leslie, & Dent, 1981), and divorce (Granvold & Welch, 1977) programs have recently emerged.

Thus the behavioral training programs are predominantly based on operant principles and social learning theory, and are mainly geared toward remediation. Most often families are trained individually. Group training is sometimes used in conjunction with individual consultation. When used alone it is usually reserved for prevention programs.

Behavioral Parent Training

Behavioral parent training is characterized by considerable diversity in its conceptualization, implementation, and evaluation. In the face of this diversity, Mash, Handy, and Hamerlynk (1976) considered the question of whether BPT represents a unitary approach. They answered the question in the affirmative, pointing to the general adherence to experimentally established behavioral principles and commitment to empirical research.

Parent involvement.   One of the key dimensions along which programs have varied is the nature and extent of parental involvement. Berkowitz and Graziano (1972) reviewed 32 experimental case studies ("N = 1 research") and sorted them into five groups based on the nature and extent of parents' involvement and degree of training, as well as the complexity of the child's problem and the methodological sophistication of the studies. The authors observed a shift from a focus on relatively uncomplicated presenting problems (such as mild conduct problems) using minimal parental involvement and no systematic evaluation, to a concern with serious clinical problems (such as psychosis) and complex multiple-problem behaviors (or syndromes) in which parents—trained to a fairly high degree of proficiency—carried out extensive home programs and in which evaluation was careful and rigorous. Even in the better developed programs, however, parents were not included in many aspects of the treatment, particularly observation, treatment planning, and evaluation, and their training was not sufficient to enable them to formulate and carry out programs independently.

In general, then, the parent's role in this training for treatment approach (BPT) stops just short of being an equal co-therapist. Whether the parent's role will develop further is uncertain. However, present trends in BPT are shifting the focus from the parent as change agent to modifying the parent–child interactional system (Berkowitz & Graziano, 1972; Graziano, 1983). Recent innovations along this theme have included training children as modifiers of their parents' behavior (Benassi & Larson, 1976) and dyadic training of parents and adolescents in problem solving and communication skills (Robin et al., 1977). This latter approach begins to extend BPT into the training as treatment area.

Nature of training programs.   A related issue is the nature of the training program. O'Dell (1974) reviewed 70 studies (most of which were $N = 1$ studies) with a focus on variations in the technology of BPT. *Training approaches* include individual consultations, educational groups, and "controlled learning environments" in which parental behavior is shaped in order to alter parents' responses to their children. *Training content* emphasized either behavioral knowledge or behavioral skills. Knowledge-oriented programs teach operant learning principles with an emphasis on how negative behavior is produced and maintained in the child's social environment through reinforcement contingencies. Skills-oriented programs teach parents to define, count, and chart behaviors and to apply consequences to either accelerate (through reinforcement) or decelerate (through extinction) their frequency. *Training techniques* include simple advice and directions; didactic instruction using programmed texts such as Patterson and Gullion's (1976) *Living with Children* and Becker's (1971) *Parents Are Teachers* (see Bernal & North, 1978, for a review of 26 commercially available parent training texts and manuals); and skill-building practices such as observation with feedback, use of videotape, modeling, and behavioral rehearsal. Finally, under the heading of *implementation and maintenance,* O'Dell discussed the use of various contingencies (such as social rewards, monetary reimbursement, and written contracts) to increase parent attendance and participation, and techniques (such as telephone contacts after treatment and periodic retraining) to promote generalization of treatment effects.

Types of child problems.   Several reviewers have discussed the type of child problems treated by BPT. Johnson and Katz (1973) listed antisocial and immature behavior, speech dysfunction, school phobia, encopresis and enuresis, seizures, self-injurious behavior, and oppositional behavior. Cone and Sloop (1974) provided detailed lists of the specific child behaviors treated in 49 studies they reviewed. Berkowitz and Graziano (1972) noted that most of the work has focused on the reduction of surplus maladaptive behavior. Finally, O'Dell (1974, p. 421), noting that the types of child problems treated by BPT have ranged from specific problem behaviors in children labeled as brain-damaged, retarded, autistic, psychotic, and school-phobic to complex behavioral syndromes, concluded that "There does not appear to be any type of overt child behaviors that parents cannot be trained to modify."

Evaluation.   In general the evaluative research indicates that parents can be used to modify their children's maladaptive behavior. Also, the sophistication of the evaluation research has increased over time. Johnson and Katz (1973) reviewed 49 studies, summarizing their methodological characteristics in tables. For each study they provided information on the number of subjects treated, the adequacy of the description of the parent training operations, whether reliability data for dependent measures was provided, whether behavioral control was demonstrated using reversal techniques in A-B-A-B experimental designs, the length of follow-up (if any), and cost efficiency data (estimate of therapist time) where available. They noted the general empirical support for BPT, but pointed out that additional research is needed not only to identify the critical components of parent training but also to determine the most efficient means to maintain positive behavior after the end of the intervention. For the latter they recommended routine follow-up and systematic programming for generalization of treatment effects.

O'Dell provided a detailed methodological critique of the 70 studies which he reviewed according to general criteria for research in applied behavioral analysis (Baer, Wolfe, & Risley, 1968). He concluded more cautiously than Johnson and Katz, noting that the usefulness of BPT is "more promise than fact" (O'Dell, 1974, p. 430). The major problem is the lack of information regarding changes in parents' behavior as a result of BPT. Evaluation has focused exclusively on changes in children's behavior. Without demonstrations that parents have acquired behavioral skills and utilized them in the home, one cannot unequivocally attribute the results of treatment to the training of the parents. Another (related) neglected area has been the generalization and maintenance of changes in parents' behavior.

Finally, Forehand and Atkeson (1977) reviewed the research on generalization of treatment effects, focusing on the procedures used to implement and assess temporal, setting, behavioral, and sibling generalization. They found few clear-cut changes, noting that the more rigorous the method of assessment, the more negative were the results. However, suggestive evidence was found for temporal generalization and setting generalization from clinic to home, whereas the evidence for setting generalization from home to school and behavioral generalization was much less compelling. Sibling generalization has been examined only infrequently, but the few studies available suggest positive changes in untreated siblings. Finally, very little is known about which training procedures promote generalization.

Behavioral Marital Therapy

Behavioral marital therapy got started a few years after BPT, in the late 1960s (Lazarus, 1968; Stuart, 1969a). Since then there have been a number of reports on the use of BMT. Although approaches vary a good deal, the central thrust is based on a combination of social learning theory and social psychological exchange theories (Homans, 1961; Thibaut & Kelley, 1959). Troubled marriages are viewed as a function of a low rate of exchange of positive reinforcers, which leads either to withdrawal (Stuart, 1969a) or to the use of aversive control strategies (Weiss, Hops, & Patterson, 1973). And whereas nondisturbed couples exchange reinforcers on an equitable basis over time (reciprocity), distressed couples have an inequitable exchange (coercion) wherein one spouse's behavior is controlled by positive reinforcement and the other's by negative reinforcement (Patterson & Reid, 1970). For example, husband yells at wife, providing an aversive stimulus; wife complies with husband's demand, positively reinforcing him; husband stops yelling, negatively reinforcing wife by withdrawing the aversive stimulus.

The central objective of BMT is to help couples learn more positive means of effecting changes in each other's behavior. Ultimately this involves a reorganization of their contingencies of reinforcement, so that positive interaction is increased and aversive interaction is decreased. Before the contingencies can be renegotiated, however, the couples must receive training in communication skills. The generally accepted rationale for this is that distressed couples are usually deficient in this area and would not be able to negotiate a meaningful contract without such skills training. Jacobson (1978) has argued, however, that skills training is the essential process and that contingency contracting may be unnecessary. Using a stimulus-control model, he argues that the conditions under which the agreement is negotiated (versus the specifics of the agreement) are the primary determinants of whether the agreement is upheld. There are some data to support his position (Jacobson & Margolin, 1979).

In any case, BMT as currently practiced involves a two-stage process of skills training followed by contingency contracting. Several modular packages have been developed, the most recent of which is the 10-session Oregon package (Weiss et al., 1973). There is also the less technical package developed by Azrin, Naster, and Jones (1973).

Skills training focuses on communication and aims at the retraining of the couple's interactional repertoire in four areas: (1) helping the couples learn to communicate more specifically (pinpointing and discrimination training) and effectively; (2) teaching problem-solving, conflict-resolution, and negotiation skills; (3) increasing the expression of appropriate feelings; and (4) increasing positive interaction. Skills training generally takes place in the clinic and utilizes the skill building practices of therapist feedback, modeling, and behavioral rehearsal. Empathy training, borrowed from the client-centered school, is often included (Epstein & Williams, 1981; O'Leary & Turkewitz, 1978).

Contingency contracting takes place in the home and involves the use of written agreements between the spouses for specific changes in behavior. The focus is on selecting positive behaviors for acceleration, rather than on decelerating negative behaviors, because the latter process requires the use of aversive stimulation. Contracts may be buttressed by the use of token economies (Stuart, 1969a, 1969b). There are two types of contracts. *Quid-pro-quo* contracts are "cross-linked," taking the form of "If you do X, I'll do Y." These are used in the Azrin et al. (1973) program. This type of contract has the disadvantage of requiring one spouse to "go first"; it also sanctions the abandonment of contractional responsibilities if one member fails to fulfill his/her responsibilities. The Oregon package (Weiss et al., 1973) uses an alternative format—the "good faith" contract, in which "If X, then W + ; if Y, then H + ." That is, each spouse is reinforced independently for performing targeted behaviors. The latter form of contract is more cumbersome, and Jacobson and Martin (1976) recommend that it be used only when it is necessary. The available research suggests that the good faith contract may be necessary with more disturbed couples or in the earlier stages of therapy (O'Leary & Turkewitz, 1978).

BMT is a brief treatment, used in a conjoint individual couple format, primarily for mildly to moderately distressed couples, although its application to severely distressed couples is being investigated (Jacobson & Weiss, 1978). As mentioned above couples groups have been used for preventive marital (Harrell & Guerney, 1976; Witkin & Rose, 1978), premarital (Markham & Floyd, 1980; Ridley et al., 1981), and divorce (Granvold & Welch, 1977) programs, but not yet for treatment programs.

The evaluative research on BMT has been reviewed several times (Bussod & Jacobson, 1983; Greer & D'Zurilla, 1975; Jacobson & Margolin, 1979; Jacobson & Martin, 1976), and the base of empirical support is increasing. Although there is some controversy about its precise empirical status (Gurman & Kniskern, 1978; Gurman, Knudson, & Kniskern, 1978; Jacobson & Weiss, 1978), BMT has demonstrated that it is an effective treatment for many couples. There is at this point an accumulating body of studies, including uncontrolled studies, controlled clinical studies, and controlled group-design analogue studies. The studies have used a combination of self-report measures of satisfaction (of which the Locke & Wallace, 1959, Marital Adjustment Scale and the Weiss et al., 1973, Spouse Observation Checklists are the most common) and behavioral observation measures of communication skills (The Marital Interaction Coding System, Weiss et al., 1973). The most impressive are Jacobson's studies (reviewed by Jacobson & Margolin, 1979), which replicated the work of the Oregon group (Weiss et al., 1973). A unique feature of Jacobson's research was the use of a series of single-subject experiments within the context of a between-groups design. Future research should aim at further replication and should include follow-up studies.

A key issue for the future of BMT concerns the effective elements within the complex treatment packages. Jacobson and Margolin (1979, p. 359) noted that available research indicates that "communication training seems to be an often necessary and at times sufficient treatment for many couples," whereas "there is some empirical basis for doubting the general effectiveness of contingency contracting." This prompted Jacobson to observe that "it may be that the most effective element of the behavioral approach is the one which is the least unique to a behavioral approach."

Parenting Programs

Parent education fits the training for enhancement paradigm. This section will review the programs focused on parenting at the pre-, neo-, and mesoparental stages. In addition, several programs will be discussed which are derived from parent education, but which focus on the family as a whole.

Preparental Programs

The preparental programs are education for parenthood courses for teenagers and young adults developed by family life educators. The *Exploring Childhood* curriculum, developed by the Education Development Center (1977) in Cambridge, Massachusetts, and financed by the Office of Education, Office of Child Development, and National Institute of Mental Health, is one of the better known programs. Designed for high school students, the program is eclectic and integrates didactic instruction in child development (written by some of the leading experts in developmental psychology) with practical experiences in child care. An extensive evaluation found gains in knowledge, attitudes, and behavior in child care, and a complex pattern of relationships between student variables (such as age, sex, race, socioeconomic status, and prior course work in child development) and gain scores (Education Development Center, 1976). However, de Lissovoy (1978) pointed out that such short-term gains do not ensure long-term preparation for parenthood. Making the case that adolescents are not ready developmentally to prepare themselves for parenthood, he argued that *Exploring Childhood* is a "white elephant in the classroom," which might be better utilized for an audience of prospective parents.

Neoparental Programs

Neoparental programs consist of various forms of childbirth education classes offered in many local communities through prenatal clinics, maternity hospitals, the Red Cross, and the Childbirth Education Association. The courses are usually led by nurses, and the content typically includes information on the health needs of pregnant women, labor and delivery, and the care of the newborn infant. These classes are designed to help prepare women for the birth process. Whether or not they go beyond this to help prospective parents cope with the developmental transition to parenthood varies a great deal, depending on the skills and awareness of the instructor. Prepared childbirth classes, especially the Lamaze Method (Bing, 1969), provide more systematic attention to these psychological needs of parents-to-be.

A recent trend is the inclusion of expectant fathers in childbirth education classes (Barnhill, Rubenstein, & Rocklin, 1979; Gearing, 1978; Resnick, Resnick, Packer, & Wilson, 1978). One of these programs has been extended to provide education for fathers of infants from birth to the preschool stage (Resnick et al., 1978). The available research literature indicates that developing a coherent father role is important for men's postpartum adjustment (Fein, 1976), and that lack of knowledge about parenting is predictive of high postpartum adjustment difficulty (Wente & Crockenberg, 1976). However, whether expectant-father education is effective in facilitating postpartum adjustment has yet to be shown.

Mesoparental Programs

Mesoparental programs are those which are most commonly thought of as parent education, or parent education proper. Parent education has been defined as "purposive learning activity of parents who are attempting to change their method of interaction with their children for the purpose of encouraging positive behavior in their children" (Croake & Glover, 1977, p. 151). The first recorded parent education group in the United States was formed in 1815. Several such groups, or "maternal associations," were soon developed for the purpose of encouraging mothers to discuss their childrearing concerns and promote the moral and religious development of their children. In 1888 the organization now known as the Child Study Association of America was founded and began to sponsor ongoing parent education groups (Croake & Glover, 1977).

By the middle of the twentieth century the parent education groups sponsored by the Child Study Association were based on Freudian psychology (especially the work of Anna Freud) and on child development research, such as was being conducted at the Gesell Institute (Cable, 1975). It was assumed that parental motives, thoughts, and feelings were more important than overt behavior (Brim, 1965). These assumptions were reflected in the structure and format of the programs. The programs utilized a discussion group format in which the parents developed the agenda based on their interests and problems and in which the group leaders attempted to provide support and advice (Auerbach, 1968). While these discussion groups varied in terms of the size of the group, the homogeneity of its members, and the length and number of meetings, they shared the following goals for parents: to be more loving and accepting of their children, to understand child development and the causes of the child's behavior, to understand the effect of parent behavior on children, to develop problem-solving skills, and to feel relaxed, secure, and natural (Brim, 1965).

Tavormina (1974) reviewed the discussion group approach to parent education, and the associated evaluative research. The initial evaluations ranged from parent testimonials and clinical impressions to evaluations of changes in parental attitudes. Although Hereford's (1963) four-year study reported changes in parent attitudes as a result of discussion group parent education, his results were not replicated in subsequent research. Moreover, other studies found that changes in parent attitudes were not consistently associated with changes in children's behavior. Furthermore, Chilman's (1973) review of parent education programs indicated that most discussion group programs failed to attract and hold many parents, especially lower socioeconomic parents. In a later review article, Tavormina (1980) criticized the discussion group approach to parent education for its lack of specificity and pointed to the more recently developed didactic/discussion and skills-training programs as the direction for the future.

Didactic/discussion groups differ from discussion groups in that more time is spent in a structured presentation of didactic material. Childrearing principles are taught from a variety of theoretical perspectives. The original didactic/discussion groups were either Adlerian Parent Study groups (Dreikurs & Soltz, 1964) or Ginottian humanistic groups (Ginott, 1957). Recently a spate of new didactic/discussion programs have appeared, described in several texts and handbooks on parent education (Abidin, 1980; Arnold, 1978a; Fine, 1980; Lamb & Lamb, 1978). These new programs include theoretically pure and eclectic programs. The theoretically pure programs include models developed from systems theory (Arnold, 1978b; Benson, Berger, & Mease, 1975), transactional analysis (James & James, 1978; Lamb & Lamb, 1978; Sirridge, 1980), rational-emotive therapy (Ellis, 1978; Lamb & Lamb, 1978), and reality therapy (Lamb & Lamb, 1978; McGuinness & Glasser, 1978). Numerous eclectic programs have been developed. Representative examples include Developing the Productive Child (Gilmore & Gilmore, 1978); Becoming Us (Carnes & Laube, 1975); the Solution Oriented Approach to Problems, or SOAP program (Lamb & Lamb, 1978); and Parenting Skills (Abidin, 1976). These didactic/discussion programs are for the most part fairly new; many have not yet developed a set of teaching materials or techniques and (with three exceptions) have not yet been evaluated. The exceptions are the programs by Benson et al. (1975), Gilmore & Gilmore (1978), and Abidin (1976), which have received some empirical support.

Regarding the skills-training programs, the more established programs include client-centered programs (Parent Effectiveness Training, Gordon, 1970; and Parent Adolescent Relationship Development, Guerney, 1977), behavioral programs (group behavioral parent training), and an Adlerian program (Systematic Training for Effective Parenting, Dinkmeyer & McKay, 1976). The client-centered and behavioral programs have been described above, and the Adlerian program will be described below in a general discussion of Adlerian parent education.

Adlerian parent education. There are two basic models of Adlerian parent education: Parent Study Groups and Systematic Training for Effective Parenting. (The Adlerian Parent Teacher Education Center is a related program, but it will not be covered because its focus is on counseling parents and children and on training teachers as Adlerian counselors; c.f. Lowe & Morse, 1977). Parent study groups have a didactic/discussion group format. Groups have been run for mothers only, fathers only, both parents, and whole families (Christensen & Thomas, 1980; Lamb & Lamb, 1978). Groups consist of 8 to 12 members, which meet once per week for two hours for 8 to 12 weeks. The content is based on the Dreikurs and Soltz (1964) text, *Children: The Challenge,* for which there is a leader's manual (Soltz, 1967). The objective is to teach Adlerian-Dreikursian principles of democratic childrearing, which, in brief, include the following: (1) understanding the four goals of children's misbehavior (attention, power, revenge, or inadequacy) and learning to use one's impulsive responses to children's misdeeds to identify the child's goal; (2) understanding that the misbehaving child is a discouraged child, and learning to use encouragement in a broad form, which communicates respect and love to the child; (3) replacing the authoritarian discipline techniques of reward and punishment with the democratic techniques of natural and logical consequences; (4) learning to hold Family Councils. The evaluative research on Adlerian Parent Study Groups, recently reviewed, was found to generally support the effectiveness of these groups in improving parents' knowledge of course content and changing parents' attitudes, perceptions of their children's behavior, and self-reported child-rearing practices (Christensen & Thomas, 1980; Croake, 1983; Croake & Glover, 1977; McDonough, 1976).

Systematic Training for Effective Parenting, or STEP (Dinkmeyer & McKay, 1976), is a skills-training version of Adlerian parent education, which also incorporates training in communicational skills. It is designed for up to 12 participants and meets once a week for two hours for nine weeks. Research so far has been very limited (Dinkmeyer & Dinkmeyer, 1979), but is clearly needed, given the widespread use of this program.

Family Programs

There are three entries in this category: Kohlbergian family education, Structured Family Enrichment, and the Understanding Us program. Although these programs are designed for whole families, they are included under parent education because of their derivation from parent education programs.

Kohlbergian family education. A unique program was recently developed which utilized components of other programs, but integrated them within an intervention framework aimed at altering the justice structure of the family according to Kohlberg's theory of moral development (Stanley, 1980).

The 10-session, 25-hour program includes elements of Parent Effectiveness Training (PET) and Adlerian Parent Education, and consists of four phases. In phase I, the PET skills of empathic listening and "I"-messages are taught. In phase II, the Adlerian Family Council is introduced in order to discuss family rules and promote more justice and democracy in the family. In phase III, PET's "no-lose" method of conflict resolution is taught. Those conflicts which could not be resolved with the "no-lose" method—namely, those having to do with basic differences in values—become grist for the mill in phase IV, which is focused on the value and moral dimensions using values clarification and the discussion of moral dilemmas. An evaluation of the program administered to families (both parents and their adolescent children), compared to parents-only and no-contact groups, indicated that while parents in both treatment groups improved their equalitarian attitudes and effectiveness in collective decision making, the family group showed greater improvement and their adolescent children showed gains in moral reasoning—gains which were maintained at one-year follow-up (Stanley, 1978).

Structured Family Enrichment. The Structured Family Enrichment program was developed by L'Abate (1977) and colleagues at Georgia State University and is based on the educational methods of programmed instruction. The theoretical base lies in general information-processing systems, communication theory, and transactional psychology. The model consists of written programs with detailed instructions that an individual specifically trained then reads to the participants. Each program consists of three to six lessons, each containing five to six exercises in which the whole family participates. All totaled there are 26 different programs with 139 structured lessons. These programs and accompanying lessons are developed around specific topics of relevance to family living (such as democratic living, financial management, values clarification, assertiveness, helpfulness, and negotiation). The selection of a particular program for each family varies according to those areas of most concern to the particular family participating. This feature allows a great deal of flexibility, as well as the ability to tailor the intervention to specific family needs. Programs also vary in complexity and can be matched to the family's educational level. Some are cognitive (or didactic), some affective (or experiential), and others problem solving in focus (combining didactic and experiential). Most of the above program elements are included in L'Abate's (L'Abate et al., 1975a) first manual.

A second manual (L'Abate et al., 1975b) contains several enrichment programs written from a developmental perspective and focusing on various issues confronting families over the life cycle. Also, programs have been developed which address unique family forms or situations (such as single parents, adoptive families, drug-problems, physically handicapped, and families of alcoholics). Preliminary research on this model provides some support for its efficacy (L'Abate, 1977).

Understanding Us. The most recently developed family education program is the Understanding Us (UU) program. UU is the first in a planned series of "Whole Family Programs," and was developed by Carnes (1981a, 1981b), one of the originators of the Becoming Us parent education program (Carnes & Laube, 1975). The UU program is sponsored by Interpersonal Communication Programs, Inc., whose first effort was the well-known Couples Communication Program. The UU program is based on the "circumplex model" of family systems, recently developed by Olson, Sprenkle, and Russell (1979). The circumplex model proposes that the dimensions of "cohesion" and "adaptability" are central to family functioning, and identifies 16 family types according to their placement in a circumplex formed by these two orthogonal dimensions. The UU program adds the individual concepts of identity development and personal responsibility in an integrated set of systems principles (Carnes, 1981a).

The program is offered to groups of 10 to 12 families (primarily parents and adolescent children), who meet with a certified UU instructor for four weekly sessions, two hours in length. The topics of the sessions are adapting, caring, growing, and changing. The program is didactic and experiential, and family members are given a book with homework assignments (*Understanding Us,* Carnes, 1981b). Given the newness of the program, it has yet to be evaluated, although such research is planned.

Marriage Programs

Marriage programs are training for enhancement programs. This section will review three groups of programs: pre- and neomarital programs; mesomarital programs (marriage enrichment); and postmarital or divorce programs.

Pre- and Neomarital Programs

The field of premarital counseling dates back to 1932 (Bagarozzi & Rauen, 1981; Mudd, Freeman, & Rose, 1941). It derives from two main sources: (1) family life education programs in high schools and colleges (Figley, 1977); (2) instructional counseling offered by clergy or family physicians (Schumm & Denton, 1979). Recently, the marital enrichment movement has contributed to the development of new premarital programs.

Programs have been developed from client-centered (PRIMES, Avery, Ridley, Leslie, & Milholland, 1980; D'Augelli et al., 1974; Ginsberg & Vogelsong, 1977; Schlien, 1971), and behavioral [Premarital Relationship Enhancement Program (PREP), Markham & Floyd, 1980; Markman, Floyd, Stephen, & Stanley, 1981; Mutual Problem Solving Program, Ridley et al., 1981] perspectives. In addition, the Couple Communication Program (discussed below) was initially designed to facilitate the developmental transition to marriage (Miller, 1971). Finally, there are numerous atheoretical programs, offered from religious (Boike, 1977) and nonreligious (Ehrentrout, 1975; Hinkle & Moore, 1971; Meadows & Taplin, 1970; Van Zoost, 1973) perspectives. Five atheoretical programs were evaluated by Olson and Norem (1977).

Bagarozzi and Rauen (1981) reviewed the evaluative research literature, limiting their review to the 13 studies in which "standardized procedures and intervention technique were . . . followed systematically," and in which "some type of outcome measure was employed" (p. 14). These 13 studies suffered from several methodological flaws: Only seven used a control or comparison group; only two of these used standardized assessment procedures, and only two studies attempted follow-ups. While there is modest support for the notion that premarital enrichment programs improve communication and problem-solving skills, there is no evidence that these programs either reduce the incidence of divorce or promote more successful marriages. Believing that existing programs have little likelihood of accomplishing these long-term goals, Bagarozzi and Rauen (1981) recommended more ambitious programs which help couples preview their upcoming developmental tasks, teach a wide range of behavioral skills, and provide an opportunity to reevaluate the decision to marry.

Schumm and Denton (1979) dealt with a related problem, namely the question raised by Emily Mudd over 40 years ago: "How far can one help to prepare another person for an experience which he has not had" (Mudd et al., 1941, p. 114). Reviewing the literature on "post-wedding" or neomarital counseling, they concluded that the most "teachable moment" probably occurs after the marriage, and that the most important result of premarital counseling may be the establishment of a positive relationship as a basis for neomarital sessions. Future work in this area thus might investigate the relative efficacy of pre versus neoversus pre + neomarital enrichment programs, utilizing some of the better developed programs and evaluative procedures, including follow-ups.

Mesomarital Programs

Mesomarital programs are marital enrichment programs. Marital enrichment is a phenomenon which emerged in the 1960s as part of the humanistic wave of that period. It has been characterized as "a response to the transition from institutional to companionship marriage in our contemporary world" (Mace & Mace, 1975, p. 131). The marital enrichment movement has its roots in humanistic psychology, the human potential movement, and affective education, and relies heavily on group process techniques developed in the encounter group movement (Hof & Miller, 1980; Smith, Shoffner, & Scott, 1979). The movement has grown tremendously. Based on a survey conducted in 1973–1974, Otto (1975) estimated that 180,000 couples had participated in a marital enrichment program. A few years later he reported an estimate of 420,000 couples (Otto, 1976). Recent estimates range around 1.2 million couples.

The marital enrichment movement was started by several religious and secular groups. Herbert and Roberta Otto first led marriage groups on the West Coast in 1961 (Otto, 1969); and David and Vera Mace began leading weekend retreats for the Quakers the following year on the East Coast (Quaker Marriage Enrichment Retreats, Mace & Mace, 1973). Leon and Antoinette Smith began their work in 1964, developing the Marriage Communication Labs sponsored by the United Methodist Church (Smith & Smith, 1976). In 1966 the Catholic Marriage Encounter program (begun in Spain in 1958) reached the United States (Bosco, 1972). Because of its strong ties to the Catholic Church and differing needs, several Protestant and Jewish versions of Marriage Encounter have been developed (Genovese, 1975). In 1968 Sherod Miller and colleagues began work on the Minnesota Couple Communication Program (now known as the Couple Communication Program, Miller, Nunnally, & Wackman, 1976a, 1976b). In 1973, the Maces (1975, 1976) founded the Association of Couples for Marriage Enrichment (ACME) in an effort to coordinate the burgeoning movement. In addition, marital enrichment programs were developed during the late 1960s and early 1970s by client-centered and behavioral workers.

At present there are a large number of programs (Hof & Miller, 1980, report a knowledge of 50 programs). Many of these programs are described in several recent texts (Garland, 1983; Hof & Miller, 1981; Mace, 1982). Unfortunately, many programs are not well developed conceptually, consisting of a "hodge-podge" or "smorgasbord" of various concepts and techniques (Hof & Miller, 1980). The emphasis in this brief overview will be on the better developed programs.

The marital enrichment programs as a group are concerned with enhancing normal (i.e., nonclinical) marriages, with attention to enhancing communication, negotiation, and conflict-resolution skills, deepening emotional and sexual satisfaction, and fostering and supporting existing marital strengths (Gurman & Kniskern, 1977). There are four types of marital enrichment programs.

First, there are the programs sponsored by religious organizations. These include the Marriage Encounter (Catholic, Jewish, and Protestant forms, Genovese, 1975), the Quaker Marital Enrichment Program (Mace & Mace, 1973), the Methodist Marriage Communication Labs (Smith & Smith, 1976), and others (cf. Otto, 1976; Ulrici, L'Abate, & Wagner, 1981). The religious programs generally take the form of intensive weekend retreats or marathons for groups of couples. But whereas Marriage Encounter involves a private encounter between husband and wife, with group interaction occurring only at religious or social levels, the Methodist and Quaker programs consist almost entirely of group interaction and are modeled after the encounter group movement. Marriage Encounter, the largest marriage enrichment program, has recently been criticized on theoretical and clinical grounds, and concerns have been raised about potential harmful effects (DeYoung, 1979; Doherty, McCabe, & Ryder, 1978).

Second, there are the nonprofessional programs offered by the Association of Couples for Marriage Enrichment (ACME). ACME offers weekend retreats similar to the Methodist and Quaker programs, as well as growth groups which meet weekly for six to eight weeks, both of which are led by nonprofessionals selected, trained, and certified by ACME (Hopkins, Hopkins, Mace, & Mace, 1978). In addition to group interaction, ACME also incorporates elements of some of the systematic skills programs, such as the Couples Communication Program.

Third, there are several theoretically based group programs which have recently emerged. These include Gestalt Marriage Enrichment (Zinker & Leon, 1976), the Transactional Analysis program (Capers & Capers, 1976), and the Rankian Marital Rebirth program (Schmitt &

Schmitt, 1976). These new programs are still in the early stages of their development.

Fourth, there are the systematic skills-training programs, of which the major ones are the Conjugal Relationship Enhancement (Collins, 1977) and group behavioral marital training (Harrell & Guerney, 1976; Witkin & Rose, 1978) programs discussed above, and the Couples Communication Program (Miller et al., 1976a, 1976b), which will be discussed below. In addition, there are several other less well known skills-training programs: The Pairing Enrichment Program (Travis & Travis, 1975); MARDILAB—the Marital Diagnostic Laboratory (Stein, 1975); the Structured Marital Enrichment Program (L'Abate, 1977); and Fair Fight Training (Bach & Bernard, 1971).

The evaluative research literature on the marital enrichment programs has been reviewed by Gurman and Kniskern (1977) and Hof and Miller (1980). Although the results of controlled studies are generally positive (67 percent of the controlled studies reviewed by Gurman and Kniskern found program effects to exceed those of control groups), there are a number of methodological flaws: lack of attention-placebo control groups; overreliance on subject self-report or trainer assessments; and relative lack of follow-ups. Thus, although there is modest support for the proposition that marital enrichment programs enhance short-term communication skills and satisfaction with the relationship, the empirical basis for this needs to be strengthened through improved studies. In addition, Gurman and Kniskern (1977) recommend attention to several related issues: (1) the durability of enrichment-induced change; (2) the generalizability of enrichment-induced change to other family relationships; (3) the range of potential participants (most research has focused on educated couples from university communities or couples closely affiliated with a religious organization); (4) the timing of enrichment programs to fit with developmental needs; (5) investigations of the relative efficacy of various program forms, and separating out the most potent program components.

More recently, Giblin (1982) conducted a meta-analysis of the enrichment literature; the results of this study are summarized in Chapter 8.

The Couple Communication Program. The Couple Communication Program has been identified as one of the most promising marital enrichment programs (Olson, 1976; Olson & Sprenkle, 1976; Otto, 1975). The program (as originally developed) is a brief (4 session, 12 hour) systematic training program based somewhat on the family sociological frameworks of family development (Hill & Rodgers, 1964) and symbolic interaction (Foote & Cottrell, 1955) but primarily on communication systems theory (Watzlawick, Beavin, & Jackson, 1967). There is a text, *Talking Together* (Miller, Wackman, & Nunnally, 1983a) and an instructor's manual (Nunnally, Miller, & Wackman, 1983). The program is designed to equip normal couples to meet the challenge of their developmental tasks, at all stages of the life cycle (premarriage, during marriage, or in anticipation of remarriage) through teaching two sets of skills: (1) speaking skills to help partners express themselves more completely and clearly; (2) listening skills to help partners understand each other more fully and accurately.

Wampler and Sprenkle (1980) reviewed prior research on the Couple Communication Program and reported the results of their follow-up study. Correcting for several of the methodological flaws of earlier studies, they found that while the program had a positive effect on communication skills (assessed behaviorally) and on relationship quality (self-reported) at post-test, only the positive changes in relationship quality persisted at four to six months follow-up. They recommended an expanded program, perhaps using booster sessions, to improve the staying power of the communication skills. A more recent review (Wampler, 1982a) and meta-analysis (Wampler, 1982b) of the research literature on the Couple Communication Program are discussed in Chapter 8. In a recent article, Miller, Wackman, and Nunnally (1983b) indicated that the program has been revised in response to research feedback and now consists of two phases: Couple Communication I and Couple Communication II.

Postmarital Programs

Divorce is a very difficult human experience, stressful and often traumatic for all members of a family. Recent studies have described the stages of the divorce process, and intervention programs have been developed for children and the separating partners at various stages of the process. Both the stage models and the intervention programs have been reviewed by Kaslow (1981). Here we will touch briefly on the structured or skills-training approaches that have been developed. More detailed discussion of these programs can be found in Chapter 9.

There are three categories of programs which I would like to highlight here. First, there are programs for the children. Open-ended discussion groups or "rap sessions" are offered to children of divorce by Parents Without Partners (P.W.P., Parks, 1977) and Children Helped in Litigated Divorce (C.H.I.L.D., Anderson, 1977). Young (1980) reported the use of court-mandated workshops (two hours in length) for adolescent children of divorcing parents, with participants reporting positive attitudes toward the program. Structured children's divorce groups for elementary school children have been described by Wilkinson and Bleck (1977), and Sonnenshein-Schneider and Baird (1980). Finally, there are two skills-training programs: Guerney and Jordan's (1979) Children of Divorce Program was offered to children 9 to 13 years of age and met for one hour for six weekly meetings; Kessler and Bostwick's (1977) assertion training program was offered to children 10 to 17 years of age, and consisted of a one-day (six-hour) workshop.

Second, there are the mediation programs (Coogler, 1978; Haynes, 1982), a recently developed alternative to the traditional legal-adversary divorce process. In one of these, a highly structured program (Coogler, 1978), couples sign a legal document which binds them to work out a mutual settlement on issues of custody, support, alimony, and division of property. If they are unable to do so, they are required to enter into binding arbitration. Couples are "walked-through" the process, using a set of "Marital Mediation Rules," which are well-worked-out methods of conflict resolution. At present, this approach utilizes very little skills training, but given its limitations found in a recent evaluation (Kressel et al., 1977), some skills training might well become a useful component of this promising approach.

Finally, there are divorce adjustment groups which utilize an educational approach. Three such programs exemplify this approach: a seven-week cognitive-behavioral treatment seminar (Granvold & Welch, 1977); an open-ended eclectic didactic/discussion group (Kessler, 1976); and a client-centered communication skills training workshop which has been offered as a 5-week, 15-hour course (Thiessen, Avery, & Joanning, 1980) and as a 2-day, 13-hour weekend workshop (Avery & Thiessen, 1982).

Conclusions

Comparative Evaluations and Future Research Directions

There is, thus, a growing array of skills-training programs for the family, for which there is also modest empirical support. The evaluative research literature of these programs will be reviewed in more detail in the subsequent chapters in this book. But before leaving this general survey, it would be well to consider the empirical literature attempting the comparative evaluation of two or more family skills-training programs. These studies are summarized in Table 1-2, grouped according to whether the focus of the program is parenting or marriage.

There are several serious problems with this literature. Some of the studies have design flaws—such as small N's, lack of random assignment to condition, use of questionable dependent measure or measures more appropriate to the objectives of one of the groups than the other, and statistical errors—which render a meaningful interpretation of their results difficult or impossible. But even more important, there are a number of

Table 1-2 Comparative Evaluation of Family Skills
Training Programs

I. *Parenting Programs*

A. Parent Effectiveness Training vs. Group Behavioral Parent Training

1. Anchor & Thomason (1977): PET vs. BPT. Design flaws, and PET course not administered in standard format.

2. Kowalewski (1977): PET vs. BPT. Design flaws.

3. Pinsker & Geoffry (1981): PET vs. BPT vs. NAC (non-attendant control) Design flaws, and treatment groups not equated for contact time.

4. Schofield (1976): PET vs. BPT vs. non-equivalent comparison group. Design flaws, and treatment groups not equated for contact time.

B. Parent Effectiveness Training vs. Adlerian Parent Study Group

1. Noble (1977): PET vs. APS vs. NAC. Design flaws, and PET not administered in standard format.

C. Parent Effectiveness Training vs. Group Behavioral Parent Training vs. Adlerian Parent Study Group

1. Schultz, Nystul, & Law (1980); Schultz & Nystul (1980): PET vs. BPT vs. APS vs. placebo control vs. NAC. Design flaws and PET not administered in standard format.

D. Parent Effectiveness Training vs. Miscellaneous Treatments

1. Hanley (1974): PET vs. Family Enrichment Groups vs. non-equivalent comparison group. Design flaws, treatment groups not equated for contact time, and alternative treatment is idiosyncratic.

2. Larsen (1972): PET vs. Achievement Motivation Group vs. Discussion Encounter Group. Design flaws, and Ach. Motiv. group not administered in standard format.

3. Miles (1975): PET vs. Verbal Reinforcement Group for Children vs. PET + VRGC vs. NAC. Design flaws, and alternative treatments are idiosyncratic.

4. Reiswig (1973): PET vs. Theme-Centered Interactional Group vs. Experiential Play. Design flaws, and alternative treatments are idiosyncratic.

E. Parent-Adolescent Relationship Development vs. Parent Discussion Groups

1. Coufal (1976); Vogelsong (1976): PARD vs. Relationship Improvement Program. Alternative treatment is not a skills training program.

F. Personal Developmental Programs vs. Behavioral Parent Training

1. Haffey & Levant (1984); Kanigsberg & Levant (1982): PDP vs. BPT vs. Non-equivalent comparison group.

    PDP parents improved their communication skills; BPT parents improved their behavioral skills; both groups improved parental attitudes and children's self-esteem at posttest and 3 month follow-up.

G. Group Behavioral Parent Training vs. Adlerian Programs (APS or STEP)

1. Frazier & Matthes (1975): BPT vs. APS vs. NAC. Design flaws.

2. Beutler, Oro-Beutler, & Mitchell (1979): BPT vs. STEP. Design flaws.

H. Behavioral Programs vs. Parent Discussion Groups.

1. Alexander & Parsons (1973); Parsons & Alexander (1973): BPT vs. client-centered parent discussion group vs. psychodynamic family counseling vs. NAC. Alternative treatments are not skills training programs, and would best be described as placebo controls.

2. Tavormina (1975): BPT vs. reflective parent discussion group. Alternative treatment is not skills training program, and would best be described as a placebo control.

3. Hampson & Tavormina (1980): BPT vs. reflective parent discussion group. Alternative treatment is not skills training program, and would best be described as a placebo control.

4. Rickel, Dudley & Berman (1980): Assertiveness training vs. parent discussion group. Alternative treatment is not skills training program, and would best be described as placebo control.

(continued)

Table 1-2 Continued

I. Adlerian Programs vs. Miscellaneous Treatments

1. Freeman (1975): APS vs. traditional parent discussion groups. Alternative treatment is not didactic/discussion program, and would best be described as placebo control.

2. Esters & Levant (1983): STEP vs. Developing the Productive Child (Gilmore & Gilmore, 1978) vs. NAC. Both groups of children showed gains in grade point average at posttest and 3 month follow-up, but only the Gilmore Method Children showed gains on self-reported and teacher-rated self-esteem at post-test and follow-up. STEP group children showed gains in teacher-rated self-esteem at post-test but not at follow-up.

J. Miscellaneous Programs

1. Campion (1973): Family Communication Systems (Benson, Berger, & Mease, 1975) vs. Adlerian-Gordon Model. Alternative treatment is an eclectic program and represents non-standard administration of PET & Adlerian programs.

II. *Marital and Premarital Programs*

A. Client-centered vs. Behavioral Programs

1. Wieman (1974): CRE vs. Reciprocal Reinforcement Therapy vs. NAC. CRE improved couples communication skills; RRT improved couples behavioral skills; and both groups resulted in gains in marital adjustment at posttest and at 10-week follow-up.

2. Ridley, Avery, Dent & Harrell (1981): PRIMES vs. Ridley Problem Solving Program vs. Lecture/discussion program. Design flaws.

3. McIntosh (1975): HRD marital skills program vs. Behavioral Exchange Training vs. client-centered couples counseling vs. NAC. Design flaws.

4. Cotton (1977): HRD marital skills program vs. BMT vs. placebo control. Very few differences found between treatment groups.

5. Venema (1976): Communication Skills Training vs. Behavioral Exchange vs. Combined Communication-Behavioral group. Very few differences found between the groups, though the combined groups showed greater change.

6. O'Leary & Turkewitz (1981): Communication Skills Training vs. BMT vs. NAC. No significant differences found between treatment groups.

B. Client-centered vs. Miscellaneous Treatments

1. Jessee (1978): CRE vs. Gestalt Relationship Awareness Facilitation. Alternative treatment is idiosyncratic.

2. Avery, Ridley, Leslie, & Milholland (1980): PRIMES vs. lecture/discussion program. Alternative treatment is not a skills training program, and would best be described as a placebo control.

3. Hines (1976): Communication skills training vs. psychodynamic group therapy vs. NAC. Alternative treatment is not skills training program and would best be described as placebo control.

4. Brock & Joanning (1983): CRE vs. Couple Communication Program vs. NAC. Very complex problems presented by this study, which attempted to compare a 10 week (20 hr) program with a 4 week (12 hr program). Results favor CRE, except at a mid-test comparison at the end of CCP, where no differences were found between the treatments.

5. Ross, Baker, & Guerney (1982): CRE compared to therapists' preferred therapy. Alternative treatments not skills training programs.

C. Behavioral vs. Miscellaneous Treatments

1. Fisher (1974): Behavioral training group vs. facilitative (combination of group-centered, Adlerian and functional group methods) vs. NAC. Alternative treatment is not skills training program and would best be described as placebo control.

2. Azrin, Besalel, Bechtel, Michalicek, Mencera, Carroll, Shuford, & Fox (1980): BMT vs. discussion group. Alternative treatment is not skills training program and would best be described as placebo control.

3. Epstein & Jackson (1978): Assertiveness Training vs. interaction insight group vs. NAC. Alternative treatment is not skills training program and would best be described as placebo control.

4. Liberman, Levine, Wheeler, Sanders, & Wallace (1976): BMT vs. interaction insight group. Alternative treatment is not a skills training program and would best be described as placebo control.

D. Miscellaneous Programs

1. Kilmann, Moreault, & Robinson (1978): Fair fight training & sexual enhancement vs. sexual enhancement & fair fight training vs. NAC. Both treatments superior to NAC in enhancing personal and marital functioning, but the sequence of treatment components did not affect outcome.

problems concerning the nature of the comparison itself: standardized treatments are administered in nonstandard formats; treatment groups are not equated for contact time; well-known treatments are compared to unknown or idiosyncratic alternative treatments, which may have been developed specifically for the purposes of assessing the better known treatments, thus appearing to be "straw men"; and skills-training programs from one theoretical orientation are compared to discussion groups from another theoretical orientation, thus confounding theoretical orientation with pedagogical method, and using as an alternative treatment an approach (discussion group) which could be considered a placebo control. Finally, a more subtle problem concerns the comparison of behavioral programs with others. These studies compare the two treatments administered in a group format and (usually) for enhancement purposes, which are the least-well-developed aspects of the behavioral programs. Behavioral parent training, a training for treatment program, would most validly be compared to Filial Therapy, in either individual or combined (individual–group) formats. And behavioral marital therapy, a training as treatment program, would most validly be compared to other marital programs designed for treatment purposes, such as CRE or the HRD program, in either an individual or group format.

These are some of the more serious problems. What then are the results? Examining only the studies free from the above problems, one finds very little evidence for the efficacy of one method over the other. Several studies find no, or only a few, differences between the treatment groups (I-I_2, II-A_4, II-A_5, II-A_6, II-D_1), whereas others find that each treatment group does well on measures tailored to its objectives, and both do well on more general measures (I-F_1, II-A_1).

There is a need for additional comparative research, but only research which is able to surmount the problems of the current literature. In addition to observing basic canons of research design, future studies should compare treatments of equal stature designed for the same objective, using standard versions of the treatments (in terms of format and program materials). The treatments should be administered by adherents of the respective approaches. An optimal approach might involve the collaboration of two or more centers, each engaged in the research and development of a particular program. The treatments should be evaluated using measures which assess both the specific objectives of each treatment and the general effects common to the programs. Measures of known psychometric properties should be employed, and a combination of participant and nonparticipant respondents utilized. No-contact and attention-placebo controls should be used to assess the effects of treatment versus no-treatment, and of specific versus nonspecific factors in treatment. Gains should be assessed in a range of settings (clinic, home, school, etc.), and follow-ups should be done to assess whether the skills are maintained and used as well as whether the other gains have been maintained.

But above all, the treatments should be compared with respect to specific populations with particular needs. The current literature indicates that the programs have general efficacy and that there is little to recommend one treatment over another with regard to the general population. What we need to know now is: "*What* treatment, by *whom,* is most effective for *this* individual with *that* specific problem and under *which* set of circumstances" (Paul, 1967, p. 111).

Directions for Future Program Development and Other Issues

There are six issues which I would like to discuss by way of closing: (1) the overselling of family skills-training programs; (2) staffing and training issues; (3) the combination of theoretically distinct program elements; (4) sex-role stereotyping in programs; (5) the family systems perspective; and (6) future developments for enhancement programs.

1. As is the case with any new intervention or method of helping people, there is the risk that the enthusiasm for skills training will outdistance its demonstrated efficacy. There are definite limits to what any intervention can accomplish, and we would do well to ensure that any claims of efficacy are founded on a solid empirical base. There is some indication that enrichment programs are being oversold (L'Abate, 1981; Smith et al., 1979) and several programs have recently been taken to task on this account (Doherty et al., 1978; Doherty & Ryder, 1980).

2. As the field of marriage and family enrichment becomes a new professional area, the questions of who provides these services and what their training should be arise. L'Abate (1981) pointed out the reluctance of many highly trained mental health practitioners to involve themselves in these kinds of activities, seeing them as "second-class" in relationship to psychotherapy; and Smith et al. (1979) noted that many current practitioners of the family skills programs have little or no training. While Durlak's (1979) review finds evidence for the efficacy of paraprofessional helpers in service activities, there is an important role for professionals in the selection and training of paraprofessionals, and in the design, evaluation, and refinement of programs. These issues are beginning to surface and hopefully will be discussed in coming years.

3. Tavormina (1980) has been one of the chief proponents of what is called the "combination format," where elements of two different programs (e.g., communication skills training and behavioral child manage-

ment) are brought together in a single program. There is a temptation in this field to do this, and at times this is done somewhat thoughtlessly, creating hodge-podges of enrichment activities. The present author does not recommend this approach, seeing value in maintaining the theoretical integrity and conceptual consistency of intervention programs. It should also be observed, however, that the better developed programs are incorporating aspects of other models, but are doing so by extending their own theoretical orientation. For example, behavioral marital therapy has incorporated communication skills training, but has conceptualized it in behavioral terms, regarding it as a means of enhancing stimulus control; so, too, Relationship Enhancement has begun to "program" generalization and maintenance effects, but does so using methods which have a client-centered flavor.

4. The issue of sex-role stereotyping has recently come into focus in regard to parent education programs (De Frain, 1977; Resnick, 1981). Parent education has usually meant "mother education," and until very recently little systematic attention was given to involving fathers in these programs. In the current "era of paternal rediscovery" (Lamb, 1979, p. 938), this is starting to change; as mentioned above, attention is now being given to fathers in childbirth education and other programs (Filial Therapy, Stollak, 1981; Parent Adolescent Relationship Development, Grando & Ginsberg, 1976; Personal Development Program, Levant & Doyle, 1983). Two recent studies evaluated the differential effects of including or excluding fathers in behavioral parent training and found no difference in mother–child interaction (Martin, 1977) and children's classroom behavior (Firestone, Kelley, & Fike, 1980) attributable to father involvement. These findings should not be interpreted as indicating that father involvement is unimportant, given the weak relationship between the criterion measures and probable father effects, and the fact that these studies are limited to one approach to working with a particular population (problem children).

Parent education has also not serviced mothers well, as Resnick (1981) has pointed out, ignoring their needs as persons and perpetuating the "motherhood mystique." Furthermore, preparental programs do not adequately address the decision to have a child, often treating motherhood as a mandate rather than a choice (Hoffman & Levant, 1985). Finally, there is very little emphasis on the later stages of parenting or on helping full-time mothers disengage from the maternal role. These are issues which should be attended to in future program development and refinement.

5. There is a limited but growing awareness in this field of the family-systems perspective. Most of the programs focus on one subsystem of the

family (usually a dyad) and do not take into account the potential consequences of such an intervention on other subsystems or the family as a whole. For instance, we have mentioned the fact that most parent education is mother education. What are the effects of training one parent on the other parent, on the parental subsystem, and on the parents–child triad? What are the effects of a training for treatment program geared to one child on the other children? What are the effects of a parent education program on the marital relationship? (Or of marriage enrichment on parenting?) Research addressing these issues is just starting to appear (Levant & Doyle, 1983; Patterson & Fleischman, 1979), and it seems that parent education does have beneficial effects on marital adjustment (Scovern et al., 1980), at least with troubled marriages (Forehand, Griest, Wells, & McMahon, 1982). This matter of system effects deserves attention in future studies.

6. The last issue concerns the future development of the training for enhancement area. While it is easy to understand why theories of therapy can serve as the foundation for the two treatment areas (training for treatment and training as treatment), it is less clear that such theories can be a viable intellectual basis for the enhancement area. Doherty and Ryder (1980) criticized PET for training parents to be therapists, but the issue is really much broader than that. The problem resides in the lack of differentiation of the objectives of enhancement programs. Most enhancement programs are designed to "improve" parenting or "enrich" marriages. Programs should become more sharply focused, as either prevention or development programs. In the case of prevention, populations at risk could be identified, their vulnerabilities and strengths assessed, and appropriate interventions designed (using therapy and other relevant theories). Good examples of this approach can be found in the new divorce programs. With regard to development, a good deal of rethinking is necessary. Parenting programs, for example, should be based to a greater degree on child development research (Griffore, 1980) and on the research regarding the adult development of parents (Newberger, 1980); different kinds of programs should be offered to parents at different stages in their own and their children's life cycles and different kinds of programs should be offered to parents in different family types (i.e., single-parent families, step-families, dual-earner/co-parents, etc.). Regarding marriage programs, little is known about the development of the marriage over the life cycle (Levant, 1982). However, the pre- and neomarital stages are key points for intervention, and future work in this area is urged, taking into account the suggestions of Bagarrozi and Rauen (1981) for improved programs and evaluations, and of Schumm and Denton (1979) regarding the timing of the intervention.

References

Abidin, R.D. (1976). *Parenting skills.* New York: Human Sciences Press.

Abidin, R.D. (Ed.). (1980). *Parent education and intervention handbook.* Springfield, IL: Charles C. Thomas.

Albee, G.W. (1967). The relationship of conceptual models to manpower needs. In E.L. Cowen, E.A. Gardner, & M. Zak (Eds.), *Emergent approaches to mental health problems.* New York: Meredith.

Alberti, R.E., & Emmons, M.L. (1974). *Your perfect right: A guide to assertive behavior.* San Luis Obispo, CA: Impact.

Alexander, J.F., & Parsons, B.V. (1973). Short-term behavioral intervention with delinquent families: Impact on family process and recidivism. *Journal of Abnormal Psychology, 81,* 219–225.

Anchor, K.M., & Thomason, T.C. (1977). A comparison of two parent-training models with educated parents. *Journal of Community Psychology, 5,* 134–141.

Anderson, H. (1977). Children of divorce. *Journal of Clinical Child Psychology,* 6(2), 41–44.

Arnold, L.E. (Ed.). (1978a). *Helping parents help their children.* New York: Brunner/Mazel.

Arnold, L.E. (1978b). Helping parents beat the system. In L.E. Arnold (Ed.), *Helping parents help their children.* New York: Brunner/Mazel.

Auerbach, A.B. (1968). *Parents learn through discussion: Principles and practices of parent group education.* New York: Wiley.

Authier, J., Gustafson, K., Guerney, B.G., Jr., & Kasdorf, J.A. (1975). The psychological practitioner as a teacher: A theoretical-historical-practical review. *The Counseling Psychologist,* 5(2), 31–50.

Avery, A.W., & Thiessen, J.D. (1982). Communication skills training for divorcees. *Journal of Counseling Psychology, 29,* 203–205.

Avery, A.W., Ridley, C.A., Leslie, L., & Milholland, T. (1980). Relationship enhancement with premarital dyads: A six month follow-up. *American Journal of Family Therapy, 8,* 23–30.

Azrin, N.H., Besalel, V.A., Bechtel, R., Michalicek, A., Mancera, M., Carroll, D., Shuford, D., & Cox, J. (1980). Comparison of reciprocity and discussion-type counseling for marital problems. *American Journal of Family Therapy, 8,* 21–28.

Azrin, N.H., Naster, B.J., & Jones, R. (1973). Reciprocity counseling: A rapid learning-based procedure for marital counseling. *Behavior Research and Therapy, 11,* 365–382.

Bach, G., & Bernard, Y. (1971). *Aggression laboratory: The fair fight training manual.* Los Angeles: Kendall Hunt Publishing.

Baer, D.M., Wolfe, M.M., & Risley, T.R. (1968). Some current dimensions of applied behavior analysis. *Journal of Applied Behavior Analysis, 1,* 91–97.

Bagarozzi, D.A., & Rauen, P. (1981). Premarital counseling: Appraisal and status. *American Journal of Family Therapy,* 9(3), 13–30.

Barnhill, L., Rubenstein, G., & Rocklin, N. (1979). From generation to generation: Fathers-to-be in transition. *The Family Coordinator, 28,* 229–235.

Becker, W.C. (1971). *Parents are teachers.* Champaign, IL: Research Press.

Benassi, V.A., & Larson, K.M. (1976). Modification of parent interaction with the child as the behavior-change agent. In E.J. Mash, L.A. Hamerlynck, & L.C. Handy (Eds.), *Behavior modification and families.* New York: Brunner/Mazel.

Bendix, L.A. (1977). The differential effectiveness on parents and their children of training parents to be helpers or life skills trainers for their children (Doctoral dissertation, Boston University). *Dissertation Abstracts International, 38,* 1869–1870 B. (University Microfilms No. 77-21, 688.)

Benson, L., Berger, M., & Mease, W. (1975). Family communication systems. *Small Group Behavior, 6*(1), 91–105.

Berkowitz, B.P., & Graziano, A.M. (1972). Training parents as behavior therapists: A review. *Behavioral Research and Therapy, 10,* 297–317.

Bergin, A.E. (1967). Some implications of psychotherapy research for therapeutic practice. *International Journal of Psychiatry, 3,* 136–150.

Bernal, M.E., & North, J.A. (1978). A survey of parents training manuals. *Journal of Applied Behavior Analysis, 11,* 533–544.

Beutler, L.E., Oro-Beutler, M.E., & Mitchell, R. (1979). Systematic comparison of two parent training programs in child management. *Journal of Counseling Psychology, 26,* 531–533.

Bing, E. (1969). *Six practical lessons for easier childbirth.* New York: Bantam Books.

Boike, D. (1977). *The impact of a premarital program on communication process, communication facilitativeness, and personality trait variables of engaged couples.* Unpublished doctoral dissertation, Florida State University.

Bosco, A. (1972). *Marriage encounter: The rediscovery of love.* St. Meinard, IN: Abbey Press.

Brim, O.G., Jr. (1965). *Education for childrearing.* New York: The Free Press.

Brock, G.W., & Joanning, H. (1983). A comparison of the relationship enhancement program and the Minnesota Couple Communication Program. *Journal of Marital and Family Therapy, 9,* 413–421.

Brockway, B.S., & Williams, W.W. (1976). Training in child management: A prevention-oriented model. In E.J. Mash, L.C. Handy, & L.A. Hamerlynck (Eds.), *Behavior modification approaches to parenting.* New York: Brunner/Mazel.

Broderick, C.B., & Schrader, S.S. (1980). The history of professional marriage and family therapy. In A.S. Gurman & D.P. Kniskern (Eds.), *Handbook of family therapy.* New York: Brunner/Mazel.

Brown, J.H., Gamboa, A.M., Jr., Birkimer, J., & Brown, R. (1976). Some possible effects of parent self-control training on parent child interactions. In E.J. Mash, L.C. Handy, & L.A. Hamerlynck (Eds.), *Behavior modification approaches to parenting.* New York: Brunner/Mazel.

Bussod, N., & Jacobson, N.S. (1983). Cognitive behavioral marital therapy. *The Counseling Psychologist, 11*(3), 57–63.

Cable, M. (1975). *The little darlings: A history of child rearing in America.* New York: Charles Scribner.

Campion, S. (1973). A comparison of two parent education models. In G.P. Miller (Ed.), *Additional studies in elementary school guidance: Psychological education activities evaluated.* St. Paul: Minnesota Department of Education.

Capers, H., & Capers, B. (1976). Transactional analysis tools for use in marriage enrichment programs. In H.A. Otto (Ed.), *Marriage and family enrichment: New perspectives and programs.* Nashville: Abington.

Caplan, G., & Grunebaum, H. (1967). Perspectives on primary prevention: A review. *Archives of General Psychiatry, 17,* 331–346.

Carkhuff, R.R. (1969a). *Helping and human relations. Vol. I: Selection and training.* New York: Holt, Rinehart & Winston.

Carkhuff, R. (1969b). *Helping and human relations. Vol. II: Practice & research.* New York: Holt, Rinehart & Winston.

Carkhuff, R.R. (1971a). Training as a preferred mode of treatment. *Journal of Counseling Psychology, 18,* 123–131.

Carkhuff, R.R. (1971b). *The development of human resources: Education, psychology, and social change.* New York: Holt, Rinehart & Winston.

Carkhuff, R.R., & Bierman, R. (1970). Training as a preferred mode of treatment of parents of emotionally disturbed children. *Journal of Counseling Psychology, 17,* 157–161.

Carnes, P.J. (1981a). *Family development instructors manual.* Minneapolis, MN: Interpersonal Communication Programs.

Carnes, P.J. (1981b). *Family development I: Understanding us.* Minneapolis, MN: Interpersonal Communication Programs.

Carnes, P.J., & Laube, H. (1975). Becoming us: An experiment on family learning and teaching. *Small Group Behavior, 6*(1), 106–119.

Chilman, C.S. (1973). Programs for disadvantaged parents. In B.M. Caldwell & H.N. Ricciuti (Eds.), *Review of child development research,* Vol. III. Chicago: University of Chicago Press.

Christensen, O.C., & Thomas, C.R. (1980). Dreikurs and the search for equality. In M.J. Fine (Ed.), *Handbook on parent education.* New York: Academic Press.

Collins, J.D. (1977). Experimental evaluation of a six-month conjugal therapy and relationship enhancement program. In B.G. Guerney, Jr., *Relationship enhancement.* San Francisco: Jossey-Bass.

Cone, J.D., & Sloop, W.E. (1974). Parents as agents of change. In A. Jacobs & W.W. Spradling (Eds.), *The group as agent of change: Treatment, prevention, personal growth in the family, the school, the mental hospital, and the community.* New York: Behavioral Publications.

Coogler, O.J. (1978). *Structured mediation in divorce settlement.* Lexington, MA: Lexington Books.

Cotton, M.C. (1977). A systems approach to marital training evaluation (Doctoral dissertation, Texas Tech University). *Dissertation Abstracts International, 37,* 5346B. (University Microfilms No. 77-8742.)

Coufal, J.D. (1976). Preventive-therapeutic programs for mothers and adolescent daughters: Skills training vs. discussion methods. (Doctoral dissertation, Pennsylvania State University.) *Dissertation Abstracts International, 37,* 3941–3942A. (University Microfilms No. 76-26-824.)

Croake, J.W. (1983). Adlerian parent education. *The Counseling Psychologist, 11*(3), 65–71.

Croake, J.W., & Glover, K.E. (1977). A history and evaluation of parent education. *The Family Coordinator, 26*(2), 151–158.

D'Augelli, A.R., Deyss, D.S., Guerney, B.G., Jr., Hershenberg, B., & Sbrofsky, S.L. (1974). Interpersonal skill training for dating couples: An evaluation of an educational mental health service. *Journal of Counseling Psychology, 21,* 385–389.

D'Augelli, J.F., & Weener, J.M. (1978). Training parents as mental health agents. *Community Mental Health Journal, 14*(1), 14–25.

De Frain, J. (1977). Sexism in parenting manuals. *Family Coordinator, 26*(3), 245–231.

de Lissovoy, V. (1978). Parent education: White elephant in the classroom? *Youth and Society, 9*(3), 315–338.

DeYoung, A.J. (1979). Marriage encounter: A critical examination. *Journal of Marital and Family Therapy, 5*(2), 27–30.

Dinkmeyer, D., & Dinkmeyer, D., Jr. (1979). A comprehensive and systematic approach to parent education. *American Journal of Family Therapy, 7*(2), 46–50.

Dinkmeyer, D., & McKay, G.D. (1976). *Systematic training for effective parenting.* Circle Pines, MN: American Guidance Service.

Doherty, W.J., & Ryder, R.G. (1980). Parent effectiveness training (PET): Criticisms and caveats. *Journal of Marital and Family Therapy, 6,* 409–419.

Doherty, W.J., McCabe, P., & Ryder, R.G. (1978). Marriage encounter: A critical appraisal. *Journal of Marriage & Family Counseling, 4*(4), 99–107.

Dreikurs, R., & Soltz, V. (1964). *Children: The challenge.* New York: Meredith Press.

Dubanoski, R.A., & Tanabe, G. (1980). Parent education: A classroom program on social learning principles. *Family Relations, 29*(1), 15–20.

Durlak, J.H. (1979). Comparative effectiveness of paraprofessional and professional helpers. *Psychological Bulletin, 66,* 80–92.

Durrett, D.D., & Kelley, P.A. (1974). Can you really talk with your child? A parental training program in communication skills toward the improvement of parent-child interaction. *Group Psychotherapy & Psychodrama, 27,* 98–109.

Education Development Center. (1976). *Exploring childhood: National field test. Summary of evaluation findings, year two.* Cambridge, MA: Education Development Center.

Education Development Center. (1977). *Exploring childhood: Program overview and catalogue of materials.* Cambridge, MA: Education Development Center.

Ehrentraut, G. (1975). The effects of premarital counseling of juvenile marriages on marital communication and relationship patterns (Doctoral dissertation, United States International University). *Dissertation Abstracts International, 36,* 3571B–3572B. (University Microfilms No. 75–29, 382.)

Ellis, A. (1978). Rational-emotive guidance. In L.E. Arnold (Ed.), *Helping parents help their children.* New York: Brunner/Mazel.

Epstein, N., & Jackson, E. (1978). An outcome study of short-term communication training with married couples. *Journal of Consulting & Clinical Psychology, 46,* 207–212.

Epstein, N., & Williams, A.M. (1981). Behavioral approaches to the treatment of marital discord. In G.P. Sholevar (Ed.), *The handbook of marriage & marital therapy.* New York: S.P. Medical & Scientific Books.

Esters, P., & Levant, R.F. (1983). The effects of two parent counseling programs on rural low achieving children. *The School Counselor, 31*(2), 159–166.

Fein, R.A. (1976). Men's entrance to parenthood. *The Family Coordinator, 25,* 341–348.

Figley, C.R. (1977). Family life education: Teacher selection, education, and training issues—a selected bibliography. *Family Coordinator, 26,* 160–165.

Fine, M.J. (Ed.). (1980). *Handbook on parent education.* New York: Academic Press.

Firestone, P., Kelley, M.J., & Fike, S. (1980). Are fathers necessary in parent training groups? *Journal of Clinical Child Psychology, 9,* 44–47.

Fisher, R.E. (1974). The effects of two group counseling methods on perceptual congruence in married pairs (Doctoral dissertation, University of Hawaii). *Dissertation Abstracts International, 35,* 885A. (University Microfilms No. 74-17, 211.)

Foote, N.H., & Cottrell, L.S., Jr. (1955). *Identity and interpersonal competence: A new direction in family research.* Chicago: University of Chicago Press.

Forehand, R., & Atkeson, B.M. (1977). Generality of treatment effects with parents as therapists: A review of assessment and implementation procedures. *Behavior Therapy, 8,* 575–593.

Forehand, R., Greist, D.C., Wells, K., & McMahon, R.J. (1982). Side effects of parent counseling on marital satisfaction. *Journal of Counseling Psychology, 29,* 104–107.

Frazier, F., & Matthes, W.A. (1975). Parent education: A comparison of Adlerian and behavioral approaches. *Elementary School Guidance & Counseling, 10,* 31–38.

Freeman, C.W. (1975). Adlerian mother study groups: Effects on attitudes and behavior. *Journal of Individual Psychology, 31,* 37–50.

Freud, S. (1959). Analysis of a phobia in a five-year old boy. In *Collected Papers.* New York: Basic Books.

Garland, D.S. (1983). *Working with couples on marriage enrichment: A guide to developing, conducting, and evaluating programs.* San Francisco: Jossey-Bass.

Gearing, J. (1978). Facilitating the birth process and father-child bonding. *The Counseling Psychologist, 7*(4), 53–56.

Genovese, R.J. (1975). Marriage encounter. *Small Group Behavior, 6,* 45–46.

Giblin, P.R. (1982). *Meta-analysis of premarital, marital, and family enrichment research.* Unpublished doctoral dissertation, Purdue University.

Gilmore, J.V., & Gilmore, E.C. (1978). *A more productive child: Guidelines for parents.* Boston: The Gilmore Institute.

Ginott, H.G. (1957). Parent education groups in a child guidance clinic. *Mental Hygiene, 41,* 82–86.

Ginsberg, G., & Vogelsong, E.L. (1977). Premarital relationship improvement by maximizing empathy and self-disclosure: The PRIMES program. In B.G. Guerney, Jr., *Relationship enhancement: Skill-training programs for therapy, problem prevention, and enrichment.* San Francisco: Jossey-Bass.

Gordon, T. (1970). *P.E.T.: Parent effectiveness training.* New York: Peter H. Wyden.

Gordon, T. (1976). *P.E.T. in Action.* New York: Peter H. Wyden.

Gormally, J., & Hill, C.E. (1974). Guidelines for research on Carkhuff's training model. *Journal of Counseling Psychology, 21*(6), 539–547.

Grando, R., & Ginsberg, B.G. (1976). Communication in the father-son relationship: The parent adolescent relationship development program. *The Family Coordinator, 4*(24), 465–473.

Granvold, D.K., & Welch, G.J. (1977). Intervention for post divorce adjustment problems. The treatment seminar. *Journal of Divorce, 1,* 81–91.

Graziano, A.M. (1983). Behavioral approaches to child and family systems. *The Counseling Psychologist, 11*(3), 47–56.

Greer, S.E., & D'Zurilla, T.J. (1975). Behavioral approaches to marital discord and conflict. *Journal of Marriage and Family Counseling, 1*(4), 299–316.

Griffore, R.J. (1980). Toward the use of child development research in informed parenting. *Journal of Clinical Child Psychology, 9,* 48–51.

Guerney, B.G., Jr. (1964). Filial therapy: Description and rationale. *Journal of Consulting Psychology, 28,* 304–310.

Guerney, B.G., Jr. (1969). *Psychotherapeutic agents: New roles for nonprofessionals, parents and teachers.* New York: Holt, Rinehart & Winston.

Guerney, B.G., Jr. (1977). *Relationship enhancement.* San Francisco: Jossey-Bass.

Guerney, B.G., Jr. (1984). Contributions of client-centered therapy to filial, marital and family Relationship Enhancement therapies. In R.F. Levant & J.M. Shlien (Eds.), *Client-centered therapy and the person-centered approach: New directions in theory, research, and practice.* New York: Praeger.

Guerney, B.G., Jr., & Vogelsong, E.L. (1980). Relationship enhancement therapy. In R. Herink (Ed.), *The psychotherapy handbook.* New York: New American Library.

Guerney, L. (1976). Filial therapy programs. In D.H. Olson (Ed.), *Treating Relationships.* Lake Mills, IA: Graphic Publishing.

Guerney, L., & Jordan, L. (1979). Children of divorce—a community support group. *Journal of Divorce, 2*(3), 283–294.

Gurman, A.S., & Kniskern, D.P. (1977). Enriching research on marital enrichment programs. *Journal of Marriage and Family Counseling, 3*(2), 3–11.

Gurman, A.S., & Kniskern, D.P. (1978). Behavior marriage therapy: II. Empirical perspective. *Family Process, 17,* 139–148.

Gurman, A.S., Knudson, R.M., & Kniskern, D.P. (1978). Behavior marriage therapy: IV. Take two aspirin and call us in the morning. *Family Process, 17,* 165–180.

Haffey, N., & Levant, R.F. (1984). The differential effortiveness of two models of skills-training for working class parents. *Family Relations, 33,* 209–216.

Hall, R.V. (1976). *Parent training: A preventive mental health program.* (Responsive Parent Training Program.) National Institute of Mental Health Grant, University of Kansas.

Hampson, R.B., & Tavormina, J.B. (1980). Relative effectiveness of behavioral and reflective group training with foster mothers. *Journal of Consulting and Clinical Psychology, 48,* 294–295.

Hanley, D.F. (1974). Changes in parent attitudes related to a parent effectiveness training and a family enrichment program (Doctoral dissertation, United States International University). *Dissertation Abstracts International, 34,* 7044A. (University Microfilms No. 74-10, 368.)

Harrell, J., & Guerney, B.G., Jr. (1976). Training married couples in conflict negotiation skills. In D.H.L. Olson (Ed.), *Treating relationships.* Lake Mills, IA: Graphic Publishing.

Haynes, J. (1982). A conceptual model of the process of family mediation. *American Journal of Family Therapy, 10,* 6–15.

Heiman, J.R., LoPiccolo, L., LoPiccolo, J. (1981). The treatment of sexual dysfunction. In A.S. Gurman & D.P. Kniskern (Eds.), *Handbook of family therapy.* New York: Brunner/Mazel.

Hereford, C.F. (1963). *Changing parental attitudes through group discussion.* Austin: University of Texas Press.

Hill, R., & Rogers, R.H. (1964). The developmental approach. In H.T. Christensen (Ed.), *Handbook of marriage and the family.* Chicago: Rand McNally.

Hines, G.A. (1976). Efficacy of communication skills training with married partners where no marital counseling has been sought (Doctoral dissertation, University of South Dakota). *Dissertation Abstracts International, 36,* 5045–5046A. (University Microfilms No. 76-2400.)

Hinkle, J.E., & Moore, M. (1971). A student couples program. *Family Coordinator, 20,* 153–158.

Hof, L., & Miller, W.R. (1980). Marriage enrichment. *Marriage & Family Review, 3,* 1–27.

Hof, L., & Miller, W.R. (1981). *Marriage enrichment: Philosophy, process & program.* Boure, MD: Robert J. Brady.

Hoffman, S.R., & Levant, R.F. (1985). A comparison of child-free and child-anticipated married couples. *Family Relations, 34,* 197–203.

Homans, C.G. (1961). *Social behavior: Its elementary forms.* New York: Harcourt Brace.

Hopkins, L., Hopkins, P., Mace, D., & Mace, V. (1978). *Toward better marriages.* Winston-Salem: ACME.

Ivey, A.E. (1971). *Microcounseling: Innovations in interviewing training.* Springfield, IL: Charles C. Thomas.

Jacobson, N.S. (1978). A stimulus control model of change in behavioral couples therapy: Implications for contingency contracting. *Journal of Marriage & Family Counseling, 4*(3), 29–36.

Jacobson, N.S. (1980). Behavioral marital therapy: Current trends in research, assessment and practice. *American Journal of Family Therapy, 8*(2), 3–5.

Jacobson, N.S., & Margolin, G. (1979). *Marital therapy: Strategies based on social learning & behavioral exchange principles.* New York: Brunner/Mazel.

Jacobson, N.S., & Martin, B. (1976). Behavioral marriage therapy. Current status. *Psychological Bulletin, 83*(4), 540–556.

Jacobson, N., & Weiss, R.L. (1978). Behavior marriage therapy: III. The contents of Gurman et al. may be hazardous to our health. *Family Process, 17,* 149–163.

James, M., & James, J. (1978). Games parents play. In L.E. Arnold (Ed.), *Helping parents help their children.* New York: Brunner/Mazel.

Jessee, R.E. (1978). A comparison of Gestalt relationship awareness facilitation and conjugal relationship enhancement programs (Doctoral dissertation, Pennsylvania State University, 1978). *Dissertation Abstracts International, 39,* 649B. (University Microfilms No. 7812055.)

Johnson, C.A., & Katz, R.C. (1973). Using parents as change agents for their children: A review. *Journal of Child Psychology & Psychiatry, 14,* 181–200.

Kagan, N. (1972). Observation and suggestions. *The Counseling Psychologist, 3*(3), 42–45.

Kanigsberg, J., & Levant, R.F. (1982). *Changes in parental attitudes, children's self-concept and behavior following parental participation in skills training programs.* Manuscript submitted for publication.

Kaslow, F.W. (1981). Divorce and divorce therapy. In A.S. Gurman & D.P. Kniskern (Eds.), *Handbook of family therapy.* New York: Brunner/Mazel.

Kerckhoff, F.G., Ulmschneider, A., & Adams, C. (1976). College and university programs in parent education. *Family Coordinator, 25*(2), 131–133.

Kessler, S. (1976). Divorce adjustment groups. *Personnel & Guidance Journal, 54*(5), 251–255.

Kessler, S., & Bostwick, S. (1977). Beyond divorce: Coping skills for children. *Journal of Clinical Child Psychology, 6,* 38–41.

Kilman, P.R., Moreault, D., & Robinson, E.A. (1978). Effects of a marriage enrichment program: An outcome study. *Journal of Sex & Marital Therapy, 4*(1), 54–57.

Kowalewski, J.F. (1977). An evaluative study of behavior modification training for parents and parent effectiveness training as methods for affecting parent-child problem resolution and parental attitude change. (Doctoral dissertation,

University of Maryland, 1976). *Dissertation Abstracts International, 37,* 6334B. (University Microfilms No. 77–13, 029.)

Kressel, K., Deutsch, M., Jaffe, N., Tuchman, B., & Watson, C. (1977). Mediated negotiations in divorce and labor disputes. *Conciliation Courts Review, 15,* 9–12.

L'Abate, L. (1977). *Enrichment: Structured interventions with couples, families, and groups.* Washington, DC: University Press of America.

L'Abate, L. (1981). Skill training programs for couples and families. In A.S. Gurman & D.P. Kniskern (Eds.), *Handbook of family therapy.* New York: Brunner/Mazel.

L'Abate, L., & Collaborators (1975a). *A manual: Family enrichment program.* Atlanta, GA: Social Research Laboratories.

L'Abate, L., & Collaborators (1975b). *Manual: Enrichment programs for the family life cycle.* Atlanta, GA: Social Research Laboratories.

Lamb, J., & Lamb, W.A. (1978). *Parent education and elementary counseling.* New York: Human Sciences Press.

Lamb, M.E. (1979). Paternal influence and the fathers' role: A personal perspective. *American Psychologist, 34,* 938–943.

Lambert, M.J., & De Julio, S.S. (1977). Outcome research in Carkhuff's Human Resource Development training programs: Where is the donut? *The Counseling Psychologist, 6*(4), 79–86.

Larson, R.S. (1972). Can parent classes affect family communications? *The School Counselor, 19,* 261–270.

Lazarus, A.A. (1968). Behavior therapy and group marriage counseling. *Journal of the American Society of Psychosomatic Medicine & Dentistry, 15,* 49–56.

Levant, R.F. (1978). Client-centered approaches to working with the family. An overview of new developments in therapeutic, educational, and preventive methods. *International Journal of Family Counseling, 6*(1), 31–44.

Levant, R.F. (1982). Developmental processes in marriage. *Medical Aspects of Human Sexuality, 16*(8), 77–94.

Levant, R.F. (1983). Client-centered skill training programs for the family: A review of the literature. *The Counseling Psychologist, 11*(3), 29–46.

Levant, R.F., & Doyle, G. (1983). An evaluation of a parent education program for fathers of school-aged children. *Family Relations, 32,* 29–37.

Levant, R.F., Slattery, S.C., & Slobodian, P.E. (1981). A systematic skills approach to the selection and training of foster parents as mental health paraprofessionals II: Training. *Journal of Community Psychology, 9,* 231–238.

Liberman, R.P., Levine, J., Wheeler, E., Sanders, N., & Wallace, C. (1976). Experimental evaluation of marital group therapy: Behavioral vs. interaction-insight formats. *Acta Psychiatrica Scandinavica, 11,* Supplement.

Locke, H.J., & Wallace, K.M. (1959). Short marital adjustment and prediction tests: Their reliability and validity. *Marriage & Family Living, 21,* 251–255.

Lowe, R.N., & Morse, C. (1977). Parent child education centers. In C. Hatcher & B.J. Brooks (Eds.), *Innovations in counseling psychology: Developing new roles, settings, techniques.* San Francisco: Jossey-Bass.

Mace, D. (1982). *Close companions: The marriage enrichment handbook.* New York: Continuum.

Mace, D., & Mace, V. (1973). *Marriage enrichment retreats: Story of a Quaker project.* Philadelphia: Friends General Conference.

Mace, D.R., & Mace, V.C. (1975). Marriage enrichment—wave of the future? *The Family Coordinator, 24,* 131–135.

Mace, D., & Mace, V. (1976). Marriage enrichment—a preventive group approach for couples. In D.H. Olson (Ed.), *Treating relationships*. Lake Mills, IA: Graphic Publishing.

Markman, H.J., & Floyd, F. (1980). Possibilities for the prevention of marital discord: A behavioral perspective. *American Journal of Family Therapy, 8*(2), 29–48.

Markman, H.J., Floyd, F., Stephen, T., & Stanley, S. (1981). *Premarital preventive intervention: Conceptual and research issues*. Paper presented at the Annual Meeting of the American Psychological Association, Los Angeles.

Martin, B. (1977). Brief family intervention: Effectiveness and the importance of including the father. *Journal of Consulting & Clinical Psychology, 45*, 1002–1010.

Mash, E.J., Handy, L.C., & Hamerlynck, L.A. (Ed.) (1976). *Behavior modification approaches to parenting*. New York: Brunner/Mazel.

McDonough, J.J. (1976). Approaches to Adlerian family education research. *Journal of Individual Psychology, 32*(2), 224–231.

McGuinness, T., & Glasser, W. (1978). Reality guidance. In L.E. Arnold (Ed.), *Helping parents help their children*. New York: Brunner/Mazel.

McIntosh, D.M. (1975). A comparison of the effects of highly structured, partially structured, and non-structured human relations training for married couples on the dependent variables of communication, marital adjustment, and personal adjustment (Doctoral dissertation, North Texas State University).

Meadows, M.E., & Taplin, J. (1970). Premarital counseling with college students: A promising triad. *Journal of Counseling Psychology, 17*, 516–518.

Miles, J.M.H. (1975). A comparative analysis of the effectiveness of verbal reinforcement group counseling and parent effectiveness training on certain behavioral aspects of potential dropouts (Doctoral dissertation, Auburn University). *Dissertation Abstracts International, 35*, 7655A. (University Microfilms No. 75-12, 493.)

Miller, G.A. (1969). Psychology as a means of promoting human welfare. *American Psychologist, 24*, 1063–1071.

Miller, S. (1971). The effects of communication training in small groups upon self-disclosure and openness in engaged couples' systems of interaction: A field experiment (Doctoral dissertation, University of Minnesota). *Dissertation Abstracts International, 32*, 2819A–2820A. (University Microfilms No. 71-28, 263.)

Miller, S., Nunnally, E.W., & Wackman, D.B. (1976a). A communication training program for couples. *Social Casework, 57*, 9–18.

Miller, S., Nunnally, E.W., & Wackman, D. B. (1976b). The Minnesota Couple Communication Program (MCCP): Premarital and married groups. In D.H. Olson (Ed.), *Treating relationships*. Lake Mills, IA: Graphic Publishing.

Miller, S., Wackman, D.B., & Nunnally, E.W. (1983a). *Talking together*. Minneapolis: Interpersonal Communication Programs.

Miller, S., Wackman, D.B., & Nunnally, E.W. (1983b). Couple communication: Equipping couples to be their own best problem solvers. *The Counseling Psychologist, 11*(3), 73–77.

Mosher, R.L., & Sprinthall, N.A. (1971). Psychological education: A means to promote personal development during adolescence. *The Counseling Psychologist, 2*(4), 3–82.

Mudd, W., Freeman, C., & Rose, E. (1941). Premarital counseling in the Philadelphia Marriage Council. *Mental Hygiene, 25*, 98–119.

Newberger, C.M. (1980). The cognitive structure of parenthood: Designing a descriptive measure. *New Directions for Child Development, 7,* 45–67.

Noble, R.D. (1977). An evaluation of parent effectiveness training and Adlerian parent groups: Changing child-rearing attitudes (Doctoral dissertation, Indiana University). *Dissertation Abstracts International, 37,* 4869A. (University Microfilms No. 77-3359.)

Nunnally, E.W., Miller, S., & Wackman, D.B. (1983). *Couple communication instructor manual.* Minneapolis: Interpersonal Communication Programs.

O'Dell, S. (1974). Training parents in behavior modification: A review. *Psychological Bulletin, 81*(7), 418–433.

O'Leary, K.D., & Turkewitz, H. (1978). Marital therapy from a behavioral perspective. In T.J. Paolino & B.S. McCrady (Eds.), *Marriage & marital therapy: Psychoanalytic, behavioral and systems theory perspectives.* New York: Brunner/Mazel.

O'Leary, K.D., & Turkewitz, H. (1981). A comparative outcome study of behavioral marital therapy and communication therapy. *Journal of Marital & Family Therapy, 7*(2), 159–169.

Olson, D.H. (1976). Treating relationships: Trends and overview. In D.H. Olson (Ed.), *Treating relationships.* Lake Mills, IA: Graphic Publishing.

Olson, D.H., & Norem, R. (1977). *Evaluation of five pre-marital programs.* Unpublished manuscript. (Available from author at Family Social Science, University of Minnesota, 218 North Hall, St. Paul, MN 55108.)

Olson, D.H., & Sprenkle, D.H. (1976). Emerging trends in treating relationships. *Journal of Marriage and Family Counseling, 2*(4), 317–329.

Olson, D.H., Sprenkle, D.H., & Russell, C. (1979). Circumplex model of marital and family systems. I. Cohesion and adaptability dimensions, family types, and clinical applications. *Family Process, 18,* 3–28.

Otto, H.A. (1969). *More joy in your marriage.* New York: Hawthorne.

Otto, H. A. (1975). Marriage and family enrichment programs in North America—report and analysis. *The Family Coordinator, 24,* 137–142.

Otto, H.A. (Ed.). (1976). *Marriage and family enrichment: New perspectives and programs.* Nashville: Abington.

Parks, A. (1977). Children and youth of divorce in Parents Without Partners, Inc. *Journal of Clinical Child Psychology, 6*(2), 44–48.

Parsons, B.V., & Alexander, J.F. (1973). Short-term family intervention: A therapy outcome study. *Journal of Consulting & Clinical Psychology, 41,* 195–201.

Patterson, G.R., & Fleischman, M.J. (1979). Maintenance of treatment effects. Some considerations concerning family systems and follow-up data. *Behavioral Therapy, 10,* 168–185.

Patterson, G.R., & Gullion, M.E. (1976). *Living with children: New methods for parents and teachers* (rev. ed.). Champaign, IL: Research Press.

Patterson, G.R., & Reid, J.B. (1970). Reciprocity and coercion: Two facets of social systems. In C. Neuringer & J.L. Michael (Eds.), *Behavior modification in clinical psychology.* New York: Appleton-Century-Crofts.

Paul, G.L. (1967). Strategy of outcome research in psychotherapy. *Journal of Consulting Psychology, 31,* 109–118.

Pierce, R.M. (1973). Training in interpersonal communication skills with the partners of deteriorated marriages. *The Family Coordinator, 21,* 223–227.

Pierce, R., & Drasgow, J. (1969). Teaching facilitative interpersonal functioning to psychiatric patients. *Journal of Counseling Psychology, 16,* 295–298.

Pinsker, M., & Geoffrey, K. (1981). A comparison of parent effectiveness training and behavior modification training. *Family Relations, 30,* 61–68.

Rappaport, A.F. (1976). Conjugal relationship enhancement program. In D.H. Olson (Ed.), *Treating relationships.* Lake Mills, IA: Graphic Publishing.

Reiswig, G.D. (1973). The parent development laboratory: A study of three group education methods and their relationship to parent-child communication (Doctoral dissertation, University of Pittsburgh). *Dissertation Abstracts International, 34,* 1054A. (University Microfilms No. 73-21, 219.)

Resnick, J.L. (1981). Parent education and the female parent. *The Counseling Psychologist, 9*(4), 55–62.

Resnick, J.L., Resnick, M.B., Packer, A.B., & Wilson, J. (1978). Fathering classes: A psychoeducational model. *The Counseling Psychologist, 7*(4), 56–60.

Resnikoff, A. (1972). A critique of the Human Resource Development model from the viewpoint of rigor. *The Counseling Psychologist, 3*(3), 46–55.

Rickel, A.U., Dudley, G., & Berman, S. (1980). An evaluation of parent training. *Evaluation Review, 4*(3), 389–403.

Ridley, C.A., Avery, A.W., Dent, J., & Harrell, J.E. (1981). The effects of relationship enhancement and problem solving programs on perceived heterosexual competence. *Family Therapy, 8*(2), 59–66.

Ridley, C.A., Avery, A.W., Harrell, J.E., Leslie, L.A., & Dent, J. (1981). Conflict management: A premarital training program in mutual problem solving. *American Journal of Family Therapy, 9*(4), 23–32.

Rinn, R.C., & Markle, A. (1977). Parent effectiveness training: A review. *Psychological Reports, 41,* 95–109.

Robin, A.L., Kent, R., O'Leary, D., Foster, S., & Prinz, R. (1977). An approach to teaching parents and adolescents problem-solving communication skills: A preliminary report. *Behavior Therapy, 8,* 639–643.

Rogers, C. (1957). The necessary and sufficient conditions of therapeutic personality change. *Journal of Consulting Psychology, 21,* 95–103.

Rogers, C.R. (1961). *On becoming a person.* Boston: Houghton Mifflin.

Ross, F.R., Baker, S.B., & Guerney, B.G., Jr. (1982). *Effects of relationship enhancement therapy versus therapists' preferred therapy.* Unpublished manuscript, Pennsylvania State University, University Park.

Scales, R. (1981). Sex education in the '70s and '80s: Accomplishments, obstacles and emerging issues. *Family Relations, 30*(4), 557–568.

Schlien, S. (1971). *Training dating couples in empathic and open communication: An experimental evaluation of a potential preventive mental health program.* Unpublished doctoral dissertation, The Pennsylvania State University.

Schmitt, A., & Schmitt, D. (1976). Marriage renewal retreats. In H.A. Otto (Ed.), *Marriage and family enrichment: New perspectives and programs.* Nashville: Abington.

Schofield, R.G. (1976). A comparison of two parent education programs: Parent effectiveness training and behavior modification and their effects upon the child's self-esteem. (Doctoral dissertation, University of Northern Colorado, 1976). *Dissertation Abstracts International,* 1976, *37,* 2087A. (University Microfilms No. 76-23, 193.)

Schultz, C.L., & Nystul, M.S. (1980). Mother-child interaction behaviors as an outcome of theoretical models of parent group education. *Journal of Individual Psychology, 36*(1), 3–15.

Schultz, C.L., Nystul, M.S., & Law, H.G. (1980). Attitudinal outcomes of theoretical models of parent group education. *Journal of Individual Psychology, 36*(2), 16–28.

Schumm, W.R., & Denton, W. (1979). Trends in premarital counseling. *Journal of Marital & Family Therapy, 5*(4), 23–32.

Scovern, A.W., Bukstel, L.H., Kilmann, P.R., Laval, R.A., Busemeyer, J., & Smith, V. (1980). Effects of parent counseling on the family system. *Journal of Counseling Psychology, 27,* 268–275.

Sirridge, S.T. (1980). Transactional analysis: Promoting OK'ness. In M.J. Fine (Ed.), *Handbook on parent education.* New York: Academic Press.

Smith, L., & Smith, A. (1976). Developing a nationwide marriage communication labs program. In H.A. Otto (Ed.), *Marriage and family enrichment: New perspectives and programs.* Nashville: Abington.

Smith, R.M., Shoffner, S.M., & Scott, J.P. (1979). Marriage and family enrichment: A new professional area. *The Family Coordinator, 28,* 87–93.

Soltz, V. (1967). *Study group leader's manual for children: The challenge.* Chicago: Alfred Adler Institute.

Sonnenschein-Schneider, M., & Baird, K.L. (1980). Group counseling children of divorce in the elementary schools: Understanding the process and technique. *Personnel & Guidance Journal, 59*(2), 88–91.

Stanley, S.F. (1978). Family education to enhance the moral atmosphere of the family and the moral development of adolescents. *Journal of Counseling Psychology, 25,* 110–118.

Stanley, S.F. (1980). The family and moral education. In R.L. Mosher (Ed.), *Adolescents' development and education: A Janus Knot.* Berkeley: McCutchan.

Stein, E.V. (1975). MARDILAB: An experiment in marriage enrichment. *Family Coordinator, 24,* 167–170.

Stollak, G.G. (1981). Variations and extensions of filial therapy. *Family Process, 20,* 305–309.

Stuart, R.B. (1969a). Operant-interpersonal treatment for marital discord. *Journal of Consulting & Clinical Psychology, 33,* 675–682.

Stuart, R.B. (1969b). Token reinforcement in marital treatment. In R.D. Rubin & C.M. Franks (Eds.), *Advances in behavior therapy.* New York: Academic Press.

Tavormina, J.B. (1974). Basic models of parent counseling: A critical review. *Psychological Bulletin, 81,* 827–835.

Tavormina, J.B. (1975). Relative effectiveness of behavioral and reflective group counseling with parents of mentally retarded children. *Journal of Consulting & Clinical Psychology, 43,* 22–31.

Tavormina, J.B. (1980). Evaluation and comparative studies of parent education. In R.R. Abidin (Ed.), *Parent education and intervention handbook.* Springfield, IL: Charles C. Thomas.

Thibaut, J.W., & Kelley, H.S. (1959). *The social psychology of groups.* New York: Wiley.

Thiessen, J.D., Avery, A.W., & Joanning, H. (1980). Facilitating post-divorce adjustment among women: A communication skills training approach. *Journal of Divorce, 4*(2), 35–44.

Travis, R.P., & Travis, P.Y. (1975). The Pairing Enrichment Program: Actualizing the marriage. *Family Coordinator, 24,* 161–165.

Truax, C.B., & Carkhuff, R.R. (1967). *Toward effective counseling and psychotherapy: Training and practice.* Chicago: Aldine.

Ulrici, D., L'Abate, L., & Wagner, V. (1981). The E-R-A Model: A heuristic framework for classification of skill training programs for couples and families. *Family Relations, 30,* 307–315.

van der Veen, F. (1977). *Three client-centered alternatives: A therapy collective, therapeutic community and skill training for relationships.* Paper presented symposium honoring Carl Rogers at 75 at the Annual Meeting of the American Psychological Association.

Van Zoost, B. (1973). Premarital communication skills education with university students. *Family Coordinator, 22,* 187–191.

Venema, H.B. (1976). Marriage enrichment: A comparison of the behavioral exchange negotiation and communication models (Doctoral dissertation, Fuller Theological Seminary). *Dissertation Abstracts International, 36,* 4184–4185B. (University Microfilms No. 76-4615.)

Vitalo, R. (1971). Teaching improved interpersonal functioning as a preferred mode of treatment. *Journal of Consulting & Clinical Psychology, 35,* 166–171.

Vogelsong, E.L. (1976). Preventive-therapeutic programs for mothers and adolescent daughters: A follow-up of relationship enhancement versus discussion and booster versus no-booster methods (Doctoral dissertation, Pennsylvania State University). *Dissertation Abstracts International, 36,* 7677A. (University Microfilms No. 76-10, 809.)

Vogelsong, E.L., Guerney, B.G., Jr., & Guerney, L.F. (1983). Relationship enhancement therapy with inpatients and their families. In R.F. Luber & C.M. Anderson (Eds.), *Family intervention with psychiatric patients.* New York: Human Sciences Press.

Wampler, K.S. (1982a). The effectiveness of the Minnesota Couple Communication Program: A review of research. *Journal of Marital & Family Therapy, 9,* 345–355.

Wampler, K.S. (1982b). Bringing the review of literature into the age of quantification: Meta-analysis as a strategy for integrating research findings in family studies. *Journal of Marriage and the Family, 44,* 1009–1023.

Wampler, K.S., & Sprenkle, D.H. (1980). The Minnesota Couple Communication Program: A follow-up study. *Journal of Marriage & the Family, 42*(3), 577–584.

Watzlawick, P., Beavin, J.H., & Jackson, D.D. (1967). *Pragmatics of human communication: A study of interactional patterns, pathologies and paradoxes.* New York: Norton.

Weiss, R.L., Hops, H., & Patterson, G.R. (1973). A framework for conceptualizing marital conflict, a technology for altering it, some data for evaluating it. In L.A. Hamerlynck, L.C. Handy, & E.J. Mash (Eds.), *Behavior change: Methodology, concepts and practice.* Champaign, IL: Research Press.

Wente, A.S., & Crockenberg, S.B. (1976). Transition to fatherhood: Lamaze preparation, adjustment difficulty and the husband-wife relationship. *The Family Coordinator, 25,* 351–357.

Wieman, R.J. (1974). Conjugal relationship modification and reciprocal reinforcement: A comparison of treatments for marital discord (Doctoral dissertation, Pennsylvania State University). *Dissertation Abstracts International, 35,* 493B. (University Microfilms No. 74-16, 197.)

Wilkinson, G.S., & Bleck, R.T. (1977). Children's divorce groups. *Elementary School Guidance & Counseling, 11,* 205–213.

Witkin, S.L, & Rose, S.D. (1978). Group training in communication skills for couples: A preliminary report. *International Journal of Family Counseling,* 6(2), 45–56.

Young, D.M. (1980). A court-mandated workshop for adolescent children of divorcing parents: A program evaluation. *Adolescence, 15,* 763–774.

Zinker, J.C., & Leon, J.P. (1976). The Gestalt perspective: A marriage enrichment program. In H.A. Otto (Ed.), *Marriage and family enrichment: New perspectives and programs.* Nashville: Abington.

2

Client-centered
Skills-training Programs
for the Family*

Ronald F. Levant

The client-centered psychoeducational, skills-training programs for the family are based on the importance of the facilitative conditions (empathy, genuineness, and regard) in the psychotherapy relationship (Bergin, 1971; Mitchell, Bozarth, & Krauft, 1977; Rogers, 1951, 1957; Truax & Mitchell, 1971) including family therapy (Gurman & Kniskern, 1978), and in human relationships in general (Carkhuff, 1971b; Rogers, 1961). During the 1960s, encouraged by the emerging psychotherapy research findings, indicating the importance of the facilitative conditions for psychotherapy outcome (Bergin, 1967), and spurred by an acute awareness of the shortages of mental health personnel (Albee, 1967), a growing number of workers began to train professional and lay helpers to enhance their interpersonal functioning in terms of the facilitative conditions (Goodman, 1972; Truax & Carkhuff, 1967). The facilitative conditions became known as skills, and systematic skills-training programs emerged (Carkhuff, 1969a, 1969b; Ivey, 1971). A general concern with having an impact beyond the individual client and on the social systems within which he/she is imbedded led to the application of skills-training to the family.

The client-centered family skills-training programs are characterized by

*This is a revised version of an earlier article: R.F. Levant (1983), "Client-centered Skills-training Programs for the Family: A Review of the Literature." *The Counseling Psychologist, 11*(3), 29–46. Reprinted by permission of *The Counseling Psychologist.*

both their content and method of training. The content involves teaching family members some variation of the facilitative conditions of empathy, genuineness, and regard. The training methods are explicitly trainee-centered, and include: "(a) Respect for judgement and autonomy of the trainee; (b) empathy with and acceptance of the trainee's feelings and wishes; and (c) genuineness with regard to the trainer's own feelings and values" (van der Veen, 1977, p. 9).

Several groups have developed family skills-training programs from or influenced by the client-centered orientation. First, there are the Relationship Enhancement (RE) programs developed at Pennsylvania State University under the leadership of Bernard Guerney, Jr. (1977). Relationship Enhancement constitutes the most highly developed and evaluated set of family skills-training programs informed or influenced by the client-centered perspective. Although aspects of social learning theory and other theoretical perspectives have shaped the RE programs (B. Guerney, 1984; Guerney & Vogelsong, 1980), I consider the influence of client-centered therapy to be of central importance. I take this position for three reasons: (1) The RE approach originated as a self-avowed part of the client-centered tradition (B. Guerney, 1964). (2) Clients in RE programs learn a set of skills which closely parallels the facilitative conditions of empathy, genuineness, and regard. (3) The RE method of training is, first and foremost, trainee-centered (van der Veen, 1977). Second, several programs have been developed which are related to RE. These include D'Augelli and Weener's (1978) Communication and Parenting Skills (CAPS) program and van der Veen's (1978) Dialoguing. Third, there are the Human Resource Development (HRD) programs developed under the leadership of Robert Carkhuff (1971b). Carkhuff is one of the pioneers of the skills-training psycho-educational approach (Carkhuff, 1971a). Kagan (1972, p. 42) wrote: "In historical perspective, I believe that Carkhuff's work will be seen not as a single enterprise, but rather as an important part of a 'new psychology.'" Despite his importance as a trailblazer, his work has been criticized on methodological grounds (Gormally & Hill, 1974; Lambert & DeJulio, 1977; Resnikoff, 1972). Fourth is Ivey's (1971) Microcounseling, conceptually related to, and a refinement in certain respects of, Carkhuff's approach. The fifth program is the Personal Developmental Program of Levant and Associates (Haffey & Levant, 1974; Kanigsberg & Levant, 1982; Levant & Doyle, 1983; Levant & Geer, 1981; Levant, Slattery, & Slobodian, 1981). Finally, there is Thomas Gordon's (1970) Parent Effectiveness Training (PET).

Following the approach taken in the overview chapter of this book, the client-centered programs will be classified according to their objective and focus. Program objectives range along a continuum from the remediation of dysfunction to the enhancement of functioning, representing the shift from the medical to the educational model for the provision of psychological services (Guerney, Stollak, & Guerney, 1971). Program focus concerns the particular problem, relationship, role, or developmental transition to which the intervention is applied.

There are three types of program objectives: (1) In training for treatment approaches, family members are trained in the application of a form of therapeutic intervention to another family member in order to treat a clinical problem. This group includes Filial Therapy, an RE program, in which mothers are trained in play therapy, which they then apply to their emotionally disturbed children; and HRD and Microcounseling approaches, in which one or both parents are trained in interpersonal communication skills in order to help their emotionally disturbed children. (2) In training as treatment approaches, the training of family members is viewed as the treatment itself. This group includes RE and HRD marital programs, in which couples are taught communication skills in order to help resolve their marital problems; Parent–Adolescent Therapy, an RE program in which parents and their adolescent children are trained in communication skills in order to resolve relationship conflicts; and Family RE and Dialoguing, which are applied to the family as a whole. (3) In training for enhancement programs, the aim is either preventing clinical problems or stimulating the development of family members, through teaching interpersonal communication and other social skills. This is the largest group of programs. In the marital area there is a premarital program (PRIMES), a marital program (Conjugal Relationship Enhancement), and two divorce programs (Children of Divorce and Communication Skills Training for Divorcees), all of which are RE programs. In the parental area there are three RE (or RE-related) programs (Filial Parent Education, Parent Adolescent Relationship Development, and Communication and Parenting Skills), an HRD program, the Personal Development Program, and Parent Effectiveness Training.

This chapter will review, in turn, program development and evaluative research on the above-delineated three sets of programs. Following a roundup of the conclusions from the point of view of future program development and research issues, an example from practice will be presented.

Training for Treatment

Rogers was the first to apply client-centered methods to the training of family members as caregivers. In this case he trained his daughter in play therapy methods, which enabled her to help her daughter overcome a toilet-training problem (Fuchs, 1957).

The more recent developments involve the systematic training of one or both parents either in the methods of play therapy or in interpersonal communication skills. In both types of programs, the intended client is the child. So far there have been no programs developed in which an adult member of the family who is experiencing personal distress is the recipient of a help-intended intervention, administered by a spouse, by a child, or by several members of the family. These types of interventions are theoretically possible and may be productive areas for future research and development.

Training Parents in Play Therapy

Aside from the case study by Fuchs (1957) and an unpublished study by Santilli (1969, mentioned in Carkhuff, 1971b, pp. 262–263), the work in this area has been done by the Guerneys and associates, in their Filial Therapy program (B. Guerney, 1964; L. Guerney, 1976; Guerney, Guerney, & Andronico, 1966).

The Filial Therapy program was started in 1962 and has continued to be an active focus for research and development. In addition to a series of studies investigating the effects of Filial Therapy itself, this program has spawned an array of Relationship Enhancement programs (Filial Parent Education, Parent–Adolescent Therapy and Relationship Development, Conjugal Therapy and Relationship Enhancement, and others).

Filial Therapy is designed for children 10 years of age or younger who have mild to severe emotional and behavioral problems. These include withdrawn, phobic, anxious, aggressive, or mixed behavior problems. Initially, children with organic impairment were excluded. Currently only autistic and severely schizophrenic children and suicidal or homicidal parents are excluded (L. Guerney, 1980).

This method involves training the couple or one parent (most commonly the mother) in the application of client-centered play therapy (Axline, 1947; Dorfman, 1951). Parents learn the elements of play therapy and develop skills in reflecting feelings, in becoming acceptant of children's feelings, and in setting limits on children's behavior in a caring and nonpunitive manner. The training process involves a combination of didactic instruction and supervised experience in the methods of play therapy and includes a client-centered group counseling experience for parents. The latter serves both to model the communication skills and to help parents cope with feelings and difficulties as they emerge in the course of Filial Therapy (Andronico, Fidler, Guerney, & Guerney, 1967). Generally the early sessions focus on training, the middle sessions focus on the play sessions conducted at home, and the last sessions focus on generalization of the experience to other areas in the parents' lives (L.

Guerney, 1976). At this later stage parents are taught self-expressive skills, which had been almost entirely excluded from the play sessions (L. Guerney, 1980).

The initial evaluation of Filial Therapy took place in two stages. The first stage was a formative evaluation, which attempted to determine the efficacy of the training procedures themselves; that is, to what extent were mothers in Filial Therapy learning to use the reflective role (similar to that of a client-centered play therapist) in play sessions with their own emotionally disturbed children (Stover & Guerney, 1967). Reflective behavior was assessed by independent judges who rated audiotaped play sessions. Comparing the training group ($N = 14$) to a no-contact control group ($N = 14$), they found that mothers did learn the reflective role by the third training play session (after 10 weeks of instruction). However, it should be noted that most of the change was accounted for by the mothers' learning to restate content in their communications to their children, which is a relatively low-order component of the reflective role. Clarification of feeling, a more subtle and empathic element of the reflective role, increased somewhat but did not become very frequent at this early stage in training. A subsequent study, using a revised measure of the same type (judges' ratings of mothers' behavior during play sessions), found mothers to have learned a more significant level of empathy in which they consistently showed "recognition and acceptance of the child's behavior, and often showed acceptance of his underlying feelings as well" (Guerney & Stover, 1971, p. 110).

The second stage of the research effort involved a summative evaluation of the effects of mother-administered Filial Therapy on the children. In a one-group pretest/post-test design ($N = 51$), Guerney and Stover (1971) found that children showed significant improvement on a variety of parent-rated measures of symptomatology and psychological adjustment. In addition, children improved significantly on two rating measures completed by therapists. On one of these (the Rutgers Maladjustment Index), all children were rated as having shown at least some improvement, and 78 percent were rated as much or very much improved.

The scores of the treatment group on two parent-report measures of child adjustment were compared with a nontreated comparison group ($N = 77$) in a separate study (Oxman, 1972). Significantly greater improvement was found in the treatment group than in the comparison group over a 12-month period. The comparison subjects, recruited from the general population, were similar to the treatment subjects with respect to a number of background variables; however, the comparison subjects were not seeking professional help and pretested at a higher level of adjustment than treatment subjects. The results were analyzed using analysis of covariance, through which post-test scores were adjusted to control for differences in pretest levels. This suggests that the results were probably not due to the fact that the treatment group started at a lower level of adjustment, but rather were due to the effects of treatment itself. This, however, is a hypothesis which needs to be tested by further studies which employ more adequate control groups.

Recognizing this problem, Sywulak (1978) utilized an own-control group design, in which subjects ($N = 32$ parents from 19 families) served as their own controls during a four-month waiting period, followed by four months of Filial Therapy. She found that treated patients increased their parental acceptance on a self-report questionnaire and rated their children as better adjusted. Sensué (1981) did a three-year follow-up study, comparing most of Sywulak's subjects ($N = 25$ parents from 16 families) to a non-equivalent comparison group ($N = 24$ parents from 24 families). She found that the gains in parental acceptance and child adjustment held up at a three-year follow-up and that parents reported continued use of the skills taught in the program.

Thus the empirical support for the efficacy of Filial Therapy is increasing. Future research should utilize more objective ratings (i.e., by nonparticipants) of the effects on children. In addition, attention should be directed to the question of how effective Filial Therapy is compared to other forms of treatment.

Recently, there have been several extensions and modifications of Filial Therapy. First, Filial Therapy—which is usually offered to families from a university community—has become a service of a community mental health clinic (Ginsberg, 1976). Second, a modified and shortened version, in which play sessions are replaced by "special times," has been used as a preventive parent education program (see below: Filial Parent Education). In addition, this course was adapted for training foster parents (L. Guerney, 1977). Third, elementary school teachers have been trained to serve as play therapists for withdrawn students (Guerney & Flumen, 1970). Fourth, it has also been applied in a Headstart program, with a neighborhood worker serving as the play therapist (Andronico & Guerney, 1969). Fifth, Filial Therapy—originally limited to children with no signs of neurological impairment—has recently been applied to learning-disabled children (L. Guerney, 1979). Sixth, Filial Therapy has also been tried with older children, using "special times" and a greater range of activities (L. Guerney, 1980). Finally, Filial Therapy—usually used in group format—has been applied in an extended program for individual families (Stollak, 1981). Both parents are included and work individually or conjointly with their child in the play session, which is immediately followed by a parental counseling session.

Training Parents in Interpersonal Communication Skills

This approach has been tried using the Human Resource Development model of Carkhuff (1971b) and the related Microcounseling model of Ivey (1971).

Human Resource Development program. Carkhuff and Bierman (1970) trained both parents of emotionally disturbed children using the Human Resource Development model. Although training included the "responsive" dimensions of empathy, respect, and genuineness, the "initiative" dimensions of self-disclosure, confrontation, and immediacy, and the general dimension of concreteness (Carkhuff, 1969a, 1969b), the emphasis of the program was on empathy. The investigators compared the results of a 25-hour systematic training program in interpersonal communication ($N = 10$ parents) with 25 hours of traditional parent therapy, using three therapy-control groups (for each, $N = 8$ parents) with therapists functioning at high, medium, and low levels of interpersonal communication. They also used a no-treatment (wait-list) control group. They found the training group to be superior in enhancing parents' interpersonal communication skills (assessed by judges' ratings of tape-recorded interactions and of written responses). There were no differences between any of the groups in the mean level of child adjustment changes. Thus, while training in communication skills is superior to traditional therapy in enhancing parents' communication skills, there is no evidence from this study that increasing parental communication skills is more effective than traditional parental therapy, or than the simple passage of time, in producing positive changes in disturbed children. Additionally, it was found that, while parents in the training group improved significantly in communication skills in a role-playing helping task with the spouse, there was no significant change in communication skills when parents conducted a play session with their child. That is, parents improved their communication with each other but were unable to generalize this to their child. The facts that the children were not included in the training program and that there was little practice in the play situation are perhaps the reasons for this finding. The importance of interpersonal skill practice was highlighted in a recent study (Renz & Cohen, 1977). As Carkhuff & Bierman concluded: "This study supports the proposition that *people learn best what they practice most*" (1970, p. 160).

Microcounseling. Durrett and Kelley (1974) used Ivey's Microcounseling program to train parents of disturbed children. They focused on the following specific communication skills: attending (eye contact, body posture, verbal follow; open invitation to talk; minimal encouragers to talk);

listening skills (paraphrasing of content; reflection of feeling); and self-expression skills (expression of content; expression of feeling; direct mutual communication). They expanded the program to include focused feedback on family communication patterns (using videotapes of the pre-test structured family interviews) and behavioral rehearsal at home, and offered 15 hours of training (2½-hour sessions twice a week). Using parents whose children were in treatment as subjects, they compared the training group ($N = 7$ parents from 5 families) to a no-contact control group ($N = 6$ parents from 5 families) on three measures of the identified child-patient's behavior in structured family interviews: total talking time, number of responses, and judge-rated attitudes toward their relationship with their parents. They found positive change on all three measures, but only the first reached statistical significance. The low N may have been a factor in the other two measures not reaching statistical significance.

Conclusions

In summary, the evidence for the efficacy of training parents in interpersonal communication skills as a mode of helping their disturbed children is weak, particularly when compared to the evidence supporting the efficacy of Filial Therapy methods. Two factors seem to account for this. The first is the brevity of the interpersonal communication skills programs in comparison to the length of Filial Therapy. When working with emotionally disturbed children, a longer program is probably necessary. Second, there is the issue of the appropriateness of specific skills to the targeted recipient of help. Training parents in verbal communication skills in order to improve their relationships with younger children may not be a wise approach. When the targeted recipients are young children, for whom communication in a play situation is the preferred mode of interaction, training parent-caregivers in play methods may be the best approach.

Training as Treatment

Carkhuff (1971a) proposed the idea of "training as a preferred mode of treatment" in and of itself. This idea was part of the shift from the medical model to the educational model, in which human problems are thought of as deficits in skills rather than as illnesses. Carkhuff's proposal received support in studies of the training of symbionts, which showed that such training had positive effects on both the client and the symbiont. Carkhuff's proposal led to investigations which attempted the direct training of the client, such as, for example, training hospitalized psychiatric patients in interpersonal skills as a means of facilitating their return to the community (Pierce & Drasgow, 1969). The application of training as treatment to the family has focused on the treatment of dysfunctional interpersonal relationships (as distinct from the treatment of troubled individuals). Two familial relationships have received attention: the marital relationship and the parent–adolescent relationship. Recently this approach has been applied to the family as a whole.

Marital Relationship Programs

Two groups have been active in the development of marital relationship programs: (1) Guerney's Relationship Enhancement program and (2) Carkhuff's Human Resource Development program.

Conjugal Relationship program. Conjugal Therapy (or Conjugal Relationship Enhancement—CRE), developed by Guerney and associates, attempts to train couples who are experiencing marital distress. The published reports of this program describe its use as a group program, although it could also be used in an individual couple format. It combines didactic and experiential exercises and utilizes homework. The program focuses on four sets of skills or behavioral modes: (1) In the *expressor mode* the individual learns to become aware of his/her thoughts and feelings as they pertain to the relationship, and to communicate these thoughts and feelings in a manner which will likely be understood and responded to compassionately. (2) In the *empathic responder mode* the individual learns to listen to the content and feelings expressed in order to understand the expressor's statement from his/her perspective at the deepest level and communicate this understanding in a warm and accepting manner. In *mode switching,* individuals learn when to use each mode and how to switch modes in a manner which facilitates productive conversation. In the *facilitator mode,* participants learn how to help others develop the other three sets of skills.

Seven studies have evaluated Conjugal Therapy. The efficacy of the training program was assessed in a study by Ely, Guerney, and Stover (1973). Comparing Conjugal Therapy (11 couples) to a no-treatment (wait-list) control group (12 couples), they found that couples with troubled marriages could learn the listener and speaker roles and the associated communication skills (as assessed by judges' ratings of taped interaction and of written statements) in a brief program (8 to 10 sessions of two hours each). A quasi-replication (10 couples), in which the results of the no-treatment control group were compared before and after they eventually participated in conjugal therapy, confirmed these results. With regard to changes in the marital relationship, in both the treatment versus control analyses and the quasi-replication analyses, training couples improved significantly more than control couples on a self-rating measure of marital communication, but did not show significant results on a self-rating measure of marital adjustment. The investigators speculated that a longer program may be necessary for significant changes in marital adjustment.

Collins (1972) took up the issue of a longer program. He used a non-clinical population, in which couples' pretest marital adjustment scores were in the mid-range. He compared a six-month (40-hour) CRE program (24 couples) to a no-contact control group (21 couples) and found that CRE resulted in significant improvement on one of two self-report measures of marital communication and on one of two self-report measures of marital adjustment. The measures which did not show significant differences favored the CRE group, and one of them (adjustment) approached statistical significance.

Rappaport (1976) developed an intensive, structured two-month (24-hour) CRE program, utilizing marathon sessions; in addition to teaching the listener and speaker roles, he also focused on the identification and resolution of specific conflict areas in the marriage. Using a sample of 20 couples who were very similar to Collins' subjects, Rappaport evaluated the program using an own-control research design. He found that the program resulted in significant improvement in listening and speaking skills (measured by judges' ratings of taped interactions), and in the quality of the marital relationship as measured by self-rating scales. These scales included ratings of marital adjustment, marital satisfaction, marital communication, trust, intimacy, and the ability to successfully resolve relationship problems.

Wieman (1973), using a similar nonclinical population, compared CRE (12 couples) to a behavioral procedure (Reciprocal Reinforcement Therapy) (12 couples), and found both eight-week programs to be superior to a no-treatment (wait-list) control group (12 couples). CRE improved communication skills (assessed by judges' ratings of taped interactions and spouse report); RRT improved behavior skills (positive statements assessed by frequency counts of taped interaction, and delivery of reciprocal reinforcement assessed by spouse-report); and both groups resulted in gains in self-rated marital adjustment at post-test and 10-week follow-up.

Jessee (1978), using a mixed clinical and nonclinical population, compared CRE (18 couples) to a new Gestalt program (Gestalt Relationship Awareness Facilitation; 18 couples), using six self-rating scales. Although both 12-week (30-hour) programs resulted in significant pre-to-post gains on all outcome measures, the CRE subjects achieved significantly higher gains than Gestalt subjects on communication, relationship satisfaction, and ability to handle problems.

Brock and Joanning (1983), using a nonclinical sample which, however, had relatively low levels of marital adjustment, compared CRE (26 couples) to the Couples Communication Program (CCP; 20 couples), and to a no-contact control group (8 couples). All leaders were certified. Due to the different lengths of CRE (10 two-hour sessions) and CCP (4 three-hour sessions), this study presented singular challenges in setting up valid comparisons. The investigators' solution was to conduct four comparisons: (1) mid-test, after the end of CCP; (2) post-test 1, in which the programs were compared as they are usually run, CRE after 10 weeks and CCP after 4 weeks; (3) post-test 2, at the end of 10 weeks, during which the CCP group received 8 hours of additional training, developed by the authors of the CC program; (4) follow-up, 3 months after the end of treatment.

At mid-test, no differences were found between CRE and CCP, although both were superior to the control group on communication skills (judge-rated). On both post-tests, CRE was superior to CCP on judge-rated communication skills, self-rated communication patterns, and marital adjustment, results which held up at follow-up. Two additional analyses provided suggestive evidence that CRE was more effective than CCP with low-adjustment couples and that CRE was associated with lower rates of deterioration.

Finally, Ross, Baker, and Guerney (1982), using a clinical sample, compared CRE individual couple format (12 couples) to traditional couple therapy (12 couples). They used a unique design, in which five therapists of orientations ranging from behavioral to Freudian provided both their own preferred therapy and CRE to an equal number of clients, who were randomly assigned to condition. At the end of 10 weeks of treatment CRE subjects had significantly higher levels of marital adjustment, relationship satisfaction, and communication patterns (all self-rated).

Thus, there is empirical support for the efficacy of CRE. Couples learn the communication skills, and rate their marriages as improved, in brief, extended, intensive, group, and individual CRE formats. Marital adjustment changes hold up over a short-term follow-up interval. And although CRE is comparable to a behavioral program, it appears to be superior to a Gestalt program, the Couples Communication Program, and traditional couples therapy. The chief weakness in this empirical literature is its almost total reliance on self-report measures (the exception being the evaluations of couples' communication skills).

Human Resource Development program.   There are several published reports on the use of Carkhuff's model of training marital couples in communication skills as treatment for marital discord. The approach involves teaching couples the "responsive" and "initiative" helping skills in a didactic and experiential format, following Carkhuff's (1972) *The Art of Helping.* Aside from one uncontrolled study (Wells, Figurel, & McNamee, 1975) and two inconclusive dissertations (Cotton, 1977; McIntosh, 1975), the principle work was done by Pierce (1973) and Valle and Marinelli (1975).

Pierce (1973) trained couples seeking marital treatment, who acknowledged a low level of communication as a major problem. The training program was conducted in groups and ran for about 12 weeks (25 hours). The program taught a variety of interpersonal communication skills but focused on the development of empathy. The results of the evaluation showed that the trained couples (5 couples) improved significantly more than a no-treatment (wait-list) control group (4 couples), and a traditional treatment group (8 couples), in their interpersonal communication skills, and in their ability to elicit self-exploration from their spouses (both measured by judges' ratings of spouse interaction). However, the impact of improved interpersonal functioning on the marriage at the end of treatment, or at a later follow-up point, was not assessed.

Valle and Marinelli (1975) combined systematic communication skills training with treatment on the premise that the improved interpersonal functioning brought about by training would facilitate the processing of problems in therapy and lead to improved overall functioning. Combined training-treatment and traditional treatment groups (5 couples per group) were formed of couples experiencing marital discord. Both groups ran for 14 weeks (50 hours). The results showed that combined training-treatment subjects experienced a significant enhancement in interpersonal communication skills (measured by a self-rating scale and a paper-and-pencil test of empathic ability) and improved significantly more than the traditional-treatment subjects in overall functioning (measured by a self-rating scale).

Both the Pierce (1973) and the Valle and Marinelli (1975) studies have several methodological limitations. In addition to the low N's, neither randomly assigned subjects to groups, and both have sampling problems. The Pierce study utilized groups from a prior study (Carkhuff & Bierman, 1970) as the traditional-treatment and no-treatment control groups. The Carkhuff–Bierman subjects were parents of an emotionally disturbed child, whereas Pierce's training group subjects were couples experiencing marital distress. Although there is some association between marital distress and disturbance in offspring, the two control groups are not equivalent to the training group. In the Valle and Marinelli study, the effects of the combined training and treatment are confounded with motivational factors. The combined training-treatment subjects had been in traditional therapy for 18 months and had expressed frustration at having reached a plateau in their therapy even though many problems remained unresolved. The researchers did recognize these problems and the attendant difficulties in interpreting the results. At this time, then, the empirical support for the Human Resource Development approach to marital treatment is weak.

Parent–Adolescent Relationship Program

Parent–Adolescent Therapy (or Parent–Adolescent Relationship Development—PARD) was developed by Guerney and associates (Ginsberg, 1972), growing out of the original Filial Therapy program. The PARD program trains parents and their adolescent children in self-expressive and empathic-responding skills, through the four skill modes (expressor, empathic responder, mode switching, and facilitator). The program has been used with an individual parent–adolescent dyad format and in a group context, although all the published studies evaluate group programs. As with the other RE programs, didactic and experiential instruction is used, and homework is assigned.

An evaluative study (Ginsberg, 1972) focusing on fathers and their adolescent sons found that father–son pairs (14 pairs) trained in a 10-week program (20 hours) improved significantly more than a no-treatment (wait-list) control group (15 pairs) on the following variables: expressive and empathic communication skills (assessed by judges' ratings of tape-recorded interactions); and general communication patterns in the home and quality of the father–son relationship (both measured by self-report questionnaires). A quasi-replication, in which the results of control subjects who later elected to participate in the program (10 pairs) were compared before and after their participation, confirmed the results of the primary study. A comparison study investigated the relationship between background variables, process measures, and outcome scores (Grando, 1972).

Two studies focusing on the mother–daughter relationship examined PARD (19 pairs) in relation to a no-treatment (wait-list) control group (17 pairs), and to a process-oriented discussion group, similar to multiple family therapy (Relationship Improvement Program—RIP; 18 pairs). Groups of two to three pairs met once per week for two hours for 12 to 15 weeks. Comparisons were made both at the end of training (Coufal, 1976) and at six-month follow-up (Vogelsong, 1976). The results were that the PARD group improved significantly more than the no-treatment control group in specific (expressive and empathic) communication skills (measured by judges' ratings of tape-recorded interactions and of written statements), in general communication patterns in the home, and in quality of the mother–daughter relationship (both measured by self-report questionnaires); these gains were maintained at a six-month follow-up. The RIP group relative to the no-treatment group did not improve in specific communication skills, but did show improvement in the general communication patterns in the home and tended to improve somewhat in the quality of the mother–daughter relationship at post-test; however, by six-month follow-up these gains had washed out. The effect of a booster program during the follow-up period was also examined (Vogelsong,

1976). The booster program was administered to half of the subjects in each of two treatment groups. It involved frequent phone contact and meetings every six weeks. For the PARD group, booster subjects improved significantly more than non-booster subjects in specific communication skills (as measured by judges' ratings of written statements but not of tape-recorded interactions) and in the quality of the mother–daughter relationship. There were no significant differences between booster and non-booster subjects for the RIP group.

The PARD program was developed to serve as both a therapeutic program with the dysfunctional parent–adolescent relationship as the target problem and as a preventive and developmental program for use with nonsymptomatic families (L. Guerney, 1976). However, thus far the evaluative research has been limited to its use with nonsymptomatic families: The Ginsberg (1972) and Grando (1972) studies utilized a middle-class university community, and Coufal (1976) and Vogelsong (1976) utilized a lower socioeconomic sample. Its use with disturbed adolescents (Vogelsong & Guerney, 1980) and psychiatric inpatients (Vogelsong, Guerney, & Guerney, 1983) has been suggested.

PARD does have some empirical support: Parent–adolescent dyads learn the communication skills and report improvements in their relationships, and these gains are held up at six-month follow-up. PARD has also been shown to be superior to an alternative treatment, ruling out nonspecific attention-placebo and group process effects as the cause for the positive changes. Future work should attempt to assess relationship changes through more objective measurement approaches than self-report questionnaires.

Family Relationship Programs

The application of communication skill training to the family, as a treatment for individual or family distress, is an emergent area. Vogelsong et al. (1983) have written about the application of RE to families of inpatients. This application has not yet been systematically implemented and evaluated. At this preliminary stage two additional sets of skills or behavioral modes are considered necessary. *Problem-solving and conflict-resolution skills* are based on the use of the expressor, empathic responder, and mode switching skills, and involve six components: (1) setting aside a time and place to work on problems; (2) taking steps to make sure participants understand the emotional and interpersonal aspects of the problem before trying to solve it; (3) attempting to maximize mutual need satisfaction in the solution; (4) reacting to the solution both cognitively and affectively so as to both achieve clarity and flush out any implicit problems; (5) forecasting any possible problems or other consequences; (6) reassessing the solution and revising as needed. *Maintenance and generalization skills* involve the use of home practice, relying primarily on the facilitator skill.

Van der Veen (1977, 1978) has also written about the application of skill training with clinical families. His program, called "Dialoguing," is an adaptation of RE, focusing on four sets of skills: congruent talking skills, empathic listening skills, interchanging skills, and facilitating skills. Again, this approach has not yet been systematically implemented and evaluated.

Conclusions

In summary, there are four main findings on training in interpersonal communication skills as treatment for dysfunctional familial relationships, specifically marital and parent–adolescent relationships. First, the communication skills can be learned effectively in a relatively short time, between 8 and 12 weeks (16 and 25 hours). Second, the dysfunctional relationship can be significantly improved in a moderate time period. The parent–adolescent relationship program demonstrated positive results in both communication in the home and quality of the relationship in 10 to 15 weeks (20 to 30 hours). For the marital relationship, improvement in communication in the home was found in 10 weeks (20 hours); improvements in the relationship were found at treatment intervals ranging from 10 weeks (20 hours) to 50 hours. Third, follow-up studies indicate that both the learned skills and the beneficial changes in communication and in the relationship are stable, at least over a short-term follow-up period: three months for CRE, and six months for PARD. Fourth, training as treatment has been compared to other approaches and has been found to be superior to a group process/discussion approach, to a Gestalt program, and to the Couples Communication Program, and equivalent in outcome to a behavioral approach. There is also evidence that training as treatment is superior to traditional couples therapy. In addition to demonstrating the robust nature of this approach, these findings obviate the need for utilizing attention-placebo control groups. This is particularly the case with the studies which show a superiority of training as treatment over discussion groups, which are similar in nature to attention-placebo groups.

The evidence supporting the efficacy of training as treatment is quite substantial at this point, although it is much stronger for the Relationship Enhancement programs than for the Human Resource Development programs. Future research could add to the foundation of empirical support for this approach in the following ways. First, there is a need to utilize more objective outcome measures in assessing the effect of skills training on the quality of the relationship. At this point, the case for the efficacy of skills training in improving the quality of or treating dysfunctional relationships rests on self-report, participant-rating scales, and question-naires. Second, there is a need for longer term follow-up studies, to determine the stability of the changes which result from training as treat-ment. Third, there is the need to evaluate certain of these programs (particularly PARD) with a clinical population, in order to demonstrate their efficacy as training as treatment programs. A related issue would be to determine to what extent duration of treatment is associated with severity of disturbance. The earlier CRE studies seemed to indicate such a relationship, yet the more recent CRE studies with low adjustment and clinic couples find changes over short treatment intervals. Fourth, al-though both PARD and CRE have been tested "off-campus," with cli-ents from the general community, more research is needed to determine these programs' efficacy with lower socioeconomic minority populations and with culturally different groups. Finally, the specific differential ef-fects and relative cost-effectiveness of the different formats (six-month weekly, three-month intensive, two-month marathon) for treating rela-tionships deserve investigation.

Training for Enhancement

The training for enhancement area includes preventive and developmen-tal programs directed at marriage and parenting at various stages of the life cycle. For the marriage there are premarital (PRIMES), marital (CRE), and divorce (Children of Divorce, and Communication Skills Training for Divorcees) programs, all of which are RE programs. For parenting there are three RE (and RE-related) programs: Filial Parent Education, PARD, and Communication and Parenting Skills. In addi-tion, there is a Human Resource Development Program, the Personal Developmental Program, and Parent Effectiveness Training.

Marital Programs

PRIMES. The Program for Relationship Improvement by Maximizing Empathy and Self-disclosure (PRIMES) is a variation of CRE, applied to dating and premarital couples. The method utilizes the four basic modes or sets of skills: expressor, empathic responder, mode switching, and facilitator (Ginsberg & Vogelsong, 1977). An evaluative study found that dating couples (15 couples) trained in a PRIMES program of 10 weeks or less (under 20 hours) improved significantly more than a no-treatment (wait-list) control group (27 couples) in the following areas: specific (ex-pressive and empathic) communication skills (measured by judges' ratings of tape-recorded interaction), and the quality of the relationship, particu-

larly the ability to handle problems (measured by self-report questionnaires) (Schlein, 1971). A related study showed that the couples' gains in
specific communication skills represented an increase from levels of skill
representative of the average college student to levels representative of
the average counselor (D'Augelli et al., 1974).

Avery, Ridley, and associates conducted a series of three investigations
of PRIMES using the same sample. First, an eight-week (24-hour)
PRIMES program (25 couples) was compared to a lecture/discussion
group (29 couples) on several self-report measures of relationship quality
(trust and intimacy; empathy, warmth, genuineness; and communication)
(Ridley, Jorgensen, Morgan, & Avery, 1982). The results showed that
the PRIMES subjects, compared to the lecture/discussion subjects, made
significantly greater gains on all dependent measures. In the second
study, the PRIMES program (19 couples) was compared to the lecture/
discussion program (19 couples) on behavioral assessments of skill level at
post-test and a six-month follow-up (Avery, Ridley, Leslie, & Milholland,
1980). The investigators found that the PRIMES couples, compared to
the lecture/discussion couples, demonstrated significantly greater gains in
both self-disclosure and empathic skills (measured by judges' ratings of
tape-recorded interaction), gains which were maintained at follow-up.
Half of the PRIMES subjects were given a one hour booster session five
months after termination, but this was not found to result in any appreciable gains at follow-up. In the third study PRIMES (24 couples) was
compared to a behavioral exchange program (the Ridley problem-solving
program) (24 couples) and to the lecture/discussion group (26 couples) on
a self-report measure of heterosexual competency (Ridley, Avery, Dent,
& Harrell, 1981). PRIMES subjects showed significantly greater improvement relative to the lecture/discussion group, whereas the behavioral exchange program showed improvement which just misssed reaching statistical significance. Although methodologically sound in most respects,
these three studies suffer from the weakness that subjects were not assigned to conditions randomly, but rather based on their class schedules.
The authors do not provide enough information to determine whether
this allowed systematic bias to enter (i.e., day versus night programs,
which might reflect working versus nonworking subjects, etc.).

Conjugal Relationship Enhancement. CRE, originally designed as a
therapeutic program, has also been used as a preventive program. The
evaluative literature has been discussed above.

Children of Divorce. L. Guerney and Jordan (1979) developed an RE
program for children of divorcing parents. This program was piloted with
a small group ($N = 9$) of children, aged 9 to 13, and consisted of six

one-hour sessions aimed at supporting children through the divorce experience. Aside from the first and last sessions (introduction and evaluation), the format consisted of the use of stimulus materials to evoke the children's feelings and opinions, and discussion of Gardner's (1970) *The Boys and Girls Book about Divorce.* The leader provided empathic understanding and helped the children disclose and come to terms with their feelings. Future programs are planned and will utilize more specific tape-recorded stimulus materials, developed by the participant-children, focusing on communication in the family.

Communication skills training for divorcees. Thiessen and associates developed a program for divorcees, which combined didactic presentations on topics of concern (e.g., emotional impact of divorce, the continued relationship with former spouse, impact on friends and family), with skills training in empathy and self-disclosure skills. They first assessed the effects of a program administered in a weekly meeting format (5 weeks, 15 hours) on women (Thiessen, Avery, & Joanning, 1980). In comparison to the control group ($N = 15$), skills training subjects ($N = 13$) showed significant improvements in empathy (measured by judges' ratings of written responses to vignettes) and self-reported divorce adjustment and self-esteem (one of two measures), but no significant changes in judge-rated self-disclosure, perceived social support, or the second measure of self-esteem. They then tried the program in a weekend marathon format (13 hours) for both sexes (Avery & Thiessen, 1982). Compared to the control group ($N = 14$), skills training subjects ($N = 13$) showed significant improvement on empathy and self-disclosure (assessed by judge's ratings of written responses to vignettes) and perceived social support. However, the findings on perceived social support may be primarily a reflection of the intensive group experience rather than actual changes in subjects' support networks. It should also be noted that this study—admittedly a preliminary investigation—did not assign subjects to condition randomly, but rather according to their available time.

Parental Programs

Filial Parent Education. L. Guerney (1976) designed a Filial Parent Education course for use as a preventive program to be taught to parents of younger children. This course is similar to and derived from Filial Therapy, with the omission of the training of parents as play therapists. The program emphasizes empathy-training and skills in limit setting. Open-ended, informal evaluation indicated that the program was of benefit to participating parents (L. Guerney, 1976). However, an evaluation of the effects on the children's self-esteem (self-reported) and behavior (teacher-rated) failed to demonstrate the efficacy of a 14-week didactic version of Filial Parent Education (Eardley, 1979).

Parent–Adolescent Relationship Development. PARD, originally designed as a therapeutic program, has also been used as a preventive program. The evaluative literature has been discussed above.

Communication and Parenting Skills. D'Augelli and Weener (1978) developed the CAPS program, which is derived from RE, particularly the earlier Filial approach. In CAPS only parents are trained. In addition to the empathic responding and self-expressive communication skills, parents are also taught methods of anticipatory structuring and limit setting. An evaluation of the short-term effects of CAPS found that parents receiving the program ($N = 36$), as compared to a control group ($N = 22$), increased their use of the skills taught in the program and decreased their use of less desirable responses (assessed by judge's ratings of parents' written responses to child statements).

Human Resource Development Programs. There are two developments here. First, Carkhuff and Pierce (1976) have developed a parents' manual, *Helping Begins at Home.* Second, Bendix (1977) compared the effects of training parents in the HRD life skills program (helper group, $N = 24$) versus training parents to train their children in these life skills (trainer group, $N = 24$), in a 10-week (30-hour) program which combined didactic and experiential instruction with skill practice at home. She found that parents in both groups, in comparison to a no-contact control group ($N = 24$), significantly improved their skills (assessed by judge's ratings of videotaped interaction and of written responses) and reported significantly fewer problem behaviors in their children. Although both groups of children significantly improved their skills (assessed by judge's ratings of written responses), the trainer group children improved significantly more than the helper group children, indicating the efficacy of training parents to train their children in interpersonal communication skills. Though statistically significant, the gains were modest; hence a longer program is probably necessary for this kind of approach.

Personal Developmental Program (PDP). This program, developed by Levant and associates at Boston University, is an eclectic synthesis of several existing skills-training programs. It consists of a set of modules focusing on specific skills, which can be used in several combinations: attending; listening and responding to content; listening and responding to feelings; speaking for oneself—self-awareness; speaking for oneself—genuiness; acceptance; structuring; rules, limits, and consequences;

conflict resolution; skill integration. The program is didactic and experiential and includes homework exercises. The initial work was done with foster parents. A pilot study of a 10-week (30-hour) course for a lower socioeconomic minority foster mother sample (N = 15) failed to demonstrate efficacy. The investigators attributed the failure to the brevity of the program (Levant, Slattery, & Slobodian, 1981).

A second phase studied the use of the program with lower income parents, as an adjunct to the individual psychotherapeutic treatment of their children. Three groups of parents whose children were in treatment were compared: (1) Those receiving an eight-week (24-hour) PDP course (N = 7); (2) an equivalent behavioral skills-training group (N = 15); and (3) a no-contact nonequivalent comparison group (N = 12). It was found that the PDP parents improved significantly more than the other two groups on communication skills (assessed by judge's ratings of written responses to child statements), and that the behavioral skills parents significantly improved more on knowledge of behavioral principles (Haffey & Levant, 1984). It was also found that both treatments were effective in enhancing children's self-esteem (self-report), changes which held up at three-month follow-up (Kanigsberg & Levant, 1982).

More recently the program was applied to fathers of school-aged children who wished to increase their parental involvement. Comparing an eight-week (24-hour) PDP course (N = 11) with a no-contact nonequivalent comparison group (N = 11), it was found that PDP fathers significantly improved their communication skills (assessed by judge's ratings of written responses to child statements), that their children perceived positive changes in their relationships, and that fathers changed their concepts of the ideal family (Levant & Doyle, 1983). A more complete description of the program for fathers is included toward the end of the chapter, as an illustration of the practical aspects of running client-centered skills programs for families.

New programs have been developed for single parents, step-parents and their spouses, and dual-career/co-parents; these are slated for evaluation.

Parent Effectiveness Training.   The best-known program in the training for enhancement area is Gordon's (1970, 1976) Parent Effectiveness Training (PET). This program is used widely throughout the country: 600,000 parents are said to have been through the course (Gordon, 1980). It is administered by a national organization, Effectiveness Training, Inc., based in California, and taught by a growing cadre of instructors (15,000; Gordon, 1980) trained and certified by E.T., Inc.

The PET course is an eight-week (24-hour) program with didactic and experiental inputs: lectures, readings from Gordon (1970), role plays, discussion, and homework exercises contained in a *Parent Notebook* (Gordon, 1972). PET emphasizes (1) "active listening," which combines empathy and acceptance; (2) "I-messages," in which the parent learns to communicate feelings clearly and directly, without blaming the child. I-messages are a more effective method of confrontation than commands (Carducci, 1975); (3) the "no-lose" method of conflict resolution, which involves a search for mutually acceptable solutions to problems. It is a democratic method as contrasted with the two win-lose or zero-sum methods—authoritarianism (parent wins) and permissiveness (child wins). The no-lose method is based on the use of active listening and I-messages, and involves six steps: identifying and defining the conflict; generating possible alternative solutions; evaluating alternative solutions; deciding on the best acceptable solution; implementing the solution; evaluating how it worked.

The evaluative research literature is complex. It consists of a large number of unpublished studies and a few published articles. In this review I will focus on the unpublished doctoral dissertations and the published articles on the outcome of PET. For the unpublished, single group, analogue, and masters thesis studies, see Gordon (1980) and Rinn and Markle (1977). The outcome studies are summarized in Table 2-1.

The group of 23 studies under consideration consists of 17 doctoral dissertations and six published studies (the latter are Nos. 1, 9, 13, 16, 21, 23 on Table 2-1). Most of these are recent; only eight appeared in Rinn and Markle's (1977) review (Nos. 2, 6, 7, 9, 10, 12, 19, 22). Most are two- or three-group designs, comparing PET to a control group or an alternative treatment. There is, however, one four-group study (No. 12), and one five-group study (No. 21). In too many of the studies, inadequate control groups are utilized. Only six studies utilized an adequate no-contact or wait-list control group formed by random assignment (Nos. 4, 5, 7, 11, 14, 21), and only one utilized a placebo control group (No. 21). With regard to alternative treatments, many of the studies have compared PET to ill-defined or idiosyncratic treatments (Nos. 2, 6, 9, 12, 13, 17). However, PET has been compared to behavior modification parent training (Nos. 1, 8, 16, 20, 21) and to Adlerian parent study groups (Nos. 14, 21).

Dependent measures are primarily of the self-report type, although three studies have used ratings by independent judges (Nos. 16, 21, 23). Both parents and children have been assessed. Parental attitudes, behavior, knowledge of course content, and personality variables have been studied. With regard to parental attitudes, the two most prominent instruments are the Hereford Parent Attitude Survey (HPAS) and The Parent Attitude Research Instrument (PARI). The HPAS (Hereford, 1963) consists of 77 forced-choice items designed to measure parental attitudes in five areas: *confidence* in the parental role, particularly in handling child problems; *causation,* natural or inherent, of the child's behavior; *acceptance* of the child's feelings, behavior, and normal developmental changes;

trust in the child's individuality; and *understanding* in the area of parent–child communication. The PARI was originally developed by Schaeffer and Bell (1958). It has also been used in a short form (Cross & Kawash, 1968), and a Q-4 form (Schluderman & Schluderman, 1977). Other measures of parent attitudes include the Porter (1954) Parental Acceptance Scale, the D-Scale (dogmatism; Rokeach, 1960), Attitudes Toward Freedom of Children Scale II (Koch, Dentler, Dysart, & Streit, 1934), and the Traditional Family Ideology Scale (Levinson & Huffman, 1955).

Parental behavior has been assessed by child-report and judge's ratings. The most common instrument is Schaeffer's (1965) Children's Report of Parent Behavior Inventory (CRPBI), which has four subscales: acceptance of individuation, rejection, acceptance, and hostile-detachment. In addition Barrett-Lennard's (1962) Relationship Inventory has also been used as a child-report on parent behavior. Judge's ratings have been applied to written parent responses to child statements using the Truax Accurate Empathy Scale (Truax & Carkhuff, 1967), and to parent–child interaction using the Patterson, Ray, Shaw, and Cobb (1969) coding scheme in one study (No. 16) and a specially designed coding scheme in another (No. 21).

With regard to children, both personality and behavioral variables have been studied. Personality variables include self-esteem, anxiety, and career maturity. Self-esteem has been assessed by several self-report measures (Piers-Harris Children's Self-Concept Sale, Piers & Harris, 1969; Coopersmith's 1967 Self-Esteem Inventory; and the Tennessee Self Concept Scale, Fitts, 1965, for older children) and by parent-reports (Coopersmith's 1967 Behavior Rating Form). Child behavior has been assessed by parent ratings, teacher ratings (Devereaux Elementary School Behavior Rating Scale and the Teacher's Behavior Rating Scale), judge's ratings (Patterson et al., 1969), and global outcome criteria (grade point averages).

The studies are typically pre-test/post-test designs, although a few have included follow-ups ranging from 6 weeks to 12 months (Nos. 18, 21, 22, 23). The samples studied have been for the most part suburban parents, but have also included parents with learning disabled, emotionally troubled, and enuretic children, Black parents of potential high school dropouts, single parents, rural subjects, and highly educated parents.

Overall, the results of these 23 studies are not encouraging. Eleven studies compared PET to a nonattendant comparison or control group (Nos. 3, 4, 5, 7, 10, 11, 15, 18, 19, 22, 23). Out of a total of 100 comparisons, 53 (53%) showed no significant differences, 36 (36%) favored PET, and 11 (11%) favored the comparison group. Twelve studies compared PET to an alternative treatment (Nos. 1, 2, 6, 8, 9, 12, 13, 14, 16, 17, 20, 21). Two of these studies were not included in this overall analysis: No. 2 was excluded because it compared PET for parents to

Table 2-1 The Outcomes of Parent Effectiveness Training

Author (Population)	Independent Variable (N = Parents/children)	Dependent Measures C = Children, P = Parents, T = Teachers as Respondents (S = Significant results) [Results at follow up]	Methodological Problems
1) Anchor & Thomason (1977) (Highly educaced parents)	a) PET (22) b) Behavior Modification Group (19)	a) P-Communication Questionnaire b) P-Child Home Behavior Checklist c) P-Adjective Checklist d) P-Rathus Assertiveness Schedule e) P-Modified Verbal Behavior Checklist	a) Means, SD's of outcome measures not reported. Although significant dropouts occured, numbers not reported c) Questionable choice of dependent measures d) No posttest; only a follow-up "5-6 months" after end of course e) Ss did not fill out all measures f) Power struggles reported in Be. Mod. group may have affected outcome g) PET course administered in nonstandard format h) no control group

2) Andelin (1975) (Suburban-children had learning disabilities and/or emotional problems)	a) PET, with children also taking PET (33/22)
	 b) PET (19/13)
		a) P-HPAS-Total Score (S. a > b)
		   1. Confidence (S. a > b)
		   2. Trust (S. a > b)
		 b) P-A Parent Problem Checklist
		   1. Child Behavior
		   2. Parents' Problems (S. a > b)
			a) Ss not randomly assigned
			 b) No controls for experimenter or demand bias (Ss & Trainers aware of design)
			 c) No control group

Study	Groups	Measures	Comments

3) Fritz (1974)	a) PET (50)
	b) Wait List Control Group (22)
	c) Nonequivalent Comparison Group (22)
		c) P-Self Concept Inventory-Parent (6 subscales plus total score)
		d) C-CRPBI
		  1. Hostile Detachment (S b>a)
		e) C-Self-Concept Inventory-Child (10 subscales plus total score)
		  1. Work Habits (S b>a)
		  2. Happy Qualities (S b>a)
			d) 40% dropout rate for children-creating selection bias

4) Geffen (1978) (Single parents)	a) PET (21/21) b) Wait List Control Group (21/21)	a) P-Cattel's 16 PFQ b) Subjective data	a) Ss not randomly assigned b) PET preceded by an Introductory lecture, deviating from standard procedures

5) Giannotti (1978) (Suburban, learning-disabled children)	a) PET (46/23)
	b) No Contact Control Group (46/23)
		a) P-HPAS-Total Score (S a>b)
		  1. Causation (S a>b)
		  2. Understanding (S a>b)
		  3. Confidence (S a>b)
		b) C-CRPB, (Aron-Cross form)
		  1. Acceptance vs. rejection
		  2. Firm vs. Lax Control
		  3. Autonomy vs. Control
		
		a) P-HPAS(S a>b)-all 5 subscales
		b) C-CRPBI (S a>b)-all 4 subscales
		c) C-Piers-Harris Children Self-Concept Scale (S a>b)
		d) T-Devereaux Elementary School Behavior Rating Scale (S a>b, P<.05, on 5/11 subscales).
			a) Children's ages had very wide range (3-16 years, which may have influenced results on CRPBI

Table 2-1 Continued

Author (Population)	Independent Variable (N = Parents/children)	Dependent Measures C = Children, P = Parents, T = Teachers as Respondents (S = Significant results) [Results at follow up]	Methodological Problems
6) Hanley (1974)	a) PET (25/38) b) Family Enrichment Program (25/15) c) Non Equivalent Comparison Group (25/14)	a) P-PHPAS Total Score (NR) 1. Acceptance (S: a $>$ c = b) 2. Understanding (S: a $>$ c = b) b) P-Parental Concerns Checklist c) C-CRPBI d) Subjective data	a) Inadequate control group b) Ss not randomly assigned c) Treatment groups not equated for contact time
7) Knight (1975) (Suburban, enuretic children)	a) PET (50/29-20b, 9g) b) Wait List Control Group (50/29-15b, 14g)	a) P,C-Family Bond Inventory 1. Mother's bond (S: a $>$ b) 2. Boy's bond (S: b $>$ a)* b) P-Manifest Anxiety Scale (S: b $>$ a) c) P-Tennessee Self-Concept Scale (S: b $>$ a, on 9/13 subtests) d) C-Children's Manifest Anxiety Scale e) C-Piers-Harris Children's Self-Concept Scale (7 subtests) f) P-Enuresis measure (S: b $>$ a, for girls)	a) Inappropriate use of post hoc statistical tests (CF*) b) Posttest only design limits our ability to know whether groups were equivalent at pretest c) PET course administered in nonstandard format
8) Kowalewski (1977)	a) PET (8) b) Behavior Modification Group (8)	a) P-HPAS (used only two variables: Causation and a summary score of the other four subscales) b) P-Larson Parent Concern Survey c) P-Self-report logs	a) Procedures for assignment to group not sufficiently described b) No control group c) Small N

Study	Groups	Measures	Comments
9) Larson (1972) (suburban)	a) PET (43) b) Achievement motivation Group (33) c) Discussion Encounter Group (11)	a) P-HPAS b) P-Self-Concept Inventory adapted from Sears' Inventory c) P-Parent Concerns Survey d) P-A Problem Checklist e) P-Self-Report logs f) Subjective data	a) No inferential statistics b) Ss not randomly assign c) Small size of discussion group d) Achievement motivation group did not use McClelland's approach e) No control group
10) Lillibridge (1972) (Suburban)	a) PET (21/18) b) Wait List Comparison Group (22/21) c) Non-Equivalent Comparison Group (26/17)	a) P-HPAS Total Score 1. Confidence $(S\ a > b = c)^*$ 2. Acceptance $(S\ a > b = c)^*$ b) C-CRPBI 1. Parents more accepting of individuation $(S\ a > b = c)$ 2. Parents more accepting $(S\ a > b = c)$ 3. Parents less rejecting $(S\ a > b = c)$	a) Ss not randomly assign b) Matching process not sufficiently described c) Pretest made after first session; posttest made before end of course d) Parents administered CRPBI to their children e) Errors in statistical analysis (CF *)
11) Mee (1977)	a) PET (97) b) No-Control Group (97)	a) P-PARI-short form $(S\ a > b)$ b) P-Porter Parental Acceptance Scale $(S\ a > b)$ c) C-Barrett-Lennard Relationship Inventory 1. Empathic Understanding $(S\ a > b)$ 2. Positive Regard $(S\ a > b)$ 3. Unconditional Regard $(S\ a > b)$ 4. Congruence $(S\ a > b)$	

Table 2-1 Continued

Author (Population)	Independent Variable (N = Parents/children)	Dependent Measures C = Children, P = Parents, T = Teachers as Respondents (S = Significant results) [Results at follow up]	Methodological Problems
12) Miles (1975) (Black students, potential high school dropouts)	a) PET (20/20) b) Verbal Reinforcement Group-Children (20/20) c) PET & Verbal Reinforcement Group-Children (12/10) d) No-Contact Control Group (10/10)	a) P,C-Tennessee Self-Concept 1. Parents 2. Children (S*) b) C-Semantic Differential Scale 1. Attitudes toward parents (S*) 2. Attitudes toward school c) T-Teachers Behavior Rating Scale (S*)	a) Incorrect interpretation of statistical tests (C F *) b) Process of matching and random assignment not sufficiently described c) TBRS-Possible poor inter-rater reliability, and teachers may not have rated blind
13) Mitchell & McManis (1977)	a) PET (26) b) Read PET book only (26) c) Nonequivalent Comparison Group (26) -2x3 factoral design, examining parents vs. nonparents as second factor	a) P-PARI-Short form (Sa > b, a > c for parents and nonparents; b > c for parents)	a) Matching procedures not sufficiently specified b) Inadequate control group c) Posttest done before end of PET course
14) Noble (1977)	a) PET (11) b) Adlerian Parent Study Group (7) c) No-Contact Control Group (9)	a) P-PARI 1. Controlling techniques (a = b > c) 2. Awareness of the emotional needs of children 3. Parent-child communications b) P-Subjective data	a) PET administered in non-standard formal and course only 12 hours long. b) Small N
15) Pelky (1977)	a) PET (33) b) No-Contact Group (33)	a) P-PARI (S- a > b) b) P-Coopersmith Behavior Rating b	a) S= not randomly assigned

Study	Groups	Measures	Methodological Criticisms

16) Pinsker & Geoffrey (1981)	a) PET (13)
	b) Behavior Modification Group (13)
	c) Wait List Control (14)
		a) P-Problem Checklist (S·b $>$ c)
		b) P-Moos Family Environment Scale
		  1. Cohesion (S·a $>$ c)
		  2. Conflict (Sa $>$ c)
		  3. Control (Sa $>$ c)
		c) P-Tennessee Self-Concept Scale
		d) P-Behavior Modification knowledge scale (Sb $>$ c = a)
		e) P-PET knowledge scale (Sa $>$ c = b)
		f) P-C-Patterson's Behavior Coding Scale
		  1. Positive parental consequences (Sa $>$ c)
		  2. Negative child behaviors (S·b $>$ c)
		c) C-Coopersmith Self-Esteem Inventory
		d) Subjective data
			a) Ss not randomly assigned
			b) Treatment groups not equated for contact time
			c) Insufficient detail reported for use of ANCOVA procedure to "equate" groups on background variables
			d) Insufficient detail reported for post-hoc tests
			e) Small N

17) Reiswig (1973)	a) PET (8) b) Theme-Centered Interactional Group (11) c) Experiential Play (8)	a) P-Attitude and Behavior Questionnaire b) P-Content analysis of group interaction	a) No control group b) Lack of standardized measures c) Small N d) No inferential statistics

18) Roots (1980) (Rural subjects)	a) PET (30/41)
	b) Nonequivalent Comparison Group (15/18)
		a) P-HPAS-Total Score (Sa $>$ b)
		  1. Understanding (Sa $>$ b)
		  2. Trust (Sa $>$ b)
		[Six month follow-up for 1/2 of PET group (15/20) showed that gains held up]
		b) C-Crites Career Maturity Inventory
		c) C-Grade point average
			a) Ss not randomly assigned
			b) Inadequate control group

19) Schmitz (1975) (Rural subjects)	a) PET (23)
	b) Nonequivalent Comparison Group (23)
		a) P-HPAS-Total Score (Sa $>$ b)
		  1. Trust (Sa $>$ b)
		  2. Causation (Sa $>$ b)*
		b) P-D-scale measuring dogmatism (Sa $>$ b)
			a) Ss not randomly assigned
			b) Inadequate control group
			c) Matching procedures not sufficiently specified
			d) Statistical errors (CF*)

Table 2-1 Continued

Author (Population)	Independent Variable (N = Parents/children)	Dependent Measures C = Children, P = Parents, T = Teachers as Respondents (S = Significant results) [Results at follow up]	Methodological Problems

20) Schofield (1976)	a) PET (14/12)
	b) Behavior Modification Group (14/14)
	c) Nonequivalent Comparison Group (14/17)
		a) P-HPAS Total Score (NR)
		  1. Acceptance (Sa>c)*
		  2. Understanding (Sa>c)
		b) P-Education Scale (Associates Progressive educational practices) (Sa>c, a>b)
		c) C-Coopersmith Self-Esteem Inventory (Sa>c)
		d) Subjective data
			a) Inadequate control group
			b) Treatment groups not equated for contact time
			c) Inappropriate use of post-hoc statistical tests (CF*)

21) Schultz, Nystul & Law (1980); Schultz & Nystul (1980)	a) PET (25)
	b) Adlerian Parent Study Group (25)
	c) Behavior Modification Group (23)
	d) Placebo Control Group (22)
	e) No-Contact Control Group (25)
		a) P-PARI-Q4 form (Sa>e)
		b) P-Attitudes Toward Freedom of Children Scale II (Sa>e, a>d)
		[12 month follow-up: a'(10), b'(9), c'(90, f-PET grad. of one month (9), g-Newly formed no-contact group (10). S, a'>g, b'>g, c'>g, a'>c, f'>c]
		c) P-Parental Rating of Improvement
		  1. Family functions better.
		  2. Households more happy Sa>d, b>d, c>d.
		d) PC- 20 behavioral measures of parent child interaction in two structured tasks (assessed
			a) PET administered in nonstandard format 10 weekly 1-1/2 hr. sessions
			b) attrition of Ss at follow-up (38%) may have introduced selection bias

22) Stearn (1971)	a) PET (18/36) b) Nonequivalent Comparison Group I (parents interested in PET) (15/30) c) Nonequivalent Comparison Group II (parents not interested in PET) (14/26)	by trained judges viewing video-tapes of interaction)-Done at follow-up only, with groups as noted under b. [12 month follow-up: $Sa > f = g$, $c > f' = g'$ both f & c fostered independence of child within warm climate] a) P-Traditional Family Ideology Test, measures autocratic/democratic dimensions of child rearing [6 week follow-up-$Sa > b$, $a > c$]* b) C-Coopersmith Self-Esteem Inventory ($S\text{-}c > a$, $c > b$)* [6 week follow-up-$S\,a > c$]* c) C-Barrett-Lennard Relationship Inventory 1) Empathy [6 week follow-up-$S\text{-}c > a$] 2) Positive Regard ($S\text{-}c > a$, $c > b$)* [(6 week follow-up-$S\text{-}c > a$, $b > a$]* 3) Unconditional Regard (NR) 4) Congruence ($S\text{-}c > a$)* [6 week follow-up-$S\text{-}c > a$]*	a) Ss not randomly assigned b) Inadequate control groups c) Parents administered dependent measures to their children d) Inappropriate use of post-hoc statistical tests (CF*)
23) Therrien (1979) Comparison Group (17)	a) PET (40) b) Nonequivalent	a) P-Truax Accurate Empathy Scale (Experienced judges rated independently + blindly written responses to child stimulus statements) ($S\text{-}a > b$) [4 month follow-up-$Sa > b$]	a) Ss not randomly assigned b) Inadequate control group

---

*Items marked with an * in the third column are examples of certain methodological problems itemized in the fourth column (CF*).

PET for parents and children; and No. 9 was excluded because no inferential statistics were used. In the remaining 10 studies, out of a total of 49 comparisons, 34 (69%) showed no significant differences, 12 (25%) favored PET, and 6 (3%) favored the alternative treatment.

However, this bleak picture is misleading because so many of the studies are rife with serious methodological problems. In fact, there are only three studies which met the following minimal criteria of methodological adequacy: use of a nonattendant control group, random assignment to condition, use of standard PET procedures, employment of standardized dependent measures, and appropriate use of inferential statistical tests (Nos. 4, 5, 11). These three studies compared PET to a control group, using a pre-post design and self-report measures. Out of 35 comparisons, 24 (69%) favored PET over the control group, 0 (0%) favored the control group, and 11 (31%) showed no significant differences.

Thus, there is a modest degree of support for the efficacy of PET, in contrast to the conclusions of the earlier review by Rinn and Markle (1977) and of a recent critique (Dohery & Ryder, 1980). To summarize the specific positive findings, PET appears to result in positive changes in parent attitudes (self-report) and behavior (child-rated) and in children's self-concept (self-report) and behavior (teacher-rated).

Clearly, many questions remain regarding the efficacy of PET. To help address these, the author and associates are undertaking a meta-analysis of the PET literature.

Conclusions

The training for enhancement area is a growing and promising field. Premarital, marital, and divorce programs have been developed, and evaluation of PRIMES and CRE indicates that couples learn the communication skills in a brief program and report improvements in their relationship. Assessments at six-month follow-up indicate that the skill level is maintained. PRIMES has demonstrated superiority over a lecture/discussion approach, and seems about equal to a behavioral exchange approach on a measure of perceived heterosexual competence. Preliminary evaluations of a communication skills program for divorcees indicate its efficacy in teaching the skills and facilitating post-divorce adjustment.

Several parental programs have been developed. With regard to RE programs, the available research does not support the efficacy of the didactic Filial Parent Education course, but the skill-training PARD and CAPS programs do have empirical support for improving communication and relationships. The Human Resource Development Program has shown its efficacy in training parents in communication skills and has been innovative in training parents to be trainers of their children. The

Personal Developmental Program has been applied to lower socioeconomic minority foster mothers, working-class parents, and fathers who wanted to increase their parental role, and has received modest empirical support. Finally, the efficacy of PET in improving parent attitudes and behavior, as well as children's self-concept and behavior, has received some support in the more adequate recent studies.

The future development of training for enhancement programs would be improved by taking a more sharply focused approach, fixing either on prevention or on development. In the former case, populations at risk could be identified and preventive programs formulated and tested (such as is being done with the divorce programs). In the latter case, programs could be aimed at particular developmental transitions (such as is being done with the premarital PRIMES program). In both cases this would lead to a series of more specifically formulated—and hopefully more helpful—programs.

Summary and Conclusions

This article has reviewed the client-centered psycho-educational skills-training programs for the family. In the two treatment areas, it has been demonstrated that effective communication skills, based on the model of the client-centered therapist, can be taught in a relatively short time. It has been shown that communication skills (particularly play therapy skills) produce positive results when applied by a parent to help a disturbed child. It has also been shown that teaching these communication skills can effectively treat dysfunctional parent–adolescent and marital relationships. Follow-up studies indicate that skill levels and other gains hold up over short- and long-term follow-up periods. Comparative studies indicate that this approach is equivalent in outcome to a behavioral approach and superior in outcome to a Gestalt program, the Couple Communication Program, and discussion group approaches. There is also evidence of the superiority of training as treatment over traditional treatment for dysfunctional marital relationships. In the enhancement area, premarital, marital, divorce, and parental programs have been demonstrated to have efficacy in teaching skills in brief programs, which then result in improvements in individuals and in family relationships. Follow-up studies indicate that skill levels and other changes are maintained over a short-term interval. Comparative studies indicate the superiority of skills training over lecture/discussion as an enhancement approach, and its approximate equivalence with a behavioral approach.

Thus there is support for the efficacy of these approaches. Future research should incorporate the following points. First, much of the literature is so plagued by basic design flaws (such as inadequate or no control groups, lack of random assignment, and statistical errors) that it is necessary to state that minimal methodological criteria should be met in future research of this kind. Second, although several studies have compared their approach to an alternative treatment, there is need for more refined studies of this type. In this regard, it should be acknowledged that some of the alternative treatments that have been used are best considered attention-placebo controls (e.g., the lecture/discussion group to which PRIMES was compared), and others are unknown or idiosyncratic treatments which appear to have been developed specifically to test the better established treatment (e.g., the Gestalt Relationship Awareness Facilitator group, to which CRE was compared). Comparisons with established treatments of comparable type and duration administered by professionals actively involved in their development and evaluation would be an optimal approach. In this regard, the comparisons of Filial Therapy versus behavioral parent training (both well-developed and researched training as treatment approaches) and CRE versus behavioral marital therapy (both well-developed and researched training for treatment approaches) would be particularly rigorous. Third, there is the need for more objective outcome measures. While the assessment of skill level is solidly based on the method of independent judge's ratings of behavioral samples, the assessment of changes in relationships is primarily based on self-report. So, too, the assessment of changes in children in the training for treatment and training for enhancement areas is similarly weak, resting on self-report or ratings of participants. Two recent studies of PET point the way toward more objective measurement strategies (Pinsker & Geoffrey, 1981; Schultz & Nystul, 1980). Fourth, there is the issue of outcome criteria, particularly in the training for enhancement area. If the programs do become more specific in their aim (as preventive *or* development programs), they should take on the task of evaluation in terms of these more specific aims. For example, a premarital program might be assessed in terms of its effects on marital stability and happiness within the first several years of marriage. Fifth, there is the related point of the need for longer term follow-ups in order to demonstrate the stability of the outcomes. Follow-ups are not done often, and those that are done are usually 6 months or less (the exceptions being a 12-month follow-up of PET, Schultz & Nystul, 1980; and a 3-year follow-up of Filial Therapy, Sensué, 1981). Finally there is the issue of client population. With a few exceptions these methods have generally been applied to middle and upper-middle class clientele, and to clients experiencing mild to moderate distress. There is a need to investigate the potential of these approaches with a broader population, including lower income and minority groups, and with more severely disturbed clients.

An Example from Practice:
A Parent Education Course For Fathers*

As a counterpoint to the preceding discussion of program development and evaluative research, a more complete description of one program will now be presented. I have chosen a program with which I am most familiar, and one which has stimulated a great deal of interest recently in the popular media: The Personal Development Program for Fathers.

Description of the Program

Until recently, men's active participation in parenting has been viewed as of minimal importance, and even as inappropriate. However, the importance of the father's role in child development has gained increasing recognition during the 1970s. Moreover, increasing men's participation in parenting is a key issue for contemporary families and for society as a whole as women increase their participation in the paid labor force.

The initial thinking of our group was that a psycho-educational program might help facilitate men's increased participation in parenting. Traditionally, men have not been prepared for an extensive role in parenting, through either family socialization or formal education. This lack of preparation poses a difficult and even insurmountable obstacle for many men. Price-Bonham and Skeen (1979) have suggested that "fathers may be spending great amounts of time in their work role in order to avoid responsibilities of the father role because they lack the knowledge/skills to be comfortable in the role" (p. 58). Indeed, the difficulties which many men experience in developing an active parenting role are quite profound, as has been highlighted in recent popular and professional examinations of fathering after marital separation (*Kramer vs. Kramer,* Jaffrey, 1979; Keshet & Rosenthal, 1978).

In turning to the literature we found that parent education for fathers has been a badly neglected area. First of all, the vast majority of popular parenting manuals explicitly or implicitly endorse the traditional roles of father as dominant breadwinner and mother as nurturant caregiver (De-Frain, 1977). Second, parent education courses have, until very recently, almost completely ignored fathers. A search of the available reviews of the literature on parent training in 1980 found not one study which fo-

*I am indebted to Dr. Greg Doyle and Mr. Joseph Rabinovitz for their efforts, upon which this section is based. Dr. Doyle was a colleague in the original development and evaluation of the Parent Education Program for Fathers. Mr. Rabinovitz served as a co-leader of the course with me during the Spring semester of 1984, and developed the section on suggestions for leaders based on this experience.

cused on the training of fathers, or which even indicated whether the "parent" group included fathers (Loiselle, 1980).

With this as backdrop, we developed a parent education program for fathers, based on our Personal Developmental Program. The program consists of eight three-hour sessions and is designed for both married and single fathers.

The first half of the course focuses on listening and responding to one's child, whereas the second half concerns speaking for oneself and acceptance. The format for the course is detailed in the *Leader's Guide* (Levant & Doyle, 1981a). Each half of the course includes three sessions devoted to the development of specific skills followed by a fourth session devoted to synthesis and integration. The last session includes a graduation ceremony.

The listening and responding half of the course begins with a session concerning nonverbal parental behaviors which can facilitate communication, moves in the next session to listening and responding reflectively to the content of the child's message, and finishes with a session on listening and responding empathically to the child's feelings.

In the second half of the course, the speaking for oneself segment begins with a session on increasing fathers' awareness of their thoughts and feelings which emerge while interacting with their children, and concludes with a session on fathers learning to express their thoughts and feelings in a nondefensive, open manner. In the segment on acceptance, the fathers examine their personal sensitivities in order to become more accepting of their children.

The program includes didactic and experiential components. The format for the skill training sessions is as follows: Introduction and definition of the skill in a brief lecture; demonstration of the skill using videotaped and live examples, usually role-plays between the instructors; practice of the skill in role-play exercises, using videotape for immediate feedback; and consolidation and transferring the skill to the interaction with one's child through homework assignments. The homework assignments are contained in the *Father's Workbook* (Levant & Doyle, 1981b). Fathers are expected to spend one hour per week on homework, which includes readings, paper-and-pencil exercises, and experiential practice with one's child. The paper-and-pencil exercises progress from asking the fathers to discriminate good versus poor responses to asking them to formulate their own good responses. Homework assignments are discussed in class each week.

The fathers who participate in the course come from all walks of life, from laborer to plumber to lawyer to stockbroker. Ages have ranged from the late 20s to the mid 50s, with children from early infancy to young adulthood. About half the dads are married and half divorced. A few of the married fathers have remarried and are working out a "reconstituted" family. Those that are divorced have custody arrangements ranging from visitation to joint custody to sole custody.

Though the men are successful in the work place and fulfill the "good provider" role, they experience dissatisfaction with their relationships with their children. Some speak with sadness of the distance in their relationships with their own fathers, or articulate a desire not to make some of the same mistakes with their children that their fathers made with them. Others feel inadequate with their children, and marvel at how well their wives "do it." Some are very uncomfortable with feelings, both their own and their children's. Others get caught in the "anger trap" and become ensnared in unproductive repetitive patterns of testing and punishment. Most assume they know how to communicate, until the first videotaped role-play, in which a father might tower over his child, or talk from behind a newspaper. About halfway through the course, after fathers have had some success at mastering the skills, several report that they are finding the skill useful not only with their children, but with their wives and others at the work place, as well.

For example, one father said:

I found the lessons in practicing communication particularly valuable. I would add the concept—the one most people miss—that communication is generally undervalued and completely misunderstood in our society. I think that people must feel as though they are doing fine, when in fact they are not dealing with the emotional level at all, in many, many cases.

And another observed:

Like I said in the beginning, not only family members, but I'm using the listening skills on my job. I'm taking those same skills that we developed, and applying them, so that if I'm talking to an employee, and the employee is having a problem, I try to develop some trust with that person, establish eye contact, and respond to his statement by saying the statement back to let him know I'm listening.

The results of the evaluation were briefly reported earlier in the chapter (see p. 71). Some feel for these results can perhaps be garnered from considering the responses of one boy to a test which asked him to draw a picture of his family doing something together. Before the course began the child drew a picture of a roller coaster, with the tracks filling 90 percent of the page. At the very top was a tiny little car. In the front seat was the boy, legs and arms akimbo. In the next seat was Mom and then Dad. His brother was in the last seat, and appeared to be falling out of the car. After the course was over, the boy drew a picture of a spaceship running diagonally across the page in which the cockpit filled about 40 percent of the page. Seated at the controls was Dad; next to him, Mom. At opposite sides, looking out the window, were he and his brother.

Suggestions for Leaders

Leaders of client-centered parent education courses for fathers must be aware of many issues that can affect the outcome of the course. For starters there are familiar issues such as helping group members to develop trust in each other, facilitating conversation, keeping the group safe for members, and conveying the course content in a manner that can be digested by the members. The following section outlines additional factors that the leader working specifically with fathers must be aware of.

The first factor is the motivation for the father enrolling in the course. It is not enough to assume that the dad is simply there to learn the communication skills offered in the course description. The leader must consider what is the source of the father's motivation. For example, many of the fathers who enroll in the course do so because they are experiencing moderate to severe difficulties with their children. Some of the fathers who have been experiencing stress begin the course hoping to find some sort of "correct" method of dealing with their children. The leader must be able to recognize this desire, legitimize the feeling behind it, and convey to the father that there is no "correct" method, without dampening the father's enthusiasm. This is analogous to the family that presents itself for family therapy with the parents hoping the therapist will be able to "fix" the problem child. Some of the fathers in this course take time to learn the distinction between learning a technique they can use to make their child behave differently and learning a set of skills that they can use to enhance their interactions with their child. The latter is the idea the leaders try to engender in the group members.

A second factor leaders must take into account is the amount of experience the group members have had in similar situations. Because men have not typically been involved in parent education courses, it is not surprising to find that the majority of any given group will have had little experience in this type of group learning situation. Thus, members may be reluctant to participate because they are not sure of the rules by which the group operates. It is helpful for the leaders to present their agenda for the session at the start of the class in order to put members at ease. It is also recommended to structure some kind of warm-up exercise for the first session to help reduce anxiety. One technique that has proved helpful involves pairing the fathers up, giving them 10 to 15 minutes to talk together about such things as the reasons why they are taking the course, their home situation, and their children, and then have the group reform and have each father introduce his "partner" to the group.

A related issue is how long it has been since the father participated in some kind of classroom learning situation. Some fathers will not have been in a classroom since they were in high school or college. They may feel somewhat inhibited or nervous about being in a class situation, and this nervousness may be compounded by the fact that much of the learning centers around group discussion and role-plays. The leader can get an idea of both the members' experience in groups and how long it has been since they were in a classroom situation by simply asking the question during his introduction to the course. Care must be taken to ensure that a member is not put on the spot.

One strength of this course is that it is designed in such a way that it does not require group members to be versed in theories of child development. The theoretical aspects are presented in a straightforward manner with each succeeding week building on the material from the previous session. Leaders have found that sometimes members come with a wide range of knowledge of child development. This can affect the group process in a positive or negative manner depending on the particular style of the "advanced" group member and the leader's ability to integrate the more advanced material offered by this member in a way that enhances the group process. The leader must take care not to engage this member in "high level" discussions to the exclusion of other group members.

During the first session it is helpful for the leader to get a sense of the home and family situation of the fathers in the group. A typical group will consist of fathers who are married, divorced, and separated. The leader must be able to blend the concerns brought up by different members so that all will profit from ensuing discussions. One common issue is the fact that some of the fathers are single parents while others have a partner to whom they may or may not be married. It is important for the leader to help the fathers on one side of the coin understand what the issues are for the person on the other side and vice versa.

The leader must be aware that the home situation may affect the father's ability to practice the skills with his child and do the assigned homework. Some fathers may report that they have difficulty because of occupations and other circumstances to practice the skills. These fathers should be encouraged to find the time, and they can be reminded that similar to any other skill they have learned, these communication skills must be practiced.

The amount of support the fathers receive from significant adults in their lives may affect the process. A number of married fathers report experiencing significant amounts of support and encouragement from their wives, which they say helps them stay motivated. Other, unmarried fathers have reported feeling supported from significant adults in their lives. However, a few fathers report skeptical reactions from friends and family members concerning their participation in the course.

One very helpful factor is that the members of the group tend to become very supportive of each other. Comments like, "I like how you handled that," and "I don't blame you for getting angry," are commonly heard throughout the sessions. The leader is also in a position to offer support and encouragement.

One last point that the leader must keep in mind is that many of the fathers are going to come to class directly from work, so that energy level is an important factor. Allowing for differences in personal style, it is important for the leader to be energized and enthusiastic. Many fathers report that they often came to the class extremely tired, but found the class an upbeat, highly energizing experience.

References

Albee, G.W. (1967). The relationship of conceptual models to manpower needs. In E.L. Cowan, E.A. Gardner, & M. Zak (Eds.), *Emergent approaches to mental health problems*. New York: Meredith.

Anchor, K.M., & Thomason, T.C. (1977). A comparison of two parent-training models with educated parents. *Journal of Community Psychology, 5,* 134–141.

Andelin, S. (1975). *The effects of concurrently teaching parents and their children with learning adjustment problems the principles of parent effectiveness training.* Unpublished doctoral dissertation, Utah State University.

Andronico, M.P., Fidler, J., Guerney, B., Jr., & Guerney, L.F. (1967). The combination of didactic and dynamic elements in filial therapy. *International Journal of Group Psychotherapy, 17,* 10–17.

Andronico, M.P., & Guerney, B.G., Jr. (1969). A psychotherapeutic aide in a Headstart program. *Children, 16*(1), 14–22.

Avery, A.W., Ridley, C.A., Leslie, L., & Milholland, T. (1980). Relationship Enhancement with premarital dyads: A six month follow-up. *American Journal of Family Therapy, 8,* 23–30.

Avery, A.W., & Thiessen, J.D. (1982). Communication skills training for divorcees. *Journal of Counseling Psychology, 29,* 203–205.

Axline, V.M. (1947). *Play therapy.* Boston: Houghton Mifflin.

Barrett-Lennard, G.F. (1962). Dimensions of therapist response as causal factors in therapeutic change. *Psychological Monographs, 76.*

Bendix, L.A. (1977). The differential effects on parents and their children of training parents to be helpers or life skill trainers for their children (Doctoral dissertation, Boston University, 1977). *Dissertation Abstracts International, 38,* 1869–1870B. (University Microfilms No. 77-21, 688.)

Bergin, A.E. (1967). Some implications of psychotherapy research for therapeutic practice. *International Journal of Psychiatry, 3,* 136–150.

Bergin, A.E. (1971). The evaluation of therapeutic outcomes. In A.E. Bergin & S.L. Garfield (Eds.), *Handbook of psychotherapy and behavior change: An empirical analysis.* New York: Wiley.

Brock, G.W., & Joanning, H. (1983). A comparison of the Relationship Enhancement Program and the Minnesota Couple Communication Program. *Journal of Marital and Family Therapy, 9,* 413–421.

Carducci, R. (1975). *A comparison of I-messages with commands in the control of disruptive classroom behavior.* Unpublished doctoral dissertation, University of Nevada.

Carkhuff, R.R. (1969a). *Helping and human relations. Vol. I: Selection and training.* New York: Holt, Rinehart & Winston.

Carkhuff, R.R. (1969b). *Helping and human relations Vol. II: Practice and research.* New York: Holt, Rinehart & Winston.

Carkhuff, R.R. (1971a). Training as a preferred mode of treatment. *Journal of Counseling Psychology, 18,* 123–131.

Carkhuff, R.R. (1971b). *The development of human resources: Education, psychology, and social change.* New York: Holt, Rinehart & Winston.

Carkhuff, R.R. (1972). *The art of helping.* Amherst, MA: Human Resource Development Press.

Carkhuff, R.R., & Bierman, R. (1970). Training as a preferred mode of treatment of parents of emotionally disturbed children. *Journal of Counseling Psychology, 17,* 157–161.

Carkhuff, R.R., & Pierce, R.M. (1976). *Helping begins at home.* Amherst, MA: Human Resource Development Press.

Collins, J. (1972). The effects of conjugal relationship modification method on marital communication and adjustment (Doctoral dissertation, Pennsylvania State University). *Dissertation Abstracts International, 32,* 6674B. (University Microfilms No. 72-13, 836.)

Coopersmith, S. (1967). *The antecedents of self-esteem.* San Francisco: Freeman.

Cotton, M.C. (1977). A systems approach to marital training evaluation (Doctoral dissertation, Texas Tech University). *Dissertation Abstracts International, 37,* 5346B. (University Microfilms No. 77-8742.)

Coufal, J.D. (1976). Preventive-therapeutic programs for mothers and adolescent daughters: Skills training versus discussion methods (Doctoral dissertation, Pennsylvania State University). *Dissertation Abstracts International, 37,* 3941–3942A. (University Microfilms No. 76-26, 824.)

Cross, H., & Kawash, G. (1968). A short form of PARI to assess authoritarian attitudes toward child rearing. *Psychological Reports, 23,* 91–98.

D'Augelli, A.R., Deyss, C.S., Guerney, B.G., Jr., Herschenberg, B., & Sborofsky, S.L. (1974). Interpersonal skill training for dating couples: An evaluation of an educational mental health service. *Journal of Counseling Psychology, 21,* 385–389.

D'Augelli, J.F., & Weener, J.M. (1978). Training parents as mental health agents. *Community Mental Health Journal, 14*(1), 14–25.

DeFrain, J.D. (1977). Sexism in parenting manuals. *The Family Coordinator, 26,* 245–251.

Doherty, W.J., & Ryder, R.G. (1980). Parent effectiveness training (PET): Criticisms and caveats. *Journal of Marital and Family Therapy, 6*(4), 409–419.

Dorfman, E. Play therapy. (1951). In C.R. Rogers (Ed.), *Client-centered therapy.* Boston: Houghton Mifflin.

Durrett, D.D., & Kelley, P.A. (1974). Can you really talk with your child? A parental training program in communication skills toward the improvement of parent–child interaction. *Group Psychotherapy and Psychodrama, 27,* 98–109.

Eardley, D.A. (1979). An initial investigation of a didactic version of filial therapy dealing with self-concept increase and problematic behavior decrease (Doctoral dissertation, Pennsylvania State University). *Dissertation Abstracts International, 39,* 5942B. (University Microfilms No. 7909061.)

Ely, A.L., Guerney, B.G., Jr., & Stover, L. (1973). Efficacy of the training phase of conjugal therapy. *Psychotherapy: Theory, Research, and Practice, 10,* 201–207.

Fitts, W.H. (1965). *Tennessee self-concept scale manual.* Nashville: Counselor Recordings and Tests.

Fritz, E.J. (1974). Parent effectiveness training: The measurement of change on participants' personality traits (Doctoral Dissertation, United States International University). *Dissertation Abstracts International, 35,* 1380–1381B. (University Microfilms No. 74-20, 517.)

Fuchs, N.R. (1957). Play therapy at home. *Merrill-Palmer Quarterly, 3,* 89–95.

Gardner, R. (1970). *The boys and girls book about divorce.* New York: Bantam.

Geffen, M.S. (1978). The value of a course in parent effectiveness training for single parents (Doctoral dissertation, California School of Professional Psychology-Fresno). *Dissertation Abstracts International, 35,* 3877–3878B. (University Microfilms No. 7732249.)

Giannotti, T.J. (1979). Changes in self-concept and perception of parental behavior among learning disabled elementary school children as a result of parent effectiveness training (Doctoral dissertation, St. Johns University). *Dissertation Abstracts International, 39,* 4137–4138A. (University Microfilms No. 7900261.)

Ginsberg, B.G. (1972). Parent-adolescent relationship development. A therapeutic and preventive mental health program. (Doctoral dissertation, Pennsylvania State University). *Dissertation Abstracts International, 33,* 426–427A. (University Microfilms No. 72-19, 306.)

Ginsberg, B. (1976). Parents as therapeutic agents: The usefulness of filial therapy in a community psychiatric clinic. *American Journal of Community Psychology, 4*(1), 47–54.

Ginsberg, B., & Vogelsong, E.L. (1977). Premarital relationship improvement by maximizing empathy and self-disclosure: The PRIMES Program. In B.G. Guerney, Jr. (Ed.), *Relationship Enhancement.* San Francisco: Jossey-Bass.

Goodman, G. (1972). *Companionship therapy: Studies in structured intimacy.* San Francisco: Jossey-Bass.

Gordon, T. (1970). *P.E.T.: Parent effectiveness training.* New York: Peter H. Wyden.

Gordon, T. (1972). *Parent effectiveness training: Parent notebook.* Pasadena, CA: Effectiveness Training Associates.

Gordon, T. (1976). *P.E.T. in Action.* New York: Wyden.

Gordon, T. (1980). Parent effectiveness training: A preventive program and its effects on families. In M. Fine (Ed.), *Handbook on parent education.* New York: Academic Press.

Gormally, J., & Hill, C.E. (1974). Guidelines for research on Carkhuff's training model. *Journal of Counseling Psychology, 21*(6), 539–547.

Grando, R.M. (1972). The parent adolescent relationship development program: Relationships among pretraining variables, role performance and improvement (Doctoral dissertation, Pennsylvania State University, 1972). *Dissertation Abstracts International, 34,* 1385A. (University Microfilms No. 73-21, 265.)

Guerney, B., Jr. (1964). Filial therapy: Description and rationale. *Journal of Consulting Psychology, 28,* 304–310.

Guerney, B.G., Jr. (1977). *Relationship enhancement.* San Francisco: Jossey-Bass.

Guerney, B.G., Jr. (1984). Contributions of client-centered therapy to filial, marital, and family relationship enhancement therapies. In R.F. Levant & J.M. Shlien (Eds.), *Client-centered therapy and the person-centered approach: New directions in theory, research, and practice.* New York: Praeger.

Guerney, B.G., Jr., & Flumen, A.B. (1970). Teachers as psychotherapeutic agents for withdrawn children. *Journal of School Psychology, 8*(2), 107–113.

Guerney, B.G., Jr., Guerney, L.F., & Andronico, M.P. (1966). Filial therapy. *Yale Scientific Magazine,* March.

Guerney, B.G., Jr., Stollak, G., & Guerney, L. (1971). The practicing psychologist as educator—An alternative to the medical practitioner model. *Professional Psychology, 2*(3), 276–282.

Guerney, B.G., Jr., & Stover, L. (1971). *Final report on filial therapy* (Grant MH18264-1). Rockville, MD: National Institute of Mental Health.

Guerney, B.G., Jr., & Vogelsong, E.L. (1980). Relationship enhancement therapy. In R. Herink (Ed.), *The psychotherapy handbook.* New York: New American Library.

Guerney, L.F. (1976). Filial therapy program. In D.H.L. Olson (Ed.), *Treating relationships.* Lake Mills, IA: Graphic Publishing.

Guerney, L.F. (1977). A description and evaluation of a skills training program for foster parents. *American Journal of Community Psychology, 5*(3), 361–371.

Guerney, L.F. (1979). Play therapy with learning disabled children. *Journal of Clinical Child Psychology, 8,* 242–244.

Guerney, L.F. (1980). Filial therapy. In R. Herink (Ed.), *The psychotherapy handbook.* New York: New American Library.

Guerney, L., & Jordon, L. (1979). Children of divorce—A community support group. *Journal of Divorce, 2*(3), 283–293.

Gurman, A.S., & Kniskern, D.P. (1978). Research on marital and family therapy: Progress, perspective and prospect. In S. Garfield & A. Bergin (Eds.), *Handbook of psychotherapy and behavior change* (2nd ed.). New York: Wiley.

Haffey, N., & Levant, R.F. (1984). The diffential effectiveness of two models of skills training for working class parents. *Family Relations, 33,* 209–216.

Hanley, D.F. (1974). Changes in parent attitudes related to a parent effectiveness training and a family enrichment program (Doctoral dissertation, United States International University). *Dissertation Abstracts International, 34,* 7044A. (University Microfilms No. 74-10, 368.)

Hereford, C.F. (1963). *Changing parent attitudes through group discussion.* Austin: University of Texas Press.

Ivey, A.E. (1971). *Microcounseling: Innovations in interviewing training.* Springfield, IL: Charles C. Thomas.

Jaffrey, S. (Producer). (1979). *Kramer vs. Kramer.* New York: Columbia Pictures.

Jessee, R.E. (1978). A comparison of Gestalt relationship awareness facilitation and conjugal relationship enhancement programs (Doctoral dissertation, Pennsylvania State University). *Dissertation Abstracts International, 39,* 649B. (University Microfilms No. 7812055.)

Kagan, N. (1972). Observations and suggestions. *The Counseling Psychologist, 3*(3), 42–45.

Kanigsberg, J., & Levant, R.F. (1982). *Changes in parental attitudes, children's self-concept and behavior following parental participation in skills training programs.* Manuscript submitted for publication.

Keshet, H.F., & Rosenthal, K.M. (1978). Fathering after marital separation. *Social Work, 23,* 11–18.

Knight, N.A. (1975). The effects of changes in family interpersonal relationships on the behavior of enuretic children and their parents (Doctoral dissertation, University of Hawaii). *Dissertation Abstracts International, 36,* 783A. (University Microfilms No. 75-17, 120.)

Koch, N.L., Dentler, M., Dysart, B., & Streit, H. (1934). A scale towards measuring attitudes: The question of children's freedom. *Child Development, 5,* 253–266.

Kowalewski, J.F. (1977). An evaluative study of behavior modification training for parents and parent effectiveness training as methods for affecting parent–child problem resolution and parental attitude change (Doctoral dissertation, University of Maryland). *Dissertation Abstracts International, 37,* 6334B. (University Microfilms No. 77-13, 029.)

Lambert, M.J., & DeJulio, S.S. (1977). Outcome research in Carkhuff's Human Resource Development training programs: Where is the donut? *The Counseling Psychologist, 6*(4), 79–86.

Larson, R.S. (1972). Can parent classes affect family communication? *The School Counselor, 19,* 261–270.

Levant, R.F. (1983). Client-centered skills-training programs for the family: A review of the literature. *The Counseling Psychologist, 11*(3), 29–46.

Levant, R.F., & Doyle, G.F. (1981a). *Parent education for fathers: A personal developmental approach. Leader's Guide.* Unpublished manuscript, Boston University.

Levant, R.F., & Doyle, G.F. (1981b). *Parent education for fathers: A personal developmental approach. Father's Workbook.* Unpublished manuscript, Boston University.

Levant, R.F., & Doyle, G. (1983). An evaluation of a parent education program of fathers of school-aged children. *Family Relations, 32,* 29–37.

Levant, R.F., & Geer, M.F. (1981). A systematic skills approach to the selection and training of foster parents as mental health paraprofessionals. I: Project overview and selection component. *Journal of Community Psychology, 9,* 224–230.

Levant, R.F., Slattery, S.C., & Slobodian, P.E. (1981). A systematic skills approach to the selection and training of foster parents as mental health paraprofessionals. II: Training. *Journal of Community Psychology, 9,* 231–238.

Levinson, D., & Huffman, P. (1955). Traditional family ideology and its relationship to personality. *Journal of Personality, 23, 251–273.*

Lillibridge, E.M. (1972). The relationship of a parent effectiveness training program to change in parents' self-assessed attitudes and children's perceptions of parents (Doctoral dissertation, United States International University). *Dissertation Abstracts International, 32,* 5613A. (University Microfilms No. 72-10, 520.)

Loiselle, J.E. (1980). *A review of the role of fathers in parent training programs.* Unpublished manuscript, Boston University.

McIntosh, D.M. (1975). A comparison of the effects of highly structured, partially structured, and non-structured human relations training for married couples on the dependent variables of communication, marital adjustment, and personal adjustment (Doctoral dissertation, North Texas State University). *Dissertation Abstracts International, 36,* 2636–2637A. (University Microfilms No. 75-24, 158.)

Mee, C.B. (1977). Parent effectiveness training: Assessment of the developmental gains in parents' capacity to counsel their children (Doctoral dissertation, Catholic University of America). *Dissertation Abstracts International, 32*, 115–116A. (University Microfilms No. 77-14, 586.)

Miles, J.M.H. (1975). A comparative analysis of the effectiveness of verbal reinforcement group counseling and parent effectiveness training in certain behavioral aspects of potential drop-outs (Doctoral dissertation, Auburn University). *Dissertation Abstracts International, 35*, 7655A. (University Microfilms No. 75-12, 493.)

Mitchell, J., & McManis, D.L. (1977). Effects of P.E.T. on authoritarian attitudes toward child-rearing in parents and non-parents. *Psychological Reports, 41*, 215–218.

Mitchell, K.M., Bozarth, J.D., & Krauft, C.C. (1977). A reappraisal of the therapeutic effectiveness of accurate empathy, non-possessive warmth and genuineness. In A.S. Gurman & A.M. Razin (Eds.), *Effective psychotherapy: A handbook of research*. Oxford: Pergamon Press.

Noble, R.D. (1977). An evaluation of parent effectiveness training and Adlerian parent groups: Changing child-rearing attitudes. (Doctoral dissertation, Indiana University). *Dissertation Abstracts International, 37*, 4869A. (University Microfilms No. 77-3359.)

Oxman, L.K. (1972). The effectiveness of filial therapy: A controlled study (Doctoral dissertation, Rutgers University). *Dissertation Abstracts International, 32*, 6656B. (University Microfilms No. 72-16, 093.)

Patterson, G.R., Ray, R.S., Shaw, D.A, & Cobb, J.A. (1969). *Manual for coding of family interaction* (National Auxillary Publications Service Document No. 01234). New York: Microfiche Publications.

Pelkey, G.F. (1977). The effect of parent effectiveness training and teacher effectiveness training on student self-image. (Doctoral dissertation, University of Southern California). *Dissertation Abstracts International, 37*, 5590A.

Pierce, R.M. (1973). Training in interpersonal communication skills with the partners of deteriorated marriages. *The Family Coordinator, 21*, 223–227.

Pierce, R., & Drasgow, J. (1969). Teaching facilitative interpersonal functioning to psychiatric patients. *Journal of Counseling Psychology, 16*, 295–298.

Piers, E., & Harris, D. (1969). *The Piers-Harris Children's Self-Concept Scale*. Nashville: Counselor Recordings and Tests.

Pinsker, M., & Geoffrey, K. (1981). A comparison of parent effectiveness training and behavior modification training. *Family Relations, 30*, 61–68.

Porter, B.M. (1954). Measurement of parental acceptance of children. *Journal of Home Economics, 46*(3), 176–182.

Price-Bonham, S., & Skeen, P. (1979). A comparison of black and white fathers with implications for parent education. *The Family Coordinator, 28*, 53–59.

Rappaport, A.F. (1976). Conjugal relationship enhancement program. In D.H.L. Olson (Ed.), *Treating relationships*. Lake Mills, IA: Graphic Publishing.

Reiswig, G.D. (1973). The parent development laboratory: A study of three group education methods and their relationship to parent-child communication (Doctoral dissertation, University of Pittsburgh). *Dissertation Abstracts International, 34*, 1054A. (University Microfilms No. 73-21, 219.)

Renz, L., & Cohen, M. (1977). Interpersonal skill practice as a component in effective parent training. *Community Mental Health Journal, 13*, 54–57.

Resnikoff, A. (1972). A critique of the Human Resource Developmental model from the viewpoint of rigor. *The Counseling Psychologist, 3*(3), 46–55.

Ridley, C.A., Avery, A.W., Dent, J., & Harrell, J.E. (1981). The effects of relationship enhancement and problem solving programs on perceived hetero-sexual competence. *Family Therapy, 8*(2), 59–66.

Ridley, C.A., Jorgensen, S.R., Morgan, A.C., & Avery, A.W. (1982). Relationship enhancement with premarital couples: An assessment of effects on relationship quality. *American Journal of Family Therapy, 10*(3), 41–48.

Rinn, R.C., & Markle, A. (1977). Parent effectiveness training: A review. *Psychological Reports, 41*, 95–109.

Rokeach, M. (1960). *The open and closed mind.* New York: Basic Books.

Rogers, C.R. (1951). *Client-centered therapy.* Boston: Houghton Mifflin.

Rogers, C.R. (1957). The necessary and sufficient conditions of therapeutic personality change. *Journal of Consulting Psychology, 21*, 95–103.

Rogers, C.R. (1961). *On becoming a person.* Boston: Houghton Mifflin.

Root, R.W., II. (1980). *The effects upon rural parental attitudes, old-rural versus new-rural parental attitudes, a child's career maturity, and a child's scholastic grade point average of a rural parent taking parent effectiveness training.* Unpublished doctoral dissertation, Boston University.

Ross, E.R., Baker, S.B., & Guerney, B.G., Jr. (1982). *Effects of relationship enhancement therapy versus therapists' preferred therapy.* Unpublished manuscript, Pennsylvania State University, University Park.

Schaeffer, E.S. (1965). Children's report of parental behavior: An inventory. *Child Development, 36*, 413–424.

Schaeffer, E.S., & Bell, R.Q. (1958). Development of a parental attitude research instrument. *Child Development, 29*(3), 339–361.

Schlein, S. (1971). *Training dating couples in empathic and open communication: An experiment evaluation of a potential preventative mental health program.* Unpublished doctoral dissertation, Pennsylvania State University.

Schluderman, S., & Schluderman, E. (1977). A methodological study of a revised maternal attitude research instrument. *The Journal of Psychology, 95*, 77–86.

Schmitz, K.P. (1975). A study of the relationship of parent effectiveness training to changes in parent's self-assessed attitudes and behavior in a rural population (Doctoral dissertation, University of South Dakota). *Dissertation Abstracts International, 36*, 3526A. (University Microfilms No. 75-28, 917.)

Schofield, R.G. (1976). A comparison of two parent education programs: Parent effectiveness training and behavior modification and their effects upon the child's self-esteem. (Doctoral dissertation, University of Northern Colorado). *Dissertation Abstracts International, 37*, 2087A. (University Microfilms No. 76-23, 193.)

Schultz, C.L., & Nystul, M.S. (1980). Mother-child interaction behaviors as an outcome of theoretical models of parent group education. *Journal of Individual Psychology, 36*(1), 3–15.

Schultz, C.L., Nystul, M.S., & Law, H.G. (1980). Attitudinal outcomes of theoretical models of parent group education. *Journal of Individual Psychology, 36*(1), 16–28.

Sensué, M.E. (1981). *Filial therapy follow-up study: Effects on parental acceptance and child adjustment.* Unpublished doctoral dissertation, Pennsylvania State University.

Stearn, M.B. (1971). The relationship of parent effectiveness training to parent attitudes, parent behavior and child self-esteem (Doctoral dissertation, United States International University). *Dissertation Abstracts International, 32*, 1883–1886B. (University Microfilm No. 71-24, 506.)

Stollak, G.G. (1981). Variations and extensions of filial therapy. *Family Process,* *20,* 305–309.

Stover, L., & Guerney, B.G., Jr. (1967). The efficacy of training procedures for mothers in filial therapy. *Psychotherapy: Theory, research and practice, 4,* 110–115.

Sywulak, A.E. (1978). The effect of filial therapy on parental acceptance and child adjustment (Doctoral dissertation, Pennsylvania State University). *Dissertation Abstracts International, 38,* 6180–6181B. (University Microfilms No. 7808432.)

Therrien, M.E. (1979). Evaluating empathy skill training for parents. *Social Work, 24,* 417–419.

Thiessen, J.D., Avery, A.W, & Joanning, H. (1980). Facilitating post-divorce adjustment among women: A communication skills training approach. *Journal of Divorce, 4*(2), 35–44.

Truax, C.B., & Carkhuff, R.R. (1967). *Toward effective counseling and psychotherapy: Training and practice.* Chicago: Aldine.

Truax, C.B., & Mitchell, K.M. (1971). Research on certain therapist interpersonal skills in relation to process and outcome. In A.E. Bergin & S.L. Garfield (Eds.), *Handbook of psychotherapy and behavior change.* New York: Wiley.

Valle, S.K., & Marinelli, R.P. (1975). Training in human relations skills as a preferred mode of treatment for married couples. *Journal of Marriage and Family Counseling, 1,* 359–365.

van der Veen, F. (1977). *Three client-centered alternatives: A therapy collective, therapeutic community and skill training for relationships.* Paper presented in symposium honoring Carl Rogers at 75 at the Annual Meeting of the American Psychological Association.

van der Veen, F. (1978). *Dialoguing: A way of learning to relate constructively in close relationships.* Unpublished manuscript. (Available from author at Center for Studies of the Person, 1125 Torrey Pines Road, La Jolla, CA 92037.)

Vogelsong, E.L. (1976). Preventive-therapeutic programs for mothers and adolescent daughters: A follow-up of relationship enhancement versus discussion and booster methods (Doctoral dissertation, Pennsylvania State University). *Dissertation Abstracts International, 36,* 7677A. (University Microfilms No. 76-10, 809.)

Vogelsong, E.L., & Guerney, B.G., Jr. (1980). Working with parents of disturbed adolescents. In R.R. Abidin (Ed.), *Parent education and intervention handbook.* Springfield, IL: Charles C. Thomas.

Vogelsong, E., Guerney, B.G., Jr., & Guerney, L.F. (1983). Relationship enhancement therapy with inpatients and their families. In R. Luber & C. Anderson (Eds.), *Communication training approaches to family intervention with psychiatric patients.* New York: Human Sciences Press.

Wells, R.A., Figurel, J.A., & McNamee, P. (1975). Group facilitation training with conflicted marital couples. In A.S. Gurman & D.G. Rice (Eds.), *Couples in conflict: New directions in marital therapy.* New York: Jason Aronson.

Wieman, R.J. (1973). Conjugal relationship modification and reciprocal reinforcement: A comparison of treatments for marital discord (Doctoral dissertation, Pennsylvania State University). *Dissertation Abstracts International, 35,* 493B. (University Microfilms No. 74-16, 097.)

3

Behavioral Approaches to Child and Family Systems*

Anthony M. Graziano

In 1963 a new journal, *Behaviour Research and Therapy,* appeared. Edited by H. J. Eysenck and Stanley Rachman, it marked the reemergence of a major behavioral emphasis in applied psychological research and intervention. The new journal did not launch the behavioral field, but, as intended by its editors, it provided a forum for the long-developing behavioral trends which had begun more than a half century earlier. As discussed elsewhere (Graziano, 1975), behavior modification had emerged by the late 1920s as the systematic application of psychology to human functional problems. Its conceptual beginnings included the work of Thorndike, Watson, Pavlov, some precursors in E. L. Witmer's psychoeducation, and the treatment applications to children by Jones (1924a, 1924b), Jersild and Holmes (1935a, 1935b), Holmes (1936), and Mowrer and Mowrer (1938), to name only a few. Those early behavioral approaches were constructed around combinations of S-R concepts, a powerful environmental emphasis, a focus on teaching methods and learning processes, objective psychology, and interest in the development and functioning of the "normal" child. The term "behavior modification" appears to have been coined by J. Stanley Gray in 1932. Writing about the application of psychology to teaching children in schools, Gray gave his article the impressively contempo-

*This is a revised version of an earlier article: A. M. Graziano (1983), "Behavioral Approaches to Child and Family Systems," *The Counseling Psychologist, 11*(3), 47–56. Reprinted by permission of *The Counseling Psychologist.*

rary-sounding title, "A Biological View of Behavior Modification." As discussed by Graziano (1970b), Gray urged teachers to avoid the use of subjective concepts such as insight, feelings, willpower, consciousness, and intuition and to instead focus on behavior, determining for each child *what* behavior is to be modified and then, with careful attention to details, controlling the relevant learning variables in that environment. Any failure of the child to learn, Gray maintained, is due to the failure of the teacher to effectively manipulate the relevant variables.

By the early 1930s behavior modification had developed a conceptual base, had been applied to both clinical and educational issues, and had revealed a strong interest in children's functioning. Almost immediately, however, these developments were overshadowed by psychoanalysis, Freud's revival, and popularization of the romantic psychiatry of a century earlier (Graziano, 1975). Behavior modification had originated and developed in academic psychology, which might have been one reason for its lack of influence on the medically dominated mental health field. After all, psychology, compared with psychiatry, was a relative newcomer, basically an academic rather than applied discipline with little precedent in therapeutics and, perhaps more importantly, virtually no political/professional power. The American mental health field, already well-committed to its organic models, embraced psychoanalysis, which emphasized, in good eighteenth-century romantic philosophy tradition, humanity's irrationality, and which viewed human behavior as driven by unfolding instincts. Although both behavioral and psychoanalytic positions are deterministic models, they differ enormously in their respective emphases on internal versus external determinants of human behavior.

Psychodynamic theory continued to dominate psychiatry, social work, and, after World War II, professional (especially clinical) psychology until well into the 1970s. The modern mental health field has grown into a medically dominated profession espousing organic and psychodynamic models. Although other social science disciplines were developing in academic settings, they had little influence in providing the mental health field with alternative models.

It seems clear that World War II, with its heavy demands for selection, evaluation, and treatment of military personnel, was a major factor in the admission of large numbers of psychologists into the mental health field and contributed to the rapid postwar growth of professional psychology. There were, of course, reciprocal effects of psychologists entering the medically dominated mental health field. At first severely restricted to ancillary psychiatrically supervised functions, psychologists eventually developed a reasonably independent status with recognized skills in psychological evaluation, treatment, consultation, and research. However, perhaps in some professional compromise with the dominant discipline of psychiatry, psychologists adopted the psychiatrists' psychodynamic models, their focus on pathology, and their one-to-one verbal interaction, post disorder psychotherapy approaches. As noted elsewhere (Graziano & Katz, 1982), psychologists were very much ancillary to psychiatrists. But while the postwar psychologists were molding their professional identity in imitation of their psychiatric models, they were also bringing with them their own academic psychology background. Their studies of perception and cognition, psychology of learning, and their general training in research constituted an infusion of modern, academic-based psychology, with heavy emphasis on objective study of learning. The psychological content and research emphases were new to psychiatry, and psychiatry's applied focus was a major redirection of interests for psychologists. In essence, the war and the postwar demands constituted a professional conduit which brought psychologists, along with their academic psychological content and research skills, into the medical field. Simultaneously many psychologists were stimulated to focus on human psychopathology. In this process both the mental health field and the discipline of psychology were to be significantly altered.

A detailed discussion of psychology's postwar entry into the mental health field is not appropriate in this chapter. The main point here is that with their entry into the mental health field psychologists both adopted much of psychiatry's professional stance, and soon, using their own academic and research background, began to critically evaluate that position and to propose variations and even alternative models. The post–World War II revival of the 1920s behavior modification constituted one of those psychological alternatives.

By the mid 1960s most psychologists were aware of the "new" behavior modification. Some viewed it as an important alternative to psychodynamic approaches. It was also the target of a great deal of criticism by more traditional colleagues and frequently was viewed as being only a temporary, somewhat faddist interest in a "shallow" approach. The model endured, however, and by 1974 Hoon and Lindsley could write, "the growth rate of publication activity in behavior therapy has been so dramatic that in 1972 [behavior therapy publications] surpassed the number . . . indexed under psychoanalysis" (p. 696). Thousands of published titles, many college courses, several graduate programs, countless workshops, some 10 new behavioral journals, and a large membership in the Association for Advancement of Behavior Therapy add to the evidence that behavior modification is a significant development, providing real alternatives to the traditional psychodynamic and organic models.

In that surging growth many important lines of development can be discerned, and the discussion from this point could take many directions, depending upon one's interests. In this chapter I will briefly make some distinctions among several important areas and terms (behavior modification, behavior therapy, applied behavior analysis, and child behavior modification) and then focus the rest of the chapter on child behavior modification with particular attention to behavioral parent training.

Behavior Modification

Behavior modification is a term used as a general label for this entire field, encompassing many subsets (e.g., programmed learning, behavior therapy, applied behavior analysis). Behavior modification includes those models which focus primarily upon changing behavior, using variations of learning theory paradigms, and with strong commitments to empirical validation. Modern behavior modification has advanced far beyond the 1920s' essentially Watsonian behavior modification. It now encompasses many theoretical variations and admits cognitive, perceptual, motivational, developmental, and social data and concepts, while remaining extremely conservative in making inferences much beyond observable behavioral data. Behavior modification is now a large, varied field with a spectrum of concepts about, and approaches to, human functioning and issues in education, clinical problems, social programming, counseling, and rehabilitation. Most recently interest has developed in the application of behavior modification to issues in prevention, community psychology, and health psychology. Whatever these variations and behavior modification subsets, the basic characteristics common to all of them include a strong commitment to empiricism, a focus on behavioral events and analysis of S-R relationships, and a general aim of systematically bringing about improvements in human functioning.

Behavior Therapy

Behavioral concepts can be applied in various settings and toward different issues, the nature of which helps to define behavior modification's subsets. Thus, behavior modification applied in clinical settings, and aimed at postdisorder, ameliorative goals, constitutes the subset, *behavior therapy*. By definition, therapy of any model occurs after the disorder has become apparent and is clearly pathology oriented. Behavior therapy in this regard is no different from other models of psychological therapy. The major goal in any therapy is to recognize and understand the pathological condition and to apply therapeutic procedures aimed at reducing that pathology and restoring the individual to a better level of functioning than had presumably prevailed before the disorder occurred. A variety of behavioral procedures have been successfully applied to adults and children toward such goals (i.e., as behavior therapy). Interestingly, behavior therapy, like psychodynamic therapy, seems to have developed from original interest in adult neurotic conditions and treatment issues. Only later were those concepts and approaches generalized and applied to children. This, of course, creates major problems (as seems characteristic in the history of psychodynamic therapy) of treating children as if they are but miniature adults. Behavior *therapy,* then, has been historically the development of adult-oriented, pathology-tied, post disorder ameliorative concerns, within behavior modification.

Applied Behavior Analysis

While behavior therapy is pathology linked and post disorder, remedially aimed, applied behavior analysis can focus on any human behavior. While applicable to the treatment of disorders, applied behavioral analysis can also focus on enhancement of normal functioning such as academic achievement, skills training, social problem solving, and so on. The major, but not the only, concepts used are those of operant functional analysis, with the major aims of establishing new behaviors and increasing or decreasing the strength of existing behavior. Unlike behavior therapy, which developed primarily within the mental health area in close alliance with psychiatric treatment of adult neurotic, anxiety-mediated conditions, applied behavior analysis has developed primarily within school settings, focused on children's issues. Applied behavior analysis, compared with behavior therapy, seems to have developed a far more child-oriented stance and appears to have greater potential for wider applications to child development and functioning.

Child Behavior Modification

This subset includes all behavior modification applied to children rather than to adults. The various other subsets, behavior therapy, applied behavior analysis, and others, can all be included when applied to children. The distinguishing factor is the application to children, which leads, of course, to concepts, issues, and procedures that may be quite different from those more appropriate for adults.

Training Parents in Behavior Modification

Training parents in the use of behavioral skills with their own children is yet another behavioral subset and includes elements of both behavior therapy and applied behavior analysis, depending upon the goals of any particular intervention. Parent training in behavior analysis to enhance a child's normal functioning is not well developed but is an interesting and potentially useful area of investigation which offers, in this writer's opinion, one of the most exciting potentials for future research in applied psychology. Most of the parent training, however, has been carried out to augment therapeutic goals in cases where a child has been identified as having a psychological problem. As noted elsewhere (Graziano, 1977), training parents to carry out therapeutic work at home with their own children is not original with behavior modification, nor is current parent training limited to behavioral models. However, the most systematic and extensive empirical investigations and research literature have been developed since the early 1960s by behavior modifiers, making parent behavioral training a rapidly growing subset of behavior modification.

As this parent behavioral training endeavor matures and its trends coalesce, a field is emerging that is radically different from the more traditional psychodynamic approaches of the pre-1965 child-treatment field. In this process of change some of the most basic and traditional professional–client roles and relationships have been redefined to the extent that we now have not only a changed field, but a new field. What are these changes? Briefly, the professional is becoming more of a family consultant and teacher and less of a therapist or treatment specialist; the parents and other significant people in the child's life have become active change agents rather than passive recipients of professional services; the child has begun to edge close to active assumption of personal life control; the expectations of each party concerning the roles of the others are changing from those of the traditional models; the child's home and school have become major settings for intervention, displacing the artificialities of professionals' offices; far more attention is now being paid to the realities of external environmental control and the child–environment interaction compared with the earlier focus on inferences about internal psychodynamics; cognitive problem-solving and self-control skills among family members are emphasized more; and the whole model is easily congruent with our contemporary focus on prevention in natural settings.

These and other changes and their implications have so radically recast the psychological treatment of children from traditional psychotherapy to that in which parents are trained to function as the change agents as to require new technology, new personnel and training, new research directions, and even some new constructions of ethical and legal issues; and these changes have occurred well within our current professional generation. We hesitate to label it "revolutionary" because of the catastrophic imagery evoked by that term, but there certainly appears to be more break with the past here than in other areas of behavioral treatments.

Among the earliest examples of parents' active participation in behavior therapy for their own children are the numerous cases of successful parental use of the Mowrer and Mowrer (1938) alarm device for treating enuretic children (see DeLeon & Mandell, 1966; Lovibond, 1964); single-case studies of fear reduction (Weber, 1936); and reduction of excessive crying by an infant (Williams, 1959); and, in the early 1960s, training parents to carry out programming at home for their autistic children (reported by Graziano, 1970a, 1974; Lovaas, Koegel, Simmons, & Long, 1973).

Most of the parent behavioral training literature has been published since 1965, and the field has shown a marked increase in both publication volume and methodological sophistication. Parents have been trained individually and in groups, through lectures, assigned readings, programmed materials, group discussions, modeling, and direct coaching. Nearly all of the children have been boys. In most papers (1) mothers and not fathers were the primary persons trained and bore the major responsibility for implementing home programs; (2) training consisted primarily of operant approaches to contingency management; (3) home programs have been aimed mostly at reduction of maladaptive surplus behavior such as aggressive and hyperactive behavior rather than aimed at behavioral enhancement goals. Many clinical strategies have been transferred from professional to parental control, and an abundance of treatment strategies for virtually all classes of child behavioral problems is being made available to parents. These and other shifts, as Levant (1983) reminds us, are consistent with Miller's (1969) advice to "give psychology away" to the public, and they represent a major change from the traditional medical treatment model to an educational, teaching model in psychological practice. In our judgment, utilizing parents as cooperative change agents and training them in therapeutic skills may be the single most important development in the child therapy field.

Problems Addressed by Behavioral Parent Training

Virtually all classes of child behavior problems have by now been approached through parent-training strategies, and these have been reviewed several times (Berkowitz & Graziano, 1972; Graziano, 1977; Graziano & Mooney, 1984; Johnson & Katz, 1973). In this section we will review briefly several of the major categories of these problem behaviors.

Problems Grouped in Complex Syndromes

Many children display highly generalized, global, complex problems of severe disturbance and/or marked deficiency. Labels used (retardation, brain damage, hyperactivity, autism, schizophrenia, etc.) imply some common behavioral syndrome, characteristics of which are supposedly shared by all members of each relatively homogeneous class. Here, although the therapist's or teacher's focus may be on discreet behavior, it is seldom limited to a single behavioral category. Unlike, for example, the direct treatment of enuresis in otherwise normal children, treatment in the present category involves multiple and highly generalized surplus and deficit functioning. An underlying physiological base might be assumed, but the treatment approaches are functionally aimed.

The most complete behavioral intervention programs for these children are carried out in classroom-like settings, programmed for group applications at least several hours daily, and include parent training for home behavioral programming. The latter range through basic self-care, toileting, use of utensils, speech and language training, basic social skills training, academics, control of aggression, and so on. Many parents of retarded, schizophrenic, or autistic children have become proficient in such home training of their own children, contributing to their children's progress. Parent-training programs for autistic children, for example, have been frequently reported and are becoming nearly standard aspects of interventions with this group. These parent programs are based primarily on operant principles and involve the parents in the design, operation, and monitoring of the home programming. Two early 1960s parent-training program components for autistic children were those reported by Graziano (1970a, 1974) and by Lovaas et al. (1973). As reviewed by Graziano and Mooney (1984) virtually all behavioral investigators now accept the importance of parent training and the careful development of ancillary or posttreatment programs in the child's natural environment of the home and school.

It appears in such severe conditions where the disturbed behavior is so powerfully overlearned and generalized, and appropriate alternative skills undeveloped, that daily, complex, and long-term programming is probably necessary for both behavioral improvement and long-term maintenance. Both Graziano (1974) and Lovaas et al. (1973), for example, noted that upon leaving their structured school and/or hospital-based behavioral program, autistic children whose parents had been trained in behavioral management maintained their gains, while those whose parents had not been trained, or those children who were released to nonbehavioral treatment settings, regressed.

The home programming tasks for parents (almost always the mothers) are demanding, and the children's gains are slow and small-stepped. All, and probably more, of the frustrations, inefficiencies, regressions, and failures that professional behavior modifiers encounter are met by the parents as well. Considering the gains/effort ratio, parent-training programs for these severely limited or severely disturbed children cannot be considered as very "efficient" for bringing about major functional improvement. However, "efficiency" in raising children has seldom been accorded high value. Perhaps the greatest contribution of parent training programs may lie in their potentials not as behavioral change programs, but as programs for the generalization and maintenance of improvements brought about in more structured, professional programming.

In our judgment the treatment of choice at this time for children included in this large-syndrome category must include structured, daily, behavioral programming, integrated with environment, carried out by trained parents. As we have suggested elsewhere (Graziano, 1974), much of the parents' personal commitment to their children might constitute a thus far untapped resource, one which might serve to sustain the too often "low-return" and professionally too costly efforts that might nevertheless be of great personal value for both child and parents, and, in the parents' value systems, well worth the time and effort required.

Psychological Problems Related to Somatic Conditions

Causal relationships between psychological processes and somatic problems are not clear, but we know the two systems are related in many cases. Psychophysiological conditions include child problems such as skin disorders, digestive and elimination problems, and tics and motor-habit disorders such as nailbiting. Other behavior-somatic problems include obesity, anorexia nervosa, and self-injurious behavior.

Therapists have traditionally viewed many of these problems as symptoms, the results of complex, repressed emotionality. More recently, both respondent and operant models have been applied to several psychophysiological conditions of childhood such as asthma, tracheostomy addiction in infants, rumination, encopresis, enuresis, constipation, eating disorders, and sleep problems. These childhood problems are natural environment events in which the parents are very much involved. It is reasonable, therefore, to assume that parent training may offer a major potential for treatment and maintenance of treatment gains in many of these conditions.

Enuresis is probably the most researched somatic problem in which parents have successfully treated their own children. The treatment, using variations of the Mowrer and Mowrer (1938) conditioning apparatus, has been documented in many hundreds of cases (Jones, 1960; Lovibond,

1964; Martin & Kubly, 1955); and this particular treatment has become a stock answer to the criticisms of two decades ago that conditioning treatments will result in "symptom substitution." Azrin and Foxx (1973) and their colleagues have further refined the behavioral treatment of enuresis and developed alternative behavioral approaches which are proving to be of impressive effectiveness. Bollard and Woodroffe (1977), Butler (1976), and Azrin and Besalel-Azrin (1979) have extended the new procedures to applications by parents at home. Their rapid toilet-training techniques have been tested with normal children who are enuretic and with retarded and other exceptional children. The usual training time is reported to be about four hours, with girls training somewhat faster than boys. A parent-training manual by Azrin and Besalel-Azrin (1979) is available.

Parental effectiveness has also been reported in a related problem, encopresis, although the research to date is not as extensive as that in enuresis (Barrett, 1969; Conger, 1970; Edelman, 1971) and in treatment of constipation (Wright & Bunch, 1977)

The history of approaches to these particular problems shows that their conceptualization and treatment have changed radically from the psychoanalytic conceptions as intrapsychic problems that generated behavioral symptoms to the concept of habit problems or learned skills deficits which can be directly treated by conditioning methods. Here is a child behavioral problem for which highly effective behavioral treatments are available, suggesting that the use of any other approach, such as psychodynamic therapy (unless specifically indicated by the particular characteristics of a case), may be crowding the edges of the ethical dictum to employ the most effective treatments available.

Several other somatic-related problems have been successfully approached through parent training for home treatment programming. These have included seizures (Gardner, 1967); self-injurious behavior (Allen & Harris, 1966; Graziano, 1974; Risley, 1968); eating problems (Bernal, 1972); and wearing dental braces (Hall et al., 1972).

Asthma, which may be the leading cause of chronic illness in youth (Coleman, 1972), has been successfully alleviated by a number of investigators using behavioral methods. A single-case study of Neisworth and Moore (1972) is of interest because the mother of a seven-year-old asthmatic boy carried out a successful operant treatment program at home. The reliable effectiveness of behavioral treatments for asthma has not yet been convincingly established and is still open to doubt (e.g., Alexander, Cropp, & Chai, 1979), but the research to date certainly encourages further development and testing of parent training in asthma treatment as a possibly important future public health measure.

A problem for which parent behavioral training appears to be extremely appropriate is childhood obesity, but until quite recently there has been little research here. Overall the success of behavioral approaches to obesity has been disappointing, particularly in terms of maintenance of weight loss, although somewhat more successful than psychodynamic therapies. Since 1976 at least 10 controlled studies for treatment of childhood obesity have appeared (Kelly, 1982), and several included parent training in home programs (e.g., Aragona, Cassady, & Drabman, 1975; Grace, 1976; Kingsley & Shapiro, 1977; Rivinus, Drummond & Combrinck-Graham, 1976). All reported consistent but modest success rates. The potential for successful employment of parent training to treat childhood obesity is certainly suggested by the earlier work, but much more research is necessary. Here, too, is a rich area for investigation and development.

Negativistic, Oppositional, and Noncompliant Behavior

A large portion of behavioral parent training has focused on the reduction of this class of behavior, and research over the past two decades has developed to fairly sophisticated levels. Earlier work reported single- and multiple-case studies of noncompliant children, where the child's behavior was clearly the target of change. Since the mid-1960s there has been a large increase in controlled group studies as well as a growing recognition that parent–child conflicts are interactive in nature, and the parents have contributed to both creating and maintaining the "child's" problem behavior. The recent research, then, focuses on parent–child interactive systems, and aims at parental as well as child behavioral and cognitive change.

A series of programmatic research reports by Forehand and colleagues (e.g., Forehand, Cheney, & Yoder, 1974; Forehand, Griest, & Wells, 1979) has focused on the noncompliant behavior of young children (i.e., on the child's failure to respond to parental requests or commands and/or their failure to inhibit disruptive responses such as screaming or fighting). This is a large category of behavior which can in many cases reach extremely disruptive levels. Forehand is one of the most important researchers in this particular training area. The literature, contributed by a large number of researchers, has grown enormously.

Overtly aggressive and "out of control" children comprise a large proportion of all referrals by parents and teachers to mental health services. A large literature has developed on parent behavior training to reduce children's aggressive behavior, and among the most important programmatic research has been that carried out at the Oregon Social Learning Center since 1965 by Patterson and colleagues. This group's publications are far too numerous to cite here, but some of their recent work includes a summary of their programs since 1965 (Horne & Patterson, 1980), a theoretical account of "coercion processes" in families of aggressive children (Patterson, 1979), and several individual research papers including a study of the maintenance of family treatment effects (Patterson & Fleischman, 1979).

Wahler and Fox (1980) present a particularly interesting suggestion in their research with four aggressive young boys and their families. Of most interest was their finding that rewarding the children for quiet, appropriate, solitary play was more effective in reducing the aggressive behavior than was reinforcement of good social interactions. Although not a definitive study, it suggests the potential value of training oppositional children in how to maintain quiet playing for short periods.

Overall, the research results of parent training with such noncompliant or aggressive children have been very positive, and it is clear that for these problems an area of appropriate treatment technology now exists.

Delinquent Behavior

Juvenile delinquency involves over two million arrests of minors annually in the United States. Both the number of juvenile violators and the seriousness and aggressiveness of their violations continue to grow. Society's responses to delinquency have included punishment and control through incarceration (including a good deal of unofficial but not less real physical and psychological punishment) and many variations of psychological treatment and rehabilitation attempts. In all the years of punishment or traditional programming, there has been little indication that any methods have been effective or have helped to reduce this social problem.

Since the early 1960s behavior modification approaches have been reported as alternatives to traditional methods, with indications of some success. Several reviews of this behavioral literature have appeared (Davidson & Seidman, 1974; Emery & Marholin, 1977; Graziano & Mooney, 1984; Stumphauzer, 1970; Zimberoff, 1968). With the development of behavioral programming we begin to see reliable and significant improvement in functioning such as academic achievement, social skills, and reduced aggressive behavior, all in special, controlled settings. This is encouraging, and certainly such improvements are worthwhile goals for delinquent youth. There is, however, little evidence that such improvements have any effect upon delinquent behavior itself.

It thus appears that traditional approaches have had little success; and although behavioral programming in institutions has had significant effects on social and academic behavior, those effects have been limited to the confines of the controlling institutions. The most important criticisms of the treatment research to date are its failure to demonstrate improvement in delinquent behavior per se or to demonstrate long-term effects of its methods on any behavior of delinquent youth. The major limitation thus appears to be that of generalization of behavioral gains from the controlled setting to the real-life settings of the youths and effects upon their subsequent delinquent behavior.

In attempting to solve the problems of generalization to natural environments, a number of investigators have developed behavioral programs in the home, with active parental participation. Contingency contracting between parents and youths has been developed (Sulzer, 1962) and applied in numerous case studies (Alvord, 1971; Frederiksen, Jenkins, & Carr, 1976; Lysaught & Burchard, 1975; Rose et al., 1970; Stuart, 1971; Stumphauzer, 1976; Tharp & Wetzel, 1969). While these researchers have reported encouraging results, a larger study involving 102 preadolescents was more cautious, pointing out that contingency contracting alone is too narrow a base for effective intervention, and a more complete package, including contingency contracting, is needed (Stuart, Tripodi, Jayaratne, & Camburn, 1976). All told, the research provides good evidence for the effectiveness of home treatment packages built around parent–adolescent contingency contracting.

One of the most important series of studies involving parent participation in delinquency treatment was carried out over a five-year period by Alexander and Parsons (1973), Parsons and Alexander (1973), and Klein, Alexander, and Parsons (1977). Eighty-six families of delinquents were assigned to either a client-centered family counseling approach, an eclectic-psychodynamic approach, a behaviorally oriented family systems approach, or a no-treatment control group. In the behavioral group the investigators applied contingency contracting, modeling, social reinforcement, and, in some families, token economies and a parent-training manual (a modification of Patterson & Gullion, 1968). Overall, these studies provide evidence that carefully detailed, short-term behavioral interventions with delinquents and their families constitute a more effective package than traditional client-centered or psychodynamic treatment. Of particular note in these three studies is the finding that three and a half years later the nontreated younger siblings of the targeted delinquent youth showed significantly less delinquent behavior. This suggests that the short-term behavioral, family intervention may have had a true primary prevention effect, that is, lowering the rate of new cases in the population. This seems to be among the most encouraging, although still tentative, research in the area. Replication with larger groups is of potentially great value, and it may be that these three papers have provided the major prototypes for future delinquency intervention programs.

Child Abuse

Aggressive parent–child interactions do not always reveal the child to be the aggressor; in child abuse we see a crime of violence against children by parents or other adults. Child abuse is a tragic and widespread problem in the United States, but, as Spinetta and Rigler (1972) point out, psychologists seem little involved in its solution. Except for the most severe cases of child abuse where the effects on the child are so drastic (i.e., death or severe or permanent injury) that attempts to "rehabilitate" the parent make little sense, this is a problem for which parent behavioral training may be an appropriate and effective intervention. To date there have been few reports of such attempts (e.g., Crozier & Katz, 1979; Sandler, VanDercar, & Milhoan, 1978), and those have been limited in their apparent effectiveness. Here, again, is a problem area in which more investigation seems warranted.

Reducing Children's Fears

As reviewed earlier (Graziano, 1975; Graziano, DeGiovanni, & Garcia, 1979), until recently children's fears have been largely neglected by psychologists, particularly in comparison with the vast literature on behavioral approaches to adult fears and phobias. This child behavioral problem, like childhood obesity, seems particularly suited for parent-administered treatment at home. The treatment of childhood fears may be relatively uncomplicated, and well within the possibility of reasonable training and supervision of parents. However, as with the problem of childhood obesity, there has been little research and clinical investigation into children's fears and, more specifically, into the effectiveness of training parents to treat their own children's fears.

One area of fear treatment in which parents have been involved for some time is that of school phobia (Ayllon, Smith, & Rogers, 1970; Hersen, 1971; Kennedy, 1965; Patterson, 1965; Smith & Sharpe, 1970). Kennedy (1965) reported on the rapid treatment of 50 school phobics in which the parents were given the treatment rationale and were carefully instructed in their supportive measures in the treatment. Although most of these reports are of case studies, they do strongly suggest that many children who suffer this particular fear (school phobia) can be fairly quickly treated by professionally supervised parents who apply relatively simple behavioral strategies at home, and by teachers at school.

In a recent series of studies (Graziano, Kelley, & White, 1982; Graziano & Mooney, 1980; Graziano, Mooney, Huber, & Ignasiak, 1979) a parent-administered home program successfully eliminated children's chronic, severe, and highly disruptive nighttime fears. In three treatment studies 53 families were assigned to immediate and delayed treatment

groups. The treatment groups attended three training meetings and practiced at home for about three minutes nightly for three weeks, using a
cognitive-behavioral self-control training sequence. Using multiple measures of fear strength including parent and child ratings and the parents'
recordings of nightly direct observations, the treated children, compared
with the controls, were statistically and "clinically" less fearful at the end
of the three-week training. The treatment was then applied to the controls, who demonstrated the same improvements. In a three-year follow-
up of 33 families, the significant treatment gains were maintained, without the development of new, related problems. A replication with a more
heterogeneous group of seriously fearful children (Graziano et al., 1982)
demonstrated comparable improvements. A follow-up will be carried out
at three years post-treatment.

These studies demonstrated that parents can eliminate their children's
severe fears at home using a simple and efficient procedure taught to them
through an intervention that emphasized direct and specific instructions on a
rational level to children and parents. The investigators suggested that
perhaps many parents of phobic children can be readily instructed.

Speech and Language Training

Few papers in the behavioral literature evaluate parent training to treat
children's language disorders, although, of course, speech therapists have
been doing so for a long time (e.g., Barron & Graziano, 1968). Several
single-case studies have involved parents in some aspects of speech training for autistic children (Hewett, 1965; Risley & Wolf, 1966), with a
"disturbed and illiterate" child (Mathis, 1971), and with cases of elective
mutism (Nolan & Pence, 1970).

Although parents of autistic, retarded, and other speech-impaired children have been urged by therapists to assist in their children's language
development, the skills needed to train language acquisition or even to
correct relatively minor problems are complex. Beyond training parents
in fairly straightforward contingency management to support improvement of existing speech in their children, more severe speech disorders,
such as those found in autistic children, seem beyond the present techniques of parent behavioral training. Perhaps at this time the most reasonable use of parents with regard to speech and language development
is as ancillary support at home in those cases of speech problems where
there is no other serious grossly interfering involvement.

Common Behavior Problems in the Home

Most parent behavioral training has involved clinical issues where the
target behavior has a clear "pathological" weighting. There are, however, many other issues for which parent training or instruction might be

valuable. Common problems solved through parents' application of contingency management and monitoring procedures include a child's refusal to wear a dental brace, keeping a child's bedroom clean, persistent whining and shouting, inordinate amount of time to dress in the morning (Hall et al., 1972), thumbsucking (Knight & McKenzie, 1974; Ross, 1975), and eating problems (Bernal, 1972). A frequently occurring problem involves parent–child conflicts in public places, particularly supermarkets. Both seem to be on their worst behavior: the child whining, crying, grabbing, loudly demanding; the mother exasperated, demanding, pleading, bribing, and punishing. In some cases mother and child have been evicted from the store by the manager. Barnard, Christophersen, and Wolf (1977) and Clark et al. (1975) applied contingency management programs for parents and children with that problem. Parents were trained across multiple baselines in the use of token reinforcement and response cost as contingencies for "good shopping" behavior. Disruptive behavior of the children and positive response of the parents improved. One of the researchers' inferences was that the mothers had apparently held unstated expectations for their children's behavior but had never before specified and reinforced them. The programming apparently taught the parents as much as it did the children.

It appears to us that to whatever degree such rational and objective behavioral techniques can reduce the often sharp conflicts that occur in virtually all homes, they are of social value and are potentially useful, particularly in terms of prevention of more serious problems in otherwise normally functioning families.

Evaluation of Parent Behavioral Training

General

Research in parent behavioral training has proliferated over the past two decades and is now a major subset of behavior modification. Like the behavioral literature in general, most of the early parent behavioral training reports involved mild or very discrete single-problem behaviors, such as tantrums and enuresis. The research consisted of uncontrolled case studies, and the parent training was usually carried out in a clinic or laboratory setting. While generalization was, of course, a major aim, there was little attention paid to maintenance of generalized gains over time. In the late 1960s investigators began to focus on more severe and multiple-problem behaviors and increasingly utilized behavioral-system models for approaching family interactions. This is seen, for example, in the work by Klein, Alexander, and Parsons (1977). At present parent behavioral training encompasses a large area in which basic behavioral concepts and approaches constitute intervention technology applied within the family's natural environment. There has been a growing emphasis on generalization and maintenance of functional improvements, parents are being trained to more sophisticated levels, and a large array of child–parent issues (from serious clinical levels to everyday vexations) has been successfully approached.

In addition to the validations provided by the growing array of empirical studies, there are several important facets of this field. Of particular interest to this reviewer is its position concerning the importance of studying and working within the clients' personal and social natural environments, thus reducing much of the artificiality and problems of generalization to real life that seem inherent in traditional therapeutic approaches.

The natural environment focus pulls the counselor in new directions: The counselor, as noted earlier, becomes a family consultant and teacher; the problems specified and the approaches used are defined largely in family interactional rather than intrapsychic terms; the natural environment demands may operate to sharpen the consultant's appreciation of the idiosyncratic factors of each case. On the latter point, consider that clients, whatever their similarities may be, differ from each other; but in this approach not only are individuals idiosyncratic but so, too, are the intervention settings. Each natural environment setting is physically and socially different from all others, and the parent training practitioner may thus be less likely than the more traditional therapist (who brings all clients into the same intervention setting of the office) to maintain overly standardized and possibly a too rigid sameness in treatment.

Of most interest to this reviewer is that parent behavioral training implicitly supports and operationalizes the concept that personal life control resides in the individual and in the family. The parents who are trained to carry out home programs and the parents and youths who develop and carry out contingency contracting agreements are not only the major participants but are also in the best position to exercise control over the situation and to do so without the continued presence of the practitioner. The model emphasizes the active teaching of personal and family life control skills and implicitly avoids the extreme dependence on the professional that may occur in some psychological therapies, particularly psychoanalysis. It is this notion of personal life control that is implicitly operationalized in the parent behavior training model. Personal life control is its major implicit goal; a family-systems model provides the major conceptual surround; behavior modification is its major technology; and teaching is its primary activity. While not yet fully developed in each of its components, this emerging intervention approach appears to involve major changes in the ways in which we think about and implement our psychological treatment of children.

Social Standards

At minimum, any therapeutic approach must demonstrate that it is feasible, consistent with prevailing moral, ethical, and legal standards, and results in at least some stated client satisfaction. These minimum social standards are necessary but far from sufficient conditions, and they have been met by virtually all modern therapy systems. In this regard parent behavior training fares at least as well as any other approach. Therapists and researchers have amply demonstrated the feasibility of parent behavior training for a variety of childhood problems, and many parents have reported satisfaction with the results. Ethical issues regarding behavior modification in general are currently debated, but these issues do not discriminate among the various therapy models. Rather, they apply as well to all modern therapy (London, 1964).

Parent behavior training has joined the variety of other face-valid clinical approaches and, at this level of evaluation, parent behavior training appears to be at least equal to any other approach.

Research Standards

Feasibility, ethical consistency, and apparent client satisfaction are the very *least* to be expected of any therapy approach. When more demanding criteria of effectiveness are applied, parent behavior training shows mixed results but considerable promise. The available evidence amply justifies continued, expanded research in parent behavior training.

The major methodological issues involved in behavior therapy research (e.g., Baer, Wolf, & Risley, 1968; Paul, 1969) and those specific to parent training (Johnson & Katz, 1973; O'Dell, 1974) have been frequently discussed elsewhere. Basically the criteria demand clear, replicable demonstrations of control over selected variables. Generally, in parent training research, control has been adequately demonstrated over only a limited portion of the important variables—for example, over children's targeted behavior—while other important variables remain unexplored. Thus there has been reasonably good demonstration that certain problem behaviors have improved after parent training, but much is yet to be done to determine reliability of measurements, replication of results, generalization and maintenance of improved behavior, parent characteristics, changes in parent behavior, and clear specification of the antecedent operations (e.g., parent-training procedures and child therapy manipulations) in order to determine if they are, indeed, responsible for the observed improvements.

Those issues seem to cluster around several main factors: (1) assessment of change; (2) replicability; and (3) relative effectiveness.

Assessment of change. A modern psychotherapeutic approach must at least demonstrate that (see Paul, 1969, p. 41): (1) the client's distressing problems have changed significantly in the desired direction; (2) new problems have not been created (see the discussion of negative second-order effects in therapy by Graziano & Fink, 1973); (3) the improved behaviors have generalized and become stable outside the treatment settings; and (4) the improved behaviors have been maintained over a substantial time period.

These are the minimum level criteria for therapy validation. Necessary to these criteria is the clear specification of target behaviors and their reliable measurement at least at pre- and post-treatment and at follow-up.

Overall, parent behavior trainers have done quite well in specifying target child behaviors, thus establishing a good basis for the needed assessment of change. This is particularly true with discrete problems such as enuresis (e.g. DeLeon & Mandell, 1966; Lovibond, 1964), self-injury (Allen & Harris, 1966), and thumbsucking (Knight & McKenzie, 1974). Their discreteness minimized problems of definition, quantification, reliability, and assessment of generalization and maintenance.

Thus, with many discrete problems, parent training has met this minimum level of validation fairly well, showing good generalization and maintenance over quite long periods. In the enuresis literature, for example, follow-ups for as long as three years (Lovibond, 1964) and four years (DeLeon & Sacks, 1972) have been reported in fairly large group studies, and six years (Graziano, 1974) in a case study.

Specificity of problem behavior has been generally good, and the problems of obtaining reliability may be less in behavior modification than in other approaches because of behavioral specificity. However, no matter how clearly the target behavior might be defined, measurement reliability is also needed and, although often reported, has not been consistently demonstrated (O'Dell, 1974). Johnson and Katz (1973), for example, noted that slightly less than one-third of the parent-training studies they reviewed had reported reliability estimates. When reported, reliability estimates usually entail calculating the percentage of agreement, often exceeding 90 percent, between two or more trained, independent observers. Thus, one continuing problem involves the periodic retraining of observers to prevent reliability from drifting downward. Stability of parent observations over time or agreement between parent and professional observations has not been sufficiently studied. Likewise, there has been little investigation of agreement between parent and child observations. Grace (1976) is an exception and reports high parent–child agreement.

Overall, the parent trainers can be commended for their specificity in defining target behaviors, but can also be rightly criticized for not routinely reporting reliability data on their behavioral observations. It is clear that reliability estimates can be easily obtained, and there should be no great difficulties involved in including reliability measures routinely in future studies, even in case studies and single-subject designs.

The specificity of target behaviors and the existence of easily applied reliability measures provide an excellent base for subsequent demonstrations of effectiveness. Pre and post measures of behavior, showing improvements, are common in this literature. What has been demonstrated thus far is that many problem behaviors of children have, indeed, been improved through parent behavior training.

However, the remaining criteria at this minimum level of research validation have been less completely met. Are the observed changes significant in a psychological or personal sense? Have they been achieved without creating new problems? Do they generalize beyond the training setting? Are they durable?

Psychological significance and avoidance of unintended negative effects are difficult to assess and, by and large, have not been adequately dealt with by any current therapeutic model. In psychotherapy research, "significance" has been defined in statistical terms and, when demonstrated, has been questionably equated with clinical effectiveness. Lick (1973) and Lick and Unger (1975) have pointed out that, although an experimental manipulation in a factorial design may be significantly more effective according to statistical criteria, it is not necessarily adequate in accomplishing its clinical goal. Those authors argue that the "discovery" or "exploratory" phase of research (Miller, 1972) has been insufficiently developed and requires greater attention from psychotherapy researchers, while the ". . . literature is filled with studies employing multiple control groups and reporting very weak (but statistically significant) treatment effects" (Lick, 1973, p. 34). Parent behavioral training is still largely in this exploratory or discovery phase; it might be valuable for it to remain there for some time. However, there is need to focus on the development of parental-training "packages" for relatively homogeneous subject populations. More important, there is the need to show that behavioral changes are both of large magnitude and of clinical significance before moving on to more sophisticated validation of what might be personally unimportant effects. Parent-training packages dealing with enuresis provide examples of large and clinically important changes. But, as discussed by Berkowitz and Graziano (1972), there are still numerous problems involved in clearly specifying the precise variables involved in the treatments.

Negative, second-order, or unintended effects of psychotherapy must also be guarded against, but therapists and researchers seem not to have paid sufficient attention to this issue (Graziano & Fink, 1973). In behavior therapy, "symptom substitution" as a direct result of behavioral treatment does not routinely occur and, until it is demonstrated, is not a serious issue. However, consistent with the argument by Graziano and Fink, there may be numerous possible negative effects of intervening in the complicated ecology of a family or the relationships between a mother and her child. Papers by Wahler (1969), Sajwaj, Twardosz, and Burke (1972), and Herbert et al. (1973) suggest adverse side effects of behavioral training in several cases. The last-mentioned authors studied six mother–child pairs, training the mothers in contingent use of differential attention to reduce maladaptive behavior in their children. Contrary to previous findings, differential attention did not reduce the maladaptive behavior. In fact, for four of the six children, deviant behavior actually increased in a "substantial and durable manner." More to the point of this present section, the authors reported negative "side-effects" for all of the children that included: (1) the emergence of new deviant behavior that had not been in evidence during the baseline evaluations, and (2) for four children, decreases in the appropriate behavior that had been monitored.

The above study clearly cautions against the possible overgeneralization of even "basic" contingency management in family settings, and against the assumption that a therapy enterprise is always benign. Thus, although behavioral change associated with parent training has been demonstrated, we have not yet sufficiently demonstrated that those improvements are either clinically or personally significant, or that they have been brought about without creating new problems. Those issues must be dealt with before we invest more confidence in our parent-training "packages."

This field also lacks consistent data on the generalization of observed improvements and their maintenance over time. On the latter point many studies have no follow-ups, few exceed eight months, and most follow-ups seem to be quite informal. The longest follow-ups, as noted earlier, are reported in studies of enuresis.

Generalization of change can be measured in terms of generalizing new behavior (parent's or child's) from one problem to another or from the training setting to other settings. Research by Bernal, Delfini, North, and Kreutzer (1974), Wahler (1969), Martin (1974), and Johnson, Bolstad, and Lobitz (1974) strongly cautions against the assumption that observed behavior, or improved behavior after behavioral training, necessarily generalizes from one setting to others. Generalization of improved behavior, then, must be empirically demonstrated and not merely assumed to occur. Patterson, Cobb, and Ray (1972) found that neither skills taught to parents nor behavioral improvements brought about in children necessarily generalize from one child problem to another. Even the most careful research (e.g., Hanf's parent training in controlled learning environments) does not attempt to evaluate the generalization of either parent or child behavior changes. However, Forehand and King (1974, 1975) and

Peed, Roberts, and Forehand (1975) reported generalization of improved mother–child interactions from the clinical training setting to the home. Forehand and Atkeson (1977) reviewed the research literature on generalization of treatment effects and concluded as did Graziano (1977) and Graziano and Mooney (1984) that few studies had systematically examined procedures to institute treatment generalization. Since 1977 there has been more attention paid to generalization issues, but it is still apparent that, overall, generalization of improved parent and child behavior has not yet been consistently established.

A related issue, maintenance of improved behavior, has also not yet been well demonstrated. Some studies have included data on maintenance effects. McMahon and Forehand (1978) reported maintenance of family changes over a 6-week follow-up; Patterson and Fleischman (1979) summarized 12-month maintenance findings for 50 of the families with which they worked; Alexander and Parsons (1973), Parsons and Alexander (1973), and Klein et al. (1977) presented data on 86 delinquents, showing maintenance effects as long as 3½ years later. Webster-Stratton (1982) reports maintenance for as long as 3 to 9 years post-treatment. Maintenance of treatment effects for 1 and 2 years were reported by Graziano and Mooney (1980, 1982) following a 3-week home-training parent–child program to reduce children's nighttime fears. As Patterson and Fleischman (1979) concluded in their review, the data on the persistence of treatment effects are very encouraging, but much more research is needed. We need to investigate the contribution to maintenance of treatment effects of specific parent-training and family treatment techniques and of specific, measured behavior changes in family systems and in individual behavior.

We must conclude that parent behavior training only incompletely meets the criteria at even this minimum level of validation. Desirable and predicted changes in well-specified problem behavior has been repeatedly demonstrated, but reliability of measurement, the personal significance of the changes, their generalization and maintenance, and the lack of negative effects have not yet been well established. At this level the strongest part of the literature is that dealing with highly discrete problems (such as enuresis) where definitional and observational difficulties are minimized. That is no small gain, for ameliorating such problems can be of considerable personal value to the children and their families. It is clear that a great deal of research is still needed at this essentially exploratory, minimum level of validation.

Replicability. The minimum criteria proposed above leave many other issues unresolved, issues that cluster mainly around replicability. If uniformly met, those minimum criteria would provide evidence that significant, generalizable, stable behavior changes, without negative side-effects, follow various parent-training packages. Those criteria do not help to isolate the variables responsible for the observed changes, do not allow for replicability of the studies, and leave no basis for judging the generalization of the methods to individuals and groups beyond those already studied. Continued research must (1) specify therapeutic operations both in the professionals' training of the parents, and the parents' training of their children, and specify changes in parents' behavior, so as to (a) demonstrate that those operations were responsible for the observed improvements, and (b) make replications possible; (2) specify both demographic information and parent and child characteristics so as to (a) generalize the approaches to different client groups, and (b) make predictive statements within client groups, that is, discriminate between and predict successful and unsuccessful clients.

Basic here is the clear specification of training and therapeutic operations, of demographic, behavioral, and personal characteristics of parents and children. Without such specificity, the necessary demonstrations of control over independent variables, replications, and generalizations to other groups cannot be made. Overall, when evaluated in accordance with these criteria, parent behavior training does not fare too well.

Two of the major criticisms by O'Dell (1974) are (1) the marked lack of specific descriptions of the parent-training procedures used, and (2) the lack of data on parent behavior changes. In addition there is little information provided on parent characteristics.

Johnson and Katz (1973) noted that about 65 percent of the studies they reviewed presented "clear" descriptions of parent-training operations. Overall, however, despite their clarity, the studies presented global rather than specific and operationalized descriptions. Until parent-training procedures are clearly operationalized, replication of the research will not be possible, leaving a string of only vaguely comparable studies.

As we noted earlier, some of the more recent studies have included measures of parent changes. These were relatively minor parts of each study, and some were limited to changes in attitude measures rather than changes in observed behavior. It has yet to be adequately demonstrated that parents' behavior does change through training, that their new behavior is both generalized and stable over time, and that it is, indeed, responsible for improved child behavior.

In addition to the basic and severe limitation of poor specification of training procedures, design weaknesses further reduce the possibility of replications and demonstration of control over the independent variables. Each of the three earlier reviews cited throughout this chapter noted that most of the studies have been uncontrolled case reports providing virtually no demonstrations of control over variables. Johnson and Katz (1973) concluded that in approximately 64 percent of the studies they reviewed, treatment operations were "hopelessly confounded" with extraneous, uncontrolled variables, precluding the "unambiguous interpretation of results" (p. 195).

Experimental control has been demonstrated in a number of studies (e.g. Hall & Broden, 1967; Hall, Cristler, Cranston, & Tucker, 1970; Wahler, 1969). These have included single-subject or small-sample single- or multiple-baseline reversal studies. A general problem in many of these studies is the limitation in generalizing from the experimental to the clinical situation. Further, some studies (e.g., Risley, 1968; Wahler, 1967) have introduced successive multiple treatments, without return-to-baseline conditions, making it impossible to sort out cumulative from individual treatment effects.

A major problem common to all of the single-subject and small-sample studies and experiments is their limited sampling, which makes it impossible to draw inferences about populations. As O'Dell (1974) points out, the sampling procedures throughout this literature are weak, often consisting of volunteers or clinic referrals. Systematic, unbiased sampling procedures, adequate sample size, and information concerning demographic characteristics are needed.

Relative effectiveness. If all of these criteria were met, the effectiveness of various specific parent-training procedures with known populations would be well established. However, tests against other criteria would still be necessary to determine the social value of the procedures. If these procedures are effective, what are their costs? Are they any more effective than other, currently available therapeutic approaches to children?

Neither of these two issues has been sufficiently studied but, as reviewed by Johnson and Katz (1973), some estimates are available of the time required to train parents. Overall, the investment of time in each parent-training case seems surprisingly small and suggests good efficiency. But with severely disturbed or psychotic children, the situation is different, and a vast expenditure of professional time is required to bring about even minor gains. The difference suggests that what is required to adequately evaluate efficiency is a careful analysis of the distribution of time over many cases, grouped by problem behavior and demographic variables. Data are needed for the professional time required to train parents and the parents' time required to train children. Further, the total time must be gauged against the magnitude and personal or clinical significance of the observed behavioral gains, a difficult assessment that requires the comparison of very different classes of events. Finally, an analysis of time required by different therapeutic approaches is needed.

One attempt at economic cost-effective analysis of a parent-implemented mental health program was reported by Hester (1977). The analysis was carried out by a university industrial engineering department, which concluded that the State of Tennessee realized a gain of well over a million dollars over expenditures for the three years of operation that were studied. These gains were largely brought about by the outpatient service precluding the necessity of institutionalizing approximately 64 seriously disturbed children, and by the savings from the parents' participation, compared with the costs of professional time that would be needed to provide those services. Hester discusses program evaluation in terms of economic costs-benefits, evaluation of specific organizational goals, client objectives, data-based assessment of child progress, and accountability to a consumer-based evaluation committee. Her proposed evaluation system is ambitious and promising.

Despite such promising beginnings at cost-efficiency evaluation, the data are yet too sparse to permit clear assessment of the efficiency of parent behavior training, and the field is still very far from answering that question. The same holds for its effectiveness relative to other therapeutic approaches, for example, psychodynamic child therapy. Approaches based on different models might be compared directly in factorial designs, or indirectly, against some known standard of "natural" improvement of specific behavior problems. Few investigators have made such comparisons, and when they do, there are often design problems that limit the conclusions.

Walder et al. (1967) compared behavioral and psychodynamic counseling but did not adequately specify training and therapy procedures for behavioral data on children and parents. DeLeon and Mandell (1966) reported that an automated buzzer conditioning device applied by parents with minimal professional supervision or training was superior to professional psychodynamic psychotherapy in treating enuresis. The design problems included grossly unequal group size of the two treatment conditions, uncontrolled parent–child interactions, and failure to specify the psychotherapy procedures, making it difficult to attribute the observed improvements solely to the superiority of the conditioning apparatus.

Papers by Alexander and Parsons (1973), Parsons and Alexander (1973), Tavormina (1975), and Bernal, Klinnert, and Schultz (1980) provide more complete, better designed group comparisons, but their results, too, are somewhat equivocal. In the latter study, for example, both parent training and the client-centered counseling were specified and controlled by researchers, and the therapists were specifically trained, a considerable improvement over the earlier research. However, because of problems in obtaining subjects, the no-treatment control group was not randomly assigned, and thus the only valid comparisons are those between the two treatment conditions. It is not known from this study whether either treatment was superior to no treatment. Their major finding was that behaviorally trained parents reported more child improvement and more satisfaction with the outcomes than did the client-centered counseling group. However, behavioral observations made in the home did not support the differences and found no measurable difference in outcome between the two treatment conditions. Further, at two-year follow-up the parental report differences had disappeared. Thus, while parental reports indicated greater effectiveness for behavioral training in comparison with client-centered treatment, the observation data indicated no difference, and the researchers concluded that, at the two-year follow-up, "behavioral therapy was no more effective than client-centered therapy in reducing child conduct problems" (Bernal et al., 1980, p. 688).

Client-centered parent counseling appears to be a fairly common approach in the applied clinical field. It is feasible and appears to be quite effective when evaluated, as reviewed by Tavormina (1974). Data such as presented by Bernal et al. (1980) suggested that client-centered parent counseling and parent behavioral training do not differ in outcome effectiveness. Further controlled comparisons of these two approaches appear critical in our continuing efforts to evaluate parent behavioral training.

The data available, with all of their design limitations, tend to support the effectiveness of parent behavioral training over other approaches. However, the differences, as in comparisons with client-centered parent counseling, may be too small to be of practical significance or may be only temporary. As with nearly all other evaluation issues, this field is still a long way from clear, unequivocal answers.

Conclusions

Parent–child behavior training as developed over the past two decades may be the single most important development in the child mental health field. Its critical commitment to empirical research has evolved from earlier, uncontrolled case demonstrations or behavioral change to more recent, sophisticated and well controlled investigations. It has done this in an impressively short time, compared with other models. Improvements in child behavior across a wide variety of child problems have been repeatedly demonstrated. The field's continuing commitment to research pushes toward the model's limits and is actively testing beyond demonstrated effectiveness in behavior change. As the research continues, concern is seen with the issue of personal significance of those changes, their maintenance and generalization, comparative effectiveness, and cost efficiency. It may be that no other model of psychological treatment of children's problems has ever been scrutinized so closely or completely as the child–parent behavioral training model.

This commitment to research, with its continually growing body of knowledge, tempts us to suggest, albeit with caution, particularly in comparison with client-centered parent counseling, that child–parent behavioral training may become the most appropriate general mode of psychological treatment for children. Of greatest importance are those research attempts to answer the question of specificity: under what conditions (what problem behaviors, family conditions, etc.) are which technologies most effective and appropriate? The very prospects for success and continuing research refinements must, however, also carry a strong cautionary admonition: we hope that the field's strong commitment to research will continue to guard against uncritical, overgeneralized clinical application.

References

Alexander, A. G., Cropp, G. J., & Chai, H. (1979). Effects of relaxation training on pulmonary mechanics in children with asthma. *Journal of Applied Behavior Analysis, 12,* 27–35.

Alexander, J. F., & Parsons, B. V. (1973). Short-term behavioral intervention with delinquent families: Impact on family processes and recidivism. *Journal of Abnormal Psychology, 81,* 219–225.

Allen, K. E., & Harris, F. R. (1966). Elimination of a child's excessive scratching by training the mother in reinforcement procedures. *Behaviour Research and Therapy, 4,* 79–84.

Alvord, J. R. (1971). The home token economy: A motivational system for the home. *Corrective Psychiatry and Journal of Social Therapy, 17,* 6–13.

Aragona, J., Cassady, J., & Drabman, R. S. (1975). Treating overweight children through parental training and contingency contracting. *Journal of Applied Behavior Analysis, 8,* 269–278.

Ayllon, T., Smith, D., & Rogers, M. (1970). Behavioral management of school phobia. *Journal of Behavior Therapy and Experimental Psychiatry, 1,* 125–138.

Azrin, N. H., & Besalel-Azrin, V. (1979). *Bedwetting eliminated through training.* New York: Simon & Schuster.

Azrin, N. H., & Foxx, R. M. (1973). A rapid method of toilet training children. *Behaviour Research and Therapy, 11,* 422–435.

Baer, D. M., Wolf, M. M., & Risley, T. R. (1968). Some current dimensions of applied behavior analysis. *Journal of Applied Behavior Analysis, 1,* 91–97.

Barnard, J. T., Christophersen, E. R., & Wolf, M. M. (1977). Teaching children appropriate shopping behavior through parent training in the supermarket setting. *Journal of Applied Behavior Analysis, 10,* 49–59.

Barrett, B. (1969). Behavior modification in the home: Parents adapt laboratory-developed tactics to bowel-train a 5 year old. *Psychotherapy: Theory, Research, and Practice, 6,* 172–176.

Barron, D. P., & Graziano, A. M. (1968). Parent participation in speech therapy. *Speech Journal, 9,* 46–50.

Berkowitz, B. P., & Graziano, A. M. (1972). Training parents as behavior therapists: A review. *Behaviour Research and Therapy, 10,* 297–317.

Bernal, M. E. (1972). Behavioral treatment of a child's eating problem. *Journal of Behavior Therapy and Experimental Psychiatry, 3,* 43–50.

Bernal, M. E., Delfini, L. F., North, J. A., & Kreutzer, S. L. (1974). Comparisons of boys' behavior in homes and classrooms. Paper presented at the Banff International Conference on Behavior Modification, Banff, Canada, 1974.

Bernal, M. E., Klinnert, M. D., & Schultz, L. A. (1980). Behavioral parent training and client-centered parent counseling for children with conduct problems. *Journal of Applied Behavior Analysis, 13,* 677–691.

Bollard, R. J., & Woodroffe, P. (1977). The effect of parent-administered dry-bed training on nocturnal enuresis in children. *Behaviour Research Therapy, 15,* 159–165.

Butler, J. F. (1976). The toilet training success of parents after reading "Toilet training in less than a day." *Behavior Therapy, 7,* 185–191.

Clark, H., Green, B. F., Macrae, J. W., McNees, P., Davis, J. L., & Risley, T. R. (1975). A parent advice package for family shopping trips: Development and evaluation. *Journal of Applied Behavior Analysis, 8,* 67–76.

Coleman, J. C. (1972). *Abnormal psychology and modern life.* Glenville, IL: Scott Foresman.

Conger, J. C. (1970). The treatment of encopresis by the management of social consequences. *Behavior Therapy, 1,* 386–390.

Crozier, J., & Katz, R. (1979). Social learning treatment of child abuse. *Journal of Behavior Therapy and Experimental Psychiatry, 10,* 213–220.

Davidson, W. A., & Seidman, E. (1974). Studies of behavior modification and juvenile delinquency: A review, methodological critique, and social perspective. *Psychological Bulletin, 81,* 998–1011.

DeLeon, G., & Mandell, W. (1966). A comparison of conditioning and psychotherapy in the treatment of functional enuresis. *Journal of Clinical Psychology, 22,* 326–330.

DeLeon, G., & Sacks, S. (1972). Conditioning functional enuresis: a four year follow-up. *Journal of Consulting and Clinical Psychology, 39,* 299–300.

Edelman, R. I. (1971). Operant conditioning treatment of encopresis. *Journal of Behavior Therapy and Experimental Psychiatry, 7,* 71–73.

Emery, R. E., & Marholin, E. (1977). An applied analysis of delinquency: The irrelevancy of relevant behavior. *American Psychologist, 32,* 860–873.

Forehand, R., & Atkeson, B. M. (1977). Generality of treatment effects with parents as therapists: A review of assessment and implementation procedures. *Behavior Therapy, 8,* 575–594.

Forehand, R., Cheney, T., & Yoder, P. (1974). Parent behavior training: Effects on the non-compliance of a deaf child. *Journal of Behavior Therapy and Experimental Psychiatry, 5,* 281–283.

Forehand, R., Griest, D. L., & Wells, K. C. (1979). Parent behavioral training: An analysis of the relationships among multiple outcome measures. *Journal of Abnormal Child Psychology, 7,* 229–242.

Forehand, R., & King, H. E. (1974). Pre-school children's non-compliance: Effects of short-term behavior therapy. *Journal of Community Psychology, 2,* 42–44.

Forehand, R., & King, H. E. (1975). *Noncompliant children: Effects of parent training on behavior and attitude change.* Unpublished manuscript, University of Georgia.

Frederiksen, L. W., Jenkins, J. O., & Carr, C. R. (1976). Indirect modification of adolescent drug abuse using contingency contracting. *Journal of Behavior Therapy and Experimental Psychiatry, 7,* 377–378.

Gardner, J. E. (1967). Behavior therapy treatment approach to a psychogenic seizure case. *Journal of Consulting Psychology, 31,* 209–212.

Grace, D. L. (1976). Self-monitoring in the modification of obesity in children. (Doctoral dissertation, State University of New York, Buffalo.) *Dissertation Abstracts International, 37,* 2505B. (University Microfilms No. 76–26, 527.)

Gray, J. S. (1932). A biological view of behavior modification. *Journal of Educational Psychology, 23,* 611–620.

Graziano, A. M. (1970a). A group treatment approach to multiple problem behaviors of autistic children. *Exceptional Child, 36,* 765–770.

Graziano, A. M. (1970b). An historical note on J. Stanley Gray's "A biological view of behavior modification." *Journal of the History of the Behavioral Sciences, 6,* 156–158.

Graziano, A. M. (1974). *Child without tomorrow.* Elmsford, NY: Pergamon Press.

Graziano, A. M. (Ed.). (1975). *Behavior therapy with children.* Hawthorne, NY: Aldine.

Graziano, A. M. (1977). Parents as behavior therapists. In M. Hersen, R. M. Eisler, & B. M. Miller (Eds.), *Progress in behavior modification* (Vol. III, pp. 251–298). New York: Academic Press.

Graziano, A. M. (1983). Behavioral approaches to child and family systems. *The Counseling Psychologist, 11*(3), 47–56.

Graziano, A. M., DeGiovanni, T. S., & Garcia, K. S. (1979). Behavioral treatment of children's fears: A review. *Psychological Bulletin, 86,* 804–830.

Graziano, A. M., & Fink, R. (1973). Second-order effects in mental health treatment. *Journal of Consulting and Clinical Psychology, 40,* 356–364.

Graziano, A. M., & Katz, J. N. (1982). Training paraprofessionals. In M. Hersen, A. Bellack, & A. Kazdin (Eds.), *International handbook of behavior modification and therapy.* New York: Plenum.

Graziano, A. M., Kelley, R. J., & White, R. (1982). *Behavioral treatment of parent-child night fears: Replication and generalization.* Buffalo, NY: SUNY, unpublished report.

Graziano, A. M., & Mooney, K. C. (1980). Family self-control instruction for children's nighttime fear reduction. *Journal of Consulting and Clinical Psychology, 48,* 206–213.

Graziano, A. M., & Mooney, K. C. (1982). Behavioral treatment of child-family night fears: A 2½ to 3 year follow-up. *Journal of Consulting and Clinical Psychology, 50*(3), 598–599.

Graziano, A. M., & Mooney, K. C. (1984). *Children and behavior therapy.* Hawthorne, NY: Aldine.

Graziano, A. M., Mooney, K. C., Huber, C., & Ignasiak, D. (1979). Self-control instruction for children's fear reduction. *Journal of Behavior Therapy and Experimental Psychiatry, 10,* 221–227.

Hall, R. V., Axelrod, S., Tyler, L., Grief, E., Jones, F. C., & Robertson, R. (1972). Modification of behavior problems in the home with a parent as observer and experimenter. *Journal of Applied Behavior Analysis, 5,* 53–64.

Hall, R. V., & Broden, M. (1967). Behavior changes in brain-damaged children through social reinforcement. *Journal of Behavior Therapy and Experimental Psychiatry, 5,* 463–474.

Hall, R. V., Cristler, C., Cranston, S. S., & Tucker, B. (1970). Teachers and parents as researchers using multiple baseline designs. *Journal of Applied Behavior Analysis, 3,* 247–255.

Herbert, E. W., Pinkston, E. M., Hayden, M. L., Sajwaj, T. E., Pinkston, S., Cordua, G., & Jackson, D. (1973). Adverse effects of differential parental attention. *Journal of Applied Behavior Analysis, 6,* 15–30.

Hersen, M. (1971). The behavioral treatment of school phobia. *Journal of Nervous and Mental Disease, 153,* 99–107.

Hester, P. (1977). Evaluation and accountability in a parent-implemented early intervention service. *Community Mental Health Journal, 13,* 261–267.

Hewett, F. M. (1965). Teaching speech to autistic children through operant conditioning. *American Journal of Orthopsychiatry, 35,* 927–936.

Holmes, F. B. (1936). An experimental investigation of a method of overcoming children's fears. *Child Development, 7,* 6–30.

Hoon, P. W., & Lindsley, O. R. (1974). A comparison of behavior and traditional therapy publication activity. *American Psychologist, 29,* 694–697.

Horne, A. M., & Patterson, G. R. (1980). Working with parents of aggressive children. In R. R. Abidin (Ed.), *Parent education and intervention handbook.* Springfield, IL: Thomas, pp. 159–184.

Jersild, A. T., & Holmes, F. B. (1935a). Children's fears. *Child Development Monograph,* No. 20.

Jersild, A. T., & Holmes, F. B. (1935b). Methods of overcoming children's fears. *Journal of Psychology, 1,* 75–104.

Johnson, C. A., & Katz, C. (1973). Using parents as change agents for their children: A review. *Journal of Child Psychology and Psychiatry, 14,* 181–200.

Johnson, S. M., Bolstad, O. D., & Lobitz, G. K. (1974). *The generalization of children's behavior change across settings.* Paper presented at the International Conference of Behavior Modification, Banff, Canada.

Jones, H. G. (1960). The behavioral treatment of enuresis nocturna. In H. J. Eysenck (Ed.), *Behavior therapy and the neuroses.* Oxford, England: Pergamon.

Jones, M. C. (1924a). A laboratory study of fear: The case of Peter. *Pedagogical Seminar, 31,* 308–315.

Jones, M. C. (1924b). The elimination of children's fears. *Journal of Experimental Psychology, 7,* 382–390.

Kelly, R. J. (1982). Childhood obesity. In A. M. Graziano & K. C. Mooney (Eds.), *Children and behavior therapy.* Hawthorne, NY: Aldine.

Kennedy, W. A. (1965). School phobia: Rapid treatment of fifty cases. *Journal of Abnormal Psychology, 70,* 285–289.

Kingsley, R. G., & Shapiro, J. A. (1977). Comparison of three behavioral programs for the control of obesity in children. *Behavior Therapy, 8,* 30–36.

Klein, N. C., Alexander, J. F., & Parsons, B. V. (1977). Impact of family systems intervention on recidivism and sibling delinquency: A model of primary prevention and program evaluation. *Journal of Consulting and Clinical Psychology, 45,* 469–474.

Knight, M., & McKenzie, H. S. (1974). Elimination of bedtime thumb-sucking in home settings through contingent readings. *Journal of Applied Behavior Analysis, 7,* 33–38.

Levant, R. F. (1983). Toward a counseling psychology of the family: Psychological-educational and skills training programs for treatment, prevention, and development. *The Counseling Psychologist, 11*(3).

Lick, J. (1973). Statistical vs. clinical significance in research on the outcome of psychotherapy. *International Journal of Mental Health, 2,* 26–37.

Lick, J., & Unger, T. (1975). The external validity of laboratory fear assessment:

Implications from two case studies. *Journal of Consulting and Clinical Psychology, 43,* 864–866.

London, P. (1964). *The modes and morals of psychotherapy.* New York: Holt, Rinehart & Winston.

Lovaas, O. I., Koegel, R., Simmons, J. Q., & Long, J. S. (1973). Some generalizations and follow-up measures on autistic children in behavior therapy. *Journal of Applied Behavior Analysis, 6,* 131–161.

Lovibond, S. H. (1964). *Conditioning and enuresis.* New York: Pergamon.

Lysaught, T. V., & Burchard, J. D. (1975). The analysis and modification of a deviant parent-youth communication pattern. *Journal of Behavior Therapy and Experimental Psychiatry, 6,* 339–342.

Martin, B., & Kubly, D. (1955). Results of treatment of enuresis by a conditioned response method. *Journal of Consulting Psychology, 19,* 71–73.

Martin, S. (1974). *The comparability of behavioral data in laboratory and natural settings.* Paper presented at the Banff International Conference on Behavior Modification, Banff, Canada.

Mathis, M. I. (1971). Training of a "disturbed" boy using the mother as a therapist: A case study. *Behavior Therapy, 2,* 233–239.

McMahon, R. J., & Forehand, R. (1978). Nonprescription behavior therapy: Effectiveness of a brochure in teaching mothers to correct their children's inappropriate mealtime behaviors. *Behavior Therapy, 9,* 814–820.

Miller, G. A. (1969). Psychology as a means of promoting human welfare. *American Psychologist, 24,* 1063–1075.

Miller, N. E. (1972). Comments on strategy and tactics of research. In A. E. Bergin & H. H. Strupp (Eds.) *Changing frontiers in the science of psychotherapy.* New York: Aldine-Atherton.

Mowrer, O. H., & Mowrer, W. M. (1938). Enuresis: A method for its study and treatment. *American Journal of Orthopsychiatry, 8,* 436–459.

Neisworth, J. T., & Moore, F. (1972). Operant treatment of asthmatic responding with the parent as therapist. *Behavior Therapy, 3,* 95–99.

Nolan, D. J., & Pence, C. (1970). Operant conditioning principles in the treatment of a selectively mute child. *Journal of Consulting and Clinical Psychology, 35,* 265–268.

O'Dell, S. L. (1974). Training parents in behavior modification: A review. *Psychological Bulletin, 81,* 418–433.

Parsons, B. V., & Alexander, J. F. (1973). Short-term family intervention: A therapy outcome study. *Journal of Consulting and Clinical Psychology, 41,* 195–201.

Patterson, G. R. (1965). A learning theory approach to the treatment of the school phobic child. In L. P. Ullmann & L. Krasner (Eds.), *Case studies in behavior modification* (pp. 279–284). New York: Holt.

Patterson, G. R. (1979). A performance theory for coercive family interaction. In R. Cairns (Ed.), *Social interactional analysis: Methods and illustrations.* New York: Lawrence Erlbaum Associates.

Patterson, G. R., Cobb, J. A., & Ray, R. S. (1972). A social engineering technology for retraining aggressive boys. In H. E. Adams & I. P. Unikel (Eds.), *Issues and trends in behavior therapy* (pp. 139–224). Springfield, IL: Thomas.

Patterson, G. R., & Fleischman, M. J. (1979). Maintenance of treatment effects: Some considerations concerning family systems and follow-up data. *Behavior Therapy, 10,* 168–185.

Patterson, G. R., & Gullion, M. E. (1968). *Living with children: New methods for parents and teachers.* Champaign, IL: Research Press.

Paul, G. L. (1969). Behavior modification research: Design and tactics. In C. M. Franks (Ed.), *Behavior therapy: Appraisal and status* (pp. 29–62). New York: McGraw-Hill.

Peed, S., Roberts, M., & Forehand, R. (1975). *Generalization to the home of behavior modified in a parent training program for non-compliant children.* Unpublished manuscript, University of Georgia Psychological Clinic.

Risley, T. R. (1968). The effects and side effects of punishing the autistic behaviors of a deviant child. *Journal of Applied Behavior Analysis, 1,* 21–34.

Risley, T. R., & Wolf, M. M. (1966). Experimental manipulation of autistic behaviors and generalizations in the home. In R. Ulrich, T. Stachnick, & J. Mabry (Eds.), *Control of human behavior* (pp. 187–198). Glenview, IL: Scott, Foresman.

Rivinus, T. M., Drummond, T., & Combrinck-Graham, L. (1976). A group behavior treatment program for overweight children: Results of a pilot study. *Pediatric and Adolescent Endocrinology, 1,* 55–61.

Rose, S. D., Sundel, M., DeLange, J., Corwin, L., & Palumbo, A. (1970). The Hartwig project: A behavioral approach to the treatment of juvenile offenders. In R. Ulrich, R. Stachnic, & J. Mabry (Eds.), *Control of human behavior* (Vol. 2, pp. 220–230). Glenville, IL: Scott, Foresman.

Ross, J. A. (1975). Parents modify thumbsucking: A case study. *Journal of Behavior Therapy and Experimental Psychiatry, 6,* 248–249.

Sajwaj, T., Twardosz, S., & Burke, M. (1972). Side effects of extinction procedures in a remedial pre-school. *Journal of Applied Behavior Analysis, 5,* 163–175.

Sandler, J., VanDercar, C., & Milhoan, M. (1978). Training child abusers in the use of positive reinforcement practices. *Behaviour Research and Therapy, 16,* 169–175.

Smith, R. E., & Sharpe, T. O. (1970). Treatment of a school phobia with implosive therapy. *Journal of Consulting and Clinical Psychology, 35,* 239–243.

Spinetta, J., & Rigler, D. (1972). The child-abusing parent: A psychological review. *Psychological Bulletin, 77,* 296–304.

Stuart, R. B. (1971). Behavioral contracting within families of delinquents. *Journal of Behavior Therapy and Experimental Psychiatry, 2,* 1–11.

Stuart, R. B., Tripodi, T., Jayaratne, S., & Camburn, D. (1976). An experiment in social engineering in serving the families of predelinquents. *Journal of Abnormal Child Psychology, 4,* 243–261.

Stumphauzer, J. S. (1970). Behavior modification with juvenile delinquents: A critical review. *Federal Correctional Institution Technical and Treatment Notes, 1,* 1–22.

Stumphauzer, J. S. (1976). Elimination of stealing by self-reinforcement of alternate behavior and family contracting. *Journal of Behavior Therapy and Experimental Psychiatry, 7,* 265–268.

Sulzer, E. S. (1962). Reinforcement and the therapeutic contract. *Journal of Counseling Psychology, 9,* 271–276.

Tavormina, J. B. (1974). Basic models of parent counseling: A review. *Psychological Bulletin, 81,* 827–835.

Tavormina, J. B. (1975). Relative effectiveness of behavioral and reflective group counseling with parents of mentally retarded children. *Journal of Consulting and Clinical Psychology, 43,* 22–31.

Tharp, R. G., & Wetzel, R. J. (1969). *Behavior modification in the natural environment.* New York: Academic Press.

Wahler, R. G. (1967). *Behavior therapy with oppositional children: Attempts to increase their parents' reinforcement value.* Paper presented at the Southwestern Psychological Association.

Wahler, R. G. (1969). Oppositional children: A quest for parental reinforcement control. *Journal of Applied Behavior Analysis, 2,* 159–170.

Wahler, R. G., & Fox, J. (1980). Solitary toy play and time-out: A family treatment package for children with aggressive and oppositional behavior. *Journal of Applied Behavior Analysis, 13,* 23–39.

Walder, L. O., Cohen, S. I., Breiter, D. E., Daston, P. G., Hirsch, I. S., & Leibowitz, J. M. (1967). *Teaching behavioral principles to parents of disturbed children.* Paper presented at the meetings of the Eastern Psychological Association, Boston.

Weber, H. (1936). An approach to the problem of fear in children. *Journal of Mental Science, 82,* 136–147.

Webster-Stratton, C. (1982). The long-term effects of a videotape modeling parent-training program: Comparison of immediate and 1-year follow-up results. *Behavior Therapy, 13,* 702–714.

Williams, C. D. (1959). The elimination of tantrum behaviors by extinction procedures. *Journal of Abnormal and Social Psychology, 59,* 269–270.

Wright, D. F., & Bunch, G. (1977). Parental intervention in the treatment of chronic constipation. *Journal of Behavior Therapy and Experimental Psychiatry, 8,* 93–95.

Zimberoff, S. J. (1968). Behavior modification with delinquents. *Correctional Psychologist, 3,* 11–25.

4

Cognitive Behavioral Marital Therapy*

Nicole Bussod
Neil S. Jacobson

Conjoint marital therapy represents a relatively recent development in psychotherapy. The pervasive influence of psychoanalysis and intrapersonal models of psychopathology obfuscated the importance of current interpersonal dynamics in the maintenance of dysfunctional behavior and led therapists to treat distressed spouses individually and/or concurrently (Broderick & Schrader, 1981; Gurman & Kniskern, 1978; Jacobson & Bussod, in press.) Marital therapists lacked a theory of relationships on which to base their interventions and derived their practice from pragmatic considerations.

Though behavioral marital therapy (BMT) developed quite differently from other marital therapy approaches, it was at first no exception to the rule. Early writings simply transposed operant conditioning principles which had been utilized with children onto the problems faced by adult couples (Jacobson, 1981). Thus the standard BMT fare included contingency contracting, quid pro quo agreements, and token economies (cf. Stuart, 1969).

Since its birth in the late 1960s, the developments of BMT have been numerous and substantial. This heady pace of growth is due in part to the fact that BMT, like the field of behavior therapy in general, is defined

*This is a revised version of an earlier article: N. Bussod and N. S. Jacobson (1983), "Cognitive Behavioral Marital Therapy." *The Counseling Psychologist, 11*(3), 57–63. Reprinted by permission of *The Counseling Psychologist*.

by its method of inquiry, the application of a specific scientific methodology to the treatment of couples. Thus it has progressed even in the absence of a comprehensive theory of relationships. The burgeoning of analogue and outcome research in recent years, together with cognitive trends in behavior therapy (Meichenbaum, 1977), have begun to refine the understanding and the treatment of marital distress.

The present chapter will articulate the major developments in the field of behavioral marital therapy. The first section will summarize the theories of interpersonal relationships which form the backbone of BMT. The next three sections will describe in detail the major components of BMT which constitute its practice, with a particular emphasis on its recent and sometimes tentative cognitive integrations. Finally, future directions in research and practice will be suggested.

Social Exchange and Social Learning Theories of Marital Distress

Social exchange theory posits that the birth, maintenance, and termination of a relationship are contingent upon the ratio of benefits to costs incurred in that relationship, as perceived by its members (Kelley, 1979; Thibaut & Kelley, 1959). The evaluation of the *satisfaction* derived in a particular relationship by an individual has been termed comparison level (CL) by Thibaut and Kelley (1959). This comparison level is equivalent to a personal bottom line against which the current relationship is evaluated. The criteria which comprise this bottom line can range from personal-historical to sociocultural. Thus a particular wife may consider herself dissatisfied because of her husband's lack of emotional support, while another may consider divorce only if physical abuse occurs.

Divorce, however, is not always based on dissatisfaction with the relationship, and reciprocally, dissatisfaction is not necessarily grounds for divorce (Jacobson, 1981a). In addition, the *stability* of a relationship depends on the individual's comparison level for alternatives (CL_{ALT}) (Thibaut & Kelley, 1959). The comparison level for alternatives essentially answers the question, "How much better off would I be if I were out of this relationship?" Further, the person's perceptions of alternatives are as important as the objective conditions, and these perceptions may propel or hinder the termination of a marriage. Thus a relatively nonproblematic relationship may be terminated because the partners consider it more beneficial to pursue their endeavors separately or within a different kind of relationship, while another couple deems it preferable to be miserable together than to be unhappy alone. It should be clear that internal events such as attributions about the partner and the relationship play a central role in the formulations of social exchange theory. Further, these cognitive mediations can change over time for the partners, at different rates and in different directions, and sometimes independently of events occurring in the relationship (Jacobson, 1981b). Thus, while it is understandable that a couple became distressed when one of its members began drinking to excess, it is equally understandable that a marriage which has not undergone any changes becomes distressed because the wife has met an attractive third party, or because societal factors have heightened her expectations of marital bliss.

Social learning theory takes the ratio of costs and benefits incurred by the relationship from a global to a more specific level, namely the ratio of rewarding and punishing behaviors which are exchanged on a daily basis, and how these are objectively delivered and subjectively received. Research on nondistressed (Jacobson, Follette & McDonald, 1982; Jacobson, McDonald, & Follette, 1981) as well as distressed couples (Birchler, 1973; Gottman et al., 1976; Jacobson, Waldron & Moore, 1980; Patterson & Reid, 1970; Robinson & Price, 1980) has shown that the two groups can be distinguished in several ways.

First, distressed couples engage in fewer positive exchanges and more negative exchanges than nondistressed couples, both verbally (Birchler, Weiss, & Vincent, 1975; Gottman, Markman & Notarius, 1977; Gottman et al., 1976; Klier & Rothberg, 1977; Vincent, Weiss, & Birchler, 1975; Wills, Weiss, & Patterson, 1974) and nonverbally (Jacobson, et al., 1980; Robinson & Price, 1980; Wills et al., 1974). At the cognitive level, distressed couples seem to nullify the impact of positive behavior by failing to notice it altogether, a phenomenon which has been termed negative tracking (Margolin & Weiss, 1978; Robinson & Price, 1980). Consequently, distressed couples also frequently underestimate the rate of positive behaviors exchanged (Jacobson & Moore, 1981).

Second, distressed couples differ from their nondistressed counterparts in their reactivity to negative behaviors (Jacobson et al., 1981; Jacobson et al., 1982; Weiss, 1978). While findings on reactivity to positive events are inconclusive, it is clear that distressed couples not only engage in a greater number of negative exchanges but also react more strongly to such exchanges when they occur. It is unclear at present how nondistressed couples avoid overreacting to negative events. To take verbal behavior as an example, one spouse could attribute a negative remark from her partner to external factors (e.g., John is irritable because of problems at work), or could register the negative impact and "edit" it out of her subsequent response, as suggested by Gottman (1979). Both kinds of cognitive processes seem to be diminished in distressed couples, and as a result they are hypersensitive and vulnerable to negative events.

Third, distressed couples can also be differentiated from happy couples by their tendency to reciprocate negative behavior (Gottman, 1979; Margolin & Wampold, 1981). A negative event therefore is the potential antecedent for a negative response from the partner, and distressed couples tend to escalate. Another way of describing this process is to say that distressed couples tend to rely on aversive control strategies (Weiss, Hops, & Patterson, 1973).

Fourth, the passage of time may also enter into the onset or maintenance of marital distress in the form of reinforcement erosion (Jacobson, 1981a; Jacobson & Moore, 1981). Fortunate are the partners for whom the thousandth time they make love is as exciting as the first. More commonly, it takes a couple's unrelenting ingenuity and imagination to develop new ways of rewarding each other and maintaining a mutual high level of satisfaction. If for no other reason, status quo in marriage is tantamount to regression, and many disillusions would be averted if this simple universal truth were appended as a postscript following "and they lived happily ever after."

Fifth, distressed couples frequently exhibit poor communication and problem-solving skills when compared to nondistressed couples (Gottman, 1979; Jacobson & Margolin, 1979; Jacobson et al., 1980; Markman, 1979). Nondistressed couples are not excessively alarmed by the occurrence of conflict and will tend to speak openly and directly to one another about conflict issues when they occur. When they do talk to each other about conflict, they will tend to keep the issue in perspective and focus specifically on the behaviors that are of concern to them. They will attempt to understand the spouse's point of view and listen carefully to what is being said. They will tend to establish such a process early in their married lives and use it to maintain a viable union.

Finally, socially induced expectations and cultural myths not only play the role of comparative gauge mentioned above but can also increase the pressures on a marriage in a variety of ways: Smaller, unigenerational households put the burden on the couple to satisfy a plethora of economic, interpersonal, and intrapersonal needs which only a century ago were fulfilled by several groups of people in different settings. The plight of the suburban housewife described in the feminist literature (e.g., Friedan, 1963; Millet, 1969) is but one example of this phenomenon. Further, mate selection based exclusively on romantic feelings have added fuel to the Romeo and Juliet myth. That the maintenance of a viable intimate relationship requires constant care and diligence is not only an unfamiliar idea, but one which runs counter to the expectation that love will conquer all (Jacobson, 1981a). Thus couples, when they are told that therapy requires daily efforts to acquire relationship skills, often restate the societal belief by wondering where they will find the time, given all their other commitments.

To summarize this section, we have seen that the theoretical underpinnings of behavioral marital therapy are derived from psychological exchange and social learning theory. Both theories form a comprehensive model of close relationships and help elucidate the multidimensional character of marital distress. General deficits which have been identified empirically include mediational processes such as attributional dysfunctions, negative tracking, and faulty perceptions; reactivity to negative exchanges and reciprocity of immediate negative behaviors; aversive control strategies; impaired communication and conflict resolution skills; reinforcement erosion; and unrealistic expectations. The unique history of each relationship and that of its members puts constraints on the generalizations outlined above, as social exchange and social learning theory would predict. Though researchers and practitioners would generally agree with the idea that most distressed couples are twice removed from marital happiness, behaviorally and cognitively, the topography of each couple's distress remains idiosyncratic. It is these considerations which have led the field of behavioral marital therapy to develop multidimensional assessment methods.

Assessment in Behavioral Marital Therapy

The prominence of assessment in BMT derives naturally from its theoretical foundations and serves a variety of purposes, which we will examine below. The term *assessment* implies a form of evaluation at the beginning or the end of a project and, in the case of BMT, is somewhat of a misnomer. Indeed, one of the characteristics of BMT is that interventions are evaluated in a continuous manner throughout the course of therapy. Assessment therefore includes procedures specific to the phase prior to and after therapy, as well as evaluations during treatment.

The aims of assessment are many. First, BMT holds that the most efficacious way to understand a relationship is through a careful analysis of the relationship's environment as well as the characteristics of the marriage itself, since both endogenous and exogenous factors can account for marital distress. It is clear that individual differences brought into the relationship give it its distinctive features and flavor, and in that sense this analysis constitutes more of a strategic focus than a philosophical belief. It still is the case, however, that developing a viable treatment plan is contingent upon knowing the history of the development of the relationship and its current dynamics.

Second, the social learning model is inherently reciprocal (Jacobson, 1981a; Jacobson & Moore, 1981; Jacobson et al., 1980; Margolin & Weiss, 1978). Each interpersonal event functions as both antecedent and consequence of behavior and renders a functional analysis of the problem areas necessary to the understanding of the couple's distress and to the formulation of a treatment plan.

Third, BMT's model of distress is mediational. That is to say, a functional analysis incorporates the spouses' cognitive and perceptual processes which provide behaviors with their reinforcement value (Jacobson & Moore, 1981; Weiss, 1980). An exploration of the spouses' cognitive processes will, in addition to identifying the response classes which are uniquely rewarding to them, also specify how and under which conditions a behavior is likely to be perceived as rewarding. For example, if a spouse says that he or she does not like sex, is this true only after an argument, or only when no foreplay precedes it; and does foreplay signify caring, consideration, or simply additional physical stimulation?

Finally, factors external to the relationship are given particular attention with regard to their role in the onset or maintenance of marital distress. Such factors include economic hardships, the birth of a child, or a change in a partner's role (e.g., going back to school, starting a new career).

A variety of self-report measures have been devised to provide information about the spouses' subjective appraisal of the current strengths and weaknesses of their relationship. Questionnaires include measures of global satisfaction such as the Dyadic Adjustment Scale (Spanier, 1976), the Locke-Wallace Marital Adjustment Test (Locke & Wallace, 1959), and the Areas of Change questionnaire (Weiss et al., 1973). Self-report measures such as the Marital Status Inventory (Weiss & Cerreto, 1980), which assesses how close a spouse is to terminating the relationship, and Sexual Interaction Inventory (LoPiccolo & Steger, 1974), which probes the couple's frequency and enjoyment of their sexual relationship, serve to evaluate more specific potential areas of distress.

As mentioned, distressed couples tend to have poor communication and problem-solving skills. The extent to which the treatment plan will focus on these skills is assessed by direct observation of the couple's communication process.

Throughout the assessment phase couples are also asked to collect data about particular behaviors delivered by their partner at home. To do so spouses can complete the Spouse Observation Checklist (SOC) (Patterson, 1976; Weiss et al., 1973), which includes both a global index of Daily Satisfaction and a list of 400 items subsumed under categories such as companionship, affection, communication, child management, and sex. The SOC is the therapist's lifeline to the daily events of the relationship and allows him or her to ascertain the frequency of behaviors delivered as well as the manner in which they are perceived by the receiver.

Together these assessment procedures give the counselor a detailed profile of the partner's current reinforcement capacity, their subjective appraisals, and their communication skills, and provide the researcher with a series of pre and post measures by which to evaluate treatment efficacy. With the bulk of information gathered through these means, the counselor retains more latitude to establish the therapeutic relationship with the couple, explore the nature of the presenting problems, induce positive expectancies, and attend to cognitive and perceptual processes which hinder the establishment of a collaborative set (Jacobson & Margolin, 1979).

At the end of the assessment phase, couple and therapist decide on a treatment plan which takes into account the relationship's current strengths and weaknesses, the cognitive and behavioral antecedents and consequences of problem behaviors, the couple's reinforcement potential, and the presenting problems. With respect to the latter, BMT differs fundamentally from both psychodynamic and systems perspectives in its conception of couples' willingness to, and capacity for, change. Rather than symbolic displacements or functional metaphors masquerading as overt willingness to change (e.g., Haley, 1976), presenting problems are taken as the genuine complaints. In addition, BMT's formulation of the couple's capacity for change separates it from other approaches in an equally distinctive manner. The circular and rather cynical construct of resistance (Jacobson, 1981b) is conceptualized in BMT in terms of the salience of short-term costs versus the desired but distal benefits of change.

To summarize, marital distress is a multidimensional phenomenon expressed idiosyncratically by each couple, thus precluding the application of a standard set of technologies. An exhaustive assessment of the relationship's strengths and weaknesses at the content level (behavioral exchanges) and the process level (communication skills) provides the foundation on which the treatment goals are formulated. In addition, the assessment phase, by emphasizing the dyadic nature of the current distress, articulating and enforcing new relationship rules, and exposing and challenging dysfunctional cognitions and appraisals, paves the couple's way to the demanding task of improving the marriage.

Behavior Exchange Strategies

Empirical findings and clinical refinements have altered behavior exchange procedures considerably since their inception (Jacobson, 1981a, in press; Stuart, 1980; Weiss, 1980). The major critiques leveled against early strategies such as quid pro quo agreements and contingency contracting were that insufficient attention was paid to the context in which they were presented and that contingency contracting itself may be teaching distressed couples "more of the same" (Jacobson & Moore, 1981). Successful couples characteristically perceive themselves as rewarding each other unilaterally and noncontingently (cf. Weiss, 1980). The perceived absence of contingency allows them to make internal attributions about the delivered behavior (Jacobson et al., 1981; Jacobson et al., 1982). By contrast, distressed spouses tend to make external and unstable attributions regarding positive behavior. In addition, it has been argued that the quality of some relationships does not improve even in the face of overt behavior change, because cognitive and perceptual processes have remained dysfunctional (Jacobson et al., 1982; Weiss, 1980). Dysfunctional cognitions at times hinder the very enactment of behavior change. The context in which behavior exchange procedures are instigated has therefore been altered to better accommodate cognitive and perceptual changes.

The goals of behavior exchange interventions are to teach each spouse to positively track and reward the other, and to do so unilaterally and noncontingently. This particular focus has the benefit of addressing both the negative reciprocity and the negative reactivity spirals: It attacks reciprocity by instructing the spouses to pursue their rewarding efforts regardless of what the spouse is doing, and it short-circuits reactivity by underscoring that these efforts are hypotheses to be tried, which may or may not be proven useful. Hence the expectations of the receiving spouses are adjusted such that any change will be seen as a pleasant surprise, while those of the giver are set to attribute a potential negative or lack of positive reaction in the receiver to factors more benign than ingratitude.

Early sessions consist of spouses attempting to pinpoint those behaviors which may be rewarding for the partner. Once a number of them have been identified, each spouse is then instructed to decide, without input from the partner or from the therapist, which of those to engage in or increase. The lack of specificity in the assignment helps increase the compliance by giving each spouse maximum choice in deciding which changes to implement. At the same time, the absence of specific directives from the therapist fosters internal attributions on the part of the receiving spouse (John served me coffee in bed because he wanted to, versus John served me coffee in bed because Dr. X told him to).

If the increase in positive behaviors does not improve relationship satisfaction, the assignment is clarified or other potential reinforcers are encouraged. The therapist can also engage in cognitive exploration with the receiver to ascertain whether reinforcing behaviors were delivered but not noticed (negative tracking), or whether his or her cognitive processes prevented him or her from acknowledging the impact of the reinforcers (e.g., Susan was nice to me, but it's not going to last).

Throughout the assignment spouses are assisted in focusing on themselves while tracking positive behavior. Embedded in negative tracking are hopelessness about the relationship and doubts about the partner, which decrease the sense of personal efficacy and gives rise to blaming the spouse. Together with its lack of specificity, the homework increases the perceived amount of "free will" in the giver, while the receiver can save face by not asking for anything and thereby not acknowledging that the giver possesses valued reinforcers. Usually, the assignment induces a flurry of activity such that efforts, even if misdirected, challenge the couple's view of its relationship as hopeless. Thus the behavior changes instigated noncontingently induce the spouses to hold positive expectations about the potential benefits of therapy and challenge their cognitive appraisal of the partner as well as of the marriage.

As benefits have begun to accrue and commitment to change is enhanced, input from the receiving spouse is gradually worked into the interventions (Jacobson & Margolin, 1979). Request-refusal exercises teach spouses to ask for change in a nonthreatening, behaviorally specific manner, and to agree or decline in a supportive way. This exercise challenges the societal "if-you-really-loved-me-you-would-know-what-I-want" myth, and cuts short nagging litanies. Other unrealistic expectations are exposed and acknowledged by instructing the spouses to include in their request what they would ideally like and what they are willing to settle for.

To summarize, behavior exchange procedures have evolved to attend to cognitive and perceptual processes specifically and systematically in the course of changing overt behavior. The context in which the interventions are presented are as important to success as their structure. Behavior exchange procedures attempt to alter the content of the relationship's distress by expanding and increasing its reinforcement capacity. Distressed couples often enter therapy with great uncertainty about the future of their relationship. Problems seem insurmountable and attempts to resolve them have failed. Partners are cornered into an adversarial stance and fail to see the dyadic nature of their conflicts. The intensity of their distress puts couples in dire need of immediate relief, which is best brought about by direct behavior exchange techniques. Partners are then in a better position to suspend judgment about the continuation or termination of the marriage until its best features have come into clearer focus.

Problem-Solving Training

Once collaboration has been reinforced by some improvement from content-oriented strategies, couples are trained in process and communication skills which focus on problem-solving techniques. Complainants are taught to voice grievances in a supportive manner, to acknowledge their role in the maintenance of the problem, to express their feelings clearly and their complaints in specific, behavioral terms. Complainees are taught listening skills such as paraphrasing and nondefensive acceptance of the partner's plight (Jacobson & Margolin, 1979).

Skills are taught within a highly structured, three-component format: instruction, behavior rehearsal, and feedback. The ultimate goal is for couples to internalize communication rules thoroughly enough to generalize them to the home environment. As spouses master the skills and gradually hold their own problem-solving sessions within and outside of therapy, the didactic and mediational role of the therapist is faded. The rules are best imparted by having spouses practice the skills on hypothetical or minor problems in their relationship to prevent emotionally laden content from interfering with the process. Problem-solving training challenges the belief that the quality of the communication is invariably tied to the emotional charge and promotes the idea that problem-solving skills can be learned, like skiing or algebra.

BMT has traditionally structured its training with its eyes on the product of overt behavior change. The pitfalls of this emphasis have recently been articulated (Weiss, 1980). In the problem-definition phase, for example, the principle that all problems are dyadic in nature will occasionally backfire: When any problem stated by the complainant is viewed as legitimate, very little attention is given to the nature and values underlying the complainant's grievances. The risks are two-fold: First, the complainee is required to change while in fact the request is unreasonable or unjustified, and the problem really resides with the complainant's belief system. A typical example would involve the husband's request that his wife quit the career she enjoys "because wives have enough to do at home and I make enough money anyway." The second risk is that the "wrong" problem ends up being solved because of the complainant's mislabeling or misattributing the behavior in question. The same husband might make his request because he sees his wife's enjoyment of her work as a step away from him and "maybe she will leave me if she doesn't need me to have fun." Clearly then, some situations require the therapist to set the relationship aside and attend to the cognitive processes of its members.

The framework of problem-solving training is to provide spouses with means to express complaints in noncritical, supportive ways. The complaining spouse starts by expressing appreciation about what the partner does do. Expression of appreciation fulfills two functions. First, it induces the complainant to distinguish between an argument and a problem-solving format. Second, it keeps the complainee from becoming defensive and subsequently withholding or cross-complaining, thus short-circuiting the escalation loop common to distressed couples. Collaboration is further enhanced by teaching the complainant to state grievances in behavioral terms rather than global traits (e.g., "I would like it if you picked up your socks" versus "you just don't care about me"). At this point, the counselor (and later on the complainee) can "stop action" and explore what mediating conditions bring the complainant to state this problem and what meanings are attached to the partner's behavior. Thus in the course of defining the problem, cognitive restructuring can be done to foster empathy and to expose the relationship themes and unrealistic expectations. By exploring with the complainee what his or her objections are to changing, the same goals can be accomplished during the problem-solving phase.

To summarize, the skill-training approach to communication offers inherently more benign interpretations to the couple's distress and gears the spouses away from trait-like descriptions. Continuing what the behavior exchange strategies started, problem-solving training reinforces collaboration and empathy, emphasizes more benign causal explanations for relationship problems, and offers the opportunity to expose and correct dysfunctional cognitive processes, unrealistic expectations, and relationship myths. The mastery of those skills through behavior rehearsal and feedback, self-regulation, and home problem-solving sessions puts couples on their way to preventing conflicts from causing distress after termination of therapy.

Future Directions

Outcome research has repeatedly shown BMT to be an effective treatment when compared to a waiting-list control group (Hahlweg, Revenstorff, & Schindler, 1982; Jacobson, 1977, 1978; Jacobson & Anderson, 1980; Turkewitz & O'Leary, 1981) or to a credible placebo control group (Azrin et al., 1980; Crowe, 1978; Jacobson, 1978, 1979; Margolin & Weiss, 1978). Despite our emphasis throughout this chapter on the idiographic stance which BMT takes to the treatment of distressed couples, traditional research conventions lead to the evaluation of standardized treatment packages. Furthermore, results are typically reported in terms of group means, without providing information about the outcome for particular couples. Significant differences between group means are hard to interpret in the absence of specific information about the couples. Significance could be reached by each treatment couple changing a little while those in the control group fail to change at all, by some treatment couples changing dramatically while others do not change or deteriorate, or by couples remaining stationary while the control group deteriorates. Clearly, ingenuity and sophistication are needed in both the design and presentation of data to provide information about the effects of BMT on specific couples.

At the other end of the spectrum, limits need to be defined regarding the applicability of BMT to certain populations as well as certain types of relationships. Some evidence, for example, points to the age of the couple as a variable influencing outcome (Baucom, 1982; Turkewitz & O'Leary, 1981). Very little has been reported on the socioeconomic level as a mediator of outcome. Finally, cross-cultural research and research on special populations such as gay couples would further define the limits of the applicability of BMT.

Emphasis has been placed in this chapter on the cognitive components which have been weaved into the fabric of BMT. It is believed that this integration can improve both the success rate and the quality of the relationship of distressed couples. Research is needed to clarify whether and to what extent cognitive and perceptual processes induce or maintain marital distress, and whether, when their function has been specified, it necessarily follows that the most effective approach to alleviate distress is through strategies which include cognitive components.

Reciprocally, the active ingredients of BMT need to be determined more precisely. Findings have so far been inconclusive as to which components are effective when compared to their combination (Baucom, 1982; Hahlweg et al., 1982; Jacobson, 1979; Turkewitz & O'Leary, 1981). The fact that isolated components proved almost as effective as the complete treatment begs the question of what other, nonspecific variables are operating to induce change.

Communication training has been identified as one important component in the treatment of marital distress (Jacobson, 1978). This seems to parallel the findings in the area of prevention that the impact of communication has some predictive value for relationship satisfaction and that problem-solving deficits may precede marital distress (Markman, 1979, 1981; Gottman et al., 1977). Prevention research is still in its beginning stages, and most efforts until now have been directed toward behavior change techniques after distress has drawn couples to therapy (Markman, 1978). Yet prevention may be the way for marital therapists to reach their loftiest goal: to put themselves out of a job.

References

Azrin, N. H., Besalel, V. A., Bechtel, R., Michaliceck, A., Mancera, M., Carroll, D., Shuford, D., & Cox, J. (1980). Comparison of reciprocity and discussion-type counseling for marital problems. *American Journal of Family Therapy, 8,* 21–28.

Baucom, D. H. (1982). A comparison of behavioral contracting and problem-solving/comunications training in behavioral marital therapy. *Behavior Therapy, 13,* 162–174.

Birchler, G. R. (1973). Differential patterns of instrumental affiliative behavior as a function of degree of marital distress and level of intimacy. (Doctoral dissertation, University of Oregon, 1972). *Dissertation Abstracts International, 33,* 4499B–4500B. (University Microfilms, No. 73-7865, 102.)

Birchler, G. R., Weiss, R. L., & Vincent, J. P. (1975). A multimethod analysis of social reinforcement exchange between maritally distressed and nondistressed spouse and stranger dyads. *Journal of Personality and Social Psychology, 31,* 349–360.

Broderick, C. B., & Schrader, S. S. (1981). The history of professional marriage and family therapy. In A. S. Gurman & D. P. Kniskern (Eds.), *Handbook of family therapy*. New York: Brunner/Mazel.

Bussod, N., & Jacobson, N. S. (1983). Cognitive behavioral marital therapy. *The Counseling Psychologist, 11*(3), 57–63.

Crowe, M. J. (1978). Conjoint marital therapy: A controlled outcome study. *Psychological Medicine, 8,* 623–636.

Friedan, B. (1963). *The feminine mystique*. New York: Summit Books.

Gottman, J. M. (1979). *Marital interaction: Experimental investigations*. New York: Academic Press.

Gottman, J. M., Markman, H., & Notarius, C. (1977). The topography of marital conflicts: A sequential analysis of verbal and nonverbal behavior. *Journal of Marriage and the Family, 39,* 461–477.

Gottman, J. M., Notarius, C., Markman, H., Bank, S., Yoppi, B., & Rubin, M. E. (1976). Behavior exchange theory and marital decision making. *Journal of Personality and Social Psychology, 34,* 14–23.

Gurman, A. S., & Kniskern, D. P. (1978). Research on marital and family therapy: Progress, perspective, and prospect. In S. L. Garfield & A. E. Bergin (Eds.), *Handbook on psychotherapy and behavior change: An empirical analysis* (2nd ed). New York: Wiley.

Hahlweg, K., Revenstorff, D., & Schindler, L. (1982). Treatment of marital distress: Comparing formats and modalities. *Advances in Behavior Research and Therapy, 4,* 57–74.

Haley, J. (1976). *Problem-solving therapy*. San Francisco: Jossey-Bass.

Jacobson, N. S. (1977). Problem solving and contingency contracting in the treatment of marital discord. *Journal of Consulting and Clinical Psychology, 45,* 92–100.

Jacobson, N. S. (1978). Specific and nonspecific factors in the effectiveness of a behavioral approach to the treatment of marital discord. *Journal of Consulting and Clinical Psychology, 46,* 442–452.

Jacobson, N. S. (1979). Increasing positive behavior in severely distressed marital relationships: The effects of problem-solving training. *Behavior Therapy, 10,* 311–326.

Jacobson, N. S. (1981a). Behavioral marital therapy. In A. S. Gurman & D. P. Kniskern (Eds.), *Handbook of family therapy*. New York: Brunner/Mazel.

Jacobson, N. S. (1981b). Marital problems. In J. L. Shelton & R. L. Levy (Eds.), *Behavioral assignments and treatment compliance: A handbook of clinical strategies*. Champaign, IL: Research Press.

Jacobson, N. S., & Anderson, E. A. (1980). The effects of behavior rehearsal and feedback on the acquisition of problem solving skills in distressed and nondistressed couples. *Behavior Research and Therapy, 18,* 25–36.

Jacobson, N. S., & Bussod, N. (In press). Marital and family therapy. In M. Hersen, A. E. Kazdin, & A. S. Bellack (Eds.), *The clinical psychology handbook*. London: Pergamon Press.

Jacobson, N. S., Follette, W. C., & McDonald, D. W. (1982). Reactivity to positive and negative behavior in distressed and nondistressed married couples. *Journal of Consulting and Clinical Psychology, 50,* 706–714.

Jacobson, N. S., McDonald, D. W., & Follette, W. C. (1981). *Attributional differences between distressed and nondistressed married couples.* Paper presented at the annual meeting of the Association for the Advancement of Behavior Therapy, November 13, Toronto.

Jacobson, N. S., & Margolin, G. (1979). *Marital therapy: Strategies based on social learning and behavior exchange principles.* New York: Brunner/Mazel.

Jacobson, N. S., & Moore, D. (1981). Behavior exchange theory of marriage: Reconnaissance and reconsideration. In J. P. Vincent (Ed.), *Advances in family intervention, assessment, and theory* (Vol. 2). Greenwich: JAI Press.

Jacobson, N. S., Waldron, H., & Moore, D. (1980). Toward a behavioral profile of marital distress. *Journal of Consulting and Clinical Psychology, 48,* 696–703.

Kelley, H. H. (1979). *Personal relationships.* New York: Wiley.

Klier, J. L., & Rothberg, M. (1977). *Characteristics of conflict resolution in couples.* Paper presented at the Annual Meeting of the Association for the Advancement of Behavior Therapy, Atlanta, December.

Locke, H. J., & Wallace, K. M. (1959). Short-term marital adjustment and prediction tests: Their reliability and validity. *Journal of Marriage and Family Living, 21,* 251–255.

LoPiccolo, J., & Steger, J. C. (1974). The sexual interaction inventory: A new instrument for assessment of sexual dysfunction. *Archives of Sexual Behavior, 3,* 585–595.

Margolin, G., & Wampold, B. E. (1981). Sequential analysis of conflict and accord in distressed and non-distressed marital partners. *Journal of Consulting and Clinical Psychology, 49*(4), 554–567.

Margolin, G., & Weiss, R. L. (1978). A comparative evaluation of therapeutic components associated with behavioral marital treatment. *Journal of Consulting and Clinical Psychology, 46,* 1476–1486.

Markman, H. J. (1978). *Possibilities for the prevention of marital discord.* Paper presented at the annual meeting of AABT, Chicago, November.

Markman, H. J. (1979). Application of a behavioral model of marriage in predicting relationship satisfaction of couples planning marriage. *Journal of Consulting and Clinical Psychology, 47,* 743–749.

Markman, H. J. (1981). Prediction of marital distress: A 5-year follow-up. *Journal of Consulting and Clinical Psychology, 49*(5), 760–762.

Meichenbaum, D. H. (1969). *Cognitive behavior modification.* New York: Plenum.

Millet, K. (1969). *Sexual politics.* New York: Doubleday.

Patterson, G. R. (1976). Some procedures for assessing changes in marital interaction patterns. *Oregon Research Institute Bulletin, 16*(7).

Patterson, G. R., & Reid, J. B. (1970). Reciprocity and coercion: Two facets of social systems. In C. Neuringer & J. L. Michael (Eds.), *Behavior modification in clinical psychology.* New York: Appleton.

Robinson, E. A., & Price, M. G. (1980). Pleasurable behavior in marital interaction: An observational study. *Journal of Consulting and Clinical Psychology, 48,* 117–118.

Spanier, G. B. (1976). Measuring dyadic adjustment: New scales for assessing the quality of marriage and similar dyads. *Journal of Marriage and the Family, 38,* 15–28.

Stuart, R. B. (1969). Operant interpersonal treatment for marital discord. *Journal of Consulting and Clinical Psychology, 33*(6), 675–682.
Stuart, R. B. (1980). *Helping couples change.* New York: Guilford.
Thibaut, J. W., & Kelley, H. H. (1959). *The social psychology of groups.* New York: Wiley.
Turkewitz, H., & O'Leary, K. D. (1981). A comparative outcome study of behavioral marital therapy. *Journal of Marital and Family Therapy, 7,* 159–170.
Vincent, J. P., Weiss, R. L., & Birchler, G. R. (1975). A behavioral analysis of problem-solving in distressed and nondistressed married and stranger dyads. *Behavior Therapy, 6,* 475–487.
Weiss, R. L. (1978). The conceptualization of marriage from a behavioral perspective. In T. J. Paolino & B. S. McCrady (Eds.), *Marriage and marital therapy: Psychoanalytic, behavioral, and systems perspectives.* New York: Brunner/Mazel.
Weiss, R. L. (1980). Strategic behavioral marital therapy: Toward a model for assessment and intervention. In J. P. Vincent (Ed.), *Advances in family intervention, assessment and theory* (Vol. 1). Greenwich, CT: JAI Press.
Weiss, R. L., & Cerreto, M. C. (1980). The marital status inventory: Development of a measure of dissolution potential. *The American Journal of Family Therapy, 8*(2), 80–85.
Weiss, R. L., Hops, H., & Patterson, G. R. (1973). A framework for conceptualizing marital conflict, technology for altering it, some data for evaluating it. In L. A. Hamerlynck, L. C. Handy, & E. J. Mash (Eds.), *Behavior change: Methodology, concepts, and practice.* Champaign, IL: Research Press.
Wills, T. A., Weiss, R. L., & Patterson, G. R. (1974). A behavioral analysis of the determinants of marital satisfaction. *Journal of Consulting and Clinical Psychology, 42,* 802–811.

5

Childbirth Education

Sylvia J. Bruce
Patricia A. Kiladis

Childbirth education programs frequently reflect the nature of present-day family values and priorities. Whether these programs actually can influence family directions or respond to societal forces is a moot issue. What is of importance is: How did we get to where we are today, what types of programs still exist from the early movement, whom do they attract, and how are they evaluated?

Origins

The childbirth education movement in the United States, as we know it today, grew from the interaction of the diverse needs and beliefs of grassroot consumer groups and changing obstetrical practices. Since the beginning of the 1900s, the tension between physicians and consumers not only paved the way for childbirth education programs but clearly directed the manner in which the birth experience would be conducted. It is doubtful that the childbirth education movement would have occurred at all or have taken the direction it did had the birth experience remained in the home and not moved to the hospital. Prior to the 1900s, birth was considered a private family event attended by close relatives, a midwife, or a physician, if one was available.

Three factors seem to have contributed to the shift from the concept of the private home birth to the notion of a safe hospital birth. First, obstetrics as a medical specialty was rapidly increasing in scope and recognition. Hospitals were expanding and updating their facilities to accommodate this new specialty; medical technology was improving and physicians were actively recruiting potential obstetrical clients to bring into the institution. Second, the country was undergoing a dramatic shift from the predominantly rural, extended family life-style to the urban, nuclear family structure. The social support commitment found in the extended family was dramatically missing. These new urban nuclear families were vulnerable and responsive to offers of assistance. The final factor which crystallized the philosophy of safe childbirth occurring only in the hospital setting was the needs of the urban poor. Physicians were pushing to bring childbirth to the hospitals to support the new obstetrical specialty. The urban wealthy responded by sending their cooks, maids, and servants who, in the absence of their own extended family network, were in desperate need of this support and care. Birth became a medical event requiring hospitalization in illness-oriented institutions where safe deliveries and the treatment of potential complications were emphasized (Wertz & Wertz, 1977). These three factors laid the foundation and created the need for an organized approach to preparing women for childbirth.

In Washington, The American Red Cross offered the first organized formal instructional course in childbirth education in 1908 (Sasmor, 1979). The program was developed to meet the needs of these new urban nuclear families, who were unlikely to receive any form of extended family "in-home" support or instruction about pregnancy, childbirth, or newborn care. Although childbirth care was moving into the hospital setting, Red Cross instruction was not associated with or sponsored by the hospital obstetrical service, as are many of today's childbirth education programs. The classes were highly structured, direct, factual, and intended to provide "how-to" information and skills. Specific topics included proper nutrition in pregnancy, suitable maternity clothing, signs of labor, and instruction on how to feed, bathe, and clothe the new baby. By 1913 Red Cross childbirth courses were offered throughout the country. Instructors were trained to teach in a prescribed manner; the curriculum sequence and content were standardized, and upon completion of the training period the instructor was certified as a Red Cross Childbirth Educator. This prototype served as a paradigm for the movement.

Early Childbirth Programs

For over 30 years, The American Red Cross Preparation for Parenthood Programs served as the major source of childbirth education for American women. Newer instructional techniques, various philosophical premises, more controlled physiological response training, and the partnership of coach-supported deliveries were all introduced between 1940 and 1960. There does not appear to be, however, any direct relationship between women's role changes attributed to World War II and the advent of major innovations in childbirth education in the early 1940s. Three dramatic departures from the Red Cross format marked the early programs: (1) childbirth without fear; (2) husband-coached childbirth; and (3) childbirth without pain.

Childbirth Without Fear

This movement actually began in England in the early 1930s but was not introduced into this country until 1944. *Childbirth Without Fear: The Principle and Practice of Natural Childbirth* (Dick-Read, 1944, 1959) became the classic textbook of the next two decades. The premise of this program turned on the notion that birth was a joy, and that women needed to be socialized appropriately into believing that fear creates tension which produces the pain of childbirth. Therefore, with appropriate knowledge, provided by the physician, a woman's fear would be eliminated, her tension would disappear, and the birth would be painless. It was essential that the woman put herself completely under the care of her physician, for he alone would help her to deal effectively with her labor. The theoretical basis of Dick-Read's approach was never tested in controlled research, yet there is sufficient evidence today to indicate that his ideas were not without merit.

Neither Dick-Read nor his method ever received wide acceptance by the medical community. A possible explanation rests in the extent of the commitment required for the educational preparation of the mother, and the time necessary to support her during labor, as well as Dick-Read's demand that analgesia and anesthesia be at a minimum or eliminated. Few physicians were willing to give that type of support or could accept childbirth as a normal or natural process . . . a problem not entirely absent today. One unfortunate outcome of the natural childbirth movement was the misinterpretation that *no* medications and *no* anesthesia were necessary if one was to be successful. Many women and health professionals believed that to "give in to the pain" was to be less of a woman, less able to be a successful mother. It is difficult to say just how many women assumed their maternal role convinced of their inadequacy.

Husband-coached Childbirth

Establishing the role of the father in childbirth preparation programs has been a slow, tedious process. The earliest efforts came from Bradley (1965), who agreed that childbirth should be painless but believed it was the husband, not the physician, who should be the most significant figure in assuring the painless birth. In Bradley's program the husband's role was to be supportive during labor. He received special training in positioning his wife for relief of labor discomfort and in giving body massage and back rubs specific to his wife's needs and preferences. The Bradley program met with considerable resistance from the medical community. Few physicians supported the husband's role as useful or legitimate, and the policies of most hospitals denied the husband access to the labor room or the delivery suite. In many parts of the country access of the father to the labor and delivery areas came about only through court-ordered mandate. The Bradley programs no longer exist as such, but his philosophy of husband participation is very much a part of today's programs.

Childbirth Without Pain

The psychoprophylactic method, so popular today, had its origins in the 1950s in the USSR. Nicolaiev (Tanzer, 1976) provided a theoretical rationale, missing in Dick-Read's approach, for the premise that women needed to be conditioned to disassociate pain from childbirth; and he attempted to accomplish this through a series of training exercises and "Pavlovian" (classical) conditioning. Breathing exercises, relaxation, and instruction about the natural process of labor and delivery served as the cues to excite the cerebral cortex of the brain to inhibit the spinal pathways from processing pain reception. Practice and repetition were critical to successful conditioning.

The psychoprophylactic method shifted the control of the conduct of childbirth from the physician to the woman. Nicolaiev's work, however, received its greatest expansion and acceptance through the efforts of the French physician Ferdinand Lamaze. Few remember Nicolaiev but none can forget Karmel's *Thank You, Dr. Lamaze* (1965). Her book became a symbol for American women and a testimonial for the Lamaze method of painless childbirth. The founding of the American Society for Psychoprophylaxis in Obstetrics (ASPO) in 1960 by Karmel and Elizabeth Bing created an organization which clearly established the Lamaze method as one of the most enduring and far-reaching approaches to childbirth education.

Expanded Childbirth Education

Current Issues

The childbirth education movement has been in flux for the past 10 years. One issue is the lack of a clear direction and purpose. Sasmor (1979), however, argues that there "are consistent commonalities in all of the approaches to educated birth" (p. 13). These commonalities are identified as providing factual knowledge about labor and delivery, along with skills-training in breathing and relaxation techniques. Other educators argue that the interactive process in leader-directed discussion groups might do more to allay anxiety about pregnancy and birth (Auerbach, 1968; Bruce, 1965; Bruce & Chard, 1977). Childbirth educators operate their programs from a variety of theoretical perspectives, usually influenced by their field of specialization and their philosophy or ideology regarding childbirth. Educators function within the rubric of such models as Selye's Stress Theory (1956), Caplan's Crisis Model (1964), Solomon's Family Development Conceptualization (1973), or Kaplan, Cassel, and Gore's Social Support Network (1977). The model most frequently suggested is Knowles' Principles of Adult Learning (1973). A variety of programs can be tolerated provided prospective parents know what the programs do and what they cannot do. Childbirth education need not be held to consensus as a test of its validity, but it should be held to clarity of purpose and demonstrated positive outcomes.

A second area of concern relates to who should be teaching childbirth education. The early educators came from the ranks of lay women who were enthusiasts of the natural approach to giving birth. Nurses, physiotherapists, and psychologists are the most frequently cited leaders today. Who teaches may not be as important an issue as what is taught and how it is taught. However, certain minimal qualifications are clearly in order. The experience of giving birth is not sufficient to establish oneself as a childbirth educator. Ideally, childbirth educators should be professional nurses with advanced training in parent-child nursing at the graduate school level, the rationale for this being that nurses have the broad-spectrum academic and clinical preparation in the total pregnancy experience. Other professions tend to lack a holistic preparation. For example, psychologists focus on the affective domain and the impact of the pregnancy experience on this domain. Physiotherapists tend to focus on muscle groups for breathing, uterine relaxation, and post-delivery muscle tone recovery—the kinesthetics of childbirth. Neither psychologists nor physiotherapists have in their professional preparation all the essential experiences necessary to provide a holistic educational program for expectant parents.

The third issue or concern influencing the scope of childbirth education programs directly relates to the emerging role of the father. In some but not all programs, fathers are viewed as a separated entity necessitating recognition for their uniqueness. Greenberg and Morris (1974), Lamb (1976), and Grossman, Eichler, and Winickoff (1980) provide empirical support for the notion that fathers have a unique role with special needs and should participate in the birthing process for their own paternal development, and not merely as ancillary figures for their female partners. Much work needs to be done in this important area.

Finally, the women served by childbirth educators generally came from white, middle- to upper-class, well-educated groups. These supporters of prepared childbirth actively determined the content of the courses and the scope of preparation and training. Today's trend sees obstetricians and hospital clinic personnel insisting that *all* pregnant women attend childbirth education classes, usually sponsored by the hospital. Nelson (1982, 1983) suggests that, as a result, we now have a dilemma whereby the content of the childbirth programs has been predetermined by one group for a class of people who do not share the same values, ethnicity, or cultural history. Perhaps in response to the increasing diversity of prospective parents, the scope of programs has expanded and there are more choices of where to attend. Extensive educational support has shifted from the private physician and the hospital clinics to the childbirth educator. Programs are now available for the adolescent, fathers, caesarean births, preparation for labor and delivery, first-time parents, or preparation for parenthood.

Institutional Programs

The majority of institutional programs are hospital-based, although some health maintenance organizations and some Red Cross chapters do sponsor childbirth programs. One criticism of this program base concerns the possible bias of the sponsor to teach only what the institution's obstetricians mandate and not present the wide selection of options prospective parents need to be aware of if they are to make intelligent choices regarding the conduct of their pregnancy, labor, and delivery. A second criticism relates to the size of the groups and the resulting difficulty in creating a rich educational experience. Therefore, some groups may have highly interactive experiences and others may be exposed to more didactic lectures with semi-formal question and answer periods. Hospital-sponsored programs tend to set their fees low, semi-require all clients delivering at the hospital to attend the groups, and include a curriculum which provides a comprehensive variety of programs with separate groups for adolescents, single parents, caesarean birth parents, or parents with specific prior high-risk factors. Most hospitals have two-hour weekly sessions, covering six to eight weeks, which include some type of skills training in relaxation and breathing techniques such as Lamaze as well as a more formal period of information giving. The scope of the programs and the quality of the experience vary according to the preparation and abilities of the childbirth educator.

Private Entrepreneurs

Although nurses still constitute the majority of this group, physical therapists, psychologists, nutritionists, and lay parents are more likely to provide
services as private individuals rather than through the sponsorship of a
formal institutional setting. Various organizations such as ASPO and local
CEAs (Childbirth Education Associations) offer courses to certify the childbirth educator. These courses generally increase the leaders' skills and
usually provide a measure of credibility to the program. Private educators
may operate from their homes, from local schools or churches, or occasionally from hospitals. The fees charged are generally higher and a specific type
of program such as ASPO (Lamaze method) or COPE's program (Coping
with the Overall Pregnancy/Parenting Experience) is generally utilized,
such that the method is frequently more important than the content.

The ASPO program has undergone refinement since its start in 1960.
The new focus is on the realization that labor contractions are often
uncomfortable but natural. Medication may or may not be used to rein-
force the birthing as a normal process. Couples tend to be exposed to
more options available to them and therefore expect to be more active in
the decision-making process regarding the conduct of the birth. Private
educators have been criticized for providing options in a way that con-
fuses parents and creates a mistrustful relationship with their obstetricians. Choice is an important factor in childbirth, provided decisions are
informed ones, and all alternative outcomes are examined.

COPE differs considerably from ASPO. Whereas ASPO is a formalized
and structured program providing knowledge, skill, and conditioning,
COPE focuses on group education processes. Prospective parents are
encouraged to examine what they know, what they need to know, how
they feel about what is happening to them, and how they might cope with
their feelings and concerns. The emphasis is on self-reliant behavior and
addresses the future demands of parenting roles. Additionally, a wide
variety of focus-specific groups are available such as groups for single
parents, the working woman and her family, older parents, and adolescent pregnancy. COPE was begun in 1972 in Boston by Maureen Turner,
a psychiatric nurse, to assist new mothers in coping with the anxieties and
isolation they experienced (COPE, 1983). The void COPE fills is a concern for the whole family, a concern which has been lost in the fragmen-
tation of obstetrical care, childbirth classes, and pediatric care.

Alternative Programs

While childbirth education methods and practices have changed in a humanistic direction, there continues to be sufficient medical intervention to
interrupt the natural order of the process. Young (1982) insists the road

to humanistic birthing is a long one and cites areas of needed change: fetal monitoring practices; the alarming increase in caesarean births; the continued excessive use of analgesics and anesthetics; and the unnatural birthing positions still in use in delivery suites. Alternative approaches have grown out of a dissatisfaction with current obstetrical practices and must be examined for their merit. For the most part these programs have not been submitted to any rigorous evaluation. Some of the programs to be monitored include home birthing (Sugarman, 1979), birthing in water (Leboyer, 1975; Teasdale, 1984), and creative visualization to ease birthing (Panuthos & Silva, 1982). It is not incumbent upon childbirth educators to fully accept and embrace each new idea or fad. It is important, however, to know that they exist and to realize that new directions come from old dissatisfactions.

Evaluation

Earlier Studies

In 1978 Beck and Hall undertook an extensive review of the literature covering the research pertaining to the various prepared approaches to childbirth education. The earliest of these studies were conducted in the late 1940s and covered a 30-year period (1948–1977). The overriding approach, testimonial in nature, attempted to support the claims that childbirth training decreased the need for analgesia and anesthesia, increased positive attitudes about labor and delivery, and produced more alert and responsive babies. According to Beck and Hall (1978), none of the research utilized unbiased, randomized, controlled designs nor produced statistically significant findings.

Although the research was lacking in scientific merit, these studies did attempt to legitimize the worth of the prepared approach to childbirth and provided an impetus to consumer efforts to make the labor and delivery experience a family affair. The early nucleus of women and their partners who participated in childbirth education programs were predominantly white, well-educated, and middle to upper class. This group was articulate and vocal in their demands to change policies governing maternity care (McCraw & Abplanalp, 1981).

More Recent Work

Beck and Hall (1978), in their review of available studies about natural childbirth programs, identified a number of methodological flaws in the research and proposed that future research include but not be limited to (1) detailed description of experimental procedures, including treatment techniques; (2) random assignment of subjects to groups; (3) control groups; (4) blind raters; (5) appropriate statistical tests; (6) use of multiple criteria in the evaluation of outcome; (7) standardized psychological tests; and (8) therapist–treatment interactions (pp. 377–378). An extensive review of the research literature published after the Beck/Hall review was undertaken to identify research that would meet, in part, these criteria. Single-group, analogue, and Master's thesis studies were not included. The results were discouraging as none of the 20 studies reviewed met at least four of the eight methodological criteria. Therefore, the studies in Table 5-1 represent a sampling of the research on childbirth education from 1978 to 1983.

The studies which are not included in Table 5-1, though interesting, were descriptive or nonstatistical or had serious methodological flaws. Some studies were reported so unclearly as to make an accurate interpretation impossible. It is obvious that childbirth education research is in need of serious upgrading. It is also clear that the proper research questions have not been posed correctly or are irrelevant or insignificant. In some instances the instruments available seem inappropriate for childbirth/labor research. The labor experience, for example, is sufficiently unique that present instruments may not be sensitive enough to measure selected variables needing study.

In Beck's (1982) research the instrument focused on postoperative surgical patients' perception of time passing and the need for pain medication over a five-day period. Labor, however, was studied over a matter of hours and the instrument was not adequately sensitive to measure this highly compressed period. This problem was also true of Cathers' (1982) research, where a standard self-esteem instrument was used to measure the relation between vaginal and unexpected caesarian section delivery and primiparous women's self-esteem. Again, the instrument was not sufficiently sensitive to determine the effect the two modes of delivery had on self-esteem. Mikhaiel's (1984) research used the health belief model (HBM) to determine the factors that might facilitate appointment-keeping in prenatal care. The HBM has been used for a long time for studies of long-term health problems such as hypertension and diabetes. Short-term pregnancy moves too quickly for discriminating measurements with present instrumentation. Adapting present instruments is not the answer for childbirth education research.

A Case in Point

The experiences of "Charlie" and "Sue" (a composite of several couples) are typical of a suburban couple attending a hospital-based Lamaze program. Charlie and Sue lived in a suburban town close to the city. They

Table 5-1 Survey of Childbirth Education Research: 1978–1983

Study	Methodology	Outcome
1. Felton & Segelman (1978). Origin of control for behavior	Three group comparison: Group I Lamaze Group II Red Cross Group III no training; Random asst. Locus of control—judge-rated	Post-test grps. I, III showed change but not significant
2. Cogan (1978). Effect of practice time on two variables: neuromuscular release and breathing techniques	Primary study compared 2 groups' practice times on 2 variables in which practice time varied 2 additional studies reported were seriously confounded $N = ?$ No statistical tests No randomization	Results: neuromuscular release for 5 min. and breathing practice for 10 min./day ↓ labor pain & seemed to be the best combination
3. Dooher (1980). Effects of Lamaze on marital adjustment	Two group comparison: Group I Lamaze method Group II non-Lamaze No control No randomization Lock-Wallace marital adjustment; Hobbs degree of crisis scale; Holmes & Rahe's social adjustment $N = ?$	Prebirth stress greater in the Lamaze group husband/wife than in non-Lamaze ($p < .05$) Postbirth stress greater in Lamaze husband group and the husband/wife non-Lamaze than the Lamaze wife group ($p < .05$)
4. Cogan & Winer (1982). Communication training for childbirth educators	Childbirth educators random assigned to Tx or control grps Tx group received communication training ($N = 21$) control ($N = 22$) Parents assigned randomly to courses led by trained/un-trained educators	Parents in teacher Tx group *reported* a significant amount more pain

had moved there from the city when they were married. Charlie worked at the garage as a mechanic while Sue did secretarial work for a local firm. Neither had been able to attend college. Charlie was 21 and Sue was 20 when she became pregnant.

They were thrilled. However, Charlie was disturbed to find out that Sue had registered them for the childbirth class at the hospital upon the recommendation of her obstetrician. Charlie hated hospitals because of childhood trips necessitated by a bee allergy. Sue said she needed Charlie there for support and so he could share labor and delivery. Charlie really hated blood and was apprehensive about his wife suffering and the possibility that he would faint.

The classes were different from what Charlie or Sue anticipated. They both found the nurses warm and the atmosphere comfortable. They were amazed at the many couples, totaling 18, but were glad because of the anonymity it promised. Charlie in particular was not fond of groups and was dismayed to find out that the 18 couples were reduced to 9 couples for exercises. Sue did not listen to much that was said because she was looking around comparing her seventh month size with others. During the break they met another couple, David and Judy, who said that they were a little nervous about this whole thing. Dave told Charlie that Judy made him come to the classes. It turned out they were in the same exercise group. Dave and Charlie were amazed to hear that some men were excited about being part of the birth process. Sue was concerned when many women talked about natural birth and no medication. She had planned on a spinal. The instructor put her at ease immediately when she emphasized that it was the positive experience and a healthy mother and child that were important rather than a particular method. Nancy, the instructor, then discussed the format for the course and made a contract with them. By the end of the evening they had all laughed at their initial attempts to relax, focus, and breathe, but they were starting to understand the concepts.

As the weeks progressed Sue liked the planned time when she learned more about her body and the labor. Not being a reader, tired of neighbors' opinions, and hesitant to ask questions of her busy OB man, she felt Nancy gave her reliable information. Sue was even comfortable with the breathing. Meanwhile, Charlie had passed the tour and movie night without any problems. However, he still felt uneasy about what he was supposed to do and felt ridiculous practicing the breathing technique with Sue.

The labor was hard. In the beginning Charlie almost left when the nurse suggested he take the suitcase to the car because Sue did not need it. But he returned to find Sue up and walking. It did not seem to matter to the staff about positions as long as she felt comfortable. Sue used the breathing and tried to relax. Sometimes it worked and other times Charlie and the nurse helped her. Then she got very sick. Both she and Charlie survived because they knew from the classes that it was due to the transitional phase of labor and would not last long.

When the baby was born two hours later Sue had pushed hard with Charlie's support. Sue even tried a special pushing chair. The spinal that Sue had originally wanted for the delivery was unnecessary, for the baby was spontaneously delivered. Charlie had seen the bald head and hoped it was a boy. But it was a girl who cried lustily. As Charlie held his newborn daughter, he experienced an elation he could not describe. Because of the classes he had been comfortable enough to share the labor and delivery and ultimately this joy. Sue felt relief and a sense of awe as she and Charlie held the baby.

Early Parenting Programs

Childbirth educators have become increasingly cognizant of the need to provide a transition service following the birth experience. In many instances mother and baby are discharged home less than 24 hours after delivery. Unless there are complications, the majority are discharged within 72 hours. Physiologically, lactation has not been established, the mother has not recovered from the delivery, and the newborn infant may not have a stabilized bilirubin, which would rule out problems of RH incompatibility. The brief hospital period does not provide time to initiate adequate support services and needed instructional programs. Many programs have initiated a planned reunion session about six weeks post-delivery. Parents have frequently viewed this as a social event where they could show off their babies. It is questionable whether the "one-shot" program can be more than a social event. Other efforts have been directed toward parenting luncheons (Croog & Zigrossi, 1983), which did not meet with success, possibly due to the extremely brief post-delivery hospitalization period. In addition, many hospitals have initiated a post-discharge hot line. All of these efforts are limited in scope, somewhat unclear as to educational purpose, and not sufficiently supportive to be of particular value to the new parents. What is clear, however, is the need for transitional programs for parents with normal infants and normal parent-development tasks. How best to introduce these programs and at what point needs to be examined. Many early parenting programs have failed because they have been offered too soon after delivery, before the new parents have had a chance to settle in or feel secure enough to leave their infant with a sitter.

Early parenting programs for special needs groups have been offered for some time now and appear to be well-attended and of supportive value to the parents. The basic purpose of the special groups has been to provide a support network of parents with similar needs and concerns. The special groups could be for parents of premature infants in Neonatal Intensive Care Units (NICU) or high-risk babies with birth defects. These groups are initiated by NICU staff and tend to be ongoing. Parents join or leave the group when they wish or when their infant is discharged home. If the infant dies, special groups are available and ongoing, in the hospital, for support during grief work. Professionals seem better able to respond when a critical medical factor exists than when it comes to the issue of normal parental development. Bridging the critical gap between delivery and early parenting programs for parents of normal infants should be one priority issue of the day.

References

Auerbach, A. (1968). *Parents learn through discussion: Principles and practices of parent group education.* Florida: Kreiger.

Beck, C. (1982). *Parturients' temporal experiences during the phases of labor.* Unpublished doctoral dissertation, Boston University.

Beck, N., & Hall, D. (1978). After office hours—Natural childbirth—A review and analysis. *Obstetrics and Gynecology, 52,* 371–379.

Bradley, R. A. (1965). *Husband-coached childbirth.* New York: Harper & Row.

Bruce, S. (1965). Do prenatal educational programs really prepare for parenthood? *Hospital Topics,* November, 104–105.

Bruce, S., & Chard, M. (1977). Teaching and counseling methods. In J. P. Clausen, M. H. Flook, B. Ford, E. S. Popiel, & M. M. Green (eds.), *Maternity nursing today* (rev. ed., Chapter 8, pp. 126–139). New York: McGraw-Hill.

Caplan, G. (1964). *Principles of preventive psychiatry.* New York: Basic Books.

Cathers, L. (1982). *The relationship between mode of delivery—vaginal or unexpected Caesarian section—and self-esteem in primiparous women.* Unpublished doctoral dissertation, Boston University.

Cogan, R. (1978). Practice time in prepared childbirth. *Journal of Obstetric, Gynecologic and Neonatal Nursing, 7,* 33–38.

Cogan, R., & Winer, J. (1982). Effect of childbirth educator communication skills training on postpartum reports of parents. *Birth, 9,* 241–244.

COPE. (1983). *Programs to strengthen families.* New Haven, CT: Yale Bush Center in Child Development and Social Policy.

Croog, E., & Zigrossi, S. (1983). Parenting luncheons on the postpartum unit. *Maternal Child Nursing, 8,* 277–279.

Dick-Read, G. (1944). *Childbirth without fear: The principles and practice of natural childbirth* New York: Harper and Brothers.

Dick-Read, G. (1959). *Childbirth without fear: The principles and practice of natural childbirth* (rev. ed.). New York: Harper & Row.

Dooher, M. (1980). Lamaze method of childbirth. *Nursing Research, 29,* 220–224.

Felton, G. S., & Segelman, F. (1978). Lamaze childbirth training and changes in belief about personal control. *Birth and the Family Journal, 5,* 141–150.

Greenberg, M., & Morris, N. (1974). Engrossment: The newborn's impact upon the father. *American Journal of Orthopsychiatry, 44,* 520–531.

Grossman, F. K., Eichler, L. S., Winickoff, S. A., & Associates (1980). *Pregnancy, birth and parenthood.* San Francisco: Jossey-Bass.

Kaplan, B. H., Cassel, J. C., & Gore, S. (1977). Social support and health. *Medical Care,* supplement, *15,* 47–58.

Karmel, M. (1965). *Thank you, Dr. Lamaze: A mother's experiences in painless childbirth* (rev. ed.) Garden City: Doubleday.

Knowles, M. (1973). *The adult learner: A neglected species.* Houston: Gulf Publishing.

Lamb, M. (1976). *The role of the father in child development.* New York: Wiley.

Leboyer, F. (1975). *Birth without violence.* New York: Knopf.

McCraw, R., & Abplanalp, J. (1981). Selection factors involved in the choice of childbirth method. *Issues in Health Care of Women, 3,* 359–369.

Mikhaiel, B. (1984). *An investigation of the psychosocial factors that may influence pregnant women's health behavior.* Unpublished doctoral dissertation, Boston University.

Nelson, M. (1982). The effect of childbirth preparation on women of different social classes. *Journal of Health and Social Behavior, 23,* 339–352.

Nelson, M. (1983). Working-class women, middle-class women, and models of childbirth. *Social Problems, 30,* 284–297.

Panuthos, C., & Silva, J. (1982). *Positive birthing.* (May be available from The People Place, Cambridge, MA.)

Sasmor, J. (1979). *Childbirth education: A nursing perspective.* New York: Wiley.

Selye, H. (1956). *Stress of life.* New York: McGraw-Hill.

Solomon, M. (1973). A developmental conceptual premise for family therapy. *Family Process, 12,* 179–188.

Sugarman, M. (1979). Regionalization of maternity and newborn care: Facts, fantasies, flaws, and fallacies. In D. Stewart & L. Stewart (Eds.), *Compulsory hospitalization or freedom of choice in childbirth?* (Vol. 1). Marble Hill: NAPSAC Reproductions.

Tanzer, D. (1976). *Why natural childbirth-psychologists report on the benefits to mothers, fathers and babies.* New York: Schocken Books.

Teasdale, C. (1984). Underwater birth—A dangerous fad or the ultimate in gentle birthing? *International Childbirth Education Association News, 23,* 9–10.

Wertz, R., & Wertz, D. (1977). *Lying-in: A history of childbirth in America.* New York: Free Press.

Young, D. (1982). *Changing childbirth—family birth in the hospital.* Rochester, NY: CB Graphics.

6

Parent Education

Wesley Lamb

During the six years since this author's last review of the parent education literature (Lamb & Lamb, 1978), the field has burgeoned, as evidenced by the greater number of articles, the development of a topic heading located in *Psychological Abstracts,* and the constant supply of new books in local bookstores aimed at reaching the parent population. Over 350 references were reviewed in the preparation of this chapter. Major works edited by Fine (1980) and Abidin (1980) further document current activity in the field. Due to space limitations, only a limited number were selected as references.

Parent education (PE) is an intervention that is usually short and based on the parent(s) picking up information and new skills. Even when affective components are included, parent education is primarily a cognitively based strategy. Parent education tends to focus on a relationship between the parent and interventionist aimed at skill acquisition based on information transfer and feedback. In contrast, traditional approaches to parent and family *therapy* have focused more on the interpersonal relationship between the parent and the interventionist. Use of this relationship and the interpretation of the transference between the partners in the enterprise rather than the acquisition of information and skills is, in therapy, a primary goal of intervention. As Christensen (1969) points out, parents are better viewed as people who need to learn than as people who are sick.

Our further definition of parent education is complicated by the very scope of the term. Parent education can be viewed as any enterprise where the goal is to impart new knowledge or skill regarding parenting to someone who is, soon will become, or is potentially a parent. Therefore, anything ranging from recent popular television movies regarding child abuse to an interaction between a parent and a specialist such as a teacher or a pediatrician can fall within the field of parent education. For the purposes of this chapter we will circumscribe our focus on parent education (PE) to any planned intervention where the goal involves change of parental behavior via educational methods (transfer of information or acquisition of skill).

Levant (in Chapter 1) has presented a classification schema for grouping skill-building programs. Parent education or training has been located in several sections of the schema, thus affirming the scope of the field. Prior to a review of Adlerian therapy, Rational-Emotive Therapy, Reality Therapy, moral education, discussion groups, Transactional Analysis, and eclectic or integrative approaches to PE, the history and current status of the entire field will be reviewed. The reader is referred to additional chapters in this book, where major contributions to the field have merited separate discussions (Parent Effectiveness Training and Guerney's Relationship Enhancement, in Chapter 2; Behavioral Parent Training, in Chapter 3).

History

Parent education appears to be at the very center of the major professional movement involving the use of psychoeducational approaches with families. The apparent exponential increase in citations in the field of psychology/education would lead one to predict a recent beginning in the PE field. A review of the literature quickly shows this to be erroneous. To the chagrin of graduate students, academic researchers, and practitioners who feel that they are extremely avant garde, the field has been traced to Galen ca. 175 by Beckman (1977). Boggs (1981) gives a thorough review of the antecedents of current-day PE, including manuscripts dating prior to the invention of the printing press. Reviews of childrearing practices have been presented by Wolfenstein (1951), Sunley (1955), Brim (1959), Auerbach (1968), Beales (1975), and Cable (1975). Both Brim and Auerbach closely tie the field of parent education into the early social history of the United States. Brim reports that the earliest PE activities in this country took the form of women meeting in religious associations to study the proper ways to bring up their children consistent with prevailing Calvinistic thought. Croake and Glover (1977) report the first recorded parent group in this country to have taken place in Maine in 1815.

Both Brim and Auerbach cite 1888 as the advent of a group that later developed into the Child Study Association of America, which became one of the central advocacy groups supporting formalized approaches to parent education. Schlossman (1976) describes the establishment of the National Council of Parent Education by the Child Study Association. Various publications, groups, and early parent manuals are also described, demonstrating a very widespread interest in parent education.

The period from approximately the mid-1800s until the beginning of World War II can be seen as a very active time in this country in terms of the development of psychology and education, as well as in the development of various social movements. The formation of parent–teacher associations in schools, the major educational programs undertaken by governmental branches, as well as the development of centers for the study of child development within major universities, all took place during this time. During this period we can trace the systematic study of children back to G. S. Hall (1883), which very likely added to the *zeitgeist*. His work gave some degree of scientific and professional legitimacy to the areas of child study and parent education.

Without going into further historical detail, the early days of parent education in this country can be characterized as focused on childrearing goals and strategies which by current standards would be seen as harsh and rigid, heavily influenced by religious thought. In contrast, a later phase from about the time of G. S. Hall to the beginning of World War II can be characterized by its attempts at application of more democratic principles, with a greater focus on the child's developmental needs than on the rules of conduct espoused by the parent. There was a great effort during these years to base childrearing practices on science rather than religious belief. The wholesale effort at parent education documented by Croake and Glover (1977) included 2,000 County Home Demonstration Agents under the U.S. Department of Agriculture and over 126 major programs involving parent education. According to the White House Conference on Child Health and Protection (1932), over 350 organizations responded to a mailed questionnaire indicating at least some parent education activities by the responding organization. Efforts and financial support during these years were sufficient to provide a fellowship program where professionals could further their own development (Witmer, 1936).

In short, the history of PE is extensive. At this point it is safe to say that the early promise of PE producing a nation of knowledgeable, skillful, sensitive, aware, committed, and responsible parents has yet to be realized. Costner (1980) has used a sociological approach to understand the history of parent education. Such approaches can assist in understanding the context of PE. Not all writers support implementation of parent education as a massive social movement. Westin (1981) describes such activity and warns parents to begin thinking for themselves. Schlossman (1976) also adds cautionary notes.

In a further analysis of background issues in PE, Levant (1983) sees that the programs arising in the last 15 years may be moving in the direction of becoming a new professional field. Carkhuff (1971) had the temerity to suggest that "training" might well become the preferred method of treatment. The recent impetus in the field in fact appears to be an amalgam from various fields such as the community mental health movement, the use of paraprofessionals, the skills-training approaches based on client-centered and humanistic approaches within psychology, the remnants of the child guidance movement started in the 1930s, the behavioral approaches promoting the use of the operant/social-learning-theory paradigm, and the various schools of family therapy. In short, forms of parent education appear to have been developing in all of these areas at approximately the same time. The lack of awareness by authors in one field of the accomplishments and paradigms in the other fields is rather remarkable.

The literature reflects an increased emphasis on the ecological, systems, and comprehensive approaches in working with children. Tavormina (1980) supported the notion of combining forms of treatment with families. Others such as Liddle (1982) and Levant (1983) caution against imprudent combinations. Levant clearly makes the point that programs can be developed by extending the scope and interests of a given intervention rather than creating a "hodgepodge."

At this point, let us look at some of the more clearly identified "schools" or "models" of parent education. As noted above, several models are extensive and influential enough to have warranted discussion elsewhere in this text, and hence will not be covered here.

Models of Parent Education

Adlerian Parent Education

Ansbacher and Ansbacher (1956), Lowe and Morse (1977), Christensen and Thomas (1980), and Croake (1983) have presented comprehensive reviews of Adlerian psychology and the full history of this approach in Europe, with its eventual importation into the United States. Most reviewers make the point that Adler was a contemporary of Freud in Vienna but take care to identify him as a peer of Freud, and not the student of Freud described in some history books.

The reviewers stress Adler's emphasis on the social nature of man and the need to belong to a group. Since the first group one is usually exposed to is the family, a person's role in the family was of utmost importance to Adler. Adler extended his theories of personality development into clinical interventions, which were the early beginnings of the Child Guidance Movement.

Adlerian Centers were established throughout Austria, Germany, and parts of Europe after World War I. As the Nazi movement began to assert itself, Adler eventually moved to the United States. A number of friends and colleagues also left the Child Guidance Movement in Europe to make the same emigration to the United States. The most noteworthy of these was Adler's friend and student, Rudolph Dreikurs.

Dreikurs extended the work begun by Adler in terms of having a group focus and continued to carry out the basic tenets of both theory and application. The basic assumptions of Adlerian psychology have been summarized by Lamb and Lamb (1978) and will not be repeated here. In this country, the applications of these principles have been seen primarily in two settings: (1) Parent–Teacher Centers and (2) Parent Study Groups. The Parent–Teacher Centers as described by Lowe and Morse (1977) combine work with teachers, parents, and families in an interesting combination. Parents come because they wish to gain insight into their child's or their own behavior. Frequently the child has presented some type of "problem." Via interviews conducted publicly in the full view of other families, teachers, and counselors, the goals and life-style of the family and the family members are reviewed. With the insight gained, the family members can respond in a different way so that the goals selected by the person can still be met while the family learns to operate in a more respectful and democratic manner.

Dreikurs had a major impact on the functioning of the Parent–Teacher Centers in a number of ways: (1) he acted as a consultant to a number of original Centers in this country; (2) his clarification of Adlerian psychology provided the theoretical underpinnings of both the work of individuals and of the Centers as well; (3) his extension of the Adlerian thoughts into the areas of short-term goals of children gave further guidance to understanding the day-to-day problems presented by children; and (4) the work in the Parent–Teacher Centers can be seen as a major influence on the second area of application mentioned above, Parent Study Groups.

Dreikurs developed formulations regarding the short-term goals of children's misbehaviors which result when children are discouraged about their ability to find a place in the family. Dreikurs (1958) and Christensen and Thomas (1980) present the most complete explanation of these goals:

1. To gain attention.
2. To demonstrate power when they were unable to get the attention they sought.

3. To have revenge, punish, or get even when the power they had used did not establish a place for them within the family.
4. To demonstrate inadequacy when the other short term goals they have tried have not succeeded.

In addition to presenting the goals of children's misbehavior, Dreikurs made a distinction between the types of consequences available for a child's behavior. The differentiation of natural and logical consequences (Dreikurs, 1958) plays a central role in training parents, teachers, or counselors in Adlerian psychology. Natural consequences are those that parents do not need to apply themselves but do need to allow to occur. An example of a natural consequence can be seen when a child is playing roughly with a toy so that it is about to break. A natural consequence is allowing the toy to break and allowing the child to learn from the natural consequences. Logical consequence is one where the parent intervenes and removes the toy while indicating that the child has decided to play without the toy for a specified period of time.

The goals of children's misbehavior and the use of natural and logical consequences are most often taught in Parent Study Groups, which can be seen as the second major contribution of Dreikurs. The Parent Study Groups generally follow either the work of Dreikurs and Soltz (1964) entitled *Children: The Challenge* or *Systematic Training for Effective Parenting (STEP)* by Dinkmeyer and McKay (1976). The STEP program is a specifically designed parent education program with nine group sessions outlined on the following topics:

1. Understanding Children's Behavior and Misbehavior.
2. Understanding More About Your Child and About Yourself as a Parent.
3. Encouragement.
4. Communication: How to Listen to Your Child.
5. Communication: Exploring Alternatives, Expressing Your Ideas and Feelings to Children.
6. Natural and Logical Consequences.
7. Applying Natural and Logical Consequences.
8. The Family Meeting.
9. Developing Confidence and Using Your Potential.

The Dinkmeyer and McKay approach to PE and Parent Study Groups can be seen to emphasize a majority of the Adlerian/Dreikursian concepts including the family meeting, or Family Council as described by Dreikurs (1958). The emphasis is on democracy within the family unit and moving away from the older authoritarian model of parenting. The STEP program can also be seen to demonstrate influence from client-centered approaches as well as an emphasis on engaging the child, along with the entire family, in the problem-solving process.

In general there has been very little empirical research presented by the Adlerians. Croake (1983) describes the Adlerian approach as placing emphasis on teaching through demonstration in both the Parent–Teacher Centers and Parent Study Groups. The emphasis on demonstration teaching and the relative lack of both research and literature production clearly distinguishes the Adlerian and Behavioral schools of PE.

Despite the lack of emphasis on research and publication, a number of articles have appeared that suggest that the Adlerian approach does have an impact, particularly in the area of changing parental attitudes. However, virtually every article reviewed either had a nonstandard application of the approach (which would be very difficult to replicate) or used outcome measures that were (1) extremely reactive, (2) unvalidated, and (3) designed in such a way that the very language of the instrument would pull for greater impact in the Adlerian group than either control or comparison groups. In addition, the studies reviewed did not follow up for a sufficient length of time, failed to demonstrate that a change in the parental reports of attitudes had a demonstrable impact on the behavior of the child or parent, and frequently did not test for possible pretraining differences between groups. In short, even though there is a growing trend to do research within the Adlerian model, the research does not meet the criteria expected in many other fields.

Dinkmeyer and Dinkmeyer (1979) give a very brief report of research done by McKay where an Adlerian group using the STEP model was reported to have resulted in more positive parental feelings toward children than were seen in the no-treatment control group. Insufficient information is presented in the article to evaluate the research. Schultz and Nystul (1980) in a study of Australian mothers compared a behavioral group, an Adlerian group, and two different PET groups (1-month and 12-month duration) and found that the behavioral and PET groups had a greater impact on mother–child interactions than did the Adlerian group. The dependent measures included observations of mother–child dyads in structured tasks involving completion of a puzzle and in problem solving. Beutler, Oro-Beutler, and Mitchell (1979) reported a major program involving 14 different school counselors comparing a behavioral program (Becker's 1971 book entitled *Parents Are Teachers*) to the Adlerian STEP program. In general, no major differences were sighted in the outcome measures. Parents who completed the training were seen as having more needs for inclusion. Parents who completed the STEP program were found to need less affection than those who completed the behavioral training.

In an earlier comparison of behavioral and Adlerian parent education, Frazier and Matthes (1975) had used the text *Children: The Challenge* (Dreikurs & Soltz, 1964) for the Adlerian group while the behavioral group studied *Changing Children's Behavior* (Krumboltz & Krumboltz, 1972). In addition, a no-treatment control group was used. At post-test the Adlerian group was found to have a less restrictive attitude than either the behavioral or no-treatment groups, and the behavioral group was less restrictive than the control group. These findings must be viewed with caution since the instrument, the Attitude Toward the Freedom of Children Scale (Shaw & Wright, 1967), has not been fully accepted as a valid measure and is clearly a reactive measure in this particular study.

In another example of the use of outcome measures which have not been fully validated, Noble (1977) used the Parent Attitude Research Instrument. Parents were assigned to either a PET group, an Adlerian group, or a control group. Both treatment groups changed in their reported attitudes about the use of controlling techniques. The author's conclusion that both treatment groups share some common elements may be correct, but in fact is only one of several possible conclusions.

The further use of the same outcome measures along with the analysis of videotapes of parental/child behaviors was reported by Moore and Dean-Zubritsky (1979). Eight control parents and eight parents trained in an Adlerian Parent Study Group were compared on both attitude and behavioral measures. The group receiving training was found to express more democratic attitudes and behaviorally demonstrated more contact with their children. In contacts with their children, the trained parents were found to use more encouragement and to be more directive. Here we find a bit of a paradox in terms of the expression of democratic attitudes while demonstrating more direction of the children.

In summary, the Adlerian literature would lead one to the conclusion that the training programs (either *Children: The Challenge* or the STEP program) *may* change attitudes. One particular study by Schultz, Nystul, and Law (1980) suggests that such attitudinal changes may be present at least one year after training. However, the attitudinal measures used have not reached the level of reliability and predictive validity that would be needed to accept the results without reservations. More attention will need to be paid to issues of reactivity in measurement (Nelson & Hayes, 1981). Having viewed and participated in Adlerian training, I am certain that it does meet a number of needs of consumers and should be continued. However, a major push toward more systematic research in the Adlerian as well as other models must be mounted if the field continues to seek scientific demonstration of efficacy.

Rational-Emotive Therapy

In spite of the promise seen in an earlier review of the potential for Rational-Emotive Therapy (RET) in the field of PE (Lamb & Lamb, 1978), there have been very few contributions and almost no empirical research. The model is included here in spite of its failing to meet earlier expectations. This inclusion is based on the opinion that RET is in fact an eclectic or integrative theory which has now developed into a recognizable model of both personality functioning and psychotherapy. The model places heavy emphasis on both cognitive and affective concepts in theoretical as well as implementation areas. As an integrative theory, it may well still hold promise in its own right or as an adjunctive theory for parent educators.

Both Ellis (1957) and a reviewer of his work and professional development (Dolliver, 1977) cite a number of philosophical and theoretical influences on the formulation of RET (Stoic philosophy, Abraham Low, Karen Horney, Alfred Adler, Sigmund Freud, semanticist Alfred Korzybski, Bertrand Russell, Carl Rogers, Eric Berne, and Fritz Perls). It is impossible at this point to determine how much weight these influences had prior to the development of RET or if they have been cited in a post hoc fashion due to some of their similarities to Ellis' theoretical position. The theory may reasonably be viewed as an integrative model.

The general assumption in RET is that people have rational and irrational components. The discomfort experienced on an emotional level comes from having irrational thoughts and coming to illogical conclusions. By training people to think more rationally and reach more logical conclusions, an increase in comfort, productivity, and happiness should be seen. Therefore, since parents are people, the theory should be entirely compatible with PE, even though it has not had a major impact on the field to date.

Ellis and Abrams (1978) propose the A-B-C theory in which our emotional reactions or consequences (C) are a result of the conscious or unconscious beliefs (B) which result primarily from the activating experiences that happened at point A. Most of our distress comes from point B rather than point A. In short, our biggest difficulties are our beliefs about ourselves and our difficulties, rather than actual external events. The reader is referred back to Ellis (1962) for a discussion on the 11 most common illogical or irrational ideas. Hauck (1972) presents what he terms as "Erroneous Beliefs of Child Management" as follows:

1. Children must not question or disagree with their superiors.
2. A child and his behavior are the same.
3. Children can upset their superiors.

4. Punishment, guilt, and blame are effective in child management.
5. Children learn from what we say rather than what we do.
6. Praise spoils a child.
7. Children must not be frustrated.
8. Heavy penalties work best if applied early.
9. A child must earn the parent's love.
10. Children should be calmed first and adults later.

Hauck further presents the reasoning showing each of the above beliefs to be indeed irrational and illogical. Parents are encouraged to drop these beliefs and instead begin to utilize an incompatible set of beliefs. Parents are further encouraged to stay with their new rational approach even though it might not get immediate results. In addition, parents are counseled to be less upset by their own mistakes and their child's behavior.

Further suggestions for the use of RET in parent education can be found in Knaus (1974), who reviewed a number of suggestions for teachers' use of RET. Many of these ideas apply directly to parent use as well. Additional suggestions for the inclusion of RET in parent education have been presented by Lamb and Lamb (1978).

With the apparent "goodness of fit" of the RET conceptual framework to the field of parent education, the lack of contribution is rather remarkable. Three explanations are offered in the most speculative sense:

1. Ellis's work in general has not had a major impact on personality or psychotherapy literatures and, therefore, is not in a position to be a major contribution.

2. Ellis appears to have more impact as a speaker than as a writer. Audiences appear to expect him to use colorful language and to be very confrontative and controversial, and do not see him as a serious social science contributor. Accordingly, his impact on clinical training and on research programs has been limited. Since most publications in the field of parent education appear to come from professionals with academic affiliations, Ellis and RET may be viewed as something less than acceptable.

3. Terms such as "irrational" and "illogical" appear to be cursed with difficulties in definition and specification as well as sounding very pejorative and value laden. Some of the early literature on impression formation might well give some explanation for the lack of heuristic value in RET.

Parent educators and researchers should be encouraged to review the RET literature with the expectation that it may offer additions to their own work. As Levant (1983) would appear to suggest, such awareness might stimulate broadening of their own theoretical perspective.

Reality Therapy

Reality Therapy, developed by Glasser (1965), is yet another theoretical model which in earlier reviews of parent education appeared to offer great promise (Brown, 1976; Lamb & Lamb, 1978). However, this promise was not fulfilled since there have been no significant contributions to the parent education literature in the last six years. Glasser continues to publish (1981) and to clarify his theory, as have others (Bassin, Bratter, & Rachin, 1976). His central focus is on a person's individual responsibility for making decisions regarding one's own behavior. Glasser applies this to both parents and children. Glasser's earlier work with parents took place in conjunction with a teacher training program. The program was called the Parent Involvement Program and according to Brown (1976) had seven major steps:

1. Making certain that a warm relationship exists between parent and child. Suggestions are presented on how to establish such a relationship via the uses of conversation.
2. Ask what the child is doing. Do not ask questions using the word "why?".
3. Support the child in evaluating his or her own behavior.
4. Assist (but do not take over) the child's planning more responsible behavior.
5. Get a strong commitment from the child to implement the planning.
6. Avoid the acceptance of any excuses. Ask the child to return to the evaluation stage.
7. Don't use punishment. Encouragement and praise are fine but punishment adds to what will be seen as irresponsible behaviors.

Glasser (1981) has elaborated his theoretical formulation to postulate that behavior functions to control perceptions. Frequently we experience what Glasser regards as perceptual errors, which within an information feedback system influence our behavior, which in turn further increases our perceptual errors. In his recent work, Glasser has added another step to reality therapy, which can best be described as *perseverance,* since behavior and perceptions take time to change.

Hall (1982) has attempted to use Glasser's concepts in the preparation of a parent guide for parents of misbehaving high school students. His guide includes concepts from Dreikurs, Glasser, and various behaviorists. The guide is unfortunately just an exhortation to parents to use a combination of principles. There are no clear programmatic suggestions other than for the parent to work with the school staff in establishing extremely clear communication and expectations. There is apparently no expectation on Hall's part other than that parents will read the guide and behave accordingly. No empirical evaluation was presented.

The Parent Involvement Program described by Brown (1976) has not continued. Accordingly, one is left with only speculations regarding the apparent lack of development of parent education within Reality Therapy. The speculations might well be similar to those presented in the section on Rational-Emotive Therapy. Regardless, further investigation into this model may be useful.

Transactional Analysis

Transactional Analysis (TA), as developed by Eric Berne (1961, 1972), focuses on the structure of a person's ego state, and on the transactions between people which are influenced by the ego states involved in the transaction. Three ego states or aspects of the person that are most identifiable are the Parent, Adult, and Child states. The Parent state is described as one where concern is shown about others and others protected from harm, and where the person expects the others to respond to him or her in an authority role. The Adult ego state is described as one where the person is able to accept responsibility for his or her own behavior and generally functions rationally and tests reality. The Child state is one that is focused more on meeting desires and avoiding fears. Most people are seen as demonstrating these three components in their functioning. Structural analysis would focus on the degree to which a given person exhibits the various states.

The transactional focus comes into play when two or more people are interacting and the attention is placed on which ego states are being used within an interaction. Transactions or communications come from one ego state in a person and are aimed at a particular ego state in the respondent. If the respondent replies to the sending ego state, the transaction is seen as complementary and meets the needs of both parties. However, when the respondent does not send a message or arouses a new ego state, dysfunction is experienced by both parties.

Obviously many of the exchanges between parents and children remain in the proper Parent to Child or Child to Parent channels. However, there may well be times when the situation actually evokes the Child ego state in the parent. When this happens, the possibility of the communication remaining complementary is slim indeed (Sirridge, 1980).

A review of the literature suggests that Berne did not work a great deal with parent groups in what we would view as formal parent education. However, all of his work would speak to the proper training and retraining of ego states including the Parent state. Therefore, it could be argued that his work involved some degree of parent education. James

(1974) speaks more directly to the issue through her book entitled *Transactional Analysis for Moms and Dads: What Do You Do with Them Now That You've Got Them?* This book reviews the various TA concepts that parents could apply to themselves and to their transactions with their children.

Several recent articles suggest ways of using TA concepts and techniques in the area of family intervention (Friedman & Shmukler, 1983; Shmukler & Friedman, 1983). A group from Argentina has addressed the ways that a person can be "reparented" in order to develop a more adequate Parent ego state (Del Casale, Munilla, de Del Casale & Fullone, 1982). However, none of these three references outlines a training program that could be replicated nor do they present any outcome data that would withstand research scrutiny. Samuels (1981) presents a position paper for therapists who are attempting to ameliorate problems in Parental ego states. Samuels feels that other theorists, including many in the TA field, have been unkind to parents and to the Parent ego state by blaming problems on earlier parental influences. He views the Parent ego state as representing a much more positive and necessary role. Samuels gives a number of suggestions for working with the Parent ego state within psychotherapy which would likely be useful for anyone applying the TA methods to parent education.

Since the book by James (1974) noted above, several articles have described the use of TA directly in parent education. Sinclair-Brown (1982) describes a TA program aimed at mothers who have either physically abused their children or have been found to be "seriously neglectful." Nine mothers were selected via court referral. Each mother had two individual interviews prior to entering into TA/Redecision group treatment for 12 weeks. The treatment involved the mothers contracting for change, receiving positive "strokes" for change, and feedback in cognitive areas, which was thought necessary since this population was particularly disturbed and exhibited low use of cognitive skills in problem solving. The core of this TA/Redecision therapy program involves the parents taking responsibility for their own decisions and therefore being placed in a position to make new decisions. Both the abusing and the neglectful mothers completed a majority of their contracts for change. They did not, however, demonstrate significant change on the MMPI, which was administered pre and post treatment. The mothers were reported to have increased their coping skills as indicated by 9 out of 18 mothers getting jobs, by therapist and social worker evaluations, and by the fact that there were no reported incidents of abuse or neglect during the study. Even though there were no control groups, variables were rather ill-defined, and the actual treatment rather poorly specified, the attempt to evaluate the efficacy of TA should be applauded.

Clarke (1982) reports on a more extensive program entitled *Self-Esteem: A Family Affair* (Clarke, 1978, 1981). This program is used in groups of 12 to 20 people (either parents or child caretakers). Clarke reports that 212 people have been trained specifically to be facilitators/leaders in these groups, and indicates that, as of two years ago, these courses were being taught in eight states. Over 1,400 people had taken the course in Minnesota alone. An ongoing research project is mentioned, but no data are presented.

Baker and Bursor (1982) present another TA program which sounds interesting but again presents no data for its support. Their approach is the use of TA Redecision Therapy in a five-session program with college students in a preparenting workshop. Baker and Bursor take a position that in order to be a "good" parent, a person has to be nurturing and accepting of their own parenting ego state. The overall program and each of the sessions is described in some detail. It is possible that a person trained in TA would be able to come close to replicating the training procedures. No information is given regarding potential measures, the length of time that the program has been running, or even any comments by the consumers. In short, this is an idea whose time *might yet come.*

When one reviews the basic concepts of the TA theory, it would be predicted to be the theory with the most impact on PE since the issues of parenting and feelings about Parent ego states are central constructs of the theory. However, the impact is again considerably less than expected. Part of this may well be traced to TA's minimal impact on both the professional literature and academic settings. This general point has been made regarding the theoretical models of Rational-Emotive Therapy and Reality Therapy. However, the specific degree of TA's impact has been charted by B. D. Wilson (1981). Wilson traced the number of dissertations on TA from the years of 1963 through 1980. Only a total of 124 were found. The years between 1975 and 1979 demonstrated a drop from 23 in 1975 to 11 in 1979. In short, the impact has been minimal and appears to be decreasing.

Kohlberg's Moral Education Model

Kohlberg (1969) has studied the development of moral judgments in children and adolescents for a number of years. The general conclusions from these studies can be summarized by the statement that the level of moral reasoning develops as an apparent function of one's ability to look at a given situation through the perspective of the other person or persons involved. Kohlberg and Turiel (1971) take this position a bit further to suggest that difficulties in families and in society at large are brought about by the lack of "moral education" of children. Improvement in the children's behavior and mental health could result from proper education regarding moral decision making.

The impact of parent training on moral judgments has been studied by Stanley (1978, 1980), who found that a combination of Adlerian and PET training had significant effects on the moral reasoning styles of adolescents who had attended the program with their parents. The difficulty with the study is the relatively small number of subjects, the use of a number of dependent measures whose validity is not well established, and the failure to report inter-rater reliability of judges' ratings of tape-recorded family meetings. However, it is noteworthy that moral judgments had not been a particular focus in the parent education program, and yet some impact was noted on moral judgments.

Kupfersmid and Wonderly (1981) take up the issue of moral education and conclude after reviewing the literature that it is too early to determine whether there exists a relationship between moral maturity and the mental health of the person. Therefore, from the perspective of parent education, it may be a bit too early to evaluate the effectiveness of training parents and/or families in decision making about moral issues. From the current author's perspective, the matter is even a bit more complex since neither mental health nor moral development has been adequately defined in a manner that has much empirical utility.

Discussion Methods

For reviews of the earliest forms of parent education in this country the reader is referred to the work of Brim (1959) and Auerbach (1968), who document the development and activities of the Child Study Association of America, which uses primary discussion methods based on the notion that each parent learns in his or her own manner. A further assumption indicates that the learning to be done by the parent is as much an emotional as it is an intellectual process. Accordingly, the major emphasis in the discussion groups is on exploration of feelings with personal insight to be gained from the process. A similar focus is described in a position paper by Ginott (1957), who had arranged discussion groups in a child guidance clinic.

Very little substantive research was done during the early years of the CSAA movement. The most comprehensive piece of research to date was conducted by Hereford (1963), who studied a major parent education project which used the discussion method. His conclusions were as follows: (1) Parents attending a group discussion series demonstrated positive attitude changes on the Parent-Attitude Survey (developed by Hereford). (2) Interviews with parents further demonstrated both behavioral and attitudinal changes. (3) Children of discussion-group parents demonstrated better relationships with peers than did the children of control-group parents (however, these improvements were noted by teachers in only a younger subset of the girls). (4) Effects of number of sessions and effects of the leader were not demonstrated.

At this point, there are no indications in the literature that attendance in a parent group discussion alone brings about demonstrable changes in either parent or child behavior. There are, however, indications that parent attitudes *may* change. The use of reactive measures of attitudes have precluded any more definitive statements.

Eclectic Parent Education

Even though "eclectic" approaches cause many purists to frown, and even though both Levant (1983) and Liddle (1982) have given some very sound precautions against adding concepts from disparate approaches, we find a number of parent education programs including both concepts and strategies from what appear to be other theories. At times it is difficult to determine whether the authors have in fact selected nonrelated concepts and have combined them in something of a patchwork quilt, or if they have in fact broadened and expanded their original theoretical framework, as proposed by Levant.

Several examples of eclectic or integrative approaches follow. Pierce (1973) incorporated both insight and behavioral elements into what appears to be a client-centered approach to working with the partners of dysfunctional marriages. His focus was helping the parents handle the situation so that the communications to and about the children remained as clear as possible. Very few empirical data to support the system are presented. Benson, Berger, and Mease (1975) presented a project whose goals involved teaching parents the following skills: listening, goal setting, identification of parenting styles, sending neutral feelings, sending positive feelings, systems-analysis skills, creative problem solving, and awareness of the roles various family members play. The approach to both the selection of these goals and the means for reaching them further demonstrates eclecticism. There was no attempt to fully evaluate the results, nor was there an attempt to critically evaluate the component parts.

Adlerian approaches have been combined with other approaches in several studies. Carlson and Russel (1982) developed what they termed an integrative approach to parent training. Their interesting position paper reviews what they see to be the strengths and weaknesses of Adlerian, behavioral, and communications models. Unfortunately, this work remains at the position paper level without systematic application or evaluation. Wolf (1983) combines Adlerian, communications, and family systems theory in her work. However, insufficient details are reported to evaluate the integration. To her credit, she presents some consumer satisfaction information to support her model. However, the level of empirical support gained from consumer satisfaction surveys and reports of change gathered in a very reactive manner is not sufficient to accept this model.

Since the behavioral model of parent education is currently developing the largest representation in the literature, it is no surprise to find that it is also well represented in eclectic versions of parent education. We find a recent review of behavioral parent education (Gordon & Davidson, 1981) reporting that the behavioral articles have been paying attention to "softer" issues. We find a number of references to the eclectic Multimodal Behavioral Therapy proposed by Lazarus (1977). Greist and Wells (1983), in a review of child behavior therapy, document the expansion of the model to one of "behavioral family therapy," which appears to be approaching behavioral eclecticism. Griest et al. (1982) had previously presented a very comprehensive piece of research involving work with the mothers of 17 noncompliant children. All of the mothers and children were seen in individual dyads for the basic behavioral training. Some of the mothers were seen for what was termed "parent enhancement therapy." By means of didactic presentations, modeling, role playing, and homework assignments, the mothers were given treatment in the areas of parental perception of the child's behavior, personal adjustment of the parent, and adjustment in the marital relationship and in relationships with people outside of the family. In short, this was a broad-spectrum treatment. Immediately post-treatment and again at a two-month follow-up, the group receiving both the parent training and the parent enhancement therapy demonstrated significantly more improvement on various measures, including in-home observations. The exact nature of the "enhancement" sessions is rather difficult to determine from the article, but whatever the treatment, it appeared to enhance the traditional behavioral training, which employed rewarding positive behavior and using time-out for noncompliance.

Nadler (1983) developed a series of workshops for people who have either recently remarried or who are contemplating remarriage. At the time the article was written, over 120 people had taken the six-session workshops, which were described as "educational, behavioral, and psychodynamic" in nature. Since many clinicians see "reconstituted" families in their practice, the article was thought to give guidelines for intervention. However, the specific interventions and the ways of combining the three components are not outlined sufficiently to give a practitioner anything other than a general framework. Evaluative research was limited entirely to an evaluation questionnaire with no follow-up.

Retarded parents have been placed in an eclectic parent education program by Peterson, Robinson, and Littman (1983). The six retarded parents attended eight group sessions in which they were taught skills of describing, praising, and making reflective comments about their children's behavior. They were also taught to be nondirective during their children's play. Observations of their responses with their children indicated that immediately post-training, the parents were less directive and increased their positive comments. However, a follow-up observation conducted at one month post-training demonstrated only the nondirective skills to be maintained.

Another rather specialized group to receive eclectic education has been high school students in a preparenting course (Moore & Robin, 1981). In comparing those receiving training to those in a wait-list control group by means of written tests and role-played analogue situations, the training group was found to be very effective in helping the high school students make gains in both behavioral and reflective skills. The entire study can be seen as an analogue study since the students are not parents and no attempt was made to determine effectiveness in actual parenting or child-care settings. However, PET and behavioral training makes an interesting combination that might well deserve further study.

The current author is very familiar with both the uses and the scientific deficits of eclectic models because of his own involvement in the development and use of such a model over the last 10 years. This model, the Solution Oriented Approach to Problems (the SOAP system) developed by Lamb and Reidy (1975) and reported by Lamb and Lamb (1978), takes a slightly different tack in the development of an eclectic approach. Originally the author used primarily a behavioral approach to working with families in both a therapeutic and an educational role. This behavioral approach was used with individual parents as well as with groups of parents. It became apparent after several years that this approach, although initially effective, was not meeting the needs of the families. The same child was being referred to the clinic for a different problem, or a sibling was being referred for a very similar problem. All this was taking place even though various behavioral techniques aimed at generalization and maintenance were being employed.

An informal survey of professional colleagues indicated that the same lack of effectiveness was being experienced not only within the behavioral model but also within the PET model and within the Adlerian model as well. After much discussion and review of literature, it was suggested that we had in fact failed to follow Miller's (1969) plan of "giving psychology away." The major contribution of psychology to that point was not any of the extant theories, but rather the "scientific approach" or the hypothetico-deductive method of viewing human behavior. Our conclusion was, therefore, that perhaps we should be working with parents to help them understand ways of approaching problems, rather than arriving on the scene with our solutions derived from theoretical positions, which we then encourage the parents to implement in order to validate our theories.

Use of general strategies of problem solving is in fact not an entirely novel approach. Initially, we used the same steps proposed by Gordon (1970) but later dropped his step involving "ownership" of the problem. Shure and Spivak (1978) developed what they termed Interpersonal Cognitive Problem Solving, a program in which they taught mothers (in low-income groups) both to use a problem-solving approach and to teach its use to their children. Shure and Spivack concluded that finding multiple solutions to problems may well be the most potent component of their program. On a one-year follow-up, children of those mothers who used the problem-solving skills improved the most in their own problem-solving abilities as well as on measures of behavioral adjustment. Further problem-solving approaches have been presented by Blechman (1980) and Breton, Welbourn, and Waters (1981).

The SOAP system has been used now for approximately 10 years in settings ranging from community mental health centers, child psychiatry clinics, public and parochial school systems, pediatric clinics, child abuse units, and the private practice sector. The populations have ranged from low to middle income, clinic to nonclinic, active to inactive children, single- to two-parent families, and "normal" to moderately disturbed children. Additional specific populations including parents of children with specific learning disabilities, hemophilia, and diabetes have been members of groups. The groups have lasted from 6 to 10 sessions ranging from 1½ to 2 hours each.

The specific content of each session, general format, and style of presentation are outlined more completely in Lamb and Lamb (1978). The portion of the program that may make the SOAP system a unique example of the eclectic approach is that each parent presents problems to the group, with the group then developing at least 10 possible solutions to that particular problem. The leader(s) of the group make certain that solutions are presented which represent concepts from behavioral, Adlerian, PET, Rational-Emotive, and other approaches. These ideas are presented to the group by means of short didactic presentations and short handouts (as the leader feels is appropriate).

It may not be possible to have all theories represented in each set of 10 solutions. However, in any given session it is most likely that some elements of almost all theories will be presented either by a parent member of the group or by a leader.

This author concluded some time ago that certain theoretical approaches *do not fit* certain families. Anyone who attempts to have a family engage in a *nonfitting* procedure is bound to be something less than successful. By having the target parents select from the array of solutions, after first stating something they like and something they do not like about each item in the array, we find parents selecting items or combinations of items that are compatible with their style. Such compatibility is prerequisite to the parent implementing the solution.

The SOAP system is subject to the criticism directed at other approaches since it is, at this point, only in the form of a proposal even though it has been in use for 10 years. The only data collected to date have been consumer satisfaction oriented and have not been subjected to external validation and long-term follow-up. However, its use to date would suggest that it could, after this number of years of development and implementation, be put to such a test.

Educational Methods

A relatively wide range of methods has been employed in training parents. A body of literature is beginning to develop focused on the differential efficacy of the various methods and on critical components of various training packages.

Lamb (1970) attempted to evaluate the relative effectiveness of didactic training, modeling, and self-observation via videotape. Mothers were trained to model descriptive language for their children and to reward the children for descriptive language. This limited study found a combination of modeling and self-observation to be the most powerful educational method. Bernal, Williams, Miller, and Reagor (1972) further review and document the use of videotape to provide parents with feedback regarding their responses to difficult-to-manage children. Successful cases are presented where the videotape was used both pre and post training in order to allow parents to become active in the assessment of the case from beginning to end.

The use of videotape and review of the possible components of the educational package are discussed more recently by Webster-Stratton (1981, 1982). The rationale for the use of videotaped models and guidelines are clearly presented and a brief report of a supporting study is included. Changes were measured both by means of reactive paper-and-pencil reports of children's behavior and by trained raters observing videotapes of the mother–child interactions.

O'Dell et al. (1982) found major differences in outcome measures when comparing training received by 100 parents assigned to either minimal training control group, written manual group, audiotape group, videotaped modeling group, or live modeling plus behavioral rehearsal group. The parents were trained to use behavioral reinforcement skills. Observations were carried out in the home by trained observers. The minimum training group scored significantly lower than all other training groups. Audiotape training was found to be significantly less effective than live modeling with rehearsal. There was no evidence that changes in observed parental behavior resulted in changes in the child's behavior.

O'Dell, Krug, Patterson and Faustman (1980b) and O'Dell, Krug, O'Quin, and Kasnetz (1980a) had previously concluded that a combination of media combined with a brief individual contact at the end of group media training appeared to be the most cost-effective method of training. McConkey, McEvoy, and Gallagher (1982) reported an evaluation of a video course for Irish parents of mentally handicapped children, which was found to be very successful. However, the measures were entirely self-report and therefore subject to the limitations of the methodology. Bradley-Johnson and Johnson (1980), studying a program to give information to mothers in maternity wards, found methods including videotape more effective than simply giving the mothers a handbook.

Other attempts to determine the relevant variables relating to the efficacy of various training methods have been reported. Pevsner (1982) found group training to be more effective in teaching behavioral principles. Sirbu, Cotler, and Jason (1978) found little difference between groups receiving a programmed text, a course, or a course plus a text. All groups were significantly better than an attention-placebo group. Scovern et al. (1980) in a very limited study concluded that the critical components of parent counseling may be just the presentation of information in a didactic manner. The limitations of the study, as noted, are great, but the issue is clearly raised. Edgar, Singer, Ritchie, and Heggelund (1981) reported consumer satisfaction when parents were used as group facilitators, which has also been noted in some of the early Adlerian work. Similarly, Ganong and Coleman (1983) found no differences between volunteers and professionals on several outcome measures. The limitations of the study are rather severe, but again the use of people other than professionals to run parent education groups is suggested and receives some limited support.

In clinical settings, repeated contact and follow-up visits are frequent. The use of "booster sessions" have been reported in the behavioral field in dealing with phobia problems. McDonald and Budd (1983) applied the use of booster sessions in the parent education of a mother with a Down's syndrome child. By use of a multiple-baseline design, the effectiveness of the booster session was demonstrated and maintained at a 10-week follow-up.

Another study which focused on feedback was reported by Packard, Robinson, and Grove (1983), who compared the results of training groups receiving placebo-control, self-instruction, and "bug-in-the-ear," for parents in a relationship-building program. Those who had received the bug-in-the-ear training were continuing to show gains in the use of nondirective skills 11 weeks after training. These results were obtained in a laboratory setting via the use of trained observers of mothers and children in a situation where the play was requested to be "child-directed." It is interesting to see *very* direct coaching being used to develop *very* nondirective responses.

Holcomb, Shearer, and Thro (1982) described a program in which parents are provided with literature designed to assist them in participation in their child's educational development, including reading-readiness skill building. The description is limited and not based on empirical results. The program is thus a typical example of the use of books and handouts by various professionals. The lack of research regarding the use of such materials is almost universal. More comments about this state of affairs will be made in the Conclusions section at the end of the chapter.

It may be a bit premature to focus our research on educational methods since there are remaining questions regarding the results of parent training. In a number of studies, it is impossible to sort out the effects of training versus effects of the specific educational methods used. Perhaps more definitive and long-term studies may be able to answer such questions in the future.

Special Populations and Scope of Parent Education

In addition to the typical populations of parents recruited from school, clinics, and community agencies, some rather specialized parents have been trained: parents of deaf children (Craig, 1983; Simmons-Martin, 1983; G. Wilson, 1981); foster parents (Engle, 1983; Guerney & Gavigan, 1981; Hill & Peltzer, 1982; Levant, Slattery & Slobodian, 1981; Simms, 1983); parents in pediatric settings (Mandell & Yogman, 1982; Rothenberg, Hitchcock, Harrison & Graham, 1983); abusive parents (Barth, Blythe, Schinke, & Schilling, 1983; Egan, 1983; Nomellini & Katz, 1983; Older, 1981); parents of retarded children (Clark, Baker, & Heifetz, 1982; Firth, 1982; Moxley-Haegert & Serbin, 1983; Singh & Kaushik, 1982); parents of children in early education or language programs (Andrews et al., 1982; Cataldo, 1980; Johnson & Breckenridge, 1982; McConkey & O'Connor, 1982); and illiterate parents interested in developmental issues (Brooks, 1981).

Additional programs, books, and empirically based research studies have been completed on the following less frequently reported specific populations or topic areas: (1) how to avoid becoming a battered parent

(Palmer, 1980); (2) a guide for becoming a step-parent (Kalter, 1979); (3) a guide for parent self-help groups (Pizzo, 1983); (4) a guide to working with adolescent parents (Halpern & Covey, 1983); (5) parents being trained to deal with issues of joint custody of their children (Mitnick, 1982); (6) description of a program to train parents of incarcerated serious juvenile offenders (Gerstein & Pittman, 1983); (7) study of the perceived parent education needs of high school students in Trinidad (Mensah, Schultz, & Hughes, 1983); (8) an Australian study of the efficacy of group parent training in behavioral techniques for enuretic children (Bollard, Nettelback, & Roxbee, 1982); (9) a well-designed study of the management of pre-meal inappropriate behavior in restaurants, which included a generalization study (Bauman, Reiss, Rogers, & Bailey, 1983); (10) a single-case clinical report of training parents to successfully treat their encopretic child (Grimes, 1983); and (11) training parents to deal with their child who had unobserved trichotillomania (Altman, Grahs, & Friman, 1982). This list is by no means exhaustive; and due to space limitations, details and evaluations of the studies cannot be provided.

The range and scope of parent education is immense. Over 10 countries have been represented in the literature reviewed for this chapter. The geographic range of parent education activities was earlier confirmed by Stern (1960), who conducted an international survey through the UNESCO organization. Thirty-five countries reported ongoing parent education programs conducted by governments, local authorities, and volunteer groups.

Parent Variables

A number of different parent variables have been studied regarding their impact on outcomes of parent education programs. Patterson (1974), Storm, Griswold, and Slaughter (1981), Firestone and Witt (1982), Bridges (1982), and Clarke and Baker (1983) all present data suggesting that parent socioeconomic class, education, or other demographic variables have an important impact on the outcome of parent training. However, at least one study, which was fairly well designed and which included behavioral observations, failed to find SES differences (Rogers, Forehand, Griest, Wells, & McMahon, 1981).

Birkel and Reppucci (1983) and Dumas and Wahler (1983) found one's social network to be an important factor in prediction of utilization of resources, as well as in the outcome of parent education. Rowland and Wampler (1983) found both race and education to be related to perceived needs for parent education. Therefore, general support for the importance of social and demographic variables can be found.

Sex of the parent receiving the parent education is an important variable. Resnick (1981) objects to the implicit assumptions involved in aiming parent education primarily at mothers. Several studies conclude that it may be unnecessary to include fathers in parent training (Budd & O'Brien, 1982; Firestone, Kelley, & Fike, 1980; Martin, 1977).

The impact of parental styles, personality, and goals prior to engaging in parent education has received limited attention to date. Brewer, Tollefson, and Fine (1981) found interactions between the mode of presentation in parent education and the mother's locus of control, which then related to the attitudinal outcome measures. Rebman (1983) found parents who felt responsible for their children's education to participate more in the child's education program. Parents who initially had low feelings of responsibility increased these feelings as a result of a parent education experience.

The issues of meeting parental needs have also been addressed by Wandersman (1982) and by Schreibman (1983). The lack of clear demonstrations of effectiveness of parent training programs might well result from a lack of agreement between the needs of the parents and the needs and constraints of the researcher. It is possible that clinicians doing parent education on a day-to-day basis do not have the same constraints and, therefore, might be more successful than the empirical researchers. In an article reviewing 45 journal articles, Forehand, Middlebrook, Rogers, and Steffe (1983) began to address the issue of dropouts, which relates to the failure to meet parental needs. Only 22 of the 45 articles reported dropout data. In those reporting, approximately 28 percent of the parents dropped out of training. This may be an important group to examine further, even though they would, by definition, be difficult to study.

Conclusions

Review of the parent education literature produces an impression that is much like the comedy routine of "some good news and some bad news." The good news—parent education is alive and flourishing. The bad news—it is suffering from the same ailments as other modes of intervention. As the review indicates, PE has had periods of very high activity and then periods of decline. The current status of high activity in both application and research may precede a period of decline.

Levant (in Chapter 1) notes several issues which may relate to the future of psychoeducational and skills-building programs for families: (1)

overselling of family skills-training programs; (2) staffing and training issues where rank, privilege, and professional roles will receive a great deal of attention; (3) combination formats versus programs with theoretical integrity; (4) sex-role stereotyping and the inclusion/exclusion of fathers in parent education; (5) development of the family systems perspective within parent education; and (6) the need for further clarification of parent education as an enhancement or prevention strategy. In short, the future and current problems of parent education as a field clearly reflect the current status of most intervention fields.

We find substantial increases in number of publications being produced in the PE field and find the majority to reflect a behavioral model, with other models falling far behind in research production. The differences clearly reflect the importance of empirical research within the behavioral framework and the relatively diminished role of research within the other models. It is rather surprising that PE has not received major research attention prior to this time since (1) it has had a sufficient length of history as well as periods of funding to make it available to research/public observation; (2) generally, PE is a time-limited intervention and, therefore, would not be subject to a number of research difficulties; (3) it may be more easily broken into component parts than a number of other interventions; (4) has a wide range of applications, as described by Levant (Chapter 1), including training for treatment, training as treatment, training for enhancement and development and/or prevention; (5) represents various fields and theoretical positions (as described by Levant) which should make it open to research from a number of perspectives; and (6) is typically seen as a cost-efficient intervention, which could be seen as a plus for both the clinician and the researcher.

Although I have no hard data to support the position, it appears that much of the research is being produced within graduate training programs where the six research advantages listed above would have very clear impact. However, from a clinical standpoint, this should bring a note of caution. Many issues become so trivialized when undertaken by academic researchers, who need to control variables and meet publication criteria, that the results have limited relevance to practical application (Ross, 1981). From my standpoint, the research in the PE area has not *yet* fallen prey to this syndrome. However, we should proceed with extreme caution since the literature is expanding so quickly as to invite what I call "me too" articles. Unfortunately, such articles are "me too" only in terms of publication and almost universally do not attempt to replicate any earlier work. Again, parent educators as a group are no more guilty of such thinking than their colleagues in other areas. We should all be reminded that psychology along with other "sciences" is ultimately based on two major tenets: (1) observation and (2) replicability of studies. A clear majority of the studies reviewed did not include observation. Many of the studies gave only general descriptions of the actual training procedures and, accordingly, never could be replicated. I am slightly embarrassed to list this as a criticism since there are almost no true replications of studies in the fields of either education or psychology. Fleischman (1981) is a rare exception when he purposefully replicates a study.

In summary, I find the general field of parent education still holding the promise of a reasonably inexpensive, consumer-compatible, common-sense idea which has demonstrated the ability to change parental reports of their own attitudes. It has yet to fully demonstrate the ability to change parental behavior over a long period of time. Even though there has been some initial success at demonstrating the ability of parents to utilize their newly acquired skills and attitudes, the full demonstration of generalization in either parents or children remains an open question.

The issue of expectations of parents, researchers, and children have been virtually ignored. Even though there have been comparisons of experimental groups to controls, and comparisons between groups based on various theoretical models, I was unable to find a single article which selected parents into a particular type of training model on the basis of parental needs, expectations, styles, and so on. Individual family training programs may be less open to this criticism since the training may be focused and designed around a specific family. However, most of the individual studies have been behavioral studies in which an attempt has been made to confirm the efficacy of a particular set of constructs and operations.

In my opinion, parent education may be better approached from a different research strategy. Rather than continuing to attempt the validation of theories, perhaps we should begin to look very carefully at the characteristics of families who apparently benefit from education, and those not benefiting. If this is done across all theoretical models, perhaps a good sociological or macroanalysis expert might be of some assistance. My final criticism involves the *insularity* of most of the researchers. Little indication of general knowledge of the field or knowledge of educational literature is demonstrated. This clearly impedes cross-model stimulation.

We must heed the warnings of our colleagues and retain a view of the forest while examining the separate trees. Without such an approach I am afraid we will be condemned to the same ill fate as many of our cohorts who spend careers analyzing the component parts of a tree but give little demonstration of either understanding or appreciation of a tree, to say nothing of the forest. Therefore, I challenge myself, researchers, and clinicians to develop research strategies able to answer real questions and able to have an impact on practitioners. In addition, we must return to the basic assumptions of science: observation and replicability.

References

Abidin, R. R. (Ed.). (1980). *Parent education and intervention handbook.* Springfield, IL: Thomas.

Altman, K., Grahs, C., & Friman, P. (1982). Treatment of unobserved trichotillomania by attention-reflection and punishment of an apparent covariant. *Journal of Behavior Therapy & Experimental Psychiatry, 13*(4), 337–340.

Andrews, S. R., Blumenthal, J. B., Johnson, D. L., Kahn, A. J., Ferguson, C. J., Lasater, T. M., Malone, P. E., & Wallace, D. B. (1982). The skills of mothering: A study of parent child development centers. *Monographs of the Society for Research in Child Development, 47*(6), 83.

Ansbacher, H. L., & Ansbacher, R. R. (Ed.). (1956). *The individual psychology of Alfred Adler: A systematic presentation in selections from his writings.* New York: Basic Books.

Auerbach, A. B. (1968). *Parents learn through discussion: Principles and practices of parent group discussion.* New York: Wiley.

Baker, M. S., & Bursor, D. E. (1982). Close encounters of the best kind: A TA pre-parenting workshop for college students. *Transactional Analysis Journal, 12*(4), 243–246.

Barth, R. P., Blythe, B. J., Schinke, S. P., & Schilling, R. F. (1983). Self-control training with maltreating parents. *Child Welfare, 62*(4), 313–324.

Bassin, A., Bratter, T. E., & Rachin, R. L. (Eds.). (1976). *The reality therapy reader.* New York: Harper & Row.

Bauman, K. E., Reiss, M. L., Rogers, R. W., & Bailey, J. S. (1983). Dining out with children: Effectiveness of a parent advice package on pre-meal inappropriate behavior. *Journal of Applied Behavior Analysis, 16*(1), 55–68.

Beales, R. (1975). In search of the historical child: Miniature adulthood and youth in colonial New England. *American Quarterly, 27,* 379–398.

Becker, W. C. (1971). *Parents are teachers.* Champaign, IL: Research Press.

Beckman, D. (1977). *The mechanical baby: A popular history of the theory and practice of child raising.* Westport, CT: Lawrence Hill.

Benson, L., Berger, M., & Mease, W. (1975). Family communication systems. *Small Group Behavior, 6*(1), 91–105.

Bernal, M. E., Williams, D. E., Miller, W. H., & Reagor, P. A. (Eds.). (1972). The use of videotape feedback and operant learning principles in training parents in management of deviant children. In R. D. Rubin, H. Fernsterheim, J. D. Henderson, & L. P. Ullman (Eds.), *Advances in behavior therapy.* New York: Academic Press.

Berne, E. (1961). *Transactional analysis in psychotherapy.* New York: Grove Press.

Berne, E. (1972). *What do you say after you say hello?* New York: Grove Press.

Beutler, L. E., Oro-Beutler, M. E., & Mitchell, R. (1979). Systematic comparison of two parent training programs in child management. *Journal of Counseling Psychology, 26,* 531–533.

Birkel, R. C., & Reppucci, N. D. (1983). Special networks, information-seeking, and the utilization of sources. *American Journal of Community Psychology, 11*(2), 185–205.

Blechman, E. A. (1980). Family problem solving training. *American Journal of Family Therapy, 8*(3), 3–21.

Boggs, C. J. (1981). Train up a parent: A review of the research in child rearing literature. *Child Study Journal, 10*(4), 261–284.

Bollard, J., Nettelback, T., & Roxbee, L. (1982). Dry-bed training for childhood bedwetting: A comparison of group with individually administered parent instruction. *Behavior Research & Therapy, 20*(3), 209–217.

Bradley-Johnson, S., & Johnson, C. M. (1980). A comparison of parent-education methods in maternity wards. *Infant Mental Health Journal, 1*(1), 34–41.

Breton, M., Welbourn, A., & Waters, J. (1981). A nurturing and problem-solving approach for abuse-prone mothers. *Child Abuse & Neglect, 5*(4), 475–480.

Brewer, S., Tollefson, N., & Fine, M. J. (1918). The effects of matching locus of control and presentation mode in parent training. *Psychology in the Schools, 18*(4), 482–488.

Bridges, K. R. (1982). Social class, gender, and attitudes toward education for parenthood of high school and college students. *Psychological Reports, 51*(1), 147–154.

Brim, O. (1959). *Education for child rearing.* New York: Russell Sage Foundations.

Brooks, J. B. (1981). *The Process of Parenting.* Palo Alto, CA: Mayfield.

Brown, C. C. (1976). It changed my life. *Psychology Today, 10,* 47–57, 109–111.

Budd, K. S., & O'Brien, T. P. (1982). Father involvement in behavioral parent training: An area in need of research. *Behavioral Therapist, 5*(3), 85–89.

Cable, M. (1975). *The little darlings: A history of child rearing in America.* New York: Scribner.

Carkhuff, R. R. (1971). Training as a preferred mode of treatment. *Journal of Counseling Psychology, 18,* 123–131.

Carlson, K. L., & Russell, R. A. (1982). An integrative approach to parent training. *School Counselor, 29*(5), 396–402.

Cataldo, C. Z. (1980). The parent as learner: Early childhood parent programs. *Educational Psychologist, 15*(3), 172–186.

Christensen, O. C. (1969). Education: A model for counseling in the elementary school. *Elementary School Guidance and Counseling Journal, 4,* 12–19.

Christensen, O. L., & Thomas, C. R. (1980). Dreikurs and the search for equality. In M. J. Fine (Ed.), *Handbook on parent education.* New York: Academic Press.

Clark, D. B., & Baker, B. L. (1983). Predicting outcome in parent training. *Journal of Consulting & Clinical Psychology, 51*(2), 309–311.

Clark, D. B., Baker, B. L., & Heifetz, L. J. (1982). Behavioral training for parents of mentally retarded children: Prediction of outcome. *American Journal of Mental Deficiency, 87*(1), 14–19.

Clarke, J. (1978). *Self-esteem: A family affair.* Minneapolis: Winston Press.

Clarke, J. (1981). *Self-esteem: A family affair leader guide.* Minneapolis: Winston Press.

Clarke, J. (1982). Self-esteem: A family affair. A parenting model. *Transactional Analysis Journal, 12*(4), 252–254.

Costner, H. L. (1980). *The changing folkways of parenthood.* New York: Arno Press.

Craig, H. B. (1983). Parent–infant education in schools for deaf children: Results of CEASD survey. *American Annals of the Deaf, 128*(2), 82–98.

Croake, J. W. (1983). Adlerian parent education. *The Counseling Psychologist, 11*(3), 65–71.

Croake, J. W., & Glover, K. E. (1977). A history and evaluation of parent education. *The Family Coordinator, 26*(2), 151–158.

Del Casale, F., Munilla, H. L., de Del Casale, & Fullone, E. (1982). Defective parenting and reparenting. *Transactional Analysis Journal, 12*(3), 181–184.

Dinkmeyer, D., & Dinkmeyer, D. Jr. (1979). A comprehensive and systematic approach to parent education. *American Journal of Family Therapy, 7*(2), 46–50.

Dinkmeyer, D., & McKay, G. D. (1976). *Systematic training for effective parenting.* Circle Pines, MN: American Guidance Service.

Dolliver, R. H. (1977). The relationship of rational-emotive therapy to ortho psychotherapies and personality theories. *The Counseling Psychologist, 7*(1), 57–63.

Dreikurs, R. (1958). *The challenge of parenthood.* New York: Hawthorne Press.

Dreikurs, R., & Soltz, V. (1964). *Children: the challenge.* New York: Meredith Press.

Dumas, J. E., & Wahler, R. G. (1983). Predictors of treatment outcome in parent training: Mother insularity and socioeconomic disadvantage. *Behavioral Assessment, 5*(4), 301–313.

Edgar, E., Singer, T., Ritchie, C., & Heggelund, M. (1981). Parents as facilitators in developing an individual approach to parent involvement. *Behavioral Disorders, 6*(2), 122–127.

Egan, K. J. (1983). Stress management and child management with abusive parents. *Journal of Clinical Child Psychology, 12*(3), 292–299.

Ellis, A. (1957). Outcome of employing three techniques of psychotherapy. *Journal of Clinical Psychology, 13,* 344–350.

Ellis, A. (1962). *Reason and emotion in psychotherapy.* New York: Lyle Stuart.

Ellis, A., & Abrams, E. (1978). *Brief psychotherapy in medical and health practice.* New York: Springer.

Engle, J. M. (1983). The parent therapist program: A new approach to foster care of difficult adolescents. *Children & Youth Services Review, 5*(2), 195–207.

Fine, M. J. (Ed.). (1980). *Handbook on parent education.* New York: Academic Press.

Firestone, P., Kelley, M. J., & Fike, S. (1980). Are fathers necessary in parent training groups? *Journal of Clinical Child Psychology, 9,* 44–47.

Firestone, P., & Witt, J. E. (1982). Characteristics of families completing and prematurely discontinuing a behavioral parent-training program. *Journal of Pediatric Psychology, 7*(2), 209–222.

Firth, H. (1982). The effectiveness of parent workshops in mental handicap service. *Child Care, Health & Development, 8*(2), 77–91.

Fleischman, M. J. (1981). A replication of Patterson's "Intervention for boys with conduct problems." *Journal of Consulting & Clinical Psychology, 49*(3), 342–351.

Forehand, R., Middlebrook, J., Rogers, T., & Steffe, M. (1983). Dropping out of parent training. *Behavior Research and Therapy, 21*(6), 663–668.

Frazier, F., & Matthes, W. A. (1975). Parent education: A comparison of Adlerian and behavioral approaches. *Elementary School Guidance and Counseling, 10,* 31–38.

Friedman, M., & Shmukler, D. (1983). A model of family development and functioning in a T.A. framework. *Transactional Analysis Journal, 13*(2), 90–93.

Ganong, L. H., & Coleman, M. (1983). An evaluation of the use of volunteers as parent educators. *Family Relations: Journal of Applied Family & Child Studies, 32*(1), 117–122.

Gerstein, L. H., & Pittman, J. F. (1983). A pilot education program for families of incarcerated serious juvenile offenders. *Family Relations: Journal of Applied Family & Child Studies, 32*(3), 411–418.

Ginott, H. G. (1957). Parent education groups in a child guidance clinic. *Mental Hygiene, 41,* 82–86.

Glasser, W. (1965). *Reality therapy.* New York: Harper & Row.

Glasser, W. (1981). *Stations of the mind: New directors for reality therapy.* New York: Harper & Row.

Gordon, S. B., & Davidson, D. (1981). Behavioral parent training. In A. S. Gurman & D. P. Kniskern (Eds.), *Handbook of family therapy.* New York: Brunner/Mazel.

Gordon, T. (1970). *P.E.T. Parent Effectiveness Training.* New York: Peter H. Wyden.

Griest, D. L., Forehand, R., Rogers, R., Breiner, J., Furey, W., & Williams, C. (1982). Effects of parent enhancement therapy on the treatment outcome and generalization of a parent training program. *Behavior Research & Therapy, 20*(5), 429–436.

Griest, D. L., & Wells, K. C. (1983). Behavioral family therapy with conduct disorders in children. *Behavior Therapy, 14*(1), 37–53.

Grimes, L. (1983). Application of the self-regulatory model in dealing with encopresis. *School Psychology Review, 12*(1), 82–87.

Guerney, L. F., & Gavigan, M. A. (1981). Parental acceptance and foster parents. *Journal of Clinical Child Psychology, 10*(1), 27–32.

Hall, G. S. (1883). Contents of children's minds. *Princeton Review, 11,* 272–294.

Hall, J. P. (1982). A parent guide for the misbehaving high school student. *Adolescence, 17*(66), 369–385.

Halpern, R., & Covey, L. (1983). Community support for adolescent parents and their children: The parent-to-parent program in Vermont. *Journal of Primary Prevention, 3*(3), 160–173.

Hauck, P. A. (1972). *The rational management of children.* New York: Libra Publishers.

Hereford, C. F. (1963). *Changing parental attitudes through group discussion.* Austin: University of Texas Press.

Hill, M., & Peltzer, J. (1982). A report of thirteen groups for white parents of black children. *Family Relations: Journal of Applied Family & Child Studies, 31*(4), 557–565.

Holcomb, T. F., Shearer, L., & Thro, E. G. (1982). The layperson's library: A tool for reaching teaching parents. *Elementary School Guidance & Counseling, 17*(2), 108–111.

James, M. (1974). *Transactional analysis for moms and dads.* Reading, MA: Addison-Wesley.

Johnson, D. L., & Breckenridge, J. N. (1982). The Houston Parent-Child Development Center and the primary prevention of behavioral problems in young children. *American Journal of Community Psychology, 10*(3), 305–316.

Kalter, S. (1979). *Instant parent: A guide for stepparents, part-time parents and grandparents.* New York: A & W Publishers.

Knaus, W. I. (1974). *Rational emotive education: A manual on elementary school teachers.* New York: Institute for Rational Living.

Kohlberg, L. (1969). *Stages in the development of moral thought and action.* New York: Holt, Rhinehart, & Winston.

Kohlberg, L., & Turiel, E. (1971). Moral development and moral education. In G. S. Lessor (Ed.), *Psychology and educational practice.* Glenview, IL: Scott Foresman.

Krumboltz, J., & Krumboltz, H. (1972). *Changing children's behavior.* Englewood Cliffs, NJ: Prentice-Hall.

Kupfersmid, J. H., & Wonderly, D. M. (1981). Moral maturity as an avenue to mental health: Another blind alley. *Child Study Journal, 10*(4), 285–296.

Lamb, J., & Lamb, W. (1978). *Parent education and elementary counseling.* New York: Human Sciences Press.

Lamb, W. (1970). *A comparison of various techniques of training mothers as language-concept models for their children.* Unpublished doctoral dissertation, University of Arizona.

Lamb, W., & Reidy, T. J. (1975). *The SOAP system: A proposed model for parent training.* Unpublished manuscript, DePaul University.

Lazarus, A. (1977). *Multimodal behavior therapy.* New York: Springer.

Levant, R. F. (1983). Toward a counseling psychology of the family: Psychological-educational and skills training programs for treatment, prevention, and development. *The Counseling Psychologist, 11*(3), 5–27.

Levant, R. F., Slattery, S. C., & Slobodian, P. E. (1981). A systematic skills approach to the selection and training of foster parents as mental health paraprofessionals: II. Training. *Journal of Community Psychology, 9*(3), 231–238.

Liddle, H. (1982). On the problems of eclecticism: A call for epistomological clarification and human scale theories. *Family Process, 21,* 243–250.

Lowe, R. N., & Morse, C. (1977). Parent child education centers. In C. Hacher & B. S. Brooks (Eds.), *Innovations in counseling psychology: Developing new roles, settings, techniques.* San Francisco: Jossey-Bass.

Mandell, F., & Yogman, M. W. (1982). Developmental aspects of well child office visits. *Journal of Developmental & Behavioral Pediatrics, 3*(2), 118–121.

Martin, B. (1977). Brief family intervention: Effectiveness and the importance of including the father. *Journal of Consulting and Clinical Psychology, 45,* 1002–1010.

McConkey, R., McEvoy, J., & Gallagher, F. (1982). Learning through play: The evaluation of a videocourse for parents of mentally handicapped children. *Child Care, Health & Development, 8*(6), 345–359.

McConkey, R., & O'Connor, M. (1982). A new approach to parental involvement in language intervention programmes. *Child Care, Health & Development, 8*(3), 163–176.

McDonald, M. R., & Budd, K. S. (1983). "Booster shots" following didactic parent training: Effects of follow-up using graphic feedback and instructions. *Behavior Modification, 7*(2), 211, 223.

Mensah, K. L., Schultz, J. B., & Hughes, R. P. (1983). Parent education needs of secondary students. *Family Relations: Journal of Applied Family & Child Studies, 32*(2), 181–189.

Miller, G. (1969). Psychology as a means of promoting human welfare. *Adlerian Psychologist, 24,* 1063–1071.

Mitnick, M. F. (1982). Joint custody information program. *Conciliation Courts Review, 20*(1), 41–42.

Moore, M. H., & Dean-Zubritsky, C. (1979). Adlerian parent study groups: An assessment of attitudes and behavior change. *Journal of Individual Psychology, 35*(2), 225–234.

Moore, P. E., & Robin, A. L. (1981). An approach to parent training for high school students. *American Journal of Family Therapy, 9*(4), 61–69.

Moxley-Haegert, L., & Serbin, L. A. (1983). Developmental education for parents of delayed infants: Effects on parental motivation and children's development. *Child Development, 54*(5), 1324, 1331.

Nadler, J. H. (1983). Effecting change in stepfamilies: A psychodynamic/behavior group approach. *American Journal of Psychotherapy, 37*(1), 100–112.

Nelson, R. O., & Hayes, S. C. (1981). Theoretical explanations for reactivity in self-monitoring. *Behavior Modification, 5*(1), 3–14.

Noble, R. D. (1977). An evaluation of parent effectiveness training and Adlerian parent groups: Changing childrearing attitudes. (Doctoral dissertation, Indiana University.) *Dissertation Abstracts International, 37,* 4869A. (University Microfilms No. 77–3359.)

Nomellini, S., & Katz, R. (1983). Effects of anger control training on abusive parents. *Cognitive Therapy & Research, 7*(1), 57–67.

O'Dell, S. L., Krug, W. W., O'Quin, J. A., & Kasnetz, M. (1980a). Media-assisted parent training: A further analysis. *Behavior Therapist, 3*(2), 19–21.

O'Dell, S. L., Krug, W. W., Patterson, J. N., & Faustman, W. O. (1980b). An assessment of methods for training parents in the use of time-out. *Journal of Behavior Therapy & Experimental Psychiatry, 11*(1), 21–25.

O'Dell, S. L., O'Quin, J., Alford, B. A., O'Briant, A. L., Bradlyn, A. S., & Biebenhain, J. E. (1982). Predicting the acquisition of parenting skills via four training models. *Behavior Therapy, 13*(2), 194–208.

Older, J. (1981). A restoring touch for abusing families. *Child Abuse & Neglect, 5*(4), 487–489.

Packard, T., Robinson, E. A., & Grove, D. C. (1983). The effect of training procedures on the maintenance of parental relationship building skills. *Journal of Clinical Child Psychology, 12*(2), 181–186.

Palmer, J. O. (1980). *The battered parent and how not to be one.* Englewood Cliffs, NJ: Prentice-Hall.

Patterson, G. R. (1974). Interventions for boys with conduct problems: Multiple setting, treatment and criteria. *Journal of Consulting and Clinical Psychology, 42,* 471–481.

Peterson, S. L., Robinson, A., & Littman, I. (1983). Parent–child interaction training for parents with a history of mental retardation. *Applied Research in Mental Retardation, 4*(4), 329–342.

Pevsner, R. (1982). Group parent training versus individual family therapy: An outcome study. *Journal of Behavior Therapy & Experimental Psychiatry, 13*(2), 119–122.

Pierce, R. M. (1973). Training in interpersonal communication skills with the partners of deteriorated marriages. *The Family Coordinator, 22,* 223–227.

Pizzo, P. (1983). *Parent to parent: Working together for ourselves and our children.* Boston: Beacon Press.

Rebman, V. L. (1983). The effect of parental attitudes and program duration upon parental participation patterns in a pre-school education program. *Child Study Journal, 13*(1), 57–71.

Resnick, J. L. (1981). Parent education and the female parent. *Counseling Psychologist, 9*(4), 55–62.

Rogers, T. R., Forehand, R., Griest, D. L., Wells, K. C., & McMahon, R. J. (1981). Socioeconomic status: Effects on parent and child behaviors and treatment outcome of parent training. *Journal of Clinical Child Psychology, 10*(2), 98–101.

Ross, A. O. (1981). Of rigor and relevance. *Professional Psychology, 12*(3), 318–327.

Rothenberg, B. A., Hitchcock, S. L., Harrison, M. S., & Graham, M. S. (1983). *Parentmaking: A practical handbook for teaching parent classes about babies and toddlers.* Menlo Park, CA: Banster Press.

Rowland, S. B., & Wampler, K. S. (1983). Black and white mothers' preferences for parenting programs. *Family Relations: Journal of Applied Family & Child Studies, 32*(3), 323–330.

Samuels, S. D. (1981). Parent ego states: Can a therapist take one to lunch? *Transactional Analysis Journal, 11*(1), 88–96.

Schlossman, S. (1976). Before home start: Notes toward a history of parent education in America, 1897–1929. *Harvard Educational Review, 46,* 436–467.

Schreibman, L. (1983). Are we forgetting the parent in parent training? *Behavior Therapist, 6*(6), 107–109.

Schultz, C. L., & Nystul, M. S. (1980). Mother–child interaction behavior as an outcome of theoretical models of parent group education. *Journal of Individual Psychology, 36*(1), 3–15.

Schultz, C. L., Nystul, M. S., & Law, H. G. (1980). Attitudinal outcomes of theoretical models of parent group education. *Journal of Individual Psychology, 36*(1), 16–28.

Scovern, A. W., Bukstel, L. H., Kilmann, P. R., Laval, R. A., Busemeyer, J., & Smith, V. (1980). Effects of parent counseling on the family system. *Journal of Counseling Psychology, 27,* 268–275.

Shaw, M. E., & Wright, J. M. (1967). *Scales for the measurement of attitudes.* New York: McGraw-Hill.

Shmukler, D., & Friedman, M. (1983). Clinical implications of the family systems model. *Transactional Analysis Journal, 13*(2), 94–96.

Shure, M. B., & Spivak, G. (1978). *Problem solving techniques in child rearing.* San Francisco: Jossey-Bass.

Simmons-Martin, A. (1983). Salient features from the literature, with implications for parent–infant programming. *American Annals of the Deaf, 128*(2), 107–117.

Simms, M. D. (1983). The foster parenting center: A multidisciplinary resource for special needs preschoolers. *Infant Mental Health Journal, 4*(2), 116–125.

Sinclair-Brown, W. A. (1982). TA redecision group psychotherapy treatment program for mothers who physically abuse and/or seriously neglect their children. *Transactional Analysis Journal, 12*(1), 39–45.

Singh, R., & Kaushik, S. S. (1982). Parent training techniques in acquisition and generalization of behavior modification skills to train the retardate. *Indian Journal of Clinical Psychology, 9*(2), 193–201.

Sirbu, W., Cotler, S., & Jason, L. A. (1978). Primary prevention: Teaching parents behavioral child rearing skills. *Family Therapy, 5*(2), 163–170.

Sirridge, S. T. (1980). Transactional analysis: Promoting OK'ness. In M. J. Fine (Ed.), *Handbook on parent education.* New York: Academic Press.

Stanley, S. F. (1978). Family education to enhance the moral atmosphere of the family and the moral development of adolescents. *Journal of Counseling Psychology, 25,* 110–118.

Stanley, S. F. (1980). The family and moral education. In R. L. Mosher (Ed.), *Adolescents' development and education: A Janus knot.* Berkeley: McCutchan.

Stern, H. H. (1960). *Parent education: An international survey.* Hamburg, Germany: UNESCO Institute for Education and Hull University.

Strom, R., Griswold, D., & Slaughter, H. (1981). Parental background: Does it matter in parent education? *Child Study Journal, 10*(4), 243–260.

Sunley, R. (1955). Early nineteenth century American literature on child rearing. In M. Mead & M. Wolfenstein (Eds.), *Childhood in contemporary cultures.* Chicago: University of Chicago, Phoenix Book.

Tavormina, J. B. (1980). Evaluation and comparative studies of parent education. In R. R. Abidin (Ed.), *Parent education and intervention handbook.* Springfield, IL: Thomas.

Wandersman, L. P. (1982). An analysis of the effectiveness of parent–infant support groups. *Journal of Primary Prevention, 3*(2), 99–115.

Webster-Stratton, C. (1981). Videotape modeling: A method of parent education. *Journal of Clinical Child Psychology, 10*(2), 93–98.

Webster-Stratton, C. (1982). Teaching mothers through videotape modeling to change their children's behavior. *Journal of Pediatric Psychology, 7*(3), 279–294.

Westin, J. (1981). *The coming parent revolution.* Chicago: Rand-McNally.

White House Conference on Child Health and Protection, Section III. (1932). Education and training committee on the family and parent education. *Parent Education: Types, Content and Method.* New York: Century.

Wilson, B. D. (1981). Doctoral dissertations on TA. *Transactional Analysis Journal, 11*(3), 194–202.

Wilson, G. (1981). Guided observation: A new program for parents of hearing-impaired children. *Volta Review, 83*(4), 236–239.

Witmer, H. L. (1936). Analysis of fellowship program of the National Council of Parent Education. *Parent Education, 2,* 16–19.

Wolf, M. C. (1983). Integrated family systems model for parent education. *Social Work in Education, 5*(3), 188–199.

Wolfenstein, M. (1951). The emergence of fun morality. *Journal of Social Issues, 7,* 15–25.

7

Programs for Premarital and Newlywed Couples

David G. Fournier
David H. Olson

Couples routinely experience serious conflicts early in their relationship and appear to lack the interpersonal skills required to satisfactorily resolve these problems. Although many factors influence early marital dissolution, lack of proper premarital preparation and an inability to adjust to the stresses which typically arise after marriage are clearly factors in divorce during the first few years.

Marriage and divorce rates in the United States have reached historic highs during the past decade. While many recognize that over one million individuals will end their marriage this year, few realize that nearly 300,000 of these persons will have been married for less than two years (U.S. National Center, 1984a).

In spite of these statistics, helping engaged couples prepare for the challenges of married life and helping young married couples cope with the adjustments and conflicts of marriage is mainly done by clergy and some family life educators. Marital and family therapists have generally avoided involvement with preventive programs which focus on the early identification and resolution of marital conflicts.

The purposes of this chapter are to (1) describe the context in which premarital and newlywed programs have developed; (2) identify issues for premarital programs; (3) describe the characteristics of several types of programs currently being offered; (4) summarize some of the existing research evaluating several of the programs; and (5) provide an example of a program that bridges premarital and marital stages. Since other chapters will address what Levant (1983) referred to as "skills-training approaches," particularly client-centered and behavioral approaches, this discussion will focus on other types of psychoeducational approaches.

Context for Premarital and Early Marriage Programs

Premarital and newlywed programs can serve to reduce the emotional pain and financial burden experienced by the over three million adults and children each year who directly experience divorce. Personal and interpersonal difficulties are also felt by family, friends, employers, schools, physicians, and others who come into direct contact with individuals undergoing the painful adjustment of divorce. In addition, the impact of marital dissolution is felt by government and legal institutions forced to process the caseload, social service agency personnel needed to counsel families, and the clergy, who often feel a tremendous obligation to prevent such events.

Numerous factors have evolved over time to increase the collective awareness about the need for better programs and services for engaged and newlywed couples. The remainder of this section will expand on (1) the social context for marriage and divorce and (2) the development of preventive programs by churches, educational institutions, and government agencies.

Societal Context

Unfortunately, preparing for marriage is often seen as of little importance by both couples and society. It is still easier to get a marriage license in most states than it is to get a driver's license. To obtain a driver's license, one needs to pass a test for vision, pass a written examination on driving rules and regulations, and be able to demonstrate ability to drive a car. We know, however, that being married is more difficult than driving a car, and more people are hurt by divorce than by car accidents. We should not be surprised, therefore, that about 40 percent of the couples marrying this year will eventually divorce.

While marriage rates have stabilized since a peak in 1972, divorce rates have increased steadily over the past 10 years, reaching and surpassing historical highs for this country. Trends for increased rates of marital dissolution can be attributed to a number of factors. These include (1) an increased personal and social acceptance of divorce as a viable method of ending unsatisfactory marriages; (2) a decrease in the influence of religious factors prohibiting divorce; (3) role shifts brought about by changing economic and political attitudes; and (4) decreased legal barriers to obtaining a divorce.

No-fault divorce laws initiated in the early 1970s were particularly potent factors in increasing rates of divorce. In addition to relaxed legal barriers, Norton and Glick (1976, p. 12) point out that "the phenomenal upsurge of divorce in this country during the last ten years has been stimulated by a growing acceptance of the principle that divorce is a reasonable, and at times desirable, alternative to an unhappy marriage."

In the 18-year period starting in 1960, marriage rates increased sharply (1962 to 1968) and then leveled off, while divorce rates have continued to increase dramatically, "reaching higher levels than ever previously recorded for this country" (Norton & Glick, 1976, p. 8). While divorces per year never exceeded one million prior to 1975, 1984 is expected to be the tenth consecutive year of more than one million divorces (U.S. National Center, 1984a, b).

Compared with an average of over two million marriages in a given year, the overall marriage to divorce ratio is 2:1 (U.S. National Center, 1984a). While this ratio is misleading in many ways (rates per 1,000 marriages are more stable), other methods of calculation also show dramatic increases. For example, in 1965 the divorce rate was 2.5 per 1,000 marriages. By 1976, rates had doubled to 5.0 per 1,000 marriages. While provisional statistics for 1982 indicate no increase in divorce per 1,000 marriages for the first time in a decade (U.S. National Center, 1984a), the rate of 5.4 per 1,000 in 1979 is a historical high for the United States (U.S. National Center, 1984b).

Marital dissolution for first marriages are considerably less than 50 percent with 35 to 40 percent being the most recent estimates (Norton & Glick, 1976). However, divorce rates are twice that high for first marriages that involve males married before age 20 and females married before age 18 (Norton & Glick, 1976). The median duration for marriages ending in 1979 was 6.5 years, similar to the totals for 1977 and 1978 but a full year less than the 7.5 recorded in 1963 (U.S. National Center, 1984b). Half of the 26 reporting areas in the above statistics indicated a median duration of 6.0 years or less. These figures reflect the occurrence of severe marital conflicts at points early in the development of the relationship.

An additional problem is that divorcing individuals are more likely to be parents than nonparents. The number of children annually involved in divorce more than doubled from 1960 to 1973 with respective totals of 463,000 and 1,079,000 (Bane, 1976). Using survey data on marital history to estimate children affected by marital disruption, Bane (1976) projects that 40 percent of all children may be affected in the next few decades. Current statistics estimate that *each divorce decree affects at least one child* (U.S. National Center, 1984b).

Marriage Preparation/Enrichment as Prevention

From a preventive perspective, it is essential to help couples get their relationship off to a good start. Research and clinical experience have consistently demonstrated that problems couples have during engagement are carried over into marriage (Fowers & Olson, 1983). In addition, couples develop new problems as they adjust to each other and to the experiences of married life. Therefore, unless couples learn ways of effectively dealing with their current problems, they will continue to develop more problems in their marriage and eventually feel overwhelmed and unable to cope.

High rates of marital dissolution have stimulated efforts designed to reverse current trends by helping couples better prepare for marriage (Olson, 1983). Preparation approaches currently include self-help reading, interviews with the clergy, formal educational programs (usually lasting four to eight weeks), structured group counseling programs, enrichment programs designed to increase interpersonal skills, and various types of premarital counseling. These approaches have been adopted by church groups, private educational programs, and specialized public agencies in an effort to prevent marital disruption by educating couples before problems become too severe.

Churches, schools, and government agencies have become involved in preventive programming because their daily routines are most affected by dissolving marriages. Churches typically begin the formal marriage process and then interact with couples in an ongoing relationship. Marital failures often create feelings of guilt in clergy because churches are perceived as responsible for reviewing the couple's readiness for marriage. Social service programs usually counsel couples and children who are feeling the emotional pain of separation and divorce. In summary, those involved prefer an anticipatory or preventive approach to one which merely reacts to problems that are beyond resolution.

The generally positive atmosphere of the relationship prior to marriage may also enhance a couple's ability to learn about communication skills when compared to more stressful times when marital problems become serious. Generally speaking, couples should learn that marriage is a process that takes time and energy. They need to know that, as in an occupation, they should invest time, energy, and money into their marriage if they want it to be successful. It would also be important for them to start off the marriage realizing that further enrichment, and perhaps counseling, might be necessary to keep their relationship a satisfying one for both partners.

The ultimate step in prevention of divorce is to help some couples see that it would be a disadvantage to get married at this particular time.

Churches, schools, and government agencies are intrinsically more interested in results which may help some couples decide to delay or even cancel their plans for marriage. Even if this end is not attained, couples probably will clarify their expectations about marriage and become more realistic about the difficulties and challenges of their married life together.

The development of premarital and marital enrichment services has not generally included professional marriage and family therapy (Stahmann & Hiebert, 1980; Wright, 1983). Therapists are seldom approached by engaged couples, and therapists often do not even see couples or families until the problems are so severe and pervasive that the relationship is all but over. However, some single clients who have been married and are considering remarriage are increasingly requesting premarital counseling.

Religious influences. The majority of marriages in the United States are still performed in a church. For this reason, clergy have had a certain level of control over engaged couples that is not available once a couple is married. For example, it is possible for church organizations to establish policies regarding marriage that require attendance in a marriage-preparation program that may include face-to-face discussions with a counselor or clergyperson (Doyle, 1980). The Pre Cana Programs developed by the Catholic Church are an example of large-scale marriage-preparation programs sponsored by a church (Boike, 1977). When couples desire a church wedding, they often become a captive audience for premarital preparation when they otherwise would not have sought these services.

Another influence from church groups is related to policymaking. Regin (1980) summarized several of the regulations enforced by marriage policies for 60 Catholic dioceses in the United States. These regulations include minimum ages for males and females; required time for marital preparation; mandatory premarital education/counseling program; requirements for completing a relationship assessment or evaluation; mandatory waiting periods; required counseling sessions; involvement of parents; restrictions on setting the wedding date; and the possibility that a decision could be made to deny a request for a church wedding.

These policies have increased the numbers of couples who have participated in premarital educational or counseling programs and made it possible to observe some of the effects of the programs. Considering that few couples voluntarily seek premarital counseling, religious policymaking has greatly increased the opportunities to develop and evaluate programs that can make an impact on young couples.

As long as clergy continue to accept responsibility for the preparation of couples they marry, churches will provide the main setting for offering premarital programs. Ministers pioneered the practice of premarital counseling and will continue to develop and test new models of preparation and enrichment (Schumm & Denton, 1979). While attempts from religious sources are often not linked with any theoretical orientation (Bagarozzi & Rauen, 1981), the determination to do a good job and the vast numbers of couples available for teaching and evaluation should improve the quality of church-sponsored programming.

Educational influences. The educational system has produced many efforts related to marriage preparation and enrichment. These contributions range from university courses on courtship and marriage to family life educators instructing high school students. Educational efforts were clearly evident in the 1930s (Burgess & Cottrell, 1938; Rockwood, 1935; Terman, 1938) and are still continuing (Avery, Ridley, Leslie, & Handis, 1979; Fournier, 1981; Sieber, 1984).

Researchers have been instrumental in identifying key variables for the study of marital relationships and in many instances have provided counselors with theoretical insights and normative information regarding marital behavior. Beginning with the efforts of Burgess and Cottrell (1938), Burgess and Wallin (1953), and Terman (1938), who tried to predict marital success during engagement, many colleges have set up formal coursework in marriage relationships for both couples and noncouples (Avery et al., 1979; Duvall, 1965; Gilles & Lastrucci, 1954; Luckey & Neubeck, 1956; Olson & Gravatt, 1968).

At the present time, most major universities offer courses in marriage preparation; and the National Council on Family Relations (NCFR) is instituting new guidelines for the certification of Family Life Educators which will standardize the credentials of educators and, to an extent, the content of the courses. These courses will be further described later in this chapter.

Government influences. The influence of state and local governments in marriage preparation is primarily in policymaking relative to guidelines for couples seeking marriage. The guidelines range from blood tests and standard license applications to mandatory premarital counseling and waiting periods as long as 90 days (Trainer, 1979).

The State of California began the process of regulation in 1970 as part of the first no-fault divorce law in this country (Skolnick, 1975). The law stated that couples under 18 seeking marriage must undergo premarital counseling before a license could be issued (Elkin, 1977). Provisions for counselors were not made in all counties in California, and it is still common for the majority of couples to receive counseling from their clergyperson.

In the 1970s, Michigan gave probate judges the option to require counseling for males under 18 and females under 16 (Rolfe, 1976). Itasca County, Minnesota, instituted a policy which mandated a 90-day waiting period, regardless of age, and set up a private educational program including marriage counseling, which it recommended to all applicants for marriage (Druckman, Fournier, Olson, & Robinson, 1981). These and other policies are being developed to counteract the expense which is incurred by government agencies when marriages fail.

Although efforts to legislate marriage preparation appear to be both justified and timely, specific decisions by churches and governments are often not based on systematic research and thus may be somewhat premature. Future studies need to assess the effectiveness of various policies and programs for premarital couples.

Issues in Premarital Programming

Developmental Tasks in Early Marriage

Couples routinely encounter situations or events which require adjustment or adaptation. Although each couple has unique strengths and weaknesses, all couples must resolve similar issues, often referred to as developmental tasks. Three articles address these tasks (Duvall, 1971; Rappoport, 1963; Rausch, Goodrich, & Campbell, 1975). Table 7-1 provides a visual summary of these three articles to allow similarities and differences to be identified.

The developmental tasks listed by these authors are relatively consistent and provide useful guidelines for counselors and educators working with premarital couples. These are also particularly helpful for marital counseling, since it is these tasks which probably account for much of the stress in the early years of marriage. The common tasks include *sexual relationship, communication, relations with relatives and friends, educational and work plans, finances, family planning,* and *roles.* Marriage-preparation programs and counseling procedures should, therefore, address these topics.

Conflicts in Early Marriage

Several studies since the early 1940s have attempted to identify the most common sources of marital tension. Goode (1956) investigated the marital complaints of female divorcees in Detroit and described the issues. Kitson and Sussman (1982) revised the Goode codes and used a carefully selected sample of both men and women. These results provide considerable insight into the reasons that husbands and wives ended their marriages.

Table 7-1 Developmental Tasks in Early Marriage

Duvall, 1971	Rausch et al., 1975	Rappoport, 1963
Establish satisfying sexual relations	Sexual relationship	Satisfactory sexual relationships
Establish relations with relatives	Relationship with partner's family	Satisfactory relations with relatives
Establish community & friend relations	Relationships with friends	Satisfactory relations with friends
Plans for possibility of children	Plans for future parenthood	Agreement about family planning
	Education, occupation, career plans	Satisfactory work pattern
Establish ways of getting and spending money	Handling of money	
	Situations of physical intimacy (nudity, dressing, sleeping, waking)	
Establish communication		Satisfactory system of communication
Establish workable philosophy of life	Religion, political, social values	
Establish home base	Establishing a household	Establishing a couple identity
Establish acceptable role patterns	Mealtime and role expectations	Patterns of decision making
		Planning wedding, honeymoon, etc.

Springer, Fournier, and Olson (1984) completed a study on recurring relationship conflicts on a purposive sample of 977 individuals at a variety of relationship stages. The 2,004 conflicts were codified according to *Intrapersonal, Interpersonal,* and *External* levels to allow for grouping consistent with levels related to family systems.

Fournier (1979) used these categories to summarize a representative sampling of 10 articles and books that deal with conflict in relationships. Table 7-2 presents a detailed list of actual conflicts found and identifies (in parentheses) the number of studies (out of 10) that mentioned that particular topic. By combining research and clinical observations about the issues most frequently encountered by young couples, these results provide important topics for programs in marital preparation and enrichment.

Challenges in Programming for Engaged Couples

The challenge for marriage preparation is developing procedures which promote an atmosphere conducive to *meaningful dialogue* between the couple (Olson, 1983). Every attempt should be made to provide couples with something concrete to work on. Given the proper atmosphere and clearly defined issues to discuss, couples will be forced to take a closer look at themselves prior to the actual wedding date.

The saying "love is blind" is indeed applicable to many premarital couples. They are often very unrealistic about their relationship and are convinced that whatever problems they have will go away after the wedding. As a result, most couples are not interested in spending time on relationship issues. These sentiments were well summarized by Lederer and Jackson (1968, p. 375): "One can learn as much about a possible husband or wife *before* marriage as ten years after. The unpleasant fact is that the people concerned frequently do not wish to do so."

Couple expectations are rarely realized in marriage because few couples possess the resources to meet the rigors of marriage (Ball, 1981; Hill & Aldous, 1964; Mace, 1982; Sager, 1976). In general, engaged couples tend to be very idealistic in their notions about marriage, and this attitude affects the manner in which couples prepare for marriage. Since most couples are extremely busy during engagement, it is not uncommon for them to spend more time getting ready for the one-hour ceremony than for the relationship that is supposed to last a lifetime.

Few engaged couples are aware of the extent to which their marital attitudes are similar and/or different from their partner's. In addition, couples usually are not aware of the various day-to-day challenges of married life. While it is often assumed that marriage comes naturally or that we have learned about the relationship from our parents, it is painfully obvious that marriage is not always easy. Engaged couples have few

Table 7-2 Summary of Problem Areas Mentioned in 10 Studies*

Derived Categories†	Content Categories
Intrapersonal Issues	
Personality‡	Personality (4); immature (1); unstable (1); jealous (2); dependency (2); intelligence (2); esteem (1)
Personal habits & health	Daily routines (1); physical problem (2); habits (2); drinking (1); health (2); personal freedom (1); neatness (1); violence (1); energy level (2)
Incompatible backgrounds	Religion (5); background differences (4); incompatible background (2)
Interests and values	Social and political values (1); value differences (1); interests and values (3); social life (2); social activities (2); values (2); recreation (3); spare time (1)
Expectations	Expectations (2)
Idealization	Conventionalization (1)
Interpersonal Issues	
Communication	Communication (6); decision making (1); relationship maintenance (1); affection (1)
Sex	Sexual relationship (7); extramarital sex (2); sex (3); affection (2)
Commitment	Commitment (1); couple identity (1)
Marital roles	Marital roles (5); household roles (2); internal role problems (1); external role problems (1)
Arguments	Arguments (1); power struggle (1); deal with anger (1); dominance (1); boredom (1); conflict resolution (2)
External Issues	
Relatives	Partner's family (1); relatives (2); parents (1); family (2); in-laws (3)
Friends	Friends (7); out with boys/girls (1)
Children	Children (4); parenthood (2); family planning (1); no sense of family (1)
Money	Handling money (4); money (3); saving (1); house (3)
Work	Career plans (2); work pattern (1); time together (2); work (2); job (1); vacation (2)

*Rausch, Goodrich, & Campbell (1975); Rappoport (1963); Kitson & Sussman (1982); Microys & Bader (1977); Hobart (1958); Hunt & Hunt (1977); Sager (1976); Mace (1982); Stahmann & Hiebert (1980); Springer, Fournier, & Olson (1984).
†Categories from Springer, Fournier, & Olson (1984).
‡Number after term indicates the number of times that concept was referred to in the 10 studies.

opportunities to observe other premarital or married couples. They do not see single friends as frequently and, likewise, do not quite fit in with married friends or parents. Because of this relative isolation, couples are eager to discuss marital topics with other engaged couples when given the opportunity.

So while premarital couples are theoretically at a "teachable moment" in terms of helping them learn a great deal about themselves and each other, in practice they represent a "tough nut to crack." Any effective premarital program must, therefore, help them become more aware of their relationship issues and motivate them to begin working early, before their problems become too serious.

Some specific goals for programs for engaged couples should include (1) making couples more aware of strengths and potential problems; (2) helping couples more realistically perceive marital challenges; (3) increasing couple communication and developing effective skills for resolving conflicts; and (4) motivating couples to further enrich their relationships whenever the need is recognized.

Characteristics of Premarital Programs

Although hundreds of programs have been developed by churches, schools, and a variety of professionals to meet the needs mentioned above, most are very informal and have never been documented for wider distribution. The purposes of this section are (1) to describe three types of premarital and newlywed programs and (2) to identify and describe some of the key structural characteristics among programs.

Numerous programs have been developed for premarital and early marital counseling, and the structural characteristics of these programs are diverse (Bagarozzi & Rauen, 1981; Druckman et al., 1981; Norem, Schaefer, Springer, & Olson, 1980; Schumm & Denton, 1979). Table 7-3 provides an overview of the characteristics of programs categorized according to the thrusts of family life education, instructional counseling, and enrichment. An attempt has been made to provide readers with a bibliography of published resources for a sample of representative programs in each group. Some programs are described in more detail in other chapters of this book, while others are discussed in the above-mentioned review articles.

Types of Premarital Programs

Programs for premarital couples and newlyweds can be classified into the four basic approaches identified by Schumm and Denton (1979). These include (1) family life education courses; (2) instructional counseling; (3) enrichment; and (4) counseling. Since most couples do not seek therapeutic counseling in the early stages of marriage, the components which describe programs will involve primarily education, instructional counseling, and enrichment.

Family life education courses are typically offered in high schools and colleges and involve instruction in topics associated with marriage and family life. These courses usually last 6 to 20 weeks and include the reading of textbooks and facilitation by a teacher. *Instructional counseling* usually refers to programs which combine an educational and counseling format. Couples may be asked to read instructional materials or view videotapes or films and then take part in some type of group or individual counseling experience. *Enrichment* programs often refer to programs designed for couples who are functioning satisfactorily in their marriage but who may wish to more fully reach their potentials for further growth and development. Couples in need of marriage counseling are usually discouraged from attending an enrichment program. Counseling at the premarital stage is less often used because of the intense time commitment. The structural aspects of these types of programs will be described next.

Teaching Methods

Premarital programs utilize a wide range of methods to help young couples. Perhaps the most common method is the didactic approach or *lecture* even though it probably is the least effective. Lectures are usually the method of choice for programs involving a large number of couples. When 30 or more couples atttend a session, other approaches may be too cumbersome. Lectures are often held weekly and cover topics such as communication, sexuality, finances, values, roles, and conflict resolution. Many types of programs may include a lecture or two, but studies have suggested that total reliance on lectures is not very effective (Norem et al., 1980).

Another popular method of instruction in marriage programs is *group discussion*. Recently many church-sponsored and educational programs have organized workshops where couples have an opportunity to discuss marital issues with each other. Unlike lectures, discussion groups allow couples to become actively involved in the process of stating their views on marital topics and, perhaps more important, listening to how others' views might be similar or different. Since engaged couples have few opportunities to discuss these topics, most appreciate the opportunity to observe how others handle the same issues they are experiencing. Group discussions may take a counseling focus, with trained leaders and stated goals that allow for conflicts to be discussed and resolved in the group.

A method seldom used which usually involves direct input by a trained facilitator is *modeling*. Modeling requires a facilitator to behave or act in a manner which is observed and perhaps practiced by couples in the program. Examples of topics which can be modeled include positive eye contact, listening skills, role reversal, and conflict resolution. *Role playing* hypothetical or actual couple situations is also a form of modeling and may be used to illustrate common problems and misunderstandings.

Table 7-3 Characteristics of Various Premarital Programs

Structural Characteristics	Family Life Education	Instructional Counseling	Enrichment
Teaching methods	Didactic, lectures, small groups, some experiential	Lectures, group discussions, role playing, modeling, experiential, skill-enhancement training, some therapeutic counseling	Private reflections, couple dialogues, some small groups
Training of facilitators	College degree for college and high school programs	Varies greatly, skill programs usually have certified instructors, instructional programs may use untrained volunteers	Varies greatly, usually trained in facilitating a structured program, some untrained volunteers
Goals and objectives	Impart general knowledge about marriage	Specific goals unique to each program, skill development, increase awareness and preparedness	Help couples explore their relationship, share inner feelings
Range of topics	Broad coverage of topics usually comprehensive	Varies greatly, programs tend to be narrowly focused for depth of coverage, some programs are comprehensive	Limited to what couples decide to work on
Time frame	Long term, 15–20 weeks up to 50 hours total	Varies, skills training between 10 and 20 hours, instructional between 5 and 25 hours, usually short term	Few sessions, usually marathons over a weekend
Timing of program	Usually early in the relationship, dating couples and individuals	Later in relationship development, engaged and married couples	Engaged couples have encountered enrichment groups but most are for married couples

Types of couples	Generally no restrictions	Depends on program, some for teens, handicapped, certain religious groups, stable couples, others not restricted	Designed for couples who do not have serious problems
Couple risk	Low risk, not usually confrontive	Moderate to high risk, couples may be asked to speak in groups or could be denied permission to marry	Low to moderate, couples control the topics discussed and may choose low levels of disclosure
Use of assessment	Marital attitude assessments are sometimes used	Most programs do not use formal assessments, some programs are built around assessments	Depends on program, formal assessment is not a common feature
Some representative references	Avery, Ridley, Leslie, & Handis (1979); Fournier (1981); Sieber (1984); Duvall (1965)	D'Augelli, Deyss, Guerney, Hershenberg, & Sborofsky (1974); Nickols, Fournier, and Nickols (1984), Boike (1977), Freeman (1965), Glendening & Wilson (1972), Olson, Fournier, & Druckman (1980), McRae (1975), Microys & Bader (1977), Miller, Nunnally, & Wackman (1976), Ridley, Avery, Harrell, Leslie, & Dent (1982), Most & Guerney (1983)	Growth in Marriage for Newlyweds, Thompson & Thompson, 1980; Engaged Encounter; ACME by Mace (1983); Rolfe (1975, 1983)

A method used in several enrichment programs is referred to as *private reflections*. Individuals (or couples) are asked to think about specific topics and to record their ideas in writing. These reflections often involve feelings during certain relationship events which are intended to produce insights. These reflections are often followed by *couple dialogues* (private or group), which ask couples to share their private thoughts with the goal of increasing understanding.

Another group of methods could be referred to as *experiential techniques*. These could include actual skills-training or other tasks designed to provide a teachable moment for couples. These experiences could be a part of the program or a type of homework assignment. The experiential procedures are usually designed to create a common frame of reference for couples to discuss what they internalized and learned from the task. Experiential approaches allow for direct observation and feedback which can provide extremely useful insights for a couple. Video and audio equipment can enhance the feedback process by allowing couples to observe themselves in action.

Skill building in the areas of communication and problem solving are seldom used with premarital couples. However, those that have attempted such programs have demonstrated positive change in the couple's skill levels (Most & Guerney, 1983; Ridley, Avery, Harrell, Hayes-Clements, & McCunney, 1983; Ridley, Avery, Harrell, Leslie, & Dent, 1982; Ridley, Jorgensen, Morgan, & Avery, 1982).

A final method used with premarital couples is *counseling*. Counseling could be incorporated into an instructional program as a supplemental service for couples or could be used as the exclusive method of working with couples. Although this is a rare approach for engaged couples, it is becoming more common for couples where one or both had been previously married.

Training of Facilitators

Individuals with a wide range of experience and background often conduct preparation-for-marriage programs. Some programs are run by highly skilled licensed practitioners with years of experience, while others are run by well-intentioned individuals with little or no training. Compounding this problem is the fact that current articles on marriage can be found in theology, medicine, law, counseling and social psychology, applied sociology, and other interdisciplinary sources. This diversity has proved both beneficial and harmful to the delivery of premarital counseling services.

Since articles appear in diverse locations and disciplines, it is highly probable that most of these resources are never read by the majority of individuals who could benefit. This is particularly true when it is considered that the clergy performs the vast majority of all premarital preparation. As a group, the clergy range in counseling skills from rather sophisticated to untrained. In addition, time demands usually make it difficult for the clergy to keep in touch with new advances. When programs involve formal counseling or specialized skill training, it is important that the credentials of the facilitator match the intended goals of the program. Less ambitious programs could use paraprofessional or volunteer help.

Goals, Objectives, and Philosophy

Stated goals and objectives vary greatly from program to program (Bagarozzi & Rauen, 1981). Some programs do specify intended outcome, but others are so vague that they cannot be effectively evaluated by a potential user. The sponsor of the program usually determines the basic program orientation or philosophy. Religious-sponsored programs may cover several marital topics, but religion and spirituality are an essential theme. Educational programs range from specialized training programs, such as increasing communication skills, to general programs designed to increase couple knowledge and awareness in a number of topic areas not limited to specific skill areas.

Bagarozzi and Rauen (1981) pointed out that many programs were *not* based on a theoretical model of relationship development and change and were thus not as consistent or structured in their philosophy. Programs without specific goals, objectives, and/or theoretical orientation are more difficult to evaluate. Some common goals for programs are (1) to help partners clarify their expectations of each other and marriage; (2) to train couples to negotiate contracts of agreement; (3) to provide problem-solving skills to couples; (4) to increase awareness of couples' patterns of communication; (5) to help couples become more realistic; (6) to provide information about important marital topics (i.e., finances); (7) to help couples express feelings more openly; and (8) to counsel couples about individual contributions to dyadic interaction.

Range of Topics Covered

The variety of topics addressed within a program depends upon the stated goals and objectives. Since family life education programs are mostly didactic, it is crucial that they cover numerous topics, preferably many of those mentioned in Table 7-2. Skills-training programs are more effective when they cover one or two topics in depth rather than try to cover too much. Instructional counseling programs usually address several topics (6 to 10) which tend to reflect process-oriented issues such as communication and conflict resolution.

Time Frame

Programs differ markedly in the amount of time required for completion and in the structuring of the time that is allotted. For example, a program may require 12 hours of participation. This may be done in one marathon meeting or in six weekly two-hour sessions. This distinction is important because studies suggest that programs spread out over longer periods of time produce more change than those of one or two sessions. Considering that couples come to programs with 20 or more years of family and relationship experience, it is not surprising that one-day programs are not able to make appreciable changes in attitudes or behavior. The actual hours involved in various programs ranges from nearly 50 hours in family life education programs to less than 5 hours in some types of premarital programs. High school and college courses with 50 hours of instruction across 15 or so weeks have produced relatively impressive *attitude* changes in couples and individuals. Intensive counseling or skills-training programs are usually more effective in changing actual *behaviors* in the areas focused on by the program.

Timing of the Program

Research is beginning to demonstrate that the timing of when programs are offered may be very critical in determining the effectiveness. For example, evidence is mounting that any type of marriage-preparation program becomes less effective as the couple gets closer to the wedding date. Preparation 6 to 12 months prior to marriage is much more likely to succeed than preparation one month from the wedding. Avery et al. (1979) compared couples versus noncouples who took a family relations class and found that the couples studied more, were more motivated and interested in the course, and found it to be more relevant to them.

Relationships appear to go through a predictable pattern. Couples often appear to go from extreme optimism and idealism during engagement, to pessimism and realism during severe marital crises. Engaged couples often focus on relationship strengths (as though weaknesses do not exist), while married couples often fixate on marital problems and dissatisfactions (and seem to take for granted or forget about the things that are working in their relationship).

Studies that have been done provide insight into what might be considered a couple's "most teachable moments" and have increased interest in *post-wedding* counseling and education. Guldner (1971) found that couples seen *six months after marriage* were more open to counseling than were couples before or at one or three months after marriage. Baum (1978) found that his marital enrichment program was more effective with cohabiting and married couples than with engaged couples. Bader, Microys, Sinclair, Willett, & Conway (1980) found that post-wedding sessions were not only perceived by the couples as more helpful but also appeared to significantly improve conflict-resolution skills, whereas the premarital sessions did not.

While premarital programs can have impact on a couple before marriage, early marital follow-ups may be best held after six months of marriage. Enrichment or counseling approaches need to begin while the relationship is still stable rather than waiting until one partner is ready to end the relationship. A newlywed program which emphasizes the *critical first year* was developed by David and Vera Mace with Doris and Jerry Thompson (1980) in Kansas City. The program requires couples to sign up before marriage and the couple participates in couple groups after marriage. While the program has a workbook (Thompson & Thompson, 1980), the program has not been evaluated to date.

Use of Assessment

A structural component of programs is the presence or absence of objective testing or assessment. Assessments can be helpful diagnostic aids prior to commencement of the program, facilitate insights for discussion during programs, and provide measures of change after the program is completed. Helping couples to identify their unique strengths and weaknesses early in the program serves to enhance their motivation for participating and to recognize any progress which they have made.

Measurement problems in premarital counseling are difficult given the issues that impinge on both couples and counselors. This difficulty has contributed to what Stahmann and Barclay-Cope (1977) describe as an effort by many counselors to use "various inventories and questionnaires in an attempt to provide specific assessment and feedback to [their] clients. The majority of these inventories are developed specifically by counselors for their own clinical use and are not published or standardized" (p. 298). The problem becomes one of having a number of different instruments which have questionable utility and a lack of empirical validation.

An additional problem was identified by Cromwell, Olson, and Fournier (1976) when a major review of diagnostic measures in marriage and family counseling revealed only a few techniques that were specifically designed for premarital couples. Fournier (1979) critiqued tools considered appropriate for premarital diagnosis and found at least one of the following methodological problems with each technique: (1) exclusive reliance on the self-report of individuals; (2) a limited range of issues related to marital concerns; (3) a value position or bias implicit in the instrument; (4) inability to assess couple interaction; and (5) lack of information regarding reliability and validity for young couples.

It is the authors' contention that a reliable and valid diagnostic assessment of a couple's attitudes about important content areas in marriage would provide enough specific information to confront crucial issues *prior* to starting a preparation program. Armed with objective information about strengths, weaknesses, and the degree of idealization, it will be easier to *design preparation programs around the specific needs of participating couples.* This will ensure that programming decisions made by educators and counselors will be systematically determined and probably more relevant for couples.

A recent study clearly demonstrated the value of using some type of *premarital inventory* with couples (Druckman et al., 1981). The premarital inventory used was PREPARE, which is a 125-item inventory that assesses 12 content areas such as idealism, communication, conflict resolution, finances, and expectations. This inventory was administered by counselors and clergy to the premarital couples. The couples' answer sheets were scored, and a 12 to 15 page computer printout was sent to the clergyperson or counselor, who then interpreted the results.

The research clearly demonstrated that using PREPARE was more effective than traditional sessions with clergy or the group sessions offered to premarital couples. When PREPARE was used in combination with four intensive premarital counseling sessions by a trained marriage counselor, there was some additional benefit but not much more than was obtained from having couples simply take PREPARE and having one feedback session. This finding demonstrates the effectiveness of a premarital inventory in facilitating dialogue between a couple.

Evaluation of Premarital Preparation

While educational and counseling intervention in marriage preparation has been established for many years, several factors have contributed to slow progress in identifying the relative effectiveness of various components and approaches. Giblin, Sprenkle, & Sheehan (1985) reviewed 23 enrichment studies with premarital couples, married couples, and families. Using meta-analysis to assess the results across studies, he found the following effect sizes: premarital (.526), marital (.419), and family (.545). An effect size of .44 indicates that the person gained more than 67 percent of those who had no program. This demonstrates that premarital programs have at least as much of an impact as marital enrichment programs.

Of the few evaluation studies that have been conducted and reported on premarital and marital enrichment, most exhibited one or more methodological problems that severely limit the confidence that can be placed in the results (Bagarozzi & Rauen, 1981; Gurman & Kniskern, 1977; Hof &

Miller, 1981). Some of these problems include (1) lack of comparable control groups to determine whether change is due to the marriage preparation program or to normal couple maturation processes; (2) assessments that included only subjective self-reports of satisfaction with the program rather than more objective measures of change; (3) evaluations based on very short periods of time that are not reflective of long-term effect; (4) measures that do not have established research credibility or evidence of reliability and validity; and (5) research designs that lack the sophistication to isolate the comparative effectiveness of different programs.

One factor in the slow research progress has been the isolated, atheoretical, and individualistic manner in which the majority of premarital programs are developed and offered. Since approximately 80 percent of marriage preparation is done by the clergy, it is not surprising that individuals tend to counsel in ways that have proven to be personally useful and comfortable. For the clergy, these methods range from highly sophisticated and systematic counseling procedures to seat-of-the-pants authoritarianism with high levels of value bias. The difference in training and skill for this very important group is further compounded by a generally busy work load and few opportunities for discussion with peers about better methods of premarital intervention.

Although a number of approaches to premarital preparation have been advanced in detail (Clinebell, 1975; Gangsei, 1971; Mace, 1982; Olson, Fournier, & Druckman, 1980; Peterson, 1964; Rutledge, 1966; Trainer, 1979), most evaluated programs were found to be less effective than initially intended (Boike, 1977; Garland, 1981; Guldner, 1971; Norem et al., 1980; Oussoren, 1972). In general, couples interviewed after marriage remember very little about the premarital program or did not follow through with the procedures after the program was completed.

While results based on lectures were discouraging, some studies did document couple improvements as a result of premarital preparation. Changes were particularly noticeable in the area of *communication-skills* training. Studies that did utilize adequate control groups seem to produce some positive results. Most aspects of relationships seem to improve, but other areas appear to deteriorate or stay the same (Bader et al., 1980; Ginsberg & Vogelsong, 1977; Markman, 1980; Miller, Nunnally, & Wackman, 1976; Most & Guerney, 1983). Evaluations relied upon the couple's subjective report of satisfaction with the premarital-preparation program or with their global assessment of marital happiness. Most studies assessed couples only immediately following the program or the wedding and failed to examine change over time. With very few exceptions, the majority of premarital evaluation studies do not really compare and contrast the effectiveness of alternative programming strategies.

The most systematic study was conducted in Canada by Bader et al.

with a one-year (1980) and five-year follow-up (Bader, Riddle, & Sinclair, 1981). This study clearly demonstrated the superiority of an experiential program in which couples have dialogue over a lecture format. The program consisted of four sessions before marriage and three sessions which began six months after marriage. Their studies included behavioral and self-report assessment one year after marriage (Bader et al., 1981). In general, positive change increased over time for the treatment group while no change occurred for the control group. The treatment group increased their ability to resolve conflict, increased the seeking of outside resources for their marriage, and maintained higher levels of positive feelings compared to the control group.

The quality of research evaluating premarital programs needs to be improved so that practitioners can have confidence in the comparative benefits and liabilities of specific programs. Gurman and Kniskern (1981) have offered useful guidelines for doing outcome research on therapeutic intervention, and several issues are particularly relevant for premarital evaluations. For example, outcome assessments made immediately following a program will not address the issue of whether a program has long-term positive affects after marriage. Few studies attempt to ask couples who have decided not to marry to elaborate on their reasons. A more difficult issue is the adequacy of outcome measures. Assessments should tap behavioral as well as self-report perspectives from both individuals, the couple, and the program facilitator. These vantage points will provide more detail for a comprehensive evaluation of program impact.

The remainder of this section will summarize in more detail research studies on premarital preparation. Although there are admitted weaknesses, several important trends emerge to help guide future research and programming. The discussion will focus on studies involving religious programs, comparative studies of both theoretical and atheoretical programs, and studies of skill-oriented programs.

Church Programs

Church-related programs are difficult to summarize because they range from highly sophisticated and skill-oriented programs to very superficial lecture-oriented programs with heavy value bias. Research results are also mixed concerning these programs. In general, many religious-sponsored programs were not as effective as the developers intended. Although many factors influence these findings, they have been compounded when church motivations for becoming involved in preparation are examined. For example, churches have an investment in the continuation of their denomination, and this usually means that counseling sessions will involve "permission from the pastor to get married, instructions on the nature of the church marriage, instruction on the nature of the wedding service and instruction on . . . religious life" (Stahmann & Barclay-Cope, 1977, p. 29). And as Microys and Bader (1977, p. 3) pointed out, church premarriage courses "often defined marriage according to middle class values . . . [that both] confuse and alienate" other social groups. A Canadian clergyman reviewing church-related programs concluded that present systems are inadequate and not geared to the needs of the couples involved (Oussoren, 1972).

Guldner (1971) interviewed couples six months after the wedding and found that most individuals could remember very little or nothing about premarital sessions with their clergyman. Clinebell (1975) also commented on the overall lack of effectiveness in some of the approaches utilized by the clergy. Boike (1977, p. 3084) found "no evidence of significant impact of a Pre-Cana Program on communication process."

It would be simple to say that all premarital counseling should be done by trained counselors and clergymen. However, the fact is that the clergy are in the best position to reach and have an impact on premarital couples. When given choices between clergy and other counseling services, 66.6 percent of all "minors" married in California in 1976 chose church-related counseling (County of Los Angeles, 1977). As Skolnick (1975) pointed out, part of the reason for this trend is that several clergymen required only one session instead of the three to four sessions recommended by State of California guidelines. Thus, it seems obvious that new efforts should be made to develop continuing education programs for the clergy and assessment tools that can be effectively used by most clergymen. Since preparation for marriage is usually an educational as well as a counseling experience, there is no reason why the clergy cannot become more involved in evaluating the effectiveness of currently utilized approaches.

A recent study by Wright (1981) indicated that eight intensive premarital counseling sessions with couples were of benefit. After surveying 1,000 couples after marriage, he found that those who had at least six premarital sessions felt they benefited from the experience, while those who had fewer sessions did not find the experience so beneficial.

Results of church-sponsored programs with more structured goals and skills training often equal or surpass other programs (Bader et al., 1980; Nickols, Fournier, & Nickols, 1984). The critical factors appear to be structurally based rather than being due simply to sponsorship.

Premarital Lectures versus Experiential Programs

Bagarozzi and Rauen (1981) summarized the characteristics of 13 programs and concluded that most programs tended to be "atheoretical in their approach to intervention, loosely designed, and nonspecific as to their goals" (p. 13). In addition, many of the programs were not objectively evaluated, which leaves unresolved the basic question of the effectiveness of these programs in producing positive change in couples. Even though basic methodological problems exist, the research on these types of programs has been particularly insightful in terms of comparative analysis. Since the majority of programs seem to fall into this category, the results can offer suggestions which are likely to make immediate contributions to program effectiveness.

Research which evaluates family life education courses consistently identifies significant *attitude change* for individuals and couples (Avery et al., 1979; Duvall, 1965; Gilles & Lastrucci, 1954; Olson & Gravatt, 1968; Sieber, 1984). Although these courses are usually atheoretical, they are often comprehensive in coverage of marital topics, and the long-term nature of the teaching process allows individual attitudes to be confronted, modified, and reinforced across time. Short-term programs have less time to make key points and less time for thorough coverage of important topics.

Several studies have been done on the effectiveness of lecture programs. McRae (1975) compared a behavioral group approach to a lecture-discussion approach and found no major differences in outcome. Microys and Bader (1977) compared three different types of premarital programs: (1) a small-group counseling approach; (2) a lecture-format premarital education series; and (3) a premarital weekend program. The lecture format was found to be the least effective, and the small group counseling program was regarded as the most effective. However, no single approach was found to be dramatically more effective than the other.

A more systematic study of the effectiveness of lecture programs (Norem et al., 1980) evaluated the five different premarital programs which ran from six to eight weeks. Although these programs were well conceived and the lectures well presented, no attitude change was produced as a result. It is clear that large lecture courses are not effective for premarital couples, no matter how well the lectures are presented. One of the negative outcomes of the lecture format was that it discouraged most couples from considering future marriage enrichment programs. It also decreased couples' willingness to go to marriage counseling if marriage problems occurred in their relationship. In other words, these lectures disappointed rather than excited them in terms of the need for, and value of, future marriage enrichment and counseling.

These studies suggest that *lecture formats should be deemphasized* and that small-group discussion groups may offer couples a greater chance to become involved in the process. Another conclusion is that programs should be longer rather than shorter so that changes have a chance to stabilize.

Skill-enhancement Programs

Research on skill-development programs has been more consistent and prevalent. Giblin et al. (1984) completed a comprehensive meta-analysis on enrichment programs and found that the skill-building programs had the greatest impact. Programs which focused on facts, theories, and surveys had little impact on actual couple interaction, while programs which utilized counseling techniques and focused on aspects of couple behaviors did affect relationships. Process-oriented programs have also been found helpful by Avery, Ridley, Leslie, and Mulholland (1980), Gleason and Prescott (1977), and D'Augelli, Deyss, Guerney, Hershenberg, and Sborofsky (1974).

Although the question of long-term benefit skill programs still needs more systematic research, the short-term benefits have been consistently documented. Giblin et al. (1984) found that Guerney's Relationship Enhancement (RE) program proved to be very effective (effect size of .96) while Miller et al.'s (1976) Couples Communication (CC) program and Marriage Encounter were both generally effective (effective size of .44 and .42, respectively).

A series of systematic studies by Bernard Guerney (1977) has clearly demonstrated the effectiveness of their Relationship Enhancement program for both marital and premarital couples (Avery et al., 1980; Ginsberg & Vogelsong, 1977; Most & Guerney, 1983; Ridley et al., 1982). Ridley et al. (1982) clearly demonstrated that the Relationship Enhancement program increased the premarital couple's empathy and self-disclosure skills and also increased their positive feeling about the relationship. A six-month follow-up of these couples demonstrated that most of the skills persisted even though they dropped considerably from where they were right after the program was completed (Avery et al., 1980).

In addition to demonstrating that premarital couples can learn communication skills, Ridley et al. (1983) indicated that they can also learn problem-solving and conflict-resolution skills. They developed an eight-week program in which couples were trained on how to use problem-solving skills in their relationship. A six-month follow-up of these couples also demonstrated that these problem-solving skills can be learned and do persist over time (Ridley et al., 1983). Like the communication skills, couples' abilities to use the problem-solving steps diminishes after they have completed the program, but it is still considerably higher than before they took the program. A behaviorally oriented program called Premarital Relationship Enhancement Program (PREP) developed by Markman (1980) also has potential value in building a couple's relationship skill.

Programming Guidelines Based on Research Studies

The research identifies several factors which appear to have an impact on the effectiveness of premarital programs. Based on these findings, the following recommendations appear to be justified (Fournier, 1981):

1. Facilitators should incorporate *inventories* which would provide couples with specific information about their *relationship strengths and weaknesses* as early as possible in the program.
2. *Small-group discussions* should be used whenever feasible and *lectures avoided.*
3. Programs should last *several weeks* rather than be one-day programs.
4. *Timing of programs* should be at least *six months before* the wedding since couples are less open and more distracted as the wedding date nears. Ideally, premarital preparation should start *one year* before marriage.
5. Premarital programs should prime couples so that they will participate in marital programs. Ideally, this should be *several sessions before and after marriage.*
6. Programs should provide basic *relationship skills* such as skills in speaking, listening, decision making, and conflict resolution.

PREPARE: Program for Premarital Couples

Recent reviews of assessment tools revealed few diagnostic measures designed specifically for engaged couples (Cromwell, Olson, & Fournier, 1976; Fournier, 1979). Fournier (1979) used 13 criteria for evaluating assessment tools and concluded that the development of new and more reliable and valid procedures for premarital couples was needed. Olson, Fournier, and Druckman (1980) developed the PREmarital Personal And Relationship Evaluation (PREPARE) inventory to meet the methodological and clinical needs expressed by counselors and clergy.

The PREPARE program consists of the PREPARE inventory, couple feedback session, and couple dialogue. The impetus for the development of the PREPARE program was the general weakness of most premarital instruments in providing counselors and educators with a systematic and objective assessment of personal and relationship issues. The objective nature of PREPARE inventory was intended to reduce the guesswork characteristic of premarital education by identifying specific *target issues* of relevance to each couple. Feedback sessions in which couples discuss PREPARE results provide an opportunity to probe important issues frequently encountered in marriage. A goal in constructing PREPARE was to have a procedure that enhances the ability of counseling professionals to aid premarital couples in evaluating their own readiness for marriage. PREPARE results were designed to be maximally useful for counselors attempting to clarify potential problem issues and to identify specific relationship strengths and weaknesses. Results also provide information that indicates how couples compare with similar couples who have also taken PREPARE. Individual and couple scores are provided on 12 important content areas considered problematic for married couples. These 12 areas are *idealism, realistic expectations, personality issues, communication, conflict resolution, financial management, leisure activities, children and marriage, family and friends, sexual relationship, equalitarian roles,* and *religious orientations.*

The major goals of PREPARE are to:

1. Identify the extent to which relationship partners *agree* and *disagree* with each other for all 12 of the categories in PREPARE and for the entire PREPARE procedure.
2. Compare *individual adjustment scores* and *couple agreement scores* to normative data with other premarital couples.
3. Identify and list *each* item for all 12 categories where couple *disagreement* exists.

The above information can be used to identify a number of potentially problematic issues usually not considered by premarital couples. This framework is also useful because items provide a common frame of reference about important marital topics. This frame of reference not only facilitates communication between relationship partners but also promotes dialogue between the counselor and the couple.

The reliability and validity of PREPARE is very good, as is described in greater detail elsewhere (Fournier, Olson, & Druckman, 1983; Olson et al., 1980). It is one of few marital inventories that has demonstrated high levels of predictive validity (Fowers & Olson, 1983).

To test the predictive validity of PREPARE, a study was conducted to assess how well PREPARE scores could discriminate between couples who are happily married from those who were unhappily married, separated, or divorced. Couples were identified who had taken PREPARE and later ended up being happily married or unhappily married. These couples had been married an average of two years and had taken PREPARE about three or four months before marriage. There were 148 couples (296 individuals) in this study composed of 59 happily married couples; 53 unhappily married, separated, or divorced couples; and 36 couples who had canceled their wedding.

PREPARE proved to be very accurate at predicting marital success in these couples (Fowers & Olson, 1983). Using PREPARE scores (individual, positive couple agreement, and background), it was possible to predict with 86 percent accuracy those couples that eventually got divorced and, with 78 percent accuracy, those couples who were happily married. The average prediction rate for both groups was 81 percent. The PREPARE categories that were most predictive of marital success were *realistic expectations, personality issues, communication, conflict resolution,* and *religious orientation.* Couples who had relationship strengths in these categories had a higher probability of being happily married and those who had these as weak areas had a higher probability of being unhappily married.

One surprising finding was that *idealistic distortion* was high in both groups of couples and did not discriminate between the unsuccessful and successful marriages. In other words, it appears that all premarital couples are idealistic and often see their relationship through rose-colored glasses. This idealism is simply a general characteristic of all premarital couples and is caused by the fact that they are "romantically in love."

Another significant finding concerned premarital couples who took PREPARE and later decided not to marry. About 10 percent of the couples who took PREPARE eventually decided to delay or cancel their wedding. In comparing these couples with the unsuccessful and successful groups, it appears that couples who delayed were very similar to those who later got divorced and very different from those that were happily married. This indicates that couples who canceled their wedding made a good choice because they would have had a high probability of ending up being unhappily married. PREPARE, therefore, provides a useful preventive function by helping some couples decide not to marry who have a high probability of divorce.

These results clearly demonstrate that PREPARE has high predictive validity. They also demonstrate that the manner in which couples describe their relationship on PREPARE before marriage is very predictive of whether they will succeed later in their marriage. It should be remembered, however, that these are extreme groups and that the accuracy in predicting success would probably be less for couples in general. It also should be stressed that these predictions were made using complex statistical methods, and predictions should *not* be made for individual couples.

A sample of a PREPARE Couple Profile is illustrated in Table 7-4. This summary indicates the *male* and *female scores* and *positive couple agreement* scores on the 11 categories. For each content category, a detailed summary for the 10 items is provided. An example of this item summary for the "Communications" category is illustrated in Table 7-5. It identifies the specific items for the couple where there are *special focus* items (where both agree about a problem), *indecision,* and *positive couple agreement.*

Table 7-4 Prepare Couple Profile

	Male and Female Revised Scores	*Percent Positive Couple Agreement*
	0---10---20---30---40---50---60---70---80---90---100	
REALISTIC EXPECTATIONS	MMMMMMMMM 22 FFFFFFFFFFFFFFFFFFFFFFFFFFFFFFFF 80	10
PERSONALITY ISSUES	MMMMMMMMMMMMMMMMMMM 45 FFFFF 10	20
COMMUNICATION	MMMMMMMMMMMMMMMMMMMMMMMMM 52 FFFFFFFFFFFFFF 30	50
CONFLICT RESOLUTION	MMMMMMMMMMMMMMMMMMMMMMMMMMMMMMMM 67 FFFFFFFFFFFFFFFF 39	50
FINANCIAL MANAGEMENT	MMMMMMMMM 21 FFFFFF 17	20
LEISURE ACTIVITIES	MMMMMMMMMMMMMMMMMMMMMMMMMMMMMMMMMMMMMMMMMMMM 92 FFFFFFFFFFFFFFFFFFFFFFFFFFFFFFFFFF 75	80
SEXUAL RELATIONSHIP	MMMMMMMMMMMMMMMMM 43 FFFFFFFFFFFFFFFFFF 45	40
CHILDREN AND MARRIAGE	MMMMMMMMMMMMMMMMMMMMMMMMMMMMMMM 69 FFFFFFFFFFFFFFFFFFFFFFFFFFFFFFFFFFFFFFFF 88	70
FAMILY AND FRIENDS	MMMMMMMMMMMMMMMMMMMMMMMM 53 FFFFFFFFFFFFFFFFFFFFFFF 52	60
EQUALITARIAN ROLES	MMMMM 10 FFFFFFF 16	80
RELIGIOUS ORIENTATION	MMMMMMMMM 20 FFFFFF 14	40
	0---10---20---30---40---50	

Table 7-5 Communication

1	2	3	4	5
Strongly Agree	Moderately Agree	Neither Agree nor Disagree	Moderately Disagree	Strongly Disagree

DISAGREEMENT OR DIFFERENCE ITEMS

66. M = 4. F = 2. It seems like when there is a problem in our relationship, I am always the one who wants to discuss it.

109. M = 4. F = 2. My partner is always a good listener.

SPECIAL FOCUS ITEMS

6. M = 1. F = 2. When we have problems, my partner often gives me the silent treatment.

COUPLE INDECISION ITEMS

40. M = 2. F = 3. My partner sometimes makes comments which put me down.
81. M = 3. F = 4. I should know what my partner is feeling without being told.
98. M = 3. F = 4. I do not share negative feelings with partner, fear they may get angry.
120. M = 3. F = 4. Sometimes I have trouble believing everything my partner tells me.

COUPLE POSITIVE AGREEMENT ITEMS

2. M = 1. F = 1. It is very easy for me to express all my true feelings to my partner.
91. M = 2. F = 2. I am very satisfied with how my partner and I talk with each other.
118. M = 5. F = 5. I am sometimes afraid to ask my partner for what I want.

Design of an Effective
Premarital–Newlywed Program

Ideally, it would be best if a couple could first take some type of premarital inventory and receive feedback on that instrument. Second, it would be ideal if couples could then participate in some kind of small support group where they shared their feelings and concerns with each other. Finally, it would be ideal if the couples could then receive training in communication and problem-solving skills that they could use in dealing with relationship issues. This type of three-phase sequential program would take approximately six to eight weeks. The goals that could realistically be accomplished in each of these three phases are indicated in Table 7-6 (Olson, 1983).

The major problem with attempting to have couples participate in such a three-phase program is the fact that many couples do not come for premarital counseling until two to three months before their wedding date. As a result, it is often impossible to accomplish more than the first phase of the program. This highlights the importance of trying to involve couples in the process of marriage preparation *at least one year before marriage.*

When it is not possible to have couples complete the entire three phases before marriage, the process could be continued after marriage. In fact, there is some evidence (Bader et al., 1980) that couples would be more motivated and able to utilize these communication skills if they are trained within six months to a year after marriage. The important issue is that these are three valuable experiences that would help the couple get their relationship off to a good start whether they are all completed before marriage or after. The implication is that they should have these types of experiences so that they will be more prepared to face the realities and challenges of marriage.

Bridging Premarital and Marital Enrichment

Too often there is little connection between premarital and marital enrichment programs. As a result, even if premarital couples had a good premarital experience, there is little follow-up to build their relationship. Because of the difficulties in the early years of marriage and the evidence from Guldner (1971) and Bader and Sinclair (1983) regarding the openness of newlyweds at from six months to one year, it seems important to offer couples enrichment and skill-building programs during their first year of marriage.

In the last few months, three programs have been developed that can help bridge the premarital and newlywed stage. One skill-building pro-

Table 7-6 Goals of a Three-Phase Premarital Program

Premarital Inventory and Couple Dialogue	Small Group Discussion	Communication Skill Training in Couples' Groups
Increase couple's awareness of relationship strengths and potential problem areas	Increase couple's ability and willingness to share with other couples	Build communication skills like sympathy, empathy, and self-disclosure
Facilitate a couple's discussion about their relationship	Learn how other couples relate and deal with issues	Build skills for resolving conflict and problem solving
Establish relationship with clergy, counselor, or married couple	Develop other couples as friends	
Prime couple for post-wedding enrichment or counseling		
Referral to intensive counseling if serious problems arise		

gram is Training in Marriage Enrichment (TIME) developed by Dinkmeyer and Carlson (1984). This program also incorporates ENRICH, which is the parallel inventory to PREPARE that was designed for married couples.

A two-part videotape program was developed by Brusius (1984) entitled *Building a Christian Marriage*. Four premarital sessions focus on communication, realistic expectations, personality issues, and family and friends; and four marital sessions focus on conflict resolution, finances, children and marriage, and the sexual relationship. This program was designed to be used in conjunction with the premarital inventory PREPARE and the marital inventory ENRICH (Olson et al., 1980).

The videotapes from the effective premarital–newlywed program developed and evaluated by Bader et al. (1980) are also available in the program entitled *Learning to Live Together* (Bader, 1984). The four premarital sessions focus on communication, family issues, finances, and sexuality and the three marital sessions focus on sharing feelings, changing roles, and building a positive relationship. The PREPARE–ENRICH inventories can also be used with this program since the focus is on similar topics. These inventories can help motivate the couple and increase the relevance of the program by identifying meaningful relationship issues.

Delivery of Premarital Services

Based on the past, it is clear that most marriage and family therapists will not have time or interest to deliver premarital services. To date, clergy have been the individuals most involved with premarital couples. However, their programs are often limited to the time *before* the wedding. They also seldom have the time or skills to work with the couples in intensive counseling after they have married.

Lay couples who have developed a good marriage relationship and are interested in continued marriage enrichment for themselves and others are an ideal potential resource. There are several advantages in using lay couples to work with premarital couples. First, they can use their own experience to share both the joys and frustrations of marriage with these young couples. By working with these couples before marriage, the lay couples could also serve as a useful resource and support base for the couples as they enter their first year or so of marriage. This sharing experience could also be of benefit to the marriage of the lay couple.

The kinds of services lay couples could provide would include all three previously discussed—administering and interpreting the premarital inventory, which includes facilitating the couple's dialogue, leading a couples' group, and leading a communication-skill-building group. This would naturally necessitate that the lay couples be trained in each of these areas. However, these are useful skills that would likewise enrich lay leaders' own marriages. A recent study clearly demonstrated that lay couples can learn to train premarital couples in relationship-enhancement skills (Most & Guerney, 1983).

It is clear that lay couples have been an underused resource and that they could be a valuable resource for premarital preparation. Couples and clergy alike would appreciate the involvement and modeling of couples who have been able to achieve a happy and vital marriage relationship. For this actually to occur, it is important that lay couples contact their clergy or a counseling organization and offer their services in the important area of premarital preparation.

Recommendations Regarding Policies Relating to Premarital Services

1. Premarital preparation should be seen as a national priority to help marriages get off to a good start. The prevention of divorce begins with providing good premarital preparation.
2. Premarital couples should be encouraged to begin the process of preparation and dealing with relationship issues at least *one year* before marriage.
3. Premarital programs should prime couples to participate in enrichment programs after marriage. Programs can facilitate this by offering several sessions before marriage and several sessions six months after marriage.
4. Premarital and newlywed programs should ideally have three components: (a) premarital inventory and couple dialogue; (b) small-group discussion with other couples; (c) communication-skill-building program.
5. Premarital couples and their parents should be encouraged to spend as much money, time, and energy in preparing for the marriage relationship as they do for the wedding ceremony. This will help ensure that they see marriage as an important investment and as a process that continues for the life of the individuals.
6. Lay couples should be encouraged to become actively involved with premarital couples and to work with them through their first year of married life.
7. Research should be continued to find the most effective types of premarital preparation programs. It would be useful to assess the relative advantages of various types of programs to determine when each can be most appropriately and effectively offered.

References

Avery, A.W., Ridley, C.A., Leslie, L.A., & Handis, M. (1979). Teaching family relations to dating couples versus non-couples: Who learns better? *The Family Coordinator, 28,* 41–45.

Avery, A.W., Ridley, C.A., Leslie, L.A., & Mulholland, T. (1980). Relationship enhancement with premarital dyads: a six-month follow-up. *American Journal of Family Therapy, 8*(3), 23–30.

Bader, E. (1984). *Learning to Live Together* (videotape series). Toronto: Archangel Productions.

Bader, E., Microys, G., Sinclair, L., Willett, E., & Conway, B. (1980). Do marriage preparation programs really work? A Canadian experiment. *Journal of Marital and Family Therapy, 6*(2), 171–179.

Bader, E., Riddle, R., & Sinclair, L. (1981). Do marriage preparation programs really help? *Family Therapy News, 7,* 1–10.

Bader, E., & Sinclair, L. (1983). The first critical year of marriage. In David R. Mace (Ed.), *Prevention in family services.* Beverly Hills, CA: Sage.

Bagarozzi, D.A., & Rauen, P. (1981). Premarital counseling: Appraisal and status. *The American Journal of Family Therapy, 9*(3), 13–20.

Ball, J.D. (1981). Rational suggestions for premarital counseling. *Journal of Marital and Family Therapy, 7,* 1.

Bane, M.J. (1976). Marital disruption and the lives of children. *Journal of Social Issues, 32,* 103–117.

Baum, M.C. (1978). The short-term, long-term, and differential effects of group versus bibliotherapy relationship enhancement programs for couples (Doctoral dissertation, The University of Texas at Austin, 1977). *Dissertation Abstracts International, 38,* 6132B–6133B.

Boike, D.E. (1977). The impact of a premarital program on communication process, communication facilitativeness, and personality trait variables of engaged couples. (Doctoral dissertation, Florida State University, 1977). *Dissertation Abstracts International, 38,* 5-A, 3083–3084.

Brusius, R. (1984). *Building a Christian Marriage* (videotape program). Concordia Publishing House, 3558 South Jefferson Avenue, St. Louis, MO 63118.

Burgess, E.W., & Cottrell, L. (1938). *Promoting success or failure in marriage.* New York: Prentice Hall.

Burgess, E.W., & Wallin, P. (1953). *Engagement and marriage.* New York: Lippincott.

Clinebell, H.J. (1975). *Growth counseling for marriage enrichment.* Philadelphia, PA: Fortress Press.

County of Los Angeles. (1977). *The Conciliation Court: 1976 Annual Report to the Superior Court.* Author: Los Angeles.

Cromwell, R.E., Olson, D.H., & Fournier, D.G. (1976). Tools and techniques for diagnosis in marital and family therapy. *Family Process, 15,* 1–49.

D'Augelli, A.R., Deyss, C.S., Guerney, B.G., Jr., Hershenberg, B., & Sborofsky, S.L. (1974). Interpersonal skill training for dating couples: An evaluation of an educational mental health service. *Journal of Counseling Psychology, 21*(5), 385–389.

Dinkmeyer, D., & Carlson, J. (1984). *Training in Marriage Enrichment* (TIME). Circle Pines, MN: American Guidance Service.

Doyle, T.P. (1980). *Marriage studies: Reflections in canon law and theology.* Toledo, OH: Canon Law Society of America.

Druckman, J.M., Fournier, D.F., Olson, D.H., & Robinson, B.E. (1981). *Effectiveness of various premarital preparation programs.* Unpublished manuscript, Family Social Science, University of Minnesota, St. Paul.

Duvall, E.M. (1965). How effective are marriage courses? *Journal of Marriage and the Family, 27,* 176–184.

Duvall, E.M. (1971). *Family development* (4th ed.). New York: Lippincott.

Elkin, M. (1977). Premarital counseling for minors: The Los Angeles experience. *The Family Coordinator, 26*(4), 429–443.

Fournier, D.G. (1979). Validation of PREPARE: A premarital counseling inventory. (Doctoral dissertation, University of Minnesota, 1979). *Dissertation Abstracts International, 40,* 6, 2385–2386B.

Fournier, D.G. (1981). *INFORMED: The Inventory for Marriage Education.* Unpublished technical report, Department of Family Relations and Child Development, Oklahoma State University, Stillwater, OK.

Fournier, D.G. (1982). Preparation for marriage and early marital adjustment. *Oklahoma Families,* Family Study Center, Oklahoma State University, *7,* 1–2.

Fournier, D.G., Olson, D.H., & Druckman, J.M. (1983). Assessing marital and premarital relationships: The PREPARE–ENRICH inventories. In E. Filsinger (Ed.), *A sourcebook in marriage and family assessment.* Beverly Hills: Sage.

Fowers, B., & Olson, D.H. (1983). *Predicting marital success with PREPARE: A predictive validity study.* Unpublished manuscript, Family Social Science, University of Minnesota, St. Paul, MN 55108.

Freeman, D. (1965). Counseling engaged couples in small groups. *Social Work, 10,* 36–42.

Gangsei, L.B. (1971). *Manual for group premarital counseling.* New York: Association Press.

Garland, D.R. (1981). Training married couples in listening skills: Effects on behavior, perceptual accuracy and marital adjustment. *Family Coordinator, 30*(2), 297–306.

Giblin, P., Sprenkle, D.H., & Sheehan, R. (1985). Enrichment outcome research: A meta-analysis of premarital, marital and family interventions. *Journal of Marital and Family Therapy, 11,* 257–271.

Gilles, D.V., & Lastrucci, C.L. (1954). Validation of the effectiveness of a college marriage course. *Marriage and Family Living, 16,* 55–58.

Ginsberg, B., & Vogelsong, E. (1977). Premarital relationship improvement by maximizing empathy and self-disclosure: the PRIMES program. In B.G. Guerney, Jr. (Ed.), *Relationship enhancement.* San Francisco: Jossey-Bass.

Gleason, J., & Prescott, M.R. (1977). Group techniques for premarital preparation. *The Family Coordinator, 26*(3), 277–280.

Glendening, F.E., & Wilson, A. (1972). Experiments in group premarital counseling. *Social Casework, 53,* 551–562.

Goode, W.J. (1956). *Women in divorce.* New York: Free Press.

Guerney, B.G., Jr. (Ed.). (1977). *Relationship enhancement.* San Francisco: Jossey-Bass.

Guldner, C.A. (1971). The post-marital: An alternate to premarital counseling. *The Family Coordinator, 20*(2), 115–119.

Gurman, A.S., & Kniskern, D.P. (1977). Enriching research on marital enrichment programs. *Journal of Marriage and Family Counseling, 3*(2), 3–11.

Gurman, A.S., & Kniskern, D.P. (1981). Family therapy outcome research: Knowns and unknowns. In A.S. Gurman & D.P. Kniskern (Eds.), *Handbook of family therapy,* pp. 742–776. New York: Brunner/Mazel.

Hill, R., & Aldous, J. (1964). Socialization for marriage and parenthood. In H.T. Christensen (Ed.), *Handbook of marriage and the family*. Chicago: Rand McNally.

Hobart, C.W. (1958). Disillusionment in marriage, and romanticism. *Marriage and Family Living, 20*, 156–162.

Hof, L., & Miller, W. (1981). *Marriage enrichment: Philosophy, process and program*. Bowie, MD: Robert J. Brady.

Hunt, M., & Hunt, B. (1977). *The divorce experience*. New York: McGraw-Hill.

Kitson, G.C., & Sussman, M.B. (1982). Marital complaints, demographic characteristics and symptoms of mental distress among the divorcing. *Journal of Marriage and the Family, 44*(18), 87–100.

Lederer, W.I., & Jackson, D.D. (1968). *The mirages of marriage*. New York: Norton.

Levant, R. (1983). Toward a counseling psychology of the family: Psychological-educational and skill-training programs for treatment, prevention and treatment. *The Counseling Psychologist, 11*(3), 5–46.

Luckey, E., & Neubeck, G. (1956). What are we doing in Marriage Education? *Marriage and Family Living, 18*, 349–354.

Mace, D.R. (1982). *Close companions: The marriage enrichment handbook*. New York: Continuum.

Mace, D. (Ed.). (1983). *Prevention in family services*. Beverly Hills: Sage.

Markman, M.J. (1980). Possibility for the prevention of marital discord: A behavioral perspective. *American Journal of Family Therapy, 8*, 2.

McRae, B. (1975). *A comparison of a behavioral and a lecture discussion approach to premarital counseling*. (Unpublished doctoral dissertation, The University of British Columbia).

Microys, G., & Bader, E. (1977). *Do pre-marriage programs really help?* Unpublished paper, Department of Family and Community Medicine, University of Toronto.

Miller, S., Nunnally, E.W., & Wackman, D.B. (1976). Minnesota couples communication program (MCCP): Premarital and marital groups. In D.H. Olson (Ed.), *Treating relationships*. Lake Mills, IA: Graphic Publishing.

Most, R., & Guerney, P., Jr. (1983). An empirical evaluation of the training of lay volunteer leaders for premarital relationship enhancement. *Family Relations, 32*(2), 239–251.

Nickols, F.A., Fournier, D.F., & Nickols, F.Y. (1984). *Evaluation of a preparation for marriage workshop*. Family Study Center, Oklahoma State University, Stillwater, OK. (Unpublished)

Norem, R.H., Schaefer, M., Springer, J., & Olson, D.H. (1980). *Effectiveness of premarital education programs: Outcome study and follow-up evaluations*. Family Social Science, University of Minnesota. (Unpublished)

Norton, A.J., & Glick, P.C. (1976). Past, present and future marital instability. *Journal of Social Issues, 32*(1), 5–20.

Olson, D.H. (1983). How effective is marriage preparation? In D. Mace (Ed.), *Prevention in family services* (pp. 65–75). Beverly Hills: Sage.

Olson, D.H., Fournier, D.G., & Druckman, J.M. (1980). *PREPARE–ENRICH counselors manual* (rev. ed.). Stillwater, OK: PREPARE–ENRICH, P.O. Box 1363, Stillwater, OK 74076.

Olson, D.H., & Gravatt, A.E. (1968). Attitude change in a functional marriage course. *The Family Coordinator, 17*, 99–104.

Oussoren, A.H. (1972). *Education for marriage.* Unpublished manuscript.
Peterson, J. (1964). *Education for marriage* (2nd ed.). New York: Scribners.
Rappoport, R. (1963). Normal crises, family structure and mental health. *Family Process, 2,* 68–80.
Rausch, H.L., Goodrich, W., & Campbell, H. (1975). Adaptation to the first years of marriage. *Psychiatry, 26,* 368–380.
Regin, D. (1980). Overview of Diocesan regulations on adolescent marriages since Vatican II. In T.P. Doyle (Ed.), *Marriage studies.* Toledo, OH: Common Law Society of America.
Ridley, C.A., Avery, A.W., Harrell, J.E., Hayes-Clements, A.A., & McCunney, N. (1983). Mutual problem solving skills training for premarital couples: A six month follow-up. *Journal of Applied Developmental Psychology, 4,* 179–185.
Ridley, C.A., Avery, A.W., Harrell, J.E., Leslie, L.A., & Dent, J. (1982). Conflict Management: A Premarital Training Program in Mutual Problem Solving. Tucson, AZ: Human Development Laboratory, University of Arizona.
Ridley, C.A., Jorgensen, S.R., Morgan, A.C., & Avery, A.W. (1982). Relationship enhancement with premarital couples: An assessment of effects on relationship quality. *American Journal of Family Therapy, 10*(3), 41–48.
Rockwood, L.D. (1935). *Teaching family relationships.* Washington, DC: American Home Economics Association.
Rolfe, D.J. (1975). *Marriage preparation manual.* New York: Paulist Press.
Rolfe, D.J. (1976). Premarriage assessment of teenage couples. *Journal of Family Counseling, 4*(2), 32–39.
Rolfe, D.J. (1983). *Preparing couples for marriage.* Coeur d'Alene, ID: Marriage Preparation Office.
Rutledge, A.L. (1966). *Premarital counseling.* Cambridge, MA: Schenkman.
Sager, C.J. (1976). *Marriage contracts and couple therapy: Hidden forces in intimate relationships.* New York: Brunner/Mazel.
Schumm, W.R., & Denton, W. (1979). Trends in premarital counseling. *Journal of Marital and Family Therapy, 22,* 23–32.
Sieber, Y.A. (1984). *Effect of a college marriage course on marital attitudes.* Unpublished Masters Thesis, Oklahoma State University.
Skolnick, H. (1975). Premarital counseling: Three years' experience of a unique service. *The Family Coordinator, 24*(3), 321–324.
Springer, J., Fournier, D.G., & Olson, D.H. (1984). *Relationship issues from dating to married couples.* Unpublished manuscript, Family Social Science, University of Minnesota.
Stahmann, R.F., & Barclay-Cope, A. (1977). Premarital counseling: An overview. In R.F. Stahmann & W.J. Hiebert (Eds.), *Klemer's counseling in marital and sexual problems: A clinician's handbook* (2nd ed.). Baltimore, MD: Williams & Wilkins.
Stahmann, R.F., & Hiebert, W.J. (1980). *Premarital counseling.* Lexington, MA: Lexington Books.
Terman, L.M. (1938). *Psychological factors in marital happiness.* New York: McGraw-Hill.
Thompson, D., & Thompson, J. (1980). *Growth in marriage for newlyweds.* Kansas City, MO: Living Center for Family Enrichment.
Trainer, J.B. (1979). Premarital counseling and examination. *Journal of Marital and Family Therapy, 5,* 2.
U.S. National Center for Health Statistics (1984a). *Monthly Vital Statistics Re-*

port: Provisional Summary for the United States. *32*, 12, Washington, DC: U.S. Government Printing Office.

U.S. National Center for Health Statistics. (1984b). *Vital Statistics of the United States. Vol. III, 1979 Marriage and Divorce.* Washington, DC: U.S. Government Printing Office.

Wright, H.N. (1981). Premarital counseling: A follow-up study. Christian Marriage Enrichment, 1913 E. 17th St., Suite 118, Santa Ana, CA 92701.

Wright, H.N. (1983). *Premarital counseling* (rev. ed.). Chicago: Moody Press.

8

Marriage Enrichment

Myron R. Chartier

During the past 25 years there has developed a concern for strengthening marriage relationships through preventive programs (Mace, 1983). A decade ago Otto (1976) declared: "The marriage and family enrichment movement is one of the most promising contemporary developments to appear on the scene" (p. 9).

Historical Background and Development

Early Beginnings

It began in 1962 on two separate continents. In January Father Gabriel Calvo gathered a group of married couples for a weekend retreat in Barcelona, Spain. The retreat was called *Encuentro Conyugal* (or Marriage Encounter). The Spanish word, *encuentro,* can mean confrontation or fight but it also describes two persons meeting each other and discovering the other. Father Calvo had the latter meaning in mind (Bosco, 1972; Calvo, 1975; L'Abate & McHenry, 1983; Mace, 1982). Marriage Encounter had its roots in the Spanish Christian Family Movement. Shortly after World War II Pat and Patty Crowley of the United States founded the Christian Family Movement. By 1950 the Christian Family Movement had become an international movement related to the Roman Catholic Church (L'Abate & McHenry, 1983; Strickler, 1979).

In October 1962, David and Vera Mace met with a group of married couples on a weekend at Kirkridge, a religious retreat center near Bangor, Pennsylvania. At that time they were serving as joint directors of the American Association of Marriage Counselors (now known as the American Association of Marriage and Family Therapy). This retreat was an experiment in seeing if there might be ways of preventing trouble in marriage relationships (Mace, 1982).

Development of the Religious Models

Marriage Encounter. Once started, both movements grew. Marriage Encounter soon spread to many cities throughout Spain. In 1966, the program was presented at the International Confederation of Christian Family Movements in Caracas, Venezuela. Following this international meeting, Marriage Encounter was introduced to a number of other Latin American countries. In 1966, Father Calvo, assisted by a Mexican couple, presented the first Marriage Encounter in the United States in Miami, Florida, to a group of Spanish-speaking couples (Bosco, 1972; Calvo, 1975). In the same year Father Calvo with 50 Mexican and Spanish "team couples" conducted many encounter weekends in Spanish-speaking North American communities. The first English-speaking Marriage Encounter was held in August 1967 at Notre Dame University as part of the Christian Family Movement convention (Strickler, 1979). By late 1968, Marriage Encounter had spread to Detroit, Chicago, Montreal, New Jersey, and New York. By 1969, the movement was large enough to create its own national board in a meeting in Elberon, New Jersey, where the National Marriage Encounter of the United States of America was formally launched (Bosco, 1972; Mace, 1982).

In 1971, Father Charles Gallagher insisted that his New York program was unique and offered the most promise for advancement (see Gallagher, 1975). Hence, by 1974 Marriage Encounter was represented by two quite separate groups: National Marriage Encounter and Gallagher's Worldwide Marriage Encounter (Buettner, 1976). Marriage Encounter has reached four or five times as many couples as all other marriage-enrichment programs combined, and over 1,000,000 couples have been "encountered" (Strickler, 1979; Wackman, 1983). The Marriage Encounter movement has developed a variety of Protestant expressions as well as a Jewish expression (Kligfeld, 1976).

The Quaker model. Following their first marriage-enrichment weekend in 1962, David and Vera Mace had many opportunities to lead similar experiences, more than they could accept. In 1969, they held a training workshop for carefully chosen Quaker couples from across North America, who then returned and led retreats in their home areas. Through these training experiences the Maces developed a model of marriage-enrichment leadership that reflected their basic Quaker concepts. Their particular style of marriage enrichment has become known as the Quaker model (Mace, 1982).

Marriage Communication Lab. Another pioneer couple in marriage enrichment were Leon and Antoinette Smith, who put together their first marriage-enrichment experience in the spring of 1964 in Fayetteville, North Carolina. The group was composed of clergy and spouses. Due to the large number of requests to lead marital growth groups, the Smiths persuaded the Methodist Church leaders to finance a training program to prepare carefully selected clergy and spouses for leadership of such retreats. The first training program took place in Warwick, New York, in February 1966. This was the first workshop for training leadership for marriage enrichment. From this experience the Smiths developed the Marriage Communication Lab. The Disciples of Christ and the Reformed Church have adopted the Marriage Communication Lab model (Mace, 1982; Smith & Smith, 1976).

Development of Social Science Models

These three models were developed by religious groups—Catholics, Quakers, and Methodists. Nonreligious approaches have also been developed.

Ottos' model. Herbert and Roberta Otto began in 1961 what they called the Family Resource Development Program: The Key to Family Enrichment. By 1966 they had developed "The More Joy in Your Marriage Program." The book *More Joy in Your Marriage* (Otto, 1969) resulted from their work. The Ottos' model is heavily based upon concepts and techniques that have emerged from the human-potential movement; they use these to enrich marriages (Otto, 1970).

Couple Communication Program. In 1968, a small group of family theorists, researchers, and therapists from the University of Minnesota Family Study Center and the Family and Children's Services of Minneapolis began to think through a series of programs designed to enrich family living. The first was the Couple Communication Program, formerly known as the Minnesota Couples Communication Program, and was started in 1968 with engaged couples recruited through the bridal registry of Dayton's Department Store in Minneapolis. In 1969, the first program was conducted with married couples (S. Miller, personal communication, May 20, 1984). In the same year the program was standardized and field tested. In 1972 the founders of the program began training others to conduct the program. Since then the program has been strengthened by making modifications in its design. In 1981, a further development was made by designing Couple Communication II, which builds upon the framework and skills taught in Couple Communication I (Nunnally, Miller, & Wackman, 1981). Over 100,000 have been reached through this program (Wackman, 1983; see Table 8-1).

Developments Since 1970

Most approaches to marriage enrichment have come since 1970. Otto (1976) found that 90 percent had conducted their first programs in 1973 or later. Around 1970, Conjugal Relationship Enhancement was conceived by Guerney (1977). The first research study on it was reported in 1971 (Collins, 1972). In 1972, Larry and Millie Hof started work on Creative Marriage Enrichment, the model being finalized in 1977 (Hof & Miller, 1981).

In 1973, David and Vera Mace founded the Association of Couples for Marriage Enrichment (ACME). "Its purpose was, and is, to attempt to give shape and directions to the developing marriage enrichment movement, and especially to establish standards for the selection, training, and certification of leader couples" (Mace, 1983, p. 102).

In 1975, the Maces founded in Chicago the Council of Affiliated Marriage Enrichment Organizations (CAMEO). It is made up of organizations offering marriage enrichment programs on a national scale. Its purpose is to provide a forum for exchanging ideas and sharing experiences. Most of the organizations are religious in nature (Mace, 1982).

Around 1974, Stein (1975) put together Marriage Diagnostic Laboratory, MARDILAB. During this same time period Travis and Travis (1975) designed the Pairing Enrichment Program (PEP). L'Abate (1975, 1977) developed Structured Marriage Enrichment Programs.

In 1976, Otto edited a book which presented a wide variety of marriage-enrichment programs: Christian Marriage Enrichment Retreat (Green, 1976), Marriage Renewal Retreats (Schmitt & Schmitt, 1976), Positive Partners (Hayward, 1976), Gestalt Marriage Enrichment (Zinker & Leon, 1976), Marriage Enrichment Program Phase I (Vander Haar & Vander Haar, 1976), Marriage Enrichment Lab Phase II (Van Eck & Van Eck, 1976), and the Marriage Communication Labs (Hopkins & Hopkins, 1976).

In 1981, Hof and Miller wrote a landmark book on marriage enrichment in which they presented an integrated overview of the philosophy, process of, and programs for marriage enrichment. In 1982, Mace wrote *Close Companions: The Marriage Enrichment Handbook*. Written by one of the pioneers in marriage enrichment, it provides an excellent overview and conceptual rationale for the movement. It is an historic document that will provide perspective on marriage enrichment for the future.

In two works L'Abate (1981) and L'Abate and McHenry (1983) have provided the best cataloguing of the variety of programs now available in the marriage-enrichment field. In 1982, Elliott and Saunders described a marriage-enrichment program using systems theory. In their Systems Marriage Enrichment Program, they utilized both theoretical concepts and assumptions of systems theory in conjunction with the general assumptions of relationship enrichment.

Garland (1983) has made the latest contribution to the emerging movement. She has developed a sophisticated guide for professionals who desire to design, conduct, and evaluate programs. She suggested that "rather than forming a group to experience a particular program, providers of marriage enrichment services should determine the needs of a particular group of couples and then select or design a program that focuses on the group's unique composition and goals" (p. 220).

This brief historical survey has spanned over two decades. Much has occurred in this time. Many different approaches and styles of marriage enrichment have emerged. According to Hof and Miller (1981):

> The approaches to marriage enrichment are analogous to, but more varied, than, the colors of the rainbow. From a distance, each approach or color appears to be a totally distinct and unique entity. Upon closer examination, however, we realize that the various programs or colors flow from and merge with each other. Instead of being completely separate entities, each is seen to be directly related to those on either side of it, and to share certain aspects with each other. (p. xiii)

An Organizational Analysis of Differences and Likenesses in Various Marriage Enrichment Programs

The ways in which these various programs are different and similar can be understood by examining a number of organizational variables. The following analysis shows these differences and likenesses.

Goals

All marriage enrichment programs share a primary focus upon the marital relationship; their major goal is the improvement of married life. How improvement is defined and the processes by which it is thought to be accomplished may differ at times (Garland, 1983). According to Mace (1982):

> The task of marriage enrichment is to equip couples with better insights, skills, and tools than they normally possess, in order that they may appropriate, in much fuller measure than they normally do, the rewards a fully functioning companionship marriage has to offer. (p. 61)

Most, if not all, approaches to marriage enrichment seek to improve the marital relationship through assisting couples in developing a more effective approach to communication than they have known (Hof &

Table 8-1   Chronology of Marriage Enrichment Developments

Date	Event
1962	Marriage Encounter founded by Father Calvo in Spain. First married couples retreat led by the Maces.
1966	First training program in marriage enrichment led by the Smiths. Marriage Encounter introduced in Latin America. Marriage Encounter conducted in Spanish-speaking North America. "The More Joy in Your Marriage Program" developed by the Ottos.
1967	First English-speaking Marriage Encounter held at Notre Dame University.
1968	Marriage Encounter spread throughout North America. Minnesota Couples Communication Program started with engaged couples.
1969	National board for Marriage Encounter founded. Training workshop held for Quaker couples in the Mace's Quaker model. First Minnesota Couples Communication Program conducted with married couples.
1970	Conjugal Relationship Enhancement conceptualized.
1971	Father Charles Gallagher splits from National Marriage Encounter to form Worldwide Marriage Encounter.
1972	Training others in Couple Communication Program begun. Creative Marriage Enrichment started.
1973	Association of Couples for Marriage Enrichment (ACME) founded.
1974	Marriage Encounter becomes two separate groups: National Marriage Encounter and Worldwide Marriage Encounter. Marriage Diagnostic Laboratory (MARDILAB) developed. Pairing Enrichment Program (PEP) designed. Structured Marriage Enrichment Programs developed.

(continued)

Table 8-1 Continued

Date	Event
1975	Council of Affiliated Marriage Enrichment Organizations founded.
1976	Otto's edited book, *Marriage and Family Enrichment,* presented a wide variety of programs: Christian Marriage Enrichment Retreat Marriage Renewal Retreats Positive Partners Gestalt Marriage Enrichment Marriage Enrichment Program Phase I Marriage Enrichment Lab Phase II Marriage Communication Labs (Disciples of Christ)
1981	Couple Communication II developed. Hof and Miller's *Marriage Enrichment: Philosophy, Process, and Program,* a landmark book, published. L'Abate published a chapter in *Handbook of Family Therapy* which catalogued various marriage-enrichment programs.
1982	Mace published an important theoretical book: *Close Companions: The Marriage Enrichment Handbook.* Systems Marriage Enrichment Program described.
1983	L'Abate and McHenry published the latest and most complete cataloguing of marriage-enrichment programs, *Handbook of Marital Interventions.* Garland published a professional's guide to designing, conducting, and evaluating marriage enrichment, *Working with Couples for Marriage Enrichment.*

Miller, 1981). Attention is given to self-disclosure, empathic listening, and supportive feedback. Marriage enrichment seeks to teach couples how to engage in deep sharing and listening on a cognitive and emotional level using both verbal and nonverbal expression.

Theoretical Bases

The theoretical underpinnings for marriage enrichment are varied and eclectic. The philosophy of ACME has been articulated clearly by Mace (1982) with its focus upon companionship marriage. The psychodynamics of Marriage Encounter have been stated by Regula (1975). The theoretical bases and assumptions undergirding the Couple Communication Program have been articulated by those associated with it (Miller, Nunnally, & Wackman, 1976; Nunnally et al., 1981). Guerney (1977) has explicated the conceptual rationale for Relationship Enhancement. Hof (Hof & Miller, 1981) has spelled out the theories supporting the Creative Marriage Enrichment program.

Theological bases. For marriage-enrichment programs with a strong religious base, the thinking of Buber (1937, 1947), Howe (1963), and Tournier (1957) have been important. These sources among others have provided a relational theology for their enrichment work (Regula, 1975; Vander Haar & Vander Haar, 1976). They also have drawn ideas and tools from those in the pastoral care field such as Augsburger (1974), Clinebell and Clinebell (1970), and Wright (1974).

Psychological bases. Concepts have been drawn from a wide variety of psychologists by both religious and secular orientations. The ones cited most often are persons associated with the Human Potential Movement of the Sixties such as Rogers (1951, 1961), Jourard (1964), Maslow (1968), and Schutz (1967), and others such as Foote and Cottrell (1955), Berne (1964), Bach (Bach & Wyden, 1969), and Vincent (1973). Increasingly the ideas and concepts of family theory and therapy are being employed in marriage enrichment—the ideas of Satir (1964), Watzlawick, Beavin, and Jackson (1967), Lewis, Beavers, Gossett, and Phillips (1976), Olson, Fournier, and Druckman (1982), Lederer and Jackson (1968), Speer (1970), and Steinglass (1978), to name a few.

Audience

Marriage-enrichment programs have been for couples who have what they believe to be fairly well-functioning marriages and who desire to make their marriages even more mutually satisfying. Because proponents of marriage enrichment have emphasized its dynamic, experiential, educational, and preventive nature, the programs have not been perceived as being designed for people whose marriages are at a point of crisis, or who are seeking therapy for their marital difficulties (Hof & Miller, 1981; Otto, 1976). This view has been challenged by Hof and Miller (1981), who claim "that at times, the boundaries between enrichment, education, and therapy are not always very clear" (p. 48). Guerney (1977) contends that making sharp distinctions between therapy, prevention, and enrichment is counterproductive. Screening out troubled marriages is not always successful. It is probably safe to say that most programs rely on the couple's selection of the program as the screening process.

Recruitment

Recruiting people for marriage enrichment can be a difficult process. Many enrichment leaders have been disappointed by the number of couples who have responded to a marriage-enrichment opportunity. According to Mace (1982), "The average couple when invited to a marriage enrichment weekend, react by becoming defensive" (p. 166). Mace indicates that at least four factors contribute to this negative reaction.

The first is the intermarital taboo. It gets expressed as follows: "This is an invasion of our privacy. What you are asking us to do is to open up areas of our lives that are our concern alone. They are nobody else's business."

The second is the fear of being exposed. This fear is often stated as follows: "If we went on a retreat, we might have to drop our masks and be revealed for who we really are. We're not sure we can handle that."

The third is the fear of discovering things wrong with the marriage or one's self. "If we attend a marriage-enrichment retreat, we might have to deal with some painful areas in our relationship—unresolved conflicts, issues we've never talked about. Our marriage is O.K.; let sleeping dogs lie."

The fourth factor is feeling something must be wrong with the marriage by virtue of the invitation and therapy is needed. It might be expressed in this manner: "You are suggesting that we have a marital problem and need therapy. Frankly, that is somewhat of an insult and makes us angry."

Of all the enrichment programs Marriage Encounter has had the most aggressive recruitment program. As a result it has had the most success numerically (DeYoung, 1979).

Leadership Issues

Leadership styles.   The leadership for marriage enrichment varies considerably. Programs are conducted by husband/wife teams, husband/wife teams with a priest, male/female teams (not married to each other), or individuals. One survey (Otto, 1975) of leaders indicated that 90 percent of them operated as husband/wife teams or man–woman enrichment leaders teams. Marriage Encounter utilizes a leadership team consisting of an encountered couple(s) plus a priest. Couple Communication Program's leadership may be a single person, married couple, or nonmarried male–female team. Christian Marriage Enrichment Retreat is conducted by a single facilitator (Green, 1976).

Marriage enrichment may also be leaderless. Larson and Larson (1979) have designed a workbook to be used by partners at home or by self-directed groups. Mace and Mace (1977), Clinebell and Clinebell (1970), Chartier and Chartier (1984) as well as others have written books that provide basic concepts for enhancing marital relationships which are accompanied by experiential learning opportunities to be used by a couple or in groups of couples.

Mace (1982) believes that marriage enrichment conducted without the leader couple is at a decided disadvantage, for it excludes the possibility of creating an environment for openness and trust by the leadership couple's sharing their marital experiences with the group through lecturettes as well as in demonstrations.

Styles of leadership also vary from nonparticipant/leader/director(s) to full participant leader(s). The Relationship Enhancement program encourages its group leaders to be nonparticipating leaders. The style is strictly client-focused with no personal sharing from group leaders. On the other hand, ACME leaders are trained to be full participants alongside other couples. Marriage Encounter leadership couples model the basic dialogue technique. Regardless of style, most enrichment approaches would deem it important for its leaders to model the skills they propose to teach and the growth-oriented relationship they value (Hof & Miller, 1981).

Leadership training.   Requirements for leading a marriage experience vary. There is a sense in which anybody who sets up "shop" and is able to find couples who will participate can lead a marriage enrichment experience. However, the programs that have national visibility require some form of training.

The first training program for marriage enrichment was designed for pastors and wives of the Methodist Church. It was designed by Leon Smith, who was Director of Marriage and Family Ministry for the United Methodist Church in the United States, and his wife Antoinette. Since its beginning the Marriage Communication Lab Training Program has been expanded to include other couples than clergy. However, one of the partners must be a professional in the helping field. Each of the partners is expected to have a degree of competence in terms of (1) having a sound, satisfying marriage, (2) being a warm, caring person, (3) being able to communicate effectively, (4) having problem-solving skills, (4) demonstrating group process skills, and (5) having marriage counseling skills and experience. The couples prepare for a five-day training event by some reading and work on communication in their marriage. They then serve in two three-day Marriage Communication Labs and receive an evaluation of the effectiveness of the lab. Following this training period, they are to be available for labs and receive evaluation of their work (Smith & Smith, 1976).

Building upon the Maces' experience in leadership training with the Quakers in 1969 and 1971 as well as the experience of the Smiths with their Marriage Communication Lab, ACME developed standards for the selection, training, and certification of marriage-enrichment leaders. Many member organizations of CAMEO have adopted these standards. ACME's standards call for partners who are committed to marital growth, can work cooperatively as a team, can communicate warmth and caring, can self-disclose, are sensitive to others, and have some basic knowledge about human development, marital interaction, and group process. Training involves participation in one or more marriage-enrichment events, a basic training workshop, and advanced training. Evaluative feedback occurs at many points in the process. Once certification has been granted, it has to be renewed every three years (Mace, 1982).

Marriage Encounter recruits couples who report positive Marriage Encounter experiences for future team couples. They are trained minimally to take other couples through the whole process of the dialogue technique. They are taught how to communicate naturally and honestly on a feeling level with other couples (Bosco, 1972; Gallagher, 1975). This training involves couples in rehearsing their talks which follow standardized outlines into which they put examples from their own marital experience (Doherty, McCabe, & Ryder, 1978). The talks are critiqued by other team couples (L'Abate & McHenry, 1983).

The Couple Communication Program began training others to conduct their program in 1972. Its leaders developed a certification process for its trainees. In 1977, a self-study program was designed for trainees. Its leaders discovered that the knowledge and skill of potential trainees had changed over the years, and, therefore, no longer necessitated the instructor training workshop. Persons working their way through the self-instruction process satisfactorily are qualified for certification (Nunnally, Miller, & Wackman, 1981).

Structure of Marriage Enrichment

Time format. Marriage-enrichment experiences are structured in a variety of ways. They can take place as intensive weekend programs such as in Marriage Encounter or ACME retreats, which usually involve 15 hours in a single weekend; or they can be a series of weekly meetings such as in the Couple Communication Program and the Relationship Enhancement program, which meets for a limited time period (4 to 10 weeks). They can also be a marital support group, meeting every three or four weeks for a period of nine months or longer (Catron & Catron, 1982; Hof & Miller, 1981).

Program structure. Regardless of time format, marriage-enrichment events can be structured very loosely to very tightly. Worldwide Marriage Encounter through the leadership of Father Chuck Gallagher has developed a most highly structured approach to marriage enrichment. Under his approach the format for an Encounter weekend is always the same; it never varies (Gallagher, 1975). At the opposite end of the continuum is

Maces' Quaker model. There is a minimum of structure in the model; it is highly flexible in that goals and agenda are established by the group. Many enrichment approaches fall between these two poles.

Interaction pattern. Interaction patterns vary in marriage-enrichment programs. Marriage Encounter relies on couple dialogue in the privacy of a couple's motel unit. Couple-to-couple sharing is not permitted. In the Quaker model the Maces' rely on couple dialogue which takes place openly before the group. Some leaders (Evans, 1975) rely primarily on group interaction. Some utilize the total group for part of what they do and then rely on smaller groupings for other processes such as couple-to-couple sharing or four or five couples meeting with a leader couple (Mace, 1982).

Group size. The size of groups can vary a great deal. ACME sees the minimum size being four couples with eight couples being the outside limit for one leader couple (Mace, 1982). On the other hand, Marriage Encounter can take large numbers since there is no group interaction.

Educational Methods

A variety of educational methods are used in conducting marriage enrichment events. Marriage Encounter relies on leadership talks, writing down personal answers to questions, and couple dialogue in response to each other's answers (Gallagher, 1975). Other approaches like the Quaker model rely on group and couple conversation. Still others make much use of structured exercises (Hof & Miller, 1981; Nunnally et al., 1981). Films are sometimes used (Smith & Smith, 1976). The major mode of learning in marriage enrichment is experiential.

An example of such a learning approach would be the use of the structured exercise. A marriage-enrichment facilitator could give a short presentation on self-esteem in marriage and how important affirming communication between each other is for one to feel valued. From that presentation he or she could set up an exercise whereby a couple is asked to experience esteem building, such as:

> We live or die inside to the degree that we are appreciated and affirmed by our marriage partner. Use the following exercise to express appreciation to your spouse.
> *Instruction:* Complete the statement, "I appreciate it when you _____" 10 or more times. Take time to write out your personal statements of appreciation. Study them. Then, read your list to your spouse. Afterward, discuss the results. Describe how you feel about being appreciated by your spouse. (Chartier & Chartier, 1984, p. 43)

After the couple has written and shared their lists and discussed them, the total group would gather and share what the experience had meant to them as couples and what they had learned. Any problems that may have occurred in trying to do the exercise would also be discussed.

Program Content

Marriage Encounter. Although the primary focus of marriage enrichment is strengthening marriage relationships, the content of marriage-enrichment experiences vary considerably. During a Marriage Encounter weekend four themes make up the content. These themes serve as four phases for the weekend. These phases are:

1. I—This phase involves critical self-examination as to wearing of masks and likes and dislikes regarding oneself.
2. We—The second phase focuses upon the marriage relationship.
3. We–God—This phase involves seeing the marriage relationship as basic to God's love and plan; without that love coupleness is impossible.
4. We–God–World—This final phase focuses upon how the newly encountered couple may serve God through service to others (DeYoung, 1979).

The Quaker model. When David and Vera Mace lead a marriage-enrichment retreat, the content for the event is established by the participating couples. They are provided an opportunity as couples, talking privately to each other, to identify items they would like to explore. Once that is done, the group forms their agenda. Typical items included might be:

1. Working wives
2. Need to be alone
3. Expressing affection
4. Quarrels
5. Different expectations
6. Making decisions together
7. Gender roles
8. Financial policy
9. Use of time
10. Sexual attitudes (Mace, 1982, pp. 149–150)

Marriage Communication Lab. The content of a Marriage Communication Lab, according to the Smiths:

is the participating couples—their marriages, experiences, and feelings about the ways they relate to each other; their expectations of one another, and their anxieties and hopes for the future. These may be explored through considering such concerns as what is happening in our marriage, improving communication in marriage, marital role expectations, identity and intimacy, facing conflicts, expressing positive and negative feelings, deepening our spiritual life, enriching companionship, and planning our future. (Smith & Smith, 1976, pp. 241–242)

Couple Communication Program. Couple Communication I focuses upon four conceptual frameworks. Each session presents a framework with a set of behavioral skills to be practiced and linked with the framework. The first framework is the Awareness Wheel. It helps the individual identify the many different kinds of information one has about oneself. This wheel aids the participant in organizing and using self-information. Couples are taught six specific behavioral skills for verbally expressing self-awareness congruently and self-responsibly.

The second framework is the Shared Meaning Process, designed for matching messages sent with messages received. Three behavioral skills are taught for creating understanding between persons.

The third framework is upon Verbal Communication Styles. It helps learners identify the kinds of communication alternatives they have and the kinds of impact various styles have on others. Emphasis is placed upon the value of Style IV, which is focused, direct, clear, responsible, responsive, positive, honest, caring, and collaborative communication.

The last framework is called I Count Me/I Count You. Emphasis is placed on each partner's responsibility for enhancing both one's own and the other's self-esteem (Miller et al., 1976; Nunnally et al., 1981).

Couple Communication II builds upon the frameworks and skills taught in Couple Communication I, especially the Awareness Wheel with its related skills. "It also introduces ideas related to mapping issues, resolving conflicts, exploring intimacy, and building upon relationship strengths" (Nunnally et al., 1981, pp. 1–7).

Highly focused programs. Like Couple Communication, a variety of marriage-enrichment programs have been designed that have a highly focused content. Whereas Couple Communication highlights communication, other programs give attention to assertiveness (L'Abate & McHenry, 1983), conflict management (Bach & Bernhard, 1971; Kearns, 1980), problem-solving (Carkhuff, 1973), sexuality (L'Abate & McHenry, 1983; Nathan, 1982), and parenting (Winans, 1982).

Content for a target population. Some practitioners of marriage enrichment adapt the content of a given event to the content and needs of a target population rather than requiring that group needs be adapted to the content of a particular program (Garland, 1983). The goal is to provide marriage enrichment services that are appropriate to the unique needs of a given target population (Garland, 1983; Hof & Miller, 1981).

Evaluative Research on Marriage Enrichment

Methodological Shortcomings

Since 1968 there has been a growing number of research studies conducted on marriage enrichment events. Research of this kind is difficult and susceptible to several methodological shortcomings. Common limitations have been: relatively small samples; the failure to show equivalence between experimental and control groups at pretest; failure to randomize group assignments; no attempt to control for placebo and illusory effects; failure to conduct adequate follow-up evaluations; an overuse of self-report measures as opposed to objective, observational assessments; failure to use measurements of known reliability and validity; failure to use measurements designed specifically for enrichment couples as opposed to clinical couples; and no attempts to document the presence or absence of concurrent treatments from other sources (Garland, 1983; Gurman & Kniskern, 1977; Hof, Epstein, & Miller, 1980; Hof & Miller, 1981; Wampler, 1982b). There has also been a problem with an appropriate fit between theory and operational measures in the design and evaluation of marriage enrichment programs (Garland, 1983; Schumm, 1983).

Reviews of Research Findings

Several reviews on the outcomes of marital enrichment programs have been published. Two of these have focused on behavioral skills training (Birchler, 1979; Jacobson, 1978). Since these offer nothing substantial beyond the results of the review presented below, and since behavioral programs are discussed in Chapter 4, they will not be discussed here.

Beck's review. Beck (1976) presented research findings on the outcomes of marital counseling. Of the 32 studies she reviewed, 16 fit the definition of marriage enrichment. All but one (Kind, 1969) of the studies showed positive gains. In this one study "most of the tests used proved either unreliable or unrelated to marital happiness" (Beck, 1976, p. 450). Of the others, 13 showed statistically significant gains with 50 percent or more of the tests used. Three had significant gains for less han 50 percent or more of the tests made. Three had significant gains for less than 50 percent of the tests used.

Gurman and Kniskern's review. Building upon the review by Beck, Gurman and Kniskern (1977) identified 29 studies for critical review, seven of which were with premarital couples. Of these studies 86 percent were conducted in non-church-related programs, with about 75 percent of the subjects recruited from university communities. Of the programs 93 percent were facilitated in a group setting, most with weekly meetings (76 percent) over an average span of seven weeks involving an average of 14 hours of meeting time.

The outcome criteria used in most studies were (1) overall marital satisfaction and adjustment, (2) relationship skills, and (3) personality variables. Positive change was consistently shown on 60 percent of the criterion tests. Significant change was demonstrated on 57 percent of the self-report measures, in contrast to 81 percent of the objective behavioral measures. Unfortunately, such behavioral indices were outnumbered by self-report measures by a ratio of 5 to 1. Four studies (Burns, 1972; Nadeau, 1971; Swicegood, 1974; Wieman, 1973) gave mixed results on the durability of enrichment-induced change; "the results of these follow-ups suggest only moderate maintenance of gains" (p. 8). From their analysis Gurman and Kniskern determined that the results of controlled studies on marriage enrichment were quite positive, with 23 of 34 comparisons (67 percent) showing program effects to exceed those of control groups; 11 demonstrated no difference.

Hof and Miller's review. Hof and Miller (1981) identified 40 different studies that have been clearly associated with marriage enrichment programs or consist of procedures and techniques that are consistent with marriage enrichment programs. They examined outcome categories similar to Gurman and Kniskern: overall marital adjustment, perceptual and personality variables, and relationship skills. Their review showed that most of the outcome studies reported positive changes on at least some measures following a marital enrichment experience. They also discovered that significant changes are not restricted to any particular type or class of variables. The studies showed that changes following participation were due to factors other than simple passage of time. Only one study (Roberts, 1975) could demonstrate that changes resulted from the enrichment experience itself through the use of an attention-placebo control group. They found the same problem with the use of self-report measures in relation to objective observations, as did Gurman and Kniskern.

Eight of the 40 studies (20 percent) sought to determine through follow-up assessment whether outcomes from marriage enrichment are temporary or stable in nature. Hof and Miller concluded that although the results were encouraging, more research is needed before it can be concluded that marital enrichment leads to stable relational changes.

Studies seeking to demonstrate that one enrichment experience was more effective than another have had mixed results. Some studies demonstrated that both programs (Wieman, 1973) or both formats of the same program (Kilmann, Julian, & Moreault, 1978; Kilmann, Moreault & Robinson, 1978) resulted in significant changes. Two studies (McIntosh, 1975; Williams, 1975) reported no changes for any of the enrichment experiences. In contrast, Hof and Miller reported that seven studies demonstrated superiority of one experience over another. They concluded that communication training is superior to insight-oriented group experiences; however, the comparison of behavioral and communication training programs has yielded mixed results.

Very few studies have investigated program components. Roberts (1975) found a positive association between the experience level of a therapist and the quality of outcomes. Beaver (1978) found more positive changes when couples were in the same Couple Communication Program than when in separate, concurrent groups.

Hof and Miller located two studies related to how different types of people respond to marriage enrichment. Neville (1971), using the Myers-Briggs Type Indicator, found that intuitive-feeling types were more likely to volunteer for marriage enrichment than sensing-thinking personality types; however, both types responded positively to the experience. Huber (1978) found that males may be more likely to change than females as a result of Marriage Encounter. Beaver (1978) found similar results with the Couple Communication Program.

Hof and Miller concluded from their examination of research outcomes that cautious optimism about the effectiveness of marital-enrichment programs is warranted. Future studies that are well-designed are needed before reliable conclusions about marriage enrichment's efficacy can be reached.

Giblin's meta-analysis. A review by Giblin based upon his doctoral dissertation (1982) has been the most exhaustive and sophisticated critical analysis of the literature to date (Giblin, Sprenkle, & Sheehan, 1985). Rather than evaluating a large body of studies by narrative and/or box-score methods, he used meta-analysis, which is a statistical method for analyzing a large collection of empirical results from individual studies for the purpose of integrating these findings (Glass, McGaw, & Smith, 1981). He identified 130 potential studies (premarital, marital, and family) for his analysis; 107 were acquired, and 85 were submitted to meta-analysis (65 of these were unpublished studies).

The results yielded an average effect size of .44. While this statistic is much lower than that found (.85) for psychotherapy outcomes (Smith, Glass, & Miller, 1980), the results demonstrate that enrichment deserves consideration as an effective change agent. Indeed, this result is consistent with the reviews cited above. According to Giblin, the average enrichment participant is better off than 67 percent of those who do not participate.

Beyond this overall effect size, Giblin's study examined outcomes as they related to source, program, subject, design, and measurement variables. No significance was found based upon the date of the research. However, published studies demonstrated significantly higher effect sizes than unpublished ones.

With respect to program variables there were several findings. The Relationship Enhancement program was associated with the highest effect sizes (.96), which is in contrast to Couple Communication Program (.44) and Marriage Encounter (.41). Effect size was shown to be positively correlated with program structure and length. It was negatively correlated with whole family participation. Program cost, leader experience level, goal specificity, or program format were not associated with effect size.

Ten subject variables were analyzed as to effect sizes; three were significant. Larger effect sizes were associated with younger, less educated, and more troubled participants. The impact upon distressed couples challenges the assumption of marriage enrichment leaders that enrichment "works" only with healthy, nondistressed couples. These results lend support to Hof and Miller's (1981) contention that marriage enrichment is appropriate for troubled couples. However, this result with distressed couples may be due to such factors as regression to the mean and the use of clinically oriented assessment instruments which are biased toward distressed couples. Giblin found no differences related to years married, income, gender, religion, life stage, and prior enrichment experience.

Three design variables were significant—size of experimental group, quality of research design, and type of statistical analyses used. No significant differences were found for type of assignment, controls, recruitment procedures, group homogeneity, or mortality.

The 85 studies used 89 various instruments; these were primarily either behavioral or self-report in nature. Like the reviews cited above, significantly larger effect sizes were associated with behavioral measures. Outcome measures were classified according to Gurman and Kniskern's (1977) scheme with one added category: other. Relationship skills were associated with larger effect sizes. Instruments that had low ratings as to reliability and validity tended to be associated with larger effect sizes.

While follow-up scores were found to be significantly lower than post-test scores, they did not return to pretest averages.

Giblin found meta-analysis to be invaluable as a means for evaluating research, but as a post hoc procedure it leaves the investigator entirely dependent upon the existence of adequate numbers and ranges of studies and outcome measures. He was not able to test for interaction effects due to the nature of the studies.

Research Findings on Specific Programs

As pointed out above, a variety of marriage-enrichment programs have developed since 1962. Programs with national stature include Marriage Encounter, Couple Communication Program, Relationship Enhancement, and Association of Couples for Marriage Enrichment. The most thoroughly researched of these programs has been Couple Communication; the least researched has been the ACME approach.

Couple Communication Program

A thorough review of the literature on Couple Communication Program has been completed by Wampler (1982b). She included 19 research studies in her review. Although she indicated that 25 research studies had been conducted, she could gain access to the complete text of only 19.

Wampler concluded that the research evidence of the past 10 years indicates that the program is an effective tool for teaching communication skills to couples. Behavioral measures of couple interaction strongly support this conclusion. No negative outcomes were found in any study. Furthermore, the program's impact appears to be related to the program itself rather than to nonspecific factors such as attention-placebo effects or the unique skills of particular leaders. Couples indicated less use of skills after the immediate impact of the program was past; however, some studies found that the use of new communication skills persisted as long as six months after the program.

The results of self-report measures were quite mixed—some studies showing positive effects, others no effect, and others mixed. The mixed results with respect to the impact of the training on communication quality and relationship satisfaction were due partially to the quality of the research designs. The studies with better research designs reported positive effects of the Couple Communication Program on communication and/or relationship satisfaction, which persisted after the immediate impact of the training had faded. Self-report assessments of the program's effects on self-disclosure and self-esteem have received research attention, but no positive effects have been found.

Follow-up studies tended to indicate gains over pretest levels. However, further research is needed which includes follow-up comparison with a control group, as well as both self-report and behavioral measures. The studies which used a comparative treatment group in addition to a no-treatment condition as a means of testing for the effects of nonspecific factors found Couples Communication to be superior to all the tested alternatives. Wampler reviewed two studies which compared groups with husband and wife present (conjoint) and groups where the marital dyad was divided and trained in different groups (concurrent). Beaver (1978) found positive effects, but this study is methodologically flawed. Davis (1980) found positive effects for both conjoint and concurrent groups on recall accuracy, relationship satisfaction, and work style communication. However, the conjoint group was superior to the concurrent on couple's ability to predict partner's responses to the recall accuracy questionnaire.

Studies which tested for differences between training teams found no significant differences. In other words, the effects of Couple Communication Program were not attributable to the uniqueness of particular instructors.

A second review of the effectiveness of the Couple Communication Program was conducted by Wampler (1982a) utilizing meta-analysis. This study is based on 20 studies of Couple Communication, one more than her more traditional review (Wampler, 1982b). The conclusions from the meta-analysis paralleled those from the previous review. The major difference was in the area of the durability of effects. Wampler concluded that the large positive changes in behavior persisted over time, the changes in relationship satisfaction decreased, and the positive changes in communication quality increased.

In her traditional review Wampler concluded that Couple Communication had no effect on self-disclosure and self-esteem, but the meta-analysis indicated a moderately positive impact on both self-disclosure (.40) and self-esteem (.56). The conclusion must be tentative given the small number of studies utilizing these measures.

Several studies that appear to be well-designed were not reported by Wampler. Thielen, Hubner, and Schmook (1976/1981) found no significant difference between the experimental and control groups on satisfaction with partnership. The Couple Communication participants changed more than the control group on all communication measures, especially disclosing feelings and level of regard.

Hill (1982) conducted a study designed to determine the effects of the Couple Communication Instructor-Training Workshops on the decision making of instructor couples.

The Couple Communication participants scored significantly higher on self-esteem, had significantly lower disparity scores on the sex-role preference measure, and used significantly more verbal-persuasion strategies than the control group participants in bargaining and negotiating. Support was found for Couple Communication Instructor Training's influence on sex role preferences in an egalitarian direction with a somewhat greater effect for husbands than wives. (p. 5265-A)

Support was also found for the training's increase of couples' use of verbal-persuasion strategies as compared with manipulative-competitive approaches.

Dillard (1981) investigated the experiential component of Couple Communication in an attempt to determine whether it is a necessary and effective change-inducing element. She set up two treatment groups—experiential/didactic and didactic. The control group received no treatment. She used many of the standard measures common with marriage-enrichment studies. Using pretest, post-test, and three-month follow-up, the results indicated that enrichment had no effect on participants. She concluded her study with the following recommendation: "Finally, the underlying assumption that marital enrichment produces change should be examined carefully and perhaps, if indicated, eliminated" (p. 2882-A).

Several comparative studies have been conducted which were not reported by Wampler. Witkin (1976/1981) compared Couple Communication with a behavior-oriented communication-skills workshop. There was no difference on self-report measures. Couple Communication couples changed more than the behavior-oriented group on three behavioral measures—increased expression of nonverbal positives decreased expression of both nonverbal and verbal negatives on post-test; differences were stable after a two-month follow-up.

Warner (1982) compared a religious marriage-enrichment program with Couple Communication. Both self-report and behavioral measures were used. No difference was found between the treatment groups nor between them and the no-treatment control condition. On the self-report measure (the Barrett-Lennard Relationship Inventory), religious enrichment group participants scored significantly higher than Couple Communication participants and controls on the Congruence subscale. Near-significant gains over Couple Communication participants by religious enrichment participants were obtained also on the Empathy and Unconditionality subscales. These results occurred at post-test but not at the two-month follow-up.

Relationship Enhancement

According to Giblin (1982) the studies on Relationship Enhancement had the highest effect size (.96). However, only seven studies have been conducted on this highly esteemed program (Brock, 1974; Brock & Joanning, 1983; Collins, 1972; Ely, Guerney, & Stover, 1973; Jessee & Guerney, 1981; Rappaport, 1976; Wieman, 1973). The meaning of these studies is open to some question because many of the assessment tools lacked reliability or validity data (L'Abate & McHenry, 1983), and with the exception of couples' communication skills, there has been a heavy reliance on self-report measures (Levant, 1983). (See Chapter 2 for a close examination of this literature.)

The study by Brock and Joanning compared the Relationship Enhancement program and the Couple Communication Program. Recognized self-report and behavioral measures were used to assess perceptions of marital adjustment and communication as well as communication skill. Both groups plus the control group were determined to be equivalent on the basis of statistical analysis of pretests.

Following the four weeks of the Couple Communication Program, a midtest comparison of the three groups was taken. Only the behavioral measure of communication skill proved significant. Both Relationship Enhancement and Couple Communication were shown to be equally effective skills-training strategies.

Two post-test comparisons were employed, one following each program's conclusion (Couple Communication—4 weeks; Relationship Enhancement—10 weeks) and one at a 10-week period for both programs (Couple Communication participants received an extra 6 weeks of training in problem solving). In the first post-test comparison, Relationship Enhancement couples showed changes in couples' general marital satisfaction, general communication patterns, and expression of affection, whereas Couple Communication did not. Also this comparison found Relationship Enhancement more effective in increasing mates' general agreement and actual communication skills.

Follow-up testing occurred about 90 days after the second post-test and showed that Relationship Enhancement participants' gains in general marital satisfaction, general agreement, and communication skills maintained after treatment. In addition, Relationship Enhancement was found to be superior to Couple Communication with spouses who were identified in the pretest as having low marital satisfaction. Follow-up testing indicated that these couples retained the gains they had accomplished over the 10-week program.

Brock and Joanning also assessed the negative effects of the two programs. The Relationship Enhancement program was found to be less harmful to couples' relationship than was the Couple Communication Program.

ACME Retreats

Only one study has assessed the effectiveness of ACME retreats (Swicegood, 1974). The experimental group showed a significant increase on their consensus of ranked values, while the control group showed no change. Significant changes in communication were reported for 5 of the 13 communication areas. For the control group 2 of 13 communication areas showed significant change between pre- and post-test. Degree of husband–wife agreement on the communication areas increased significantly on all 13 items for the enrichment group, but no significant changes were found for the control group. Ninety-one percent of the participants agreed that their marriage had been enriched by the experience. Follow-up interviews with six couples indicated some erosion of benefits over an extended time period. No control group was used in the follow-up.

Marriage Encounter

Marriage Encounter has been the most popular as well as the most controversial of all the marriage-enrichment programs. As a result, it has drawn high praise (Bosco, 1972; Genovese, 1975; Regula, 1975) as well as sharp criticism (DeYoung, 1979; Doherty et al., 1978). The praise-givers have been persons associated with Marriage Encounter, whereas the critics have been behavioral scientists.

Doherty et al. provided a critique of Marriage Encounter's ideology as well as of the weekend experience. They also itemized six potentially harmful effects of Marriage Encounter. With respect to ideology they questioned the validity of the movement's emphasis on total unity in marriage at the expense of one's individuality. Marriage Encounter promotes one way of being married rather than seeing that varying degrees of individuality and closeness may be appropriate. They also felt the movement has vulgarized the Judaeo-Christian theology of marriage into a set of norms and rules for achieving unity. They found the weekend program to be authoritarian and restrictive, with no encouragement for independent judgment or participant feedback. The authoritarianism was expressed by the use of strong persuasion to accept the marital theology of Marriage Encounter on the part of participants and coercive tactics upon couples to make life-altering decisions and to adopt new techniques of communication.

The harmful affects they saw were:

1. The benefits of the weekend may be at best temporary and at worst illusory.
2. Couples might avoid fundamental conflicts in the name of marital unity.
3. Couples might use the dialogue technique as a ritualized crutch.
4. Couples, having had a weekend high, might be set up for a hard fall.
5. Couples might experience a burden of guilt by failing to practice the daily dialogue technique, a guilt which gets expressed in resentment toward one's mate.
6. Possible separative or divisive influences may develop with respect to a couple's relationships with their children, relatives, and friends.

DeYoung, who was a participant-observer, found the experience to strengthen his own marriage. However, he offers several caveats. First, he found the religious element in the weekend much stronger than was contended. The program clearly promotes strengthening ties to the church as well as couple relationships. Second, the experience was like an initiation ceremony whereby one learns important and mystical facts that enable one to be an adult. Third, he found the operation and the teachings to be male-centered, with females encouraged to be followers while males take the lead. Fourth, no attempt was made to understand personal and marital life in light of social and occupational structures; a unified marriage was presented as some form of salvation from the harsh realities of the world.

Stedman (1982) has responded to these two critiques. He believed that DeYoung and Doherty et al. were correct in noting that the theological-religious dimension is central to the Marriage Encounter experience; however, Stedman believed that neither properly analyzed this dimension due to their lack of theological sophistication. The emphasis on couple-ness did not in his view promote enmeshment and fusion but healthy interdependence. With regard to the weekend experience, he found many of their observations quite correct but having an outsider's perspective. He then provided an insider's perspective. He was most puzzled by De-Young's complaint of the weekend being male-centered; from Stedman's perspective the complete thrust of the weekend is toward the theory and practice of sacramental interdependence.

Stedman addressed Doherty et al.'s concern about potential harmful effects. He saw these simply as speculation without the support of empirical data but urged that each of the concerns be translated into researchable questions.

Despite its international visibility, very few empirical outcome studies on Marriage Encounter have appeared in the professional literature.

However, several dissertations have been written which have relied exclusively on self-report measures.

One post-test-only study (Becnel, 1978) found no significant differences between experimental and control groups on measures of marital need satisfaction, sexual identity, and ability to experientially focus or to self-disclose affectively.

A number of short-term follow-up studies have been conducted. With regard to overall marital satisfaction and adjustment, the studies by Costa (1981), Dempsey (1980), Huber (1978), Milholland and Avery (1982), and Taubman (1981) found positive results. Hawley (1980) found insignificant results.

A number of the follow-up studies demonstrated that Marriage Encounter had an impact on relationship skills. Marital communication increased significantly according to Costa (1981), Dempsey (1980), Neuhaus (1977), Samko (1978), Seymour (1979), and Taubman (1981). Increase in self-disclosure was found to be significant in studies conducted by Dempsey, Neuhaus, Samko, and Taubman. Milholland and Avery found no significant increase in Marriage Encounter participants over the control group on self-disclosure. Samko found that wives who did not use the dialogue technique following their Marriage Encounter weekend dropped significantly in self-disclosure in follow-up measures.

Taubman examined the effects of the technique of dialogue on self-disclosure, communication, satisfaction, and awareness, and found significant changes for the dialogue treatment group but not for the non-dialoguing treatment group. Huber found that the frequency of use of the dialogue technique between post-test and follow-up did not prove to be a significant factor.

A number of personality and perceptual studies have been conducted with Marriage Encounter. Becnel (1978) found no significant impact of Encounter upon sex-role identity. Two studies examined interpersonal perception. Hawley (1980) obtained nonsignificant results, whereas Seymour (1979) found moderate enhancement in the perceptual congruence of the marital dyad in follow-ups. Taubman (1981) found significant results related to awareness in follow-ups. Watkins (1981) obtained mixed results on a number of perceptual variables related to Marriage Encounter concepts. Powers (1982) did not detect significant changes in wives' perceptions of the marital relationship, but husbands' perceptions seemed to improve and be maintained. French (1976) found that self-esteem was effected positively and maintained by Marriage Encounter.

With respect to other variables, Milholland and Avery (1982) found that interpersonal trust between Marriage Encounter couples increased and was maintained. Seymour (1979) found that marital commitment increased.

Urbaniak (1982) investigated whether the Caring Relationship Inventory could be used to compare Marriage Encounter couples with a normative population. He demonstrated that encounter couples compared most closely to the Caring Relationship Inventory normative groups of successfully married couples and perceived their marriages to be well-functioning.

Several investigators have studied instrumentation for measuring Marriage Encounter results. Powers (1982) found that the Caring Relationship Inventory has modest short-term, test–retest reliability for both husbands and wives. It has poor long-term, test–retest reliability for both spouses. Taubman (1981) developed the Marital Data Matrix based upon the modification of other measuring devices. She demonstrated construct validity for the instrument upon the basis of a factor analytic study. Watkins (1981) developed the Marriage Encounter Relationship Inventory (MERI) to assess the congruence of couple perceptions related to concepts treated in Marriage Encounter. He concluded that the three administrations of the MERI tended to support the face validity and reliability of the instrument.

Doherty and Walker (1982) reported on 13 case reports obtained by seven marriage therapists. The purpose of the investigation was to show the relationship between participation in Marriage Encounter and subsequent marital or family distress. They provide limited evidence of marital deterioration, which may take one of the following forms: (1) increased marital conflict; (2) avoidance of constructive problem solving; or (3) marital enmeshment that excludes children. Given the small number of cases, the sample was biased; hence, the results are difficult to generalize to a larger population.

Lester and Doherty (1983) have conducted a mail-survey study on couples' long-term evaluation of the experience with Marriage Encounter. The results indicated that approximately 80 percent of the couples reported a very positive experience. Dialogue as a technique was positively valued by 66 percent of the husbands and 60 percent of the wives. With regard to negative effects, 3 percent of the husbands and 6 percent of the wives reported a global negative effect on one or more areas of marital life. The most frequently cited negative effect (6 percent of husbands and 18 percent of wives) was that needs were identified on the weekend that afterwards were not met, thus leaving the person feeling frustrated. Twelve couples (9.3 percent of the sample of 200) suffered potentially serious negative effects from the weekend experience.

In conclusion it appears that Marriage Encounter had primarily a positive impact upon marital satisfaction and relationship skills. Personality and perceptual variables were mixed and for the most part tended to be insignificant.

Conclusions

The purpose of this chapter on marital enrichment has been to review its historical origins and development, educational and group-process issues, and to evaluate research and its outcomes. The results of the review indicate that marriage enrichment is an emerging movement which has taken a variety of forms. The research outcomes to a large degree have shown that marriage enrichment is an effective agent of change for improving marital relationships. Specifically, the research has shown enrichment's greatest impact to be on communication interaction. It has also shown that relationship skills can be taught to couples and that communication satisfaction from the learning experience is maintained over time. Marital satisfaction and adjustment have also been affected by marriage enrichment. In comparative studies Couple Communication Program and Relationship Enhancement have had more impact than others. Of the two, current studies indicate that Relationship Enhancement makes the more significant changes in a couple's life together.

In the future, program development with respect to marriage enrichment needs to base its theory and program goals upon the family strengths research (Hoopes, Fisher, & Barlow, 1984; Olson et al., 1983). Certainly the goal of marriage enrichment is to enhance the building of healthier family systems.

Future research needs to take into consideration the following points. First, continued effort needs to be made to overcome methodological shortcomings in research designs. Second, there needs to be a greater coordination between theory, research hypotheses, and assessment tools. Third, since the research has relied primarily upon self-report measures, it is imperative that future studies incorporate one, preferably more, objective, observational assessment tool(s). Fourth, comparative studies of all kinds are needed, that is, types of programs, program components, leadership variables, and so on. Fifth, religious-based enrichment programs need thorough research since there is little research to indicate their efficacy. The one exception is Marriage Encounter, but little of this research has been published. Sixth, if future marriage-enrichment programs should move toward meeting the needs of target populations, attention will need to be given to methodological rigor in the research designs.

References

Augsburger, D. W. (1974). *The love-fight.* Harrisonburg, VA: Choice Books.
Bach, G., & Bernhard, Y. (1971). *Aggression lab: The fair fight training manual.* Dubuque, IA: Kendall/Hunt.

Bach, G., & Wyden, P. (1969). *The intimate enemy: How to fight fair in love and marriage.* New York: Morrow.

Beaver, W. A. (1978). Conjoint and pseudo-disjunctive treatment in communication skills for relationship improvement with marital couples. *Dissertation Abstracts International, 39,* 3361A–3362A.

Beck, D. F. (1976). Research findings on the outcomes of marital counseling. In D. H. L. Olson (Ed.), *Treating relationships* (pp. 431–473). Lake Mills, IA: Graphic Publishing.

Becnel, H. P., Jr. (1978). The effects of a Marriage Encounter program on marital need satisfaction in regard to role identity, focusing, and self-disclosure in intimacy. *Dissertation Abstracts International, 39,* 123A.

Berne, E. (1964). *Games people play.* New York: Grove.

Birchler, G. R. (1979). Communication skills in married couples. In A. S. Bellack & M. Hersen (Eds.), *Research and practice in social skills training* (pp. 273–315). New York: Plenum.

Bosco, A. (1972). *Marriage encounter: The rediscovery of love.* St. Meinrad, IN: Abbey.

Brock, G. W. (1974). *A follow-up study of an intensive conjugal relationship enhancement program.* Unpublished master's thesis, Pennsylvania State University, University Park.

Brock, G. W., & Joanning, H. (1983). A comparison of the Relationship Enhancement program and the Minnesota Couple Communication Program. *Journal of Marital and Family Therapy, 9,* 413–421.

Buber, M. (1937). *I and thou.* Edinburgh: Clark.

Buber, M. (1947). *Between man and man.* London: Routledge & Kegan Paul.

Buettner, J. (1976, February). A history of the Marriage Encounter in the United States. *Agape,* pp. 14–19.

Burns, C. W. (1972). *The effectiveness of the basic encounter group in marriage counseling.* Unpublished doctoral dissertation, University of Oklahoma, Norman.

Calvo, G. (1975). *Marriage encounter.* St. Paul, MN: Marriage Encounter, Inc.

Carkhuff, R. (1973). *The art of problem solving.* Amherst, MA: Human Resource Development Press.

Catron, D., & Catron, S. (1982). *A guide for leaders of support groups.* Winston-Salem, NC: ACME.

Chartier, J., & Chartier, M. (1984). *Trusting together in God: Living your faith, my faith, and our faith.* St. Meinrad, IN: Abbey.

Clinebell, H. J., & Clinebell, C. H. (1970). *The intimate marriage.* New York: Harper & Row.

Collins, J. D. (1972). The effects of the conjugal relationship modification method on marital communication and adjustment. *Dissertation Abstracts International, 32,* 6674B.

Costa, L. A. (1981). The effects of a Marriage Encounter program on marital communication, dyadic adjustment and the quality of interpersonal relationships. *Dissertation Abstracts International, 42,* 1850A.

Davis, G. M. (1980). The differential effect of married couple communication training in groups with the spouse present and spouse not present. *Dissertation Abstracts International, 40,* 4023B.

Dempsey, R. J. (1980). Marital adjustment, improved communication, and greater self-disclosure as the effects of a weekend Marriage Encounter. *Dissertation Abstracts International, 40,* 4258A.

DeYoung, A. J. (1979). Marriage Encounter: A critical examination. *Journal of Marital and Family Therapy, 5*(2), 27–34.

Dillard, C. K. (1981). Marriage enrichment: A critical assessment of the Couples Communication Program model. *Dissertation Abstracts International, 42,* 2882A.

Doherty, W. J., McCabe, P., & Ryder, R. G. (1978). Marriage Encounter: A critical appraisal. *Journal of Marriage and Family Counseling, 4*(4), 99–107.

Doherty, W. J., & Walker, B. J. (1982). Marriage Encounter casualties: A preliminary investigation. *American Journal of Family Therapy, 10*(2), 15–25.

Elliott, S. S., & Saunders, B. E. (1982). The systems marriage enrichment program: An alternative model based on systems theory. *Family Relations, 31,* 53–60.

Ely, A. L., Guerney, B. G., Jr., & Stover, L. (1973). Efficacy of the training phase of conjugal therapy. *Psychotherapy: Theory, Research and Practice, 10,* 201–207.

Evans, W. I. (1975). *The pastor's role in working toward a corrective for the contemporary marital crisis.* Unpublished doctoral thesis-project, The Eastern Baptist Theological Seminary, Philadelphia.

Foote, N. N., & Cottrell, L. S. (1955). *Identity and interpersonal competence.* Chicago: University of Chicago Press.

French, M. (1976). *The changes in self-esteem as a function of self-disclosure.* Unpublished doctoral dissertation, California School of Professional Psychology, San Diego.

Gallagher, C. (1975). *The marriage encounter: As I have loved you.* Garden City, NY: Doubleday.

Garland, D. S. R. (1983). *Working with couples for marriage enrichment: A guide to developing, conducting, and evaluating programs.* San Francisco: Jossey-Bass.

Genovese, R. J. (1975). Marriage Encounter. *Small Group Behavior, 6,* 45–56.

Giblin, P. R., Sprenkle, D.H. & Sheehan, R. (1985). Enrichment outcome research: A meta-analysis of premarital, marital and family findings. *Journal of Marital and Family Therapy, 11,* 245–271.

Giblin, P. R. (1982). *Meta-analysis of premarital, marital, and family enrichment research.* Unpublished doctoral dissertation, Purdue University, West Lafayette, IN.

Glass, G., McGaw, B., & Smith, M. (1981). *Meta-analysis in social research.* Beverly Hills: Sage.

Green, H., Jr. (1976). A Christian marriage enrichment retreat. In H. A. Otto (Ed.), *Marriage and family enrichment* (pp. 85–93). Nashville: Abingdon.

Guerney, B. G., Jr. (1977). *Relationship enhancement.* San Francisco: Jossey-Bass.

Gurman, A. S., & Kniskern, D. P. (1977). Enriching research on marital enrichment programs. *The Journal of Marriage and Family Counseling, 3*(2), 3–11.

Hawley, R. W. (1980). The Marriage Encounter experience and its effects on self-perception, mate-perception, and marital adjustment. *Dissertation Abstracts International, 40,* 5791A–5792A.

Hayward, D. (1976). Positive partners: A marriage enrichment communication course. In H. A. Otto (Ed.), *Marriage and family enrichment* (pp. 121–128). Nashville: Abingdon.

Hill, E.W. (1982). An analysis of the decision-making of Couple Communication instructor couples. *Dissertation Abstracts International, 42,* 5265A.

Hof, L., Epstein, N., & Miller, W. R. (1980). Integrating attitudinal and behavioral change in marital enrichment. *Family Relations, 29,* 241–248.

Hof, L., & Miller, W. R. (1981). *Marriage enrichment: Philosophy, process, and program.* Bowie, MD: Robert J. Brady.

Hoopes, M. H., Fisher, B. L., & Barlow, S. H. (1984). *Structured family facilitation programs: Enrichment, education, and treatment.* Rockville, MD: Aspen Systems Corp..

Hopkins, P., & Hopkins, L. (1976). The marriage communication labs. In H. A. Otto (Ed.), *Marriage and family enrichment* (pp. 227–240). Nashville: Abingdon.

Howe, R. L. (1963). *The miracle of dialogue.* Greenwich, CT: Seabury.

Huber, J. W. (1978). The effects of dialogue communication upon the interpersonal marital relationship. *Dissertation Abstracts International, 38,* 3883B.

Jacobson, N.S. (1978). A review of the research on the effectiveness of marital therapy. In T. J. Paolino, Jr. & B. S. McCrady (Eds.), *Marriage and marital therapy: Psychoanalytic, behavioral and systems theory perspectives.* New York: Brunner/Mazel.

Jessee, R. E., & Guerney, B. G., Jr. (1981). A comparison of gestalt and relationship enhancement treatments with married couples. *The American Journal of Family Therapy, 9*(3), 31–41.

Jourard, S. (1964). *The transparent self: Self-disclosure and well-being.* New York: Van Nostrand.

Kearns, W. P. (1980). *The development of a marriage enrichment program on conflict management for recently married couples.* Unpublished doctoral thesis-project, The Eastern Baptist Theological Seminary, Philadelphia.

Kilmann, P. R., Julian, A., & Moreault, D. (1978). The impact of a marriage enrichment program on relationship factors. *Journal of Sex and Marital Therapy, 4,* 298–303.

Kilmann, P. R., Moreault, D., & Robinson, E. A. (1978). Effects of a marriage enrichment program: An outcome study. *Journal of Sex and Marital Therapy, 4,* 54–57.

Kind, J. (1969). The relation of communication-efficiency to marital happiness and an evaluation of short-term training in interpersonal communication with married couples. *Dissertation Abstracts International, 29,* 1173B.

Kligfeld, B. (1976). The Jewish Marriage Encounter. In H. A. Otto (Ed.), *Marriage and family enrichment* (pp. 129–143). Nashville: Abingdon.

L'Abate, L. (1975). A positive approach to marital and familial intervention. In L. R. Wolberg & M. L. Aronson (Eds.), *Group therapy 1975: An overview.* New York: Stratton Intercontinental Medical Book Corp.

L'Abate, L. (1977). *Enrichment: Structured interventions with couples, families and groups.* Washington, DC: University Press of America.

L'Abate, L. (1981). Skill training programs for couples and families. In A. S. Gurman & D. P. Kniskern (Ed.), *Handbook of family therapy* (pp. 631–661). New York: Brunner/Mazel.

L'Abate, L., & McHenry, S. (1983). *Handbook of marital interventions.* New York: Grune & Stratton.

Larson, R. S., & Larson, D. E. (1979). *I need to have you know me: A guide to a better marriage.* Minneapolis: Winston.

Lederer, W. J., & Jackson, D. D. (1968). *The mirages of marriage.* New York: Norton.

Lester, M. E., & Doherty, W. J. (1983). Couples' long-term evaluations of their marriage encounter experience. *Journal of Marital and Family Therapy, 9,* 183–188.

Levant, R. F. (1983). Client-centered skills-training programs for the family: A review of the literature. *The Counseling Psychologist, 11*(3), 29–46.

Lewis, J. M., Beavers, W. R., Gossett, J. T., & Phillips, V. A. (1976). *No single thread: Psychological health in family systems.* New York: Brunner/Mazel.

Mace, D. R. (1982). *Close companions: The marriage enrichment handbook.* New York: Continuum.

Mace, D. R. (Ed.). (1983). *Prevention in family services: Approaches to family wellness.* Beverly Hills: Sage.

Mace, D., & Mace, V. (1977). *How to have a happy marriage.* Nashville: Abingdon.

Maslow, A. H. (1968). *Toward a psychology of being.* New York: Van Nostrand Reinhold.

McIntosh, D. M. (1975). A comparison of the effects of highly structured, partially structured, and non-structured human relations training for married couples on the dependent variables of communication, marital adjustment, and personal adjustments. *Dissertation Abstracts International, 36,* 2636–2637A.

Milholland, T. A., & Avery, A. W. (1982). Effects of Marriage Encounter on self-disclosure, trust and marital satisfaction. *Journal of Marital and Family Therapy, 8*(2), 87–89.

Miller, S., Nunnally, E. W., & Wackman, D. B. (1976). Minnesota Couples Communication Program (MCCP): Premarital and marital groups. In D. H. L. Olson (Ed.), *Treating relationships* (pp. 21–39). Lake Mills, IA: Graphic Publishing.

Nadeau, K. G. (1971). *An examination of some effects of the marital enrichment group.* Unpublished doctoral dissertation, University of Florida, Gainesville.

Nathan, E. P. (1982). Enhancing marital sexuality: An evaluation of a program for enriching the sexual relation of normal couples. *Dissertation Abstracts International, 43,* 1898A.

Neuhaus, R. H. (1977). A study of the effects of a Marriage Encounter experience on the interpersonal interaction of married couples. *Dissertation Abstracts International, 37,* 6793A.

Neville, W. G. (1971). An analysis of personality types and their differential response to marital enrichment groups. *Dissertation Abstracts International, 32,* 6766A.

Nunnally, E. W., Miller, S., & Wackman, D. B. (1981). *Couple communication instructor manual.* Minneapolis: Interpersonal Communication Programs.

Olson, D. H., Fournier, D. G., & Druckman, J. M. (1982). *Prepare enrich: Counselor's manual.* Minneapolis: Prepare-Enrich.

Olson, D. H., McCubbin, H. I., Barnes, H., Larson, A., Muxen, M., & Wilson, M. (1983). *Families: What makes them work.* Beverly Hills: Sage.

Otto, H. A. (1969). *More joy in your marriage.* New York: Hawthorn.

Otto, H. A. (1970). *Group methods to actualize human potential: A handbook.* Beverly Hills: Holistic Press.

Otto, H. A. (1975). Marriage and family enrichment programs in North America—report and analysis. *The Family Coordinator, 24,* 137–142.

Otto, H. A. (Ed.). (1976). *Marriage and family enrichment: New perspectives and programs.* Nashville: Abingdon.

Powers, J. R. (1982). Marriage Encounter and the Caring Relationship Inventory: An evaluation study. *Dissertation Abstracts International, 42,* 4206B.

Rappaport, A. F. (1976). Conjugal relationship enhancement program. In D. H.

L. Olson (Ed.), *Treating relationships* (pp. 41–66). Lake Mills, IA: Graphic Publishing.

Regula, R. (1975). Marriage Encounter: What makes it work? *The Family Coordinator, 24,* 153–160.

Roberts, P. V. (1975). The effects on marital satisfaction of brief training in behavioral exchange negotiation mediated by differentially experienced trainers. *Dissertation Abstracts International, 36,* 457B.

Rogers, C. R. (1951). *Client-centered therapy.* Boston: Houghton Mifflin.

Rogers, C. R. (1961). *On becoming a person.* Boston: Houghton Mifflin.

Samko, M. R. (1978). Self-disclosure and marital communication as a function of participation in a marriage workshop and the subsequent use of a communication technique. *Dissertation Abstracts International, 38,* 4478B.

Satir, V. (1964). *Conjoint family therapy* (rev. ed.). Palo Alto, CA: Science and Behavior Books.

Schmitt, A., & Schmitt, D. (1976). Marriage renewal retreats. In H. A. Otto (Ed.), *Marriage and family enrichment* (pp. 110–120). Nashville: Abingdon.

Schumm, W. R. (1983). Theory and measurement in marital communication training programs. *Family Relations, 32,* 3–11.

Schutz, W. C. (1967). *Joy: Expanding human awareness.* New York: Grove.

Seymour, T. (1979). Effectiveness of Marriage Encounter couple participation on improving qualitative aspects of marital relationships. *Dissertation Abstracts International, 39,* 5587B.

Smith, L., & Smith, A. (1976). Developing a national marriage communication lab training program. In H. A. Otto (Ed.), *Marriage and family enrichment* (pp. 241–253). Nashville: Abingdon.

Smith, M., Glass, G., & Miller, T. (1980). *Benefits of psychotherapy.* Baltimore: Johns Hopkins.

Speer, D. C. (1970). Family systems: Morphostasis and morphogenesis, or "is homeostasis enough?" *Family Process, 9,* 259–278.

Stedman, J. M. (1982). Marriage Encounter: An "insider's" consideration of recent critiques. *Family Relations, 31,* 123–129.

Stein, E. V. (1975). MARDILAB: An experiment in marriage enrichment. *The Family Coordinator, 24,* 167–170.

Steinglass, P. (1978). The conceptualization of marriage from a systems theory perspective. In T. J. Paolino, Jr., & B. S. McCrady (Eds.), *Marriage and marital therapy.* New York: Brunner/Mazel.

Strickler, J. (1979, October). *Marriage encounter: A medium of church renewal.* Paper presented at the meeting of the Society for the Scientific Study of Religion, San Antonio, TX.

Swicegood, M. L. (1974). *An evaluative study of one approach to marriage enrichment.* Unpublished doctoral dissertation, University of North Carolina, Greensboro.

Taubman, L. C. (1981). The effects of the technique of the dialogue, as taught in a Marriage Encounter weekend, upon self-disclosure, communication, satisfaction, and awareness. *Dissertation Abstracts International, 42,* 433B.

Thielen, A., Hubner, H.O., & Schmook, C. (1976/1981). Studies of the effectiveness of the German revised version of the Minnesota Couple Communication Program on relationships between partners. Unpublished manuscript, Institute of Psychology, University of Heidelberg. [Abstract in E. W. Nunnally, S. Miller, & D. B. Wackman, *Couple Communication instructor manual* (p. 7–4). Minneapolis: Interpersonal Communication Programs.]

Tournier, P. (1957). *The meaning of persons.* New York: Harper.

Travis, R. P., & Travis, P. Y. (1975). The pairing enrichment program: Actualizing the marriage. *The Family Coordinator, 24,* 161–165.

Urbaniak, L. M. (1982). Marriage Encounter: Description of participants and comparison to the Caring Relationship Inventory norm groups. *Dissertation Abstracts International, 42,* 5030A.

Vander Haar, D., & Vander Haar, T. (1976). The marriage enrichment program—phase I. In H. A. Otto (Ed.), *Marriage and family enrichment* (pp. 193–216). Nashville: Abingdon.

Van Eck, B., & Van Eck, B. (1976). The phase II marriage enrichment lab. In H. A. Otto (Ed.), *Marriage and family enrichment* (pp. 217–226). Nashville: Abingdon.

Vincent, C. E. (1973). *Sexual and marital health.* New York: McGraw-Hill.

Wackman, D. (1983). Promoting effective communication in families. In D. R. Mace (Ed.), *Prevention in family services: Approaches to family wellness* (pp. 175–189). Beverly Hills: Sage.

Wampler, K. S. (1982a). Bringing the review of literature into the age of quantification: Meta-analysis as a strategy for integrating research findings in family studies. *Journal of Marriage and the Family, 44,* 1009–1023.

Wampler, K. S. (1982b). The effectiveness of the Minnesota Couple Communication Program: A review of research. *Journal of Marital and Family Therapy, 9,* 345–355.

Warner, M. D. (1982). Comparison of a religious marriage enrichment program with an established communication training enrichment program. *Dissertation Abstracts International, 42,* 3774A–3775A.

Watkins, J. M. (1981). Development, application and evaluation of the Marriage Encounter Relationship Inventory. *Dissertation Abstracts International, 42,* 1467A–1468A.

Watzlawick, P., Beavin, J. H., & Jackson, D. D. (1967). *Pragmatics of human communication: A study of interaction patterns, pathologies and paradoxes.* New York: Norton.

Wieman, R. J. (1973). Conjugal relationship modification and reciprocal reinforcement: A comparison of treatments for marital discord. *Dissertation Abstracts International, 35,* 493B.

Williams, A. M. (1975). *Comparison of the effects of two marital enrichment programs on marital communication and adjustment.* Unpublished master's thesis, University of Florida, Gainesville.

Winans, T. R. (1982). The effect of group parent training on marital satisfaction and on compatibility between spouses: An application and investigation of systems theory. *Dissertation Abstracts International, 43,* 2119A–2120A.

Witkin, S. L. (1976/1981). The development and evaluation of a group training program in communication skills for couples. Doctoral dissertation, University of Wisconsin, 1976. [Abstract in E. W. Nunnally, S. Miller, & D. B. Wackman, *Couple Communication instructor manual* (p. 7–4). Minneapolis: Interpersonal Communication Programs.]

Wright, H. N. (1974). *Communication: Key to your marriage.* Glendale, CA: Regal.

Zinker, J. C., & Leon, J. P. (1976). The Gestalt perspective: A marriage enrichment program. In H. A. Otto (Ed.), *Marriage and family enrichment* (pp. 144–157). Nashville: Abingdon.

9

Innovative Divorce Approaches Developed by Counselors, Conciliators, Mediators, and Educators*

Cheryl L. Storm
Douglas Sprenkle
Windell Williamson

Prior to the 1970s, attorneys acted, albeit often reluctantly, as the primary counselors, conciliators, mediators, and educators in addition to legal advisors for divorcing individuals. Attorneys, therapists, and divorcing people generally believed divorce issues should be handled solely in the legal not therapeutic realm. Consequently, attorneys, ill-equipped themselves (Fisher & Fisher, 1982; Kressel, Lopez-Morillas, Weinglass, & Deutsch, 1979) but having no other professionals to turn to, often found themselves responding to clients' pleas for help in coping with their estranged spouses. Because of their adversarial position and their lack of appropriate training, their efforts to help fighting couples negotiate mutually satisfying agreements often failed, resulting in destructive, lengthy, and costly court cases.

Fortunately, the increase in the numbers of divorcing couples and the dissatisfaction of professionals with their lack of effective responses to the divorcing have interacted, leading to creative divorce interventions. Although many of these interventions are being practiced on a small scale, often in limited geographic areas, they hold promise for more effective professional response to the divorcing.

The purpose of this chapter is to address those innovative divorce inter-

*Portions of the research section and the tables of this chapter are reprinted from Volume 9, Number 3, pp. 239–259, 1983 of the *Journal of Marital and Family Therapy.* Copyright 1983 American Association for Marriage and Family Therapy. Reprinted by permission.

ventions which emphasize education and skills training. After outlining trends in divorce intervention, those approaches will be described, and a case used to illustrate the effective use of the approaches. Research findings will be reported and research methodology critiqued. Finally, recommendations will be offered for future work.

Changes in Divorce Intervention

During the last decade, views and practices of therapists concerning divorce have undergone major changes. Divorce has been recognized as a process consisting of stages (Brown, 1976; Fisher, 1974; Kressel & Duetsch, 1977; Weiss, 1975), and special attention has been given to conducting therapy at each of the stages.

Consequently, divorce therapy has emerged as a new subspecialty (Olson, Russell, & Sprenkle, 1980). While marital therapy often has the implicit assumption of "saving" marriages, divorce therapy "does not focus on improving the husband–wife relationship but on decreasing the function of that relationship with the goal of eventual dissolution of that relationship" (Brown, 1976, p. 410). Although goals of divorce therapy differ from goals of marriage therapy, "there is little that is strategically or technically unique to divorce therapy itself" (Gurman & Kniskern, 1981, p. 694). Existing marriage and family therapy approaches including symbolic-experiential (Whitaker & Miller, 1971), psychodynamic (Fisher, 1974; Kaslow, 1981), Bowenian (Musetto, 1978; Phillips, 1981), strategic (Haley, 1973), and behavioral (Stuart, 1980) have been used with clients in all stages of divorce.

An interdisciplinary approach involving attorneys and therapists has been proposed as the standard for working with the divorcing (Bernstein, 1977; Fisher & Fisher, 1982; Hancock, 1982; Kaslow & Steinberg, 1982; Ruback, 1982). Kaslow and Steinberg (1982) argue that professionals in either discipline are providing inadequate services if they do not refer to each other and are not familiar with each other's potential contributions. Financial settlements, usually involving property, pensions, taxes, and support, are too complex for even the most informed therapist. However, therapists can often help divorcing spouses to obtain an emotional stance that allows and facilitates their negotiating mutually satisfying legal agreements. Together therapists and attorneys form an effective therapeutic team.

Structured separation, a contracted time-limited separation, has been developed by private practice clinicians to use with couples in the decision-making stage of divorce. Conciliation courts and divorce-mediation programs have been established to help couples having trouble uncoupling accomplish their goal. And finally, divorce education/adjustment programs have been created to provide interested participants with information about the many changes that accompany a divorce.

Because structured separation, conciliation courts, mediation, and divorce education/adjustment programs specifically emphasize education and skill development, they will be elaborated on more fully in the following sections of this chapter.

Structured Separation Techniques

Structured separation, a technique used as an adjunct to counseling, is for spouses who need some distance from each other. This distance serves the purpose of helping couples understand their relationship, resolve conflicts, and decide on plans of action. Generally, structured separation is used with couples who do not seem to be benefiting from marriage counseling but remain doubtful that divorce is the best solution. Greene, Lee, and Lustig (1973) suggest using the technique to "clarify the status of the marriage, determine the readiness of a spouse for separation, ascertain motivation for help or when there is a therapeutic impasse" (p. 15). Structured separation can be used as "crisis intervention," which provides a release of tension, allowing couples to open up in therapy, or be used when separation may be needed to prevent violence (Hight, 1977). Shock of separation is minimized, and positive use is made of the separation process.

The process of invoking structured separation has been fairly consistent across different proponents. Most preferred a written contract specifying the terms of the agreement. A time limit is set, usually three months, to give adequate time for therapeutic value. However, too much time may decrease spouses' motivation to work on the relationship. All of the couples attend counseling, usually once a week, during the separation. Counseling remains the primary focus, while the separation contract is viewed as ancillary.

Proponents differ about the degree of separation. Toomim (1972) and Hight (1977) require the couple to live in separate residences. They are restricted from seeing a lawyer or making any permanent property or child custody arrangements. In contrast, Greene et al. (1973) advocate the use of distancing within the same house, reserving the use of separate residences for the more severe cases.

In most cases couples are encouraged to reach a decision at the end of the agreed-upon separation time. In other cases less emphasis is on an agreement being made within a certain time frame and the separation technique is used "as needed" throughout the therapeutic process (Greene et al., 1973).

Overall, the separation time allows couples to explore their relationships, provides new information that can be processed in counseling, and allows them to test out a separation. In essence, spouses are educated about separation and begin developing skills to cope with living singly should they divorce.

Conciliation Courts Services

Conciliation courts, court-sponsored counseling services, are a resource for couples experiencing difficulties divorcing. Although their services are usually available upon request, conciliation courts receive most of their referrals from the bench.

With the founding of the first conciliation court in 1954, the beginnings of a nonadversarial and interprofessional approach to divorce was established (Elkin, 1977). Originally conciliation courts were a means to encourage reconciliation. Over time the philosophy changed from preventing divorce to helping couples uncouple constructively. In addition, there has been a recognition that court counseling services should not end with the final decree. In fact, in 1980 California passed a law requiring the referral of all custody and visitation disputes to conciliation court services.

Today many conciliation courts provide a range of services including marriage, separation, and divorce therapy, custody and visitation counseling during and after divorce, and educational programs for the divorcing. Counseling provided by conciliation courts tends to be brief, usually six to eight sessions, "here and now reality oriented crisis counseling" (Elkin, 1977, p. 57). Generally, court conciliation therapists are granted privileged communication as an effort to maximize couples' participation in counseling.

Conciliation courts are the most frequently available nonadversarial resource for those divorcing. Even so, these services are limited to those living in certain geographic areas (such as the West and Midwest in the United States).

Mediation

Mediation is a relatively new nonadversarial approach in which a neutral third party assists couples in negotiating a mutually satisfying divorce agreement outside of, or preliminary to, litigation. Sometimes mediation occurs post-divorce for ongoing contested custody or visitation. Although mediation programs vary, all emphasize self-determination. Through the help of a mediator, couples determine the best financial settlements, living arrangements, and conflict-resolution strategies for their unique situations.

Proponents argue that there are numerous advantages to mediation. First, couples can avoid the traditional adversarial process, which may increase or create hostility between them (Coogler, 1978: Haynes, 1981, 1982). Second, because couples are integrally involved in the bargaining, there is increased compliance (Silberman, 1982) and more satisfaction with the end settlement (Pearson & Thoennes, 1982). Third, children may benefit because of the "increased chances for continued cooperation and communication between the parents . . ." (Saposnek, 1983, p. 19).

Fourth, mediation costs far less than litigation (Haynes, 1982; McIsaac, 1981; Pearson & Thoennes, 1982). According to McIsaac (1981) the expense of mediation is one-fourth that of a custody or visitation trial in California. Fifth, mediated settlements require far less court time. The University of Denver Mediation Project compiled data indicating that 9.8 hours of court time was used on the average in a contested case. In contrast, mediated cases generally require a short (usually 30 minutes), one-time hearing to finalize the agreed-upon settlement. And finally, successful mediation clients relitigate less often than those using the traditional process (Bahr, 1981; Milne, 1978; Pearson & Thoennes, 1982).

Mediation can be court sponsored, often as part of a conciliation court, or privately sponsored. Court-sponsored mediation is usually free and currently available in 12 states (Heymann, 1981). Usually the court specifies a period of time during which the mediation occurs and may ask the mediator for a recommendation if no agreement is reached.

In contrast, privately sponsored mediation usually entails an hourly fee and may offer additional seminars on divorce topics; rarely will private mediators make a recommendation to the court. Several models of private mediation exist: single-lawyer mediator, single mental health professional mediator, lawyer–therapist interdisciplinary team, and advisory attorney to a mental health professional (Silberman, 1982). Proponents of these models have developed set procedures, manuals, and training programs (e.g., Coogler, 1978; Haynes, 1981).

Vroom (1983) notes "in keeping with its philosophy of empowering both parties in a divorce and encouraging their self-responsibility, mediation places great emphasis on imparting information and developing client's practical skills . . ." (p. 40). Mediators teach couples skills to use in resolving their mutual problem.

Divorce Education/Adjustment Programs

Divorce adjustment programs are generally designed to assist divorcing and divorced persons through the many changes associated with a divorce. Some programs are a response to increasing requests from individuals seeking post-partnership counseling (Morris & Prescott, 1976). Others are based on the theoretical assumption that divorce creates a mourning that needs to be treated (American Institutes for Research, 1982). Still other programs are aimed at preventing more serious problems from arising as a result of the divorce (American Institutes for Research, 1982; Cantor, 1977).

Most of the divorce adjustment programs are offered to the general community and sponsored by community agencies (Goethal, Thiessen, Henton, Avery, & Joanning, 1983; Sobota & Cappas, 1979; Stephenson & Boler, 1981). Many programs stipulate that couples must have separated and filed for divorce before individuals can attend (American Institutes for Research, 1982). Some allow participants to attend who are at various stages of divorce. Others work only with divorces in which children are involved (Hozman & Froiland, 1976; Moreland, Schwebel, Fine, & Vess, 1982). Still others work only with the children of divorce (Cantor, 1977).

Although divorce adjustment programs have a wide range of treatment goals and vary in their targeted population, a group format is most freqently used. There are two main reasons for this choice. First, groups can provide support and acceptance to aid people experiencing negative emotions brought about by divorce (Stephenson & Boler, 1981). Second, groups are often more affordable than individual counseling (Granvold & Welch, 1977).

Divorce adjustment groups can be primarily skills training, therapeutic, or a combination. Those that are *educational* are short didactic courses covering topics relevant to each stage of divorce. Many consist of a formal lecture followed by group discussions of the material presented (Sobota & Cappas, 1979; Young, 1978a, 1978b). Some are compulsory and court ordered (Young, 1978a, 1978b), whereas others are voluntary (Sobota & Cappas, 1979).

Skills-training programs are most often based on the premise that divorced persons experience major changes in their social support system. Therefore, skills-training programs are intended to provide divorced persons with communication and coping skills to acquire new social support systems or strengthen old ones (Avery & Theissen, 1982). Additionally, skills-training programs can help improve the quality and effectiveness of parent–child communication following divorce and train both parents in behavioral management techniques helpful in their new single-parent roles (Moreland et al., 1982).

In *therapeutic* divorce adjustment groups a therapist conducts group therapy. For example, Morris and Prescott (1976) used Transactional Analysis in groups to help people understand their own internal dynamics. Hozman and Froiland (1976) used a loss and grieving model for therapeutic groups with children in a school setting.

Many groups have a *combination* format. Stephenson and Boler (1981) provide information and education in short-term groups for people experiencing an immediate crisis following divorce. After six weeks, many participants transfer to a long-term group and remain in the latter anywhere from two to five years. The long-term group is for people not experiencing a crisis but who are concerned about their future lives. Similarly, Granvold and Welch (1977) utilized cognitive-behavioral methods within a combined format. The program begins with a dissemination of knowledge via lectures and proceeds to specific problem-solving-skills training.

Divorce education/adjustment programs respond to the needs of divorcing and divorced persons by providing education, skills training, therapy, or some combination of these three approaches.

Case Illustration

Theoretically a divorcing couple could benefit from each of the previously mentioned interventions. The following hypothetical example illustrates this point: John and Ann sought marriage counseling after 15 years of marriage because, as Ann stated, "we seem to be married in name only." Ann was dissatisfied with their lack of communication, John's seemingly total preoccupation with his career, and her total responsibility for household and family matters. In turn, John was upset with Ann's continual complaining and lack of understanding regarding his job, and her seemingly constant demands on him. Rather than making progress in marital therapy, their conflict seemed to be escalating and their fights becoming increasingly more bitter.

Their therapist initiated structured separation to provide some distance, to help them assess their relationship without the ongoing hostility, and to educate them about separation. Each agreed to a three-month physical separation, to refrain from contacting an attorney, to work on developing the positives in their relationship, and to have weekly contact. At the end of their structured separation, John and Ann mutually decided to divorce.

Before initiating legal action, the couple decided to attend a four-week divorce education program covering legal-financial, emotional, family, and spiritual aspects of divorce. This program helped them make informed decisions, alerted them to existing community resources, and informed them about typical responses to each stage of divorce.

Although the divorce was a mutual decision, they differed considerably about what they believed was an equitable divorce agreement. Fortunately, mediation was offered in their area. By attending eight mediation sessions, the couple was able to negotiate a financial settlement and family arrangements both could live with. In addition, they set a precedent for effective conflict resolution should future disagreements occur. Upon completion of mediation, an attorney was contacted to draw up the final agreement.

John and Ann then independently decided to attend divorce adjustment programs. Ann joined a therapeutic group while John attended a program emphasizing communication-skills training, an area he had targeted as contributing to his marital problems. These programs assisted John and Ann in establishing themselves as resingled adults and accepting their divorced status.

As can be seen, each of the interventions contributed uniquely to John and Ann experiencing divorce as a constructive way to resolve their marital problems.

Effectiveness of These Interventions

In this section we will review and synthesize the substantive findings of evaluative research studies on structured separation techniques ($n = 2$), conciliation courts services ($n = 6$), mediation ($n = 6$), and divorce education/adjustment programs ($n = 9$). Tables 9-1 through 9-4 describe the studies and list their key findings.

In order to identify the studies, we searched the bibliographical references since 1970. These included the *Inventory of Marriage and Family Literature, Psychological Abstracts, Divorce in the 1970s* (Sell, 1979), *Dissertation Abstracts International,* and current journals. All published studies were located and reviewed. Funding limitations prevented the purchase of dissertations which could not be secured through interlibrary loan or directly from the authors.

Each study was rated on 10 dimensions: sample size; random sample or every case from an identified population; inclusion of a control group; use of random assignment; inclusion of an alternate treatment; follow-up; relevant client variables; specification and control of relevant therapist variables; standardization of treatment; and adequacy of outcome criterion. Ratings of each of these dimensions were completed independently by the authors and minor discrepancies were resolved by consensus. In the column entitled "Description/Critique" in Table 9-1, a plus (+) designates a given dimension as a methodological strength and a minus (−) designates a given dimension as a methodological limitation of a particular study.

Separation Technique Studies

Two studies (Greene et al., 1973; Toomin, 1972) assessed separation techniques. Neither of the studies used very clear outcome criteria. Greene et al. (1973) used global therapist ratings and Toomin (1972) used global client-satisfaction ratings. The authors assert that the techniques lead to greater satisfaction and less rancor. However, 67 percent of the Toomin sample and 44 percent of the Greene sample went on to divorce. Other methodological limitations suggest that these results must be interpreted very cautiously. (See Table 9-1.)

Conciliation Courts Counseling

In three of the six investigations (Graham, 1968; Hickman & Baldwin, 1970; Matanovich, 1970) in this category, couples, most of whom were considering divorce, had requested marital counseling. In a fourth study (Sampel & Seymour, 1980), one of the spouses indicated a desire for counseling at an initial dissolution hearing in a jurisdiction in which the judge was required by law to order mandatory counseling. Two others assessed client satisfaction with conciliation court services (Brown & Manela, 1977; Lee, 1979).

In four of six studies in this group, reconciliation was an intended outcome of intervention; indeed, the number of reconciliations was one of the outcome measures. In three studies at least two experimental counseling groups were compared to a no-treatment control group (Graham, 1968; Hickman & Baldwin, 1970; Matanovich, 1970). These studies found a significantly greater number of reconciliations in at least one of their experimental groups than in their no-treatment control groups. Time may have been a factor in biasing the results in favor of reconciliations. Reconciliation status was determined at only three, four, and nine weeks after the beginning of treatment. Since the divorce decision-making process often entails considerable ambiguity and vacillation, it would not be surprising if temporary "honeymoon" effects occurred as a result of "good" counseling sessions which were not maintained over time. We believe that a six-month follow-up period is a more reasonable minimum extension for assessing reconciliations. Interestingly, Sampel and Seymour (1980) did not find significant differences on the reconciliation criterion, which was assessed nine months after the beginning of the treatment period, though an absence of random assignment and other methodological difficulties (see Table 9-2) may have accounted for this difference.

Another commonality among these four studies was that both Graham (1968) and Matanovich (1970) found that spouses make more positive references to each other as a result of conciliation counseling.

Two studies (Brown & Manela, 1977; Lee, 1979) emphasized the respondents' satisfaction with the services rendered. The ratings were global, and certainly could have been contaminated by social desirability. Helpfulness ratings were roughly similar, with 75 percent of the Brown and Manela (1977) sample and 60 percent of the Lee (1979) sample having rated the agency as "helpful." These studies also reported that those clients who attended more sessions were more satisfied than those who attended only one or two. Although deterioration rates were not reported as such, 5 percent of the Brown and Manela (1977) sample and 40 percent of the Lee (1979) sample reported the agency was at least somewhat "unhelpful."

Although without baseline data or control groups it is difficult to assess the meaning of these percentages, the gross "helpfulness" percentages are similar to the general improvement percentages reported by Gurman and Kniskern (1978) for uncontrolled studies of nonbehavioral marital and family therapy.

Mediation Studies

With the exception of Kressel, Jaffee, Tuchman, Watson, and Deutsch (1980), all of the mediation programs helped couples mediate child custody and/or visitation conflicts. In all but one of the studies in this group (Irving, Benjamin, Bohm, & MacDonald, 1981), mediation was compared with the traditional adversary method of resolving the same kind of dispute. As can be seen from Table 9-3, the overall results of mediation were quite favorable and suggest that this procedure has considerable advantages.

In all of the studies in which there were direct comparisons, mediation produced (1) a considerably higher rate of pretrial stipulations or agreements than did control groups; (2) a significantly higher level of satisfaction with the mediated agreements than with those imposed by courts; (3) a dramatic reduction in the amount of litigation following final orders; (4) an increase in joint custody arrangements; and (5) a decrease in public expenses such as custody studies and court costs. However, one study (Pearson & Thoennes, 1982) suggests that attorney's fees may not be reduced.

These studies also present clues about those couples for whom media-

Table 9-1 Divorce Intervention Empirical Studies: Separation Techniques

Author	Description/Critique	Design	Outcome Criterion	Results
Green, Lee, & Lustig (1973)	73 couples utilized Transient Structured Distance agreement to regulate contact. Couples used either separate bedrooms or dwellings. * + :SS – :R, CG, RA, AT, F, CV, TV, ST, OC Remarks: Subjective outcome assessment. No controls for stage of divorce. Little information regarding therapist background. Unspecified counseling.	Case studies	Therapist ratings of improved, durably incompatible, reaching an equilibrium, or divorced.	(1) 23% improved; 23% couple endured the relationship rather than accept the consequences of divorce; 10% became reasonably stable without substantial improvement; and 44% divorced.
Toomim (1972)	18 couples in structured separation plus counseling. Separation lasted 3 months during which they abided by certain rules. + :F – :SS, R, CG, RA, AT, CV, TV, ST, OC Remarks: No criteria given for determining client satisfaction. No client descriptive information. Lack of control for stage of dissolution. Only one therapist used. Separation conditions were stated, but counseling was unspecified.	Case studies	Client satisfaction.	(1) 33% reconciled and 67% divorced. (2) Only 1 couple who divorced reported needing adversarial legal help with property settlement. (3) All but 1 couple reported having good feelings about each other and all felt they made the right decision concerning divorce or reconciliation.

*Note: SS = adequate SAMPLE SIZE. Sample size of at least 30.
R = RANDOM SAMPLE or every case from an identified population (e.g., all agency cases during a specified time period).
CG = CONTROL GROUP or COMPARISON GROUP if a quasi (no random assignment) rather than true experiment.
RA = RANDOM ASSIGNMENT to treatment(s) and control group.
AT = ALTERNATIVE TREATMENT group(s). A comparison of two or more treatment modalities beyond a "no-treatment" condition, or three or more modalities if there were no "no-treatment" controls.
F = FOLLOW-UP data collected at least 3 months after treatment.
CV = results analyzed as function of important CLIENT VARIABLES, e.g., age, sex, stage in the dissolution process.
TV = THERAPIST VARIABLES considered by using more than one therapist and specifying their backgrounds.
ST = STANDARDIZED TREATMENT which can be replicated.
OC = contains at least one OUTCOME CRITERION with evidence of reliability and validity (or used non-reactive measures).

Table 9-2 Divorce Intervention Empirical Studies: Conciliation Courts Counseling

Author	Description/Critique	Design	Outcome Criterion	Results
Brown & Manela (1977)	429 clients who voluntarily participated in marriage and/or divorce counseling evaluated agency services. Clients interviewed at intake and 4 months later. *+:SS, R, F (partial) −:CG, RA, AT, CV, TV, ST, OC Remarks: Large and diverse sample but no breakdowns by client variables. Possible social desirability. No standardization of treatment. No information regarding therapists' background. At second research interview only some clients had finished therapy.	Agency evaluation by client interview	Clients' report of helpfulness or nonhelpfulness of agency services.	(1) 75% reported agency as helpful or somewhat helpful; 14% as both helpful and unhelpful. (2) One-session attendees significantly less satisfied than those who saw a counselor during the 4 months but terminated prior to the second research interview. (3) Those still seeing a counselor at second research interview were most satisfied. (4) Divorcing clients just as satisfied as those reconciling. (5) Individuals whose spouses refused to attend as satisfied as those attending conjoint sessions.
Graham (1968)	12 couples in conjoint counseling for four 50-minute sessions (where counselors responded positively to all positive references to	Experimental	(1) Leary Interpersonal Check List. (2) Number of positive references to spouse in the last 100 minutes of coun-	(1) Treatment 1 clients developed greater positive references to mates than treatment 2. (2) Clients with a divorce pending per-

Study	Description	Type	Measures	Results
	spouse) were compared to 12 couples who received combination of individual and conjoint problem-centered counseling with no positive references. Both groups compared to a no-treatment control group. All couples considering divorce or had filed and requested marital counseling. +:SS, CG, RA, AT, ST, OC, TV, CV −:R, F Remarks: Use of individual assessment rather than more appropriate interactional assessment. 3 weeks is insufficient time to determine number of reconciliations. Otherwise, very good design.		seling. (3) Number of reconciliations after 3–4 weeks of treatment, or 3 weeks after study began for control group.	ceived their mates as less dominant in treatment 1 vs. 2. (3) Clients who reconciled made most positive references to mate during sessions. (4) Treatment 1 clients reconciled more frequently than either treatment 2 or the control group.
Hickman & Baldwin (1970)	30 couples requesting marriage counseling were assigned to either 8 hours of communication and problem-centered counseling, an 8-session programmed communication text group, or a nontreatment control group.	Experimental	(1) Semantic Differential. (2) Number of reconciliations after 4 weeks for treatment and control.	(1) Mean changes on the Semantic Differential were greatest for the counseled group and least for control group. Only changes between the counseled and control were statistically significant. (2) Counseled group

Continued

Table 9-2 Continued

Author	Description/Critique	Design	Outcome Criterion	Results
	+:SS, CG, RA, AT, ST, OC −:R, F, CV, TV Remarks: Diverse sample. No control for stage of divorce. Possible attitude test sensitization. 4 weeks is insufficient time to determine number of reconciliations. Only one therapist used. Otherwise, good design.			had statistically significantly more reconciliations than control group.
Lee (1979)	168 former clients who had participated in counseling for marital dissolution or post-dissolution problems, evaluated family court services. +:SS, R −:CG, RA, AT, F, CV, TV, ST, OC Remarks: Did nonrespondent analysis. No controls for sex, those desiring reconciliation, or stage of divorce. Little standardization of treatment. Little information regarding therapist.	Agency evaluation by mail survey of former clients during one year period	Client ratings of helpfulness of the service, the counselor, and the number of sessions; and helpfulness concerning differences over spousal problems, children, and co-parenting.	(1) 60% stated agency somewhat or very helpful. (2) 69% satisfied with counselor assistance. (3) 46% reported learning some or great deal about helping their children adjust to divorce. (4) 42% reported learning to work out differences with ex; 29% stated learning to be co-parents. (5) 42% expressed satisfaction with number of sessions attended. (6) Those who participated in more sessions tended to view agency as more helpful.

Matanovich (1970)	40 couples of 212 applying for counseling assigned to 4 groups of 10 couples. Encountertapes used in 2 groups, problem-centered counseling in a third, and no-treatment control group. +: SS, CG, RA, AT, ST, OC −:R, F, CV, TV Remarks: Use of individual assessment rather than more appropriate interactional assessment. No control for stage of divorce. 3 weeks is insufficient time to determine number of reconciliations. No specific criteria for observational data.	Experimental	(1) Leary Interpersonal Check List. (2) Number of reconciliations after 9 weeks.	(1) Encountertape groups perceived a greater affiliation in their mates after the experimental treatments. (2) The experimenter reported an increase in positive expression toward subjects' mates at the end of treatment. (3) The encountertape groups had statistically significantly more reconciliations than the control group.
Sampel & Seymour (1980)	Comparison of 18 couples in mandatory conciliation counseling, 18 couples in voluntary marriage counseling, and a control group. Average number of sessions in treatment groups was 8.5. Reconciliations assessed at an average of 9 months after the beginning of treatment.	Pre–post treatment assessment with comparison group	(1) Taylor-Johnson Temperament Analysis. (2) Marriage Adjustment Inventory. (3) Number of reconciliation after 9 months.	(1) Minimal differences among groups in amount and direction of changes on the two instruments. (2) Both treatment groups increased on expressive scale of Taylor-Johnson Temperament Analysis; conciliation group more than voluntary counseling group. (3) Wives in conciliation counseling

Continued

Table 9-2 Continued

Author	Description/Critique	Design	Outcome Criterion	Results
	+:SS, CG, OC −:R, RA, F, CV, TV, ST, AT Remarks: Dissimilar groups as all couples in concilia-tion group, vs. one couple in voluntary marriage counseling group, had filed for divorce. Control group composed in intact marriages. Nonrandomized self-selection of groups. No standardiza-tion of treatment.			group reported husbands' problems exceeded own on immaturity and neurotic traits of Marriage Adjust-ment Inventory. (4) Wives in voluntary marriage counseling group reported own problems exceeded husbands' on the neurotic traits of the Marriage Adjustment Inventory. (5) No significant differences on reconciliation criterion.

*Note:
SS = adequate SAMPLE SIZE. Sample size of at least 30.
R = RANDOM SAMPLE or every case from an identified population (e.g., all agency cases during a specified time period).
CG = CONTROL GROUP or COMPARISON GROUP if a quasi (no random assignment) rather than true experiment.
RA = RANDOM ASSIGNMENT to treatment(s) and control group.
AT = ALTERNATIVE TREATMENT group(s). A comparison of two or more treatment modalities beyond a "no-treatment" condition, or three or more modalities if there were no "no-treatment" controls.
F = FOLLOW-UP data collected at least 3 months after treatment.
CV = results analyzed as function of important CLIENT VARIABLES, e.g., age, sex, stage in the dissolution process.
TV = THERAPIST VARIABLES considered by using more than one therapist and specifying their backgrounds.
ST = STANDARDIZED TREATMENT which can be replicated.
OC = contains at least one OUTCOME CRITERION with evidence of reliability and validity (or used non-reactive measures).

282

tion may be contraindicated. These data are important given the popularity of divorce mediation training and the widely disseminated manuals (e.g., Coogler, 1978; Haynes, 1981; Irving, 1980).

1. Couples whose experience encompasses a wide range of economic and child-related issues which are highly disputed may be poor candidates for mediation (Doyle & Caron, 1979; Pearson & Thoennes, 1982).
2. Couples whose level of conflict is very high and in which one or both of the parties does not believe he or she has the strength or resources for self-representation may not be appropriate for mediation (Kressel et al., 1980).
3. Couples are poor candidates if they believe that they cannot communicate or that cooperation with the other spouse is impossible (Kressel et al., 1980).
4. Couples for whom there is high degree of nonmutuality in the divorce decision, and in which the parties maintain a high degree of psychic attachment, may find mediation to be difficult (Irving, Bohm, MacDonald & Benjamin, 1979; Irving et al., 1981; Kressel et al., 1980).
5. Couples who mediate late in the divorce process will have more difficulty. Preferably the process should be done before temporary court orders (Pearson, Thoennes, & Vander Kooi, 1982) and certainly before the promulgation of permanent orders (Doyle & Caron, 1979).
6. Couples whose disputes entail third parties such as new spouses, grandparents, lovers, and friends are less likely to be successful (Doyle & Caron, 1979; Pearson et al., 1982).
7. Couples who have low incomes or experience considerable financial strains are poorer prospects (Doyle & Caron, 1979; Kressel et al., 1980; Pearson et al., 1982).
8. Couples whose lawyers oppose mediation are less likely to be successful (Irving et al., 1979, 1981; Pearson & Thoennes, 1982).

Conversely, the "ideal" candidates for mediation are couples mediating around a limited number of issues, for whom the level of conflict is moderate, and in which both spouses feel able to represent themselves in the negotiations. Both accept the divorce and have begun the process of "letting go." The mediation occurs early in the dissolution process and before receiving court orders (either temporary or permanent). There are no third parties significantly involved in the dispute. Both parties sense some ability to communicate and cooperate with the other. Money is not a major issue in the divorce, and there are adequate resources to carry on as single persons. Finally, the attorneys support the mediation process.

Table 9-3 Divorce Intervention Empirical Studies: Mediation

Author	Description/Critique	Design	Outcome Criterion	Results
Doyle & Caron	686 cases of custody litigation referred to the Hennepin County, MN, Domestic Relations Department. Records representing all cases from June 1975 to June 1978 examined. Random sample of 113 cases where custody not contested used for comparison purposes. Compared custody resolution counseling (CRC) with more traditional custody study (CS). *+:SS, R, AT, F, CV, TV, ST –:CG, RA, OC Remarks: Ex post facto design prohibits inferences about causality and renders conclusions about groups tentative.	Ex post facto analysis of records	(1) Compared couples who contest custody with those who do not on gross sociological and demographic dimensions. (2) Compared types of cases designated to CRC vs. CS. (3) Compared rate of stipulations (pretrial agreements) in CRC vs. CS. (4) Compared custody awards in CRC, CS, and uncontested groups. (5) Compared percentage of cases returning to court for additional services.	(1) No significant differences on gross sociological and demographic dimensions between divorcing couples who contest custody and those who do not. (2) Court more likely to assign couples to CS if they have previous history of disputed custody, high level of conflict, or complex set of custody-related issues. Assignment to CS also more likely if custody dispute followed divorce litigation, if children from previous marriage were involved, and if husbands' education very high or very low. (3) Stipulations produced in slightly less than half of all contested custody cases, but occurred more frequently in CRC (77%) than in the CS (21%).

| Irving, Bohm, MacDonald, & Benjamin (1979) | 228 court clients quasi-randomly assigned to a Conciliation Counseling Service (CCS, $N = 106$) or a Traditional Intake Service (TIS, $N = 122$). Using a range of test instruments, data were gathered at three points during service delivery: at baseline, during counseling, and at an | Experimental except that cases were assigned to treatments based on whichever service had a worker available following a baseline interview | 39-line baseline interview schedule; 14-item interview record after each session; 40-item termination record; 76-item follow-up interview schedule. | (4) Custody awarded to mothers more frequently in uncontested sample (84%) than in either of contested modalities (CRC = 62%; CS = 52%). For contested population, court more likely to award custody to father as age of children increased. (5) CRC led to more stable decisions. Approximately 36% of those cases litigating custody returned to domestic relations for further services: 26% after CS and 10% after CRC. |
| | | | | (1) About 3 times as many CCS clients reached agreement with spouses than TIS clients (22% vs. 8%). (2) Counseling by CCS significantly more likely to involve participation of both spouses, include a greater number of interviews, and have a greater amount of cumulative interview time. (3) Three |

Continued

Table 9-3 Continued

Author	Description/Critique	Design	Outcome Criterion	Results
	average of 12 weeks after the termination of service. Follow-ups were done in the respondents' homes by the same interviewers who did the baseline interview. +:SS, R, F, CV, TV, ST, OC, CG −:RA, AT Remarks: Assignment was quasi-random. The CSS program utilized counselors who were better trained, had smaller caseloads, worked more flexible hours, and received more special training than TIS counselors. All instruments pretested for reliability and case-workers monitored to ensure uniform inter-view procedures.			times as many CCS as TIS clients (25% vs. 9%) re-ported quality of life had gotten "much better" after counseling. (4) Among CCS as opposed to TIS clients, agreement significantly related to number of problems rated "serious" or "very serious" and having been referred to the service by a profes-sional, especially a lawyer.

| Irving, Benjamin, Bohm, & MacDonald (1981) | During 10-month period from Sept. 1978 to June 1979, 193 (of 352 or 55%) of court client couples were studied where: both spouses agreed to participate; referral made by judge or lawyer (with agreement by both lawyers); both spouses read and spoke English fluently. The follow-up sample included 90 couples or 47%. Authors sought to determine if the percentage of those reaching agreement would be higher than among the 1979 study where quasi-random assignment was employed. Couples were generally seen 4–6 times and children were typically interviewed on one or more occasions. Most couples reported custody or access to children as most important problem. +:SS, R, F, CV, TV, ST, OC −:RA, CG, AT | Pre–post follow-up, uncontrolled | (1) At baseline a client Question Form and Pre-service Interview Record. (2) Interview Record and Termination Record at time of service. (3) Post-service Client Question Form and Follow-up Interview Schedule. (4) Court Record Schedule to monitor subsequent litigation. | (1) 70% of CCS couples reached agreement (vs. 22% in 1979 study). 12% reconciled. (2) 54% of couples reported they had "completely" and 28% "partially" accomplished goals regarding most important problems. (3) Regarding total life situation, clients (76%) reported things "better" or "much better" since counseling began. (4) Therapy reduced marital conflict significantly from baseline. (5) Counselors reported agreement more difficult if clients emotionally attached and easier if lawyers supportive. (6) Agreement more likely if custody and other problems rated "mild" at intake, and if child included in counseling at least once. (7) 10% of couples turned to court within the year. 78% of the lawyers felt service should be continued because it |

Continued

Table 9-3 Continued

Author	Description/Critique	Design	Outcome Criterion	Results
	Remarks: Although no alternate treatments or control groups, the previous (1979) study and the same agency served as a kind of baseline for comparisons.			helped avoid unnecessary litigation.
Kressel, Jaffee, Tuchman, Watson, & Deutsch (1980)	Comparison of 9 mediated couples using the Family Mediation Services with 5 nonmediated couples; spent 3–8 two-hour sessions with a mediator who facilitated negotiations regarding custody, visitation, child support and/or alimony, and division of property. +:CG,CV,TV,ST −:SS, R, Ra, AT, F, OC Remarks: There was a lack of information regarding content areas of questions, rating scales, and divorce-	Post-treatment assessment with comparison group	(1) Post divorce interviews for both groups. Interviews consisted of open-ended questions and bipolar rating scales. (2) Taped mediation sessions were also rated for the mediated group.	(1) Non-mediators had difficulty understanding process of structured mediation and tended to adopt extreme, inflexible positions. (2) Non-mediated couples exhibited higher degree of non-mutuality, more negative emotional climate, and less satisfying experiences with conjoint counseling. (3) Four patterns of divorcing couples emerged: enmeshed, autistic, direct conflict, and disengaged conflict. First two not good candidates

adjustment criteria. A self-selection of couples.			for mediation. (4) Mediation an unattractive alternative for couples who perceive level of conflict between them as high and their resources for effective self-representation as inadequate.
Margolin (1973)	150 consecutive previously divorced couples involved in custody litigation referred to conciliation court. A questionnaire was employed to obtain background data and subject's definition of reasonable visitation. One-half of group randomly assigned to a single experimental 2-hour counseling session. 91% of couples and 88% of control couples divorced 5 years or less when visitation suit was filed. +:SS, R, CG, RA, F, CV -:AT, TV, ST, OC	Experimental	(1) Whether or not couple reached pretrial agreement on visitation. (2) Satisfaction with visitation on a questionnaire sent to respondents after 4 months.	(1) 73/75 counseled couples reached agreement and set up visiting plan; one control couple independently formulated plan prior to the court appearance. (2) 9 experimental couples and 59 control repeated litigation in following 4 months. (3) Plans agreed upon by counseled couples more specific and expressed unique needs of subjects. (4) Follow-up demonstrated the following were facilitated by counseling: satisfaction with visits; parents and children enjoying visits; satisfaction with visitation

Continued

289

Table 9-3 Continued

Author	Description/Critique	Design	Outcome Criterion	Results
	Remarks: Only 1 therapist cannot separate treatment from therapist effect.			period; children's activities and care during visits; child's behavior during and following visits; children's and parents' anticipation of visits. (5) 86% of mothers and 77% of fathers designated counseling as helpful.
Pearson & Thoennes (1982)	Judges and lawyers in two metropolitan judicial districts were asked to refer all suspected cases of contested custody and visitation. Cases randomly assigned to mediation ($N = 125$) and control group ($N = 54$). Since one-half of disputants rejected the offer of mediation, a third category was called the "reject group" ($N = 95$). Interviews other than a	Experimental with two no-treatment	(1) Savings in attorney's fee. (2) Public cost savings. (3) Savings in time. (4) Agreement making. (5) Satisfaction with agreement. (6) Relationship with spouse. (7) Type of custody arrangement. (8) Child support arrangements.	(1) Savings in attorney's fees less than expected and highest fees for unsuccessful mediated group. (2) Public savings estimated at $5,610 to $27,510 per 100 mediated cases. 11% required custody studies vs. 35% in adversarial groups. (3) Although successful mediation clients moved most quickly through the court system (8.5 months), unsuccessful mediation moved slowest (14.2 months). (4) 80% of individuals who attempted mediation even-

tually reached an out-of-court agreement, although only 58% by end of mediation. 50% failed to stipulate in reject and control group samples. (5) Subsequent punitive legal activity occurred for 15% (successful mediated), 39% (reject group), and 35% (control group). None of the successful group initiated motions to modify permanent orders versus 12, 14, and 20% of the unsuccessful, reject, and control groups. (6) Respondents who reached agreements through mediation considerably more satisfied than those who reached agreements without mediation. (7) Mediation respondents reported the process improved interpersonal communication and understanding. (8) Mediation respondents opted for more co-parenting and visitation, and 69% of successful media-

pre-mediation assessment for the mediation group, done by phone, with follow-ups after the courts' promulgation of orders and 6–12 months later. Mediators were male–female teams comprised of attorneys and therapists.

+:SS, R, CG, RA, F, CV, TV

–:ST, OC, AT

Remarks: Some of the positive results could be due to "thank you" effects. Otherwise, excellent design.

Continued

Table 9-3 Continued

Author	Description/Critique	Design	Outcome Criterion	Results
				tion respondents achieved legal joint custody. (9) Child-support arrangements similar across groups but successful mediation clients more likely to share costs in lieu of formal support.

*Note: SS: = adequate SAMPLE SIZE. Sample size of at least 30.
R   = RANDOM SAMPLE or every case from an identified population (e.g., all agency cases during a specified time period).
CG = CONTROL GROUP or COMPARISON GROUP if a quasi (no random assignment) rather than true experiment.
RA = RANDOM ASSIGNMENT to treatment(s) and control group.
AT = ALTERNATIVE TREATMENT group(s). A comparison of two or more treatment modalities beyond a "no-treatment" condition, or three or more modalities if there were no "no-treatment" controls.
F   = FOLLOW-UP data collected at least 3 months after treatment.
CV = results analyzed as function of important CLIENT VARIABLES, e.g., age, sex, stage in the dissolution process.
TV = THERAPIST VARIABLES considered by using more than one therapist and specifying their backgrounds.
ST = STANDARDIZED TREATMENT which can be replicated.
OC = contains at least one OUTCOME CRITERION with evidence of reliability and validity (or used non-reactive measures).

Divorce Education/Adjustment Programs

Two studies by Young (1978a, 1978b) evaluated a compulsory divorce-education program sponsored by a family court in Indiana. At the time of the three-month follow-up, 84 percent stated that the workshop was of some or great value, and 16 percent indicated that it was of little or no value. Sixty-one percent of the respondents also indicated that they had experienced long-term benefits.

In six studies of this group (Avery & Thiessen, 1982; Fisher, 1976; Goethal et al., 1983; Hoopes, Molene, & Stanfield-Packard, 1979; Sobota & Cappas, 1979; Theissen, Avery, & Joanning, 1980) researchers used a variety of self-report measures to assess changes in the separated and divorced participants. One common dimension assessed in the studies, albeit with three different instruments, was self-esteem, which significantly increased from pre- to post-test in the experimental groups. Three of the studies (Fisher, 1976; Goethal et al., 1983; Thiessen et al., 1980) also found significant increases in divorce adjustment as measured by the Fisher Divorce Adjustment Scale (Fisher, 1976).

In the final study in this group (Cantor, 1977), changes were assessed by parents, teachers, and group leaders of children participating in a group. Minimal changes were reported in openness about divorce and decreased shame. (See Table 9-4.)

Conclusions

The following conclusions emerged from this review. As will be seen in the methodological critique that follows, the last two have the most solid empirical support.

1. There is suggestive evidence that structured-separation techniques may diminish rancor even if they do not prevent divorce. However, these conclusions are based on studies with severe methodological limitations.
2. Divorce education/adjustment groups appear to be helpful in aiding divorcing individuals to feel a mastery of their environment and gain more self-confidence. They are also likely to produce at least short-term gains in self-esteem and on measures of divorce adjustment.
3. Consumers of court-related counseling centers report global satisfaction ratings roughly similar to those in other uncontrolled studies of marital and family therapy.
4. Conciliation court counseling appears to increase the percentage of (at least temporary) reconciliations over the short term.
5. There is impressive evidence that mediation is superior to the tradi-

Table 9-4 Divorce Intervention Empirical Studies: Divorce Education/Adjustment Programs

Author	Description/Critique	Design	Outcome Criterion	Results
Avery & Thiessen (1982)	5 men and 8 women who were separated in experimental group given didactic information and communication-skills training. Results compared to 5 men and 9 women in a control group. *+:CG, CV, TV, ST, OC –:SS, R, RA, AT, F	Experimental, although assignments to experimental and control groups were made on the basis of availability	(1) The perceived Social Support Scale. (2) Guerney Self-Feeling Awareness Scale. (3) Guerney Acceptance of Other Scale.	(1) Experimental group significantly increased perceived level of social support. (2) Experimental group significantly increased in self-disclosure; females increased more than males. (3) Empathy results were significant based on the Guerney Acceptance of Other Scale; females increased more in empathic ability than males.
Cantor (1977)	10 children from divorcing families who were showing changes in behavior chosen by teachers to participate in 10 group sessions. +:F –:SS, R, CG, RA, AT, CV, TV, ST, OC Remarks: Follow-up was planned.	Case studies	(1) Teachers, parents, and children evaluations. (2) Group leader observations.	(1) Minimal changes reported by teachers. (2) Group leaders observed less shame in children. (3) Teachers and group leaders reported more openness re topic of divorce.

Study	Sample/Treatment	Design	Measures	Results
Fisher (1976)	30 clients in a 10-week divorce adjustment seminar compared to a control group of 30 members from a local singles group. +:SS, CG, TV, ST, OC −:R, RA, AT, F, CV. Remarks: No controls for stage of divorce. Lack of random assignment.	Pre–post treatment assessment with comparison group	(1) Fisher Divorce Adjustment Scale. (2) Tennessee Self-Concept Scale. (3) Personality Orientation Inventory.	(1) Seminar participants had more growth in self-acceptance of divorce, disentanglement of the love relationship, rebuilding social relationships, and total divorce process as measured by Fisher Divorce Adjustment Scale. (2) Seminar participation had more growth in rebuilding self-concept as measured by Tennessee Self-Concept Scale. (3) A positive correlation between self-concept and divorce adjustment scores. (4) A positive correlation between self-actualization and divorce adjustment.
Goethal, Thiessen, Henton, Avery, & Joanning (1983)	One-month follow-up of 12 separated women in experimental group given didactic information and communication-skills training. Results compared to 15 separated women in a control group. +:CG, TV, ST, OC −:SS, R, RA, AT, F, CV	Experimental, although assignments to experimental and control groups were made on the basis of availability.	(1) General post-divorce adjustment on Fisher Divorce Adjustment Scale. (2) Rosenberg Self-Esteem Scale and subscale of the Fisher. (3) Guerney Acceptance of Other Scale.	(1) Experimental group increased post divorce adjustment on Fisher Divorce Adjustment Scale. (2) Improvement in use of empathy on Guerney Acceptance of Other Scale. (3) No significant differences on self-esteem.

Continued

Table 9-4 Continued

Author	Description/Critique	Design	Outcome Criterion	Results
	Remarks: Little information given about raters.			
Hoopes, Molene, & Stanfield-Packard (1979)	42 separated or divorced men and women in an 8-week divorce-adjustment group compared to a control group of 19. −:R, AT, F, CV, TV +:SS, CG, RA, ST, OC	Experimental	(1) Depression Adjective Check List. (2) Rosenberg's Self-Esteem Scale. (3) Modified Osgood's Semantic Differential.	(1) Group participants decreased level of depression as measured by Depression Adjective Check List. (2) Group participants increased level of self-esteem as measured by social worth and social competence factors of the Modified Osgood Semantic Differential.
Sobota & Cappas (1979)	Study assessed changes in two groups (30 total participants) who attended a 4-week lecture and discussion on divorce adjustment. +:SS, R, ST, OC −:CG, RA, AT, F, CV, TV Remarks: No control for stages of divorce. Only one therapist was involved.	Uncontrolled; pre–post workshop assessment and comparison of two samples	Semantic Differential.	(1) Seven significant changes in first sample replicated in second sample. (2) Changes on evaluation and potency dimensions of "Myself" cross-validated. (3) Evaluation changes on "Divorce," "Separation," "Former Spouse," and the "Present" replicated. (4) "Potency" replicated for children.

| Thiessen, Avery, & Joanning (1980) | 13 women in experimental group given 15 hours of training in interpersonal communication skills along with didactic information. Results compared with a control group of 15 women.
+:CG, TV, ST, OC
−:SS, R, RA, AT, E, CV
Remarks: Mean length of separation of control group 6 months vs. 3 months for experimental group. Impossible to tell if gains made by experimental group due to learning communication skills, the group experience, or some combination thereof. | Experimental, although assignments to experimental and control groups were made on the basis of available times | (1) General post-divorce adjustment on Fisher Divorce Adjustment Scale. (2) Rosenberg Self-Esteem scale and subscale of the Fisher. (3) The author's Perceived Support Scale. | (1) Experimental group increased in overall divorce adjustment on Fisher Divorce Adjustment Scale. (2) Experimental group showed increase on self-esteem subscale of the Fisher but not on Rosenberg scale. (3) The experimental group increased on perceived empathy skills. (4) No significant increase on perceived social support or self-disclosure skills. |
| Young (1978a) | 75 women evaluated a compulsory divorce-education program. The 4-hour program focused on the legal-financial, parental, and emotional aspects of divorce.
+:SS, R, F, CV, TV, ST
−:CG, RA, AT, OC | Pre–post workshop questionnaire | Questionnaire focused on program evaluation, benefit received, and whether they would attend voluntarily. | (1) Participants pleased with total program and with separate parts. (2) Positive correlation between number of children and rating. (3) 91% would attend program on their own. (4) 58% said they could see future benefits, 34% were unsure, and 8% did |

Continued

297

Table 9-4 Continued

Author	Description/Critique	Design	Outcome Criterion	Results
	Remarks: Failure to use reliable and valid instrument. Possible contamination of results by maturation and history, as well as "thank you" effects.			not anticipate long-term benefits. (5) 71% said they would attend longer program.
Young (1978b)	25 participants in a divorce-education program evaluated the workshop 3 months later. (A follow-up study to Young, 1978a.) +:SS, R, F, ST −:CG, RA, AT, CV, TV, OC Remarks: Compared those who completed questionnaires with those who did not.	Workshop follow-up questionnaire	Follow-up questionnaire.	(1) 34% stated workshop of great value, 50% of some value, 8% of little value, and 8% of no value. (2) 61% had experienced long-term benefit (in Young, 1978a, 58% had predicted long-term benefits). (3) Most helpful information: 37% re children; 25% re legal information; 21% re emotional aspects. (4) 23% stated workshop should include more sessions and material. (5) 54% stated would attend a longer program (vs. 71% at time of Young, 1978a). (6) Overall, participants still satisfied but enthusiasm and value of workshop had decreased somewhat.

*Note: SS = adequate SAMPLE SIZE. Sample size of at least 30.
R = RANDOM SAMPLE or every case from an identified population (e.g., all agency cases during a specified time period).
CG = CONTROL GROUP or COMPARISON GROUP if a quasi (no random assignment) rather than true experiment.
RA = RANDOM ASSIGNMENT to treatment(s) and control group.
AT = ALTERNATIVE TREATMENT group(s). A comparison of two or more treatment modalities beyond a "no-treatment" condition, or three or more modalities if there were no "no-treatment" controls.
F = FOLLOW-UP data collected at least 3 months after treatment.
CV = results analyzed as function of important CLIENT VARIABLES, e.g., age, sex, stage in the dissolution process.
TV = THERAPIST VARIABLES considered by using more than one therapist and specifying their backgrounds.
ST = STANDARDIZED TREATMENT which can be replicated.
OC = contains at least one OUTCOME CRITERION with evidence of reliability and validity (or used non-reactive measures).

tional adversary process for custody and visitation disputes among couples with moderate conflict, relatively limited issues, and reasonable capacity to negotiate.

Methodological Adequacy of Existing Research

Since this is an infant field, it is not surprising that the methodologies utilized are generally unsophisticated. Because most of the studies did not provide the necessary data, a methodological critique utilizing a formal procedure such as a meta-analysis (Smith, Glass, & Miller, 1980) was not possible.

Since the studies are attempting to assess the effectiveness of various treatments, design ideals are not difficult to specify. The sample size should be adequate to test the effectiveness of a given intervention, and investigators should control for such important client variables as sex, socioeconomic status, and stage in the dissolution process and should have maximal control over the manipulation of the independent (treatment) variable. A no-treatment control group should be included to diminish such threats to external validity as history and maturation (Campbell & Stanley, 1963). Random assignment to treatment and control groups is necessary to ensure internal validity. Follow-up of treatment outcomes also should be included in order to assess the durability of changes. Theoretically relevant therapist characteristics and behavior, assessed both in the course of therapy and outside therapy, should be specified and measured. Treatments should be standardized to allow replication. Outcome criteria should have established reliability and validity.

Sample Size and Random Sample

As a group, the studies reviewed generally used adequate samples. All of the mediation studies except Kressel et al. (1980) and two of the conciliation counseling studies (Brown & Manela, 1979; Lee, 1979) used impressive sample sizes. Another methodological strength is that over half the studies utilized a random sample or every case from an identical population, for example, all therapy cases at a given agency during a six-month period.

Client Variables

Investigators generally did not control for important client variables when reporting results. In only four of the studies outside of the mediation group (Avery & Thiessen, 1982; Goethal et al., 1983; Graham, 1968; Thiessen et al., 1980) were there any controls for the stage of the dissolution process.

This is an extremely important variable because proximity to the separation event is highly correlated with stress (Kitson & Raschke, 1981). Since most of the mediation studies monitored subjects' progress from the time of contact with the court system, there was a built-in control for all stages among this group. Most of the studies did not analyze outcome data as a function of gender. Where social background characteristics were gathered, they were usually not utilized in the reporting of results. Brown and Manela (1977), for example, included Blacks and lower-income subjects in their sample, yet did not report results by race or income despite their large sample size.

Random Assignment and Control-Comparison Groups

Of the 23 studies, 13 included a control or comparison group and 6 used random assignment to treatment conditions. Three of the six studies in the conciliation courts counseling group were true experiments. Two in the mediation group (Margolin, 1973; Pearson & Thoennes, 1982) and one in the divorce education/adjustment program category (Hoopes et al., 1979) were also experiments. Four other studies (Avery & Thiessen, 1982; Goethal et al., 1983; Irving et al., 1979; Thiessen et al., 1980) fell just short of a true experimental design in that their method of assignment was quasi-random (based on scheduling and availability). Three studies contained quasi-"control" groups, but these were actually comparison groups (Fisher, 1976; Kressel et al., 1980; Sampel & Seymour, 1980) because there was no random assignment or matching of treatment and "control" subjects. Hence, in these studies the comparability of the treatment and "control" groups is highly suspect.

Three of the 23 studies used ex post facto analyses of treatment, thereby precluding confidence in their internal validity.

Alternate Treatment Groups

Four studies included alternate treatment groups (a comparison of two or more treatment modalities beyond the no-treatment condition, or three or more modalities if a no-treatment control group was lacking). The three (of six) conciliation court studies which were true experiments included alternate treatments. One other study with this strength (Doyle & Caron, 1979) was an ex post facto analysis of case records. Without random assignment to alternative treatments, results of this latter study must be interpreted cautiously.

Follow-up

A limitation of most (13 of 23) studies was the lack of an adequate follow-up period (three months). Two of the generally well-designed studies in the conciliation group (Brown & Manela, 1977; Sampel &

Seymour, 1980), the two separation techniques investigations (which were essentially case studies), and one divorce education/adjustment study (Young, 1978b, which was essentially a workshop follow-up investigation) met this criterion. However, in these five studies the follow-up data were of relatively short duration, and since these studies were uncontrolled, meaningful interpretation is limited. Once again, the mediation group showed the greatest strength on this dimension. Five of the studies (all except Kressel et al., 1980, which was a one-time post-treatment assessment) met this criterion. However, since the Doyle and Caron (1979) study was an ex post facto analysis of case records, its results must be interpreted cautiously.

Therapist Variables

The criterion used to evaluate the adequacy of control of therapist variables was very lenient, in that a study only had to use more than one therapist and specify the backgrounds of its therapists. Even so, only 11 studies passed this test. Five were in the mediation group. Hence, therapist factors were poorly controlled and therapist samples were insufficiently described. Typically, the studies involved the report of one therapist evaluating his or her own work, or a grouping together of the effects of multiple therapists. Only two studies (Irving et al., 1979; Pearson & Thoennes, 1982) actually reported outcomes by significant therapist variables (e.g., experience level).

Standardized Treatment

Fifteen of the 23 studies reported a standardized treatment format that could be replicated.

Outcome Criteria

Fourteen of the 23 studies utilized outcome measures with some evidence of reliability and validity (or utilized nonreactive measures which have external validity, such as records of relitigation following mediation). Of the nine studies which did not, seven used global assessments by the clients of their satisfaction or degree of helpfulness of the services rendered. The remaining two studies employed global assessments by the therapists of the effectiveness of treatment.

All but one of the outcome measures with reported reliability and validity were self-report measures. Only three of the studies (Graham, 1968; Kressel et al., 1980; Matanovich, 1970) used in-session behavioral measures such as the rating of tapes or therapists' observations. Only Graham's (1968) study reported any evidence of coding reliability. A strength of four out of six conciliation studies was their use of the nonre-active behavioral dependent variable of number of reconciliations crite-rion. Once again, the mediation group led the way with a variety of interesting nonreactive measures, including the assessment of public and private legal expenses for mediation versus nonmediation couples; the speed with which couples moved through the court system; the number and percentage of pretrial stipulations; the amount of subsequent litiga-tion; and the nature of the custody awards and child-support decisions.

Recommendations for Future Research

With the exception of the mediation and conciliation court studies, the designs of existing research studies on these interventions are generally enormously inadequate. Given the current empirical status of this re-search, several suggested guidelines for future investigations are in order.

1. There is an urgent need for more basic controlled research. While there is sufficient empirical evidence to conclude that mediation of custody and visitation disputes is preferable to the traditional adversary process, there is not a strong empirical basis on which to conclude that other forms of divorce intervention are superior to no treatment. Aside from the me-diation investigations, and the conciliation courts counseling studies, there were only two studies (Hoopes et al., 1979; Thiessen et al., 1980) which used random assignment to treatment and no-treatment conditions.

2. Other methodological refinements are necessary. Where true experi-ments are not possible, investigators should be expected to describe both their patient and therapist samples adequately. More attention needs to be given to the reliability and validity of measures and particularly to the use of valid behavioral measures. Since a number of relatively nonreac-tive dependent variables are possible in this field, their use is strongly encouraged. Controlling for theoretically significant client and therapist variables is needed. Longer follow-ups are crucial.

3. There is a particular need to control for client variables which have a theoretical and, based on prior nontherapy research, empirical relation-ship with divorce outcome. Most important, the stage in the dissolution process should be controlled in future research. It is unwise to lump together persons in crisis immediately following separation with subjects many months into the single life.

More attention also needs to be given to the possibility that there are certain patterns or types of couples who go through divorce, as suggested by Kressel et al. (1980). To date, virtually all of the divorce adjustment literature is centered on the individual.

4. Research on divorce mediation should be broadened to include investigating the mediation of such matters as child support and property settlement. Existing research centers on custody and visitation disputes. In our judgment, these additional issues have significant psychological import and are inextricably interwoven with custody and visitation disputes. For example, a person may fight for custody as a means of avoiding child-support payments.

Ironically, in the one study reviewed here in which financial matters were mediated (Kressel et al., 1980), couples were helped only with concrete issues and were referred elsewhere for emotional problems. In our judgment, all these matters reflect the inability of couples to say "good-bye" and should be mediated.

5. Eventually, investigators should compare various forms of treatment with each other. For example, there has never been an adequate empirical test of the outcomes of individual versus conjoint treatment for persons going through divorce. Elsewhere the authors have argued (Storm & Sprenkle, 1982) that specific units of treatment (individual, conjoint, family, and group) are most appropriate for persons in certain stages of the dissolution process. Research is needed to verify such speculation and to compare similar intervention methods with the same types of clients.

Implications for Practitioners

Although additional research is sorely needed, current findings of the effectiveness of these interventions indicates ways in which therapists can most effectively help divorcing clients. Therapeutic implications of current findings are discussed below.

1. Overall, interventions reviewed in this chapter are aimed at helping divorcing couples *after* problems occur. For example, conciliation court services and mediation are usually offered to couples after they begin adversarial proceedings. If these interventions were viewed as preventive rather than remedial, and more widely available to the divorcing, professionals could provide more effective services and help couples avoid some of the stress associated with divorce.

2. All divorcing couples should have the opportunity to participate in mediation. This requires that therapists become acquainted with the practices of mediation and either become skilled themselves or familiar with others who are skilled in helping couples negotiate disputes.

3. Conciliation court services and mediation programs, interventions that have the most solid empirical evidence of their effectiveness, traditionally meet with couples. This suggests that couples benefit from con-

joint meetings focused on helping them uncouple. Consequently, therapists must encourage couples to participate in therapy to help them through the early stages of divorce.

4. Therapists must recognize that anger is a normal and necessary reaction to divorce and become comfortable with working with angry couples.

5. Because education/adjustment groups appear to help individuals adjust to divorce, therapists should become actively involved in sponsoring and planning such groups. For example, the first author recruited community professionals involved with the divorcing (i.e., lawyers, child-support workers, therapists, clergy) to jointly sponsor a divorce education program. The costs were minimal as each professional group assumed responsibility for part of the program. Although these education/adjustment groups must be tailored for a specific population and locale, they should be based on preexisting programs. New education/adjustment groups should capitalize on the content, methods, and techniques that have been demonstrated to be effective in existing programs.

6. Since for many divorce imposes financial hardships, the costs of divorce programs should be minimal. Many of the divorce interventions, particularly mediation and education/adjustment groups, are privately sponsored and thus cater to the upper-middle and upper classes. Professionals must, therefore, find ways to subsidize and/or keep their costs to a minimum so that these interventions can be available to all of the divorcing.

7. Therapists should consider the structured-separation technique as an alternative for couples in marital therapy who are especially angry. However, because other studies indicate that once couples separate the likelihood of resolving their problems is greatly reduced (Levinger, 1979), this technique should be used cautiously.

Directions for the 1980s

As can be seen from this review, counselors, conciliators, mediators, and educators have created innovative and promising interventions for the divorcing. We offer the following suggestions to those wishing to continue what they have begun.

1. Divorce must continue to be recognized as a legitimate, even if difficult and painful, solution to certain marital difficulties. A bias toward viewing divorce as pathology (Raschke, 1982) has clearly affected interventions, program development, and subsequently research on divorce intervention. As divorce is increasingly accepted as a constructive alternative, additional innovative interventions will be created.

2. As noted earlier, the help available to the divorcing depends largely on where they are living. Therefore the interventions described in this chapter should be offered to more of the divorcing. To spread these interventions throughout the country may require therapists to become activists. For example, they may need to lobby for legislation mandating the funding of conciliation courts, and for changes in recent bar rulings which discourage attorneys from supporting and/or participating in mediation (Silberman, 1982).

3. Additional education and training must be offered for helping professionals about divorce. This education and training could provide helping professionals a needed foundation to encourage interdisciplinary approaches and to provide divorce interventions (e.g., divorce education, mediation) as part of their services. Perhaps, as Ruback (1982) contends, therapists should take coursework on family law while in graduate school and have supervised clinical work with families involved in the legal system.

4. Overall, research on these innovations suggests that they are helpful to the divorcing. However, better research methodology, as suggested in the guidelines given earlier, must be done to establish which interventions are (a) better than no treatment, (b) most appropriate for each stage of divorce, and (c) more effective when comparing similar treatments. We hope this chapter will increase professional enthusiasm and efforts to develop and use creative interventions with divorcing couples.

References

American Institutes for Research. (1982). Mourning the divorce: A project in Marin County, California. *International Journal of Family Therapy, 4* (3), 164–176.

Avery, A. W., & Thiessen, J. D. (1982). Communication skills training for divorcees. *Journal of Counseling Psychology, 29* (2), 203–205.

Bahr, S. J. (1981). An evaluation of court mediation: A comparison in divorce cases with children. *Journal of Family Issues, 2,* 39–60.

Bernstein, B. (1977). Lawyer and counselor as an interdisciplinary team: Preparing the father for custody. *Journal of Marriage and Family Counseling, 3,* 29–40.

Brown, E. (1976). Divorce counseling. In D. Olson (Ed.), *Treating relationships.* Lake Mills, IA: Graphic Publishing.

Brown, P., & Manela, R. (1977). Client satisfaction with marital and divorce counseling. *Family Coordinator, 26,* 294–303.

Campbell, D. T., & Stanley, J. C. (1963). *Experimental and quasi-experimental designs for research.* Chicago: Rand-McNally.

Cantor, D. W. (1977). School-based groups for children of divorce. *Journal of Divorce, 1,* 183–187.

Coogler, O. J. (1978). *Structured mediation in divorce settlement.* Lexington, MA: Lexington Books.

Doyle, P., & Caron, W. (1979). Contested custody intervention: An empirical assessment. In D. H. Olson (Ed.), *Child custody: Literature review and alternative approaches.* Department of Family Social Science, University of Minnesota.

Elkin, M. (1977). Postdivorce counseling in a conciliation court. *Journal of Divorce, 1* (1), 55–65.

Fisher, B. F. (1976). Identifying and meeting needs of formerly married people through a divorce adjustment seminar. *Dissertation Abstracts International, 37,* 7036-A. (University Microfilms No. 77-11, 057.)

Fisher, E. O. (1974). *Divorce: The new freedom.* New York: Harper & Row.

Fisher, M., & Fisher, E. (1982). Toward understanding working relationships between lawyers and therapists in guiding divorcing spouses. *Journal of Divorce, 6,* 1–16.

Goethal, K. G., Thiessen, J. D., Henton, J. M., Avery, A. W., & Joanning, H. (1983). Facilitating postdivorce adjustment among women: A one-month follow-up. *Family Therapy, 10* (1), 61–68.

Graham, J. A. (1968). The effect of the use of counselor positive responses to positive perceptions of mate in marriage counseling. *Dissertation Abstracts, 28,* 3504-A. (University Microfilms No. 68-1649.)

Granvold, D. K., & Welch, C. J. (1977). Intervention for post divorce adjustment problems: The treatment seminar. *Journal of Divorce, 1,* 183–187.

Greene, B. L., Lee, R. R., & Lustig, N. (1973). Transient structured distance as a maneuver in marital therapy. *Family Coordinator, 22,* 15–22.

Gurman, A. S., & Kniskern, D. P. (1978). Research on marital and family therapy: Progress, perspective and prospect. In S. L. Garfield & A. E. Bergin (Eds.), *Handbook of psychotherapy and behavior change* (2nd ed.). New York: Wiley.

Gurman, A. S. & Kniskern, D. P. (1981). *Handbook of family therapy.* New York: Brunner/Mazel.

Haley, J. (1973) *Uncommon therapy.* New York: W. W. Norton.

Hancock, E. (1982). Sources of discord between attorneys and therapists in divorce cases. *Journal of Divorce, 6*(7), 115–124.

Haynes, J. M. (1981). *Divorce mediation: A practical guide for therapists and counselors.* New York: Springer.

Haynes, J. (1982). A conceptual model of the process of family mediation: Implications for training. *The American Journal of Family Therapy, 10,* 6–15.

Heymann, L. (1981). Mediation helps couples. *The Humanist, 41*(5), 21.

Hickman, M. E., & Baldwin, B. A. (1970). Use of programmed instruction to improve communication in marriage. *Family Coordinator, 20,* 121–125.

Hight, E. S. (1977). A contractual, working separation: A step between resumption and/or divorce. *Journal of Divorce, 1,* 21–30.

Hoopes, M. H., Molene, M. V., & Stanfield-Packard, K. (1979). *Structured group treatment for divorce adjustment.* Unpublished manuscript, Brigham Young University.

Hozman, T. L., & Froiland, D. J. (1976). Families in divorce: A proposed model for counseling the children. *Family Coordinator, 25,* 271–276.

Irving, H. H. (1980). *Divorce mediation.* New York: Universe Books.

Irving, H., Benjamin, M., Bohm, P., & MacDonald, G. (1981). *A study of conciliation counseling in the family court of Toronto: Implications for socio-legal practice.* Toronto: Department of National Health and Welfare and the Ontario Ministry of the Attorney General.

Irving, H., Bohm, P., MacDonald, G., & Benjamin, M. (1979). *A comparative analysis of two family court services: An exploratory study of conciliation counseling.* Toronto: Department of National Health and Welfare and the Ontario Ministry of the Attorney General.

Kaslow, F. (1981). Divorce and divorce therapy. In A.S. Gurman & D.P. Kniskern (Eds.), *Handbook of family therapy.* New York: Brunner/Mazel.

Kaslow, F., & Steinberg, J. (1982). Ethical divorce therapy and divorce proceedings: A psycholegal perspective. In L. L'Abate (Ed.), *Values, ethics, legalities, and the family therapist.* Rockville, MD: Aspen Systems Corporation.

Kitson, G.C., & Raschke, H.J. (1981). Divorce research: What we know; what we need to know. *Journal of Divorce, 4,* 1–38.

Kressel, K., & Deutsch, M. (1977). Divorce therapy: An in-depth survey of therapists' views. *Family Process, 16,* 413–444.

Kressel, K., Jaffee, N., Tuchman, B., Watson, C., & Deutsch, M. (1980). A typology of divorcing couples: Implications for mediation and the divorce process. *Family Process, 19,* 101–116.

Kressel, K., Lopez-Morillas, M., Weinglass, J., & Deutsch, M. (1979). Professional intervention in divorce: The views of lawyers, psychotherapists, and clergy. In G. Levinger & O. Moles (Eds.), *Divorce and separation: Context, causes, and consequences.* New York: Basic Books.

Lee, B.E. (1979). Consumer evaluation of a family court service. *Conciliation Courts Review, 17,* 49–54.

Levinger, G. (1979). Marital cohesiveness at the brink: The fate of applications for divorce. In G. Levinger & D. Moles (Eds.), *Divorce and separation: Context, causes, and consequences.* New York: Basic Books.

Margolin, F.M. (1973). An approach to resolution of visitation disputes postdivorce: Short-term counseling. *Dissertation Abstracts International, 34,* 1754-B. (University Microfilms No. 73-22, 680.)

Matanovich, J. P. (1970). The effects of short-term group counseling upon positive perceptions of mate in marriage counseling. *Dissertation Abstracts International, 31,* 2688-A. (Microfilms No. 70-24, 405.)

McIsaac, H. (1981). Mandatory conciliation custody/visitation matters: California's bold stroke. *Conciliation Courts Review, 19*(2), 73–81.

Milne, A. (1978). Custody of children in a divorce process: A family self-determination model. *Conciliation Courts Review, 16,* 1–10.

Moreland, J., Schwebel, A. I., Fine, M. A., & Vess, J. D. (1982). Post-divorce family therapy: Suggestions for professionals. *Professional Psychology, 13*(5), 639–646.

Morris, J. D., & Prescott, M. R. (1976). Adjustment to divorce through transactional analysis. *Journal of Family Counseling, 4,* 66–69.

Musetto, A. (1978). The role of the mental health professional in contested custody: Evaluator of competence or facilitator of change. *Journal of Divorce, 4*(4), 69–79.

Olson, D. H., Russell, C. S., & Sprenkle, D. H. (1980). Marital and family therapy: A decade review. *Journal of Marriage and the Family, 42,* 973–993.

Pearson, J., & Thoennes, N. (1982). The benefits outweigh the costs. *The Family Advocate, 4,* 26–32.

Pearson, J., Thoennes, N., & Vander Kooi, L. (1982). The mediation of contested child custody disputes. *The Colorado Lawyer, 2,* 337–355.

Phillips, C. (1981). Guidelines for separation counseling. In A. Gurman (Ed.), *Questions and answers in the practice of family therapy.* New York: Brunner/ Mazel.

Raschke, H. J. (1982). *Divorce and marital separation.* Unpublished manuscript, Department of Psychology and Sociology, Austin College, Sherman, TX.

Ruback, R. (1982). Issues in family law: Implications for therapists. In L. L'Abate (Ed.), *Values, ethics, legalities, and the family therapist.* Rockville, MD: Aspen Systems Corporation.

Sampel, D., & Seymour, W. (1980). A comparative analysis of the effectiveness of conciliation counseling on certain personality variables. *Journal of Marital and Family Therapy, 6,* 269–276.

Saposnek, D. (1983). *Mediating child custody disputes.* San Francisco: Jossey-Bass.

Sell, K. D. (1979). *Divorce in the 1970's: A subject guide to books, articles, dissertations, government documents, and film on divorce in the United States.* Department of Sociology, Catawba College, Salisbury, NC.

Silberman, L. (1982). Professional responsibility problems of divorce mediation. *Family Quarterly, 2,* 107–145.

Smith, M. L., Glass, G. D., & Miller, T. I. (1980). *The benefits of psychotherapy.* Baltimore: Johns Hopkins University Press.

Sobota, W., & Cappas, A. (1979). Semantic differential changes associated with participation in a public lecture series describing the emotional and behavior consequences of divorce. *Journal of Divorce, 3,* 137–152.

Stephenson, S. J., & Boler, M. F. (1981). Group treatment for divorcing persons. *Social Work with Groups, 4,* 67–77.

Storm, C.L., & Sprenkle, D.H. (1982) Individual treatment in divorce therapy: A critique of the assumption. *Journal of Divorce, 6,* 87–97.

Stuart, R. (1980). *Helping couples change.* New York: Guilford Press.

Thiessen, J. D., Avery, A. W., & Joanning, H. (1980). Facilitating post divorce adjustment among women: A communication skills training approach. *Journal of Divorce, 4,* 35–44.

Toomin, M. K. (1972). Structured separation with counseling: A therapeutic approach for couples in conflict. *Family Process, 11,* 299–310.

Vroom, P. (1983). The anomolous profession: Bumpy going in the divorce mediation movement. *The Family Therapy Networker,* pp. 38–42.

Weiss, R. S. (1975). *Marital separation.* New York: Basic Books.

Whitaker, C., & Miller, M. (1971). A reevaluation of "psychiatric help" when divorce impends. In J. Haley (Ed.), *Changing families: A family therapy reader.* New York: Grune & Stratton.

Young, D. M. (1978a). The divorce experience workshop: A consumer evaluation. *Journal of Divorce, 2,* 37–48.

Young, D. M. (1978b). Consumer satisfaction with the divorce workshop: A follow-up report. *Journal of Divorce, 2,* 49–56.

Index

Index

Premarital and newlywed couples,
program(s) for (*continued*)
guidelines for, based on research
studies, 218
issues in, 200–204
range of topics covered in, 209
teaching methods in, 205, 208
time frame in, 210
timing of, 210–211
training of facilitators in, 208–209
types of, 204–205; *see also* Marriage
entries
PREmarital Personal and Relationship
Evaluation (PREPARE), 218–222
Premarital preparation, evaluation of,
212–218
Premarital services
delivery of, 225–226
recommendations regarding policies
relating to, 226
Preparental programs, 18
Prevention, marriage preparation/
enrichment as, 197–200
PRIMES (Program for Relationship
Improvement by Maximizing Empathy and Self-disclosure), 67–68
Private entrepreneurs, in childbirth
education, 152
Private reflections, premarital, 208
Problem-solving training, in cognitive behavioral marital therapy, 139–141
Problems, addressed by behavioral
parent training, 104–113
grouped in complex syndromes,
105–106
in home, 112–113
psychological, related to somatic
conditions, 106–108
Psychoeducational family programs,
overview of, 1–37
Psychological bases, for marriage-
enrichment programs, 240

Quaker model, of marriage enrichment, 234–235
program content in, 245

Random assignment, in divorce research, 301
Random sample, sample size and, in
divorce research, 300

Rappaport, A.F., 61
Rappaport, R., 200–201
Rational-Emotive Therapy, in parent
education, 168–169
Rauen, P., 24
Rausch, H.L., 200–201
Reality Therapy, in parent education,
170–171
Recruitment, for marriage-enrichment
programs, 240–241
Red Cross childbirth courses, 147–148
Reducing children's fears, parent
training and, 111–112
Reidy, T.J., 177
Relationship Enhancement (RE)
and related programs, 5, 8–9
research findings on, 254–255
Religious influence, on marriage prep-
aration/enrichment, 198–199
Religious models, of marriage enrich-
ment, development of, 234–235
Research
evaluative, on marriage enrichment,
247–258
existing, in divorce approaches, me-
thodological adequacy of, 300–303
Research standards, in evaluation of
parent behavior training, 115–123
Research studies, premarital program-
ming guidelines based on, 218
Ridley, C.A., 68, 217
Robin, A.L., 177
Robinson, A., 176–177
Rogers, C.R., 54
Role playing, premarital, 205
Ross, F.R., 62

Sample size, and random sample, in
divorce research, 300
Samuels, S.D., 172
Schumm, W.R., 25, 204–205
Segelman, F., 155
Separation, structured, techniques of,
268–269
effectiveness of, 276–277; *see also*
Divorce *entries*
Services
conciliation courts, 269, 274–275,
278–282
premarital, *see* Premarital services
Shure, M.B., 178